PERU

THE COOKBOOK

GASTÓN ACURIO

PERU

THE COOKBOOK

INTRODUCTION

My childhood dream was always to be a cook. At the age of nine, I would get on my bicycle and ride to the supermarket to buy ingredients to prepare at home. After all, no one liked to cook in my family. My father was a very important politician at the time and was always very busy with his noble pursuits. My mother had enough to worry about raising my sisters and me, so cooking was never one of her passions, and my four older sisters were also not enamored of cooking. Perhaps this is why, in my house, cooking and eating were never among our favorite pastimes.

How then did the cook inside me come to life? Well, there was a lady who helped my mother around the house—her name was Juana—who did not like cooking but who used to prepare lunch and pack our lunchboxes. But her dislike of cooking meant that the result was not always pleasing. So it was through necessity that I discovered the greedy little boy living inside me.

And so it was that I found the old French cookbooks that had been abandoned for years at the back of the cupboard. I discovered that the best parts of a chicken are on the back and that squid should always be purchased fresh to be sure that it is not hard and tasteless when cooked. These books inspired the cook in me at a very young age and it was thanks to the fact that cooking was not important at home that it became the most important aspect of my life.

The years passed and I was finally able to turn my dream into a reality. I became a cook. It wasn't easy. After all, in those days, a politician like my father did not necessarily understand why his son wanted to devote himself to cooking. But times were different then and cooks were not cast in the wonderful roles they play today. We never imagined then that a cook would become a messenger of peace and solidarity among people, a spokesperson for educational, nutritional, and environmental issues, and, above all, a bridge to happiness for many people in the country, at sea, and in cities.

In those days we wanted to be cooks because we loved to cook or because we fell into the profession by accident, and our greatest dream was to own a beautiful restaurant some day. For example, we never imagined that we would be able to share, through a book, a gastronomic culture as wonderful as that of Peru with all who—anywhere in this connected world—are eager and curious to discover new flavors, new recipes, and new feelings.

We, the chefs of Peru, are precisely that today: messengers. With honor and humility we are the ambassadors of our cuisine in the world, which is why we feel privileged and grateful to be able to share the treasures of Peruvian cuisine with our sister nations. We are convinced that our cuisine is the fruit of a long, tolerant relationship among people and a treasure trove of ingredients that is the result of centuries of dialogue between our ancestors and nature.

And Peruvian cuisine is just that; it is the outcome of centuries of arduous work by our farmers in harmony with nature. Peru has more than eighty different climates, which have enabled us to domesticate an enormous variety of products that today are enjoyed by the entire world: potatoes, chile peppers, beans, cacao, peanuts, pumpkins, avocados, tomatoes, quinoa, and much more.

It is also the cuisine of a country to which different peoples, immigrants from Japan, China, Africa, Spain, Italy, and the Arab world, migrated over the last 500 years, making their own contributions. All brought with them their nostalgia, customs, and products, which were beautifully assimilated into an example of unique tolerance. The result is a Peruvian cuisine that infuses a little of each of those peoples into each bite, transforming it into something new, something Peruvian. The result of this fusion was the appearance of new words, recipes, and flavors unique to Peru, which is how *ceviches* (marinated seafood dishes) and *tiraditos* (thinly sliced raw fish dishes) gave life to the world of the raw and refreshing that is found in the sea and the Andes of Peru. This is also how our regional cuisines developed; that of the north with products from ancient cultures, that of the south with flavors influenced by European and Andean customs, and the cuisine of the Amazon region, a treasure trove of exoticism still waiting to be discovered.

This is also how the meeting of two peoples gave birth to new cuisines. *Nikkei* cuisine is the melding of Japan and Peru, while *chifa* cuisine links Peru with China, and Creole cuisine brings Africa and Europe to Peru. Then you have Italian-Peruvian cuisine, with its taverns scattered across Lima, where you find dishes that look Italian but taste Peruvian.

In this book we will venture into the world of the *ceviche*, the *tiradito*, and the wonderful world of the raw and marinated dishes of our cuisine. It is a world where we Peruvians tend to feel very comfortable; a refreshing, light world very in tune with current culinary trends.

We will also discover Peruvian appetizers and snacks, as well as a world of sauces prepared with hot chiles to accompany our potatoes and tubers, and other appetizers typical of our regional cuisines.

We will travel the route of delicious Peruvian street food, with its sandwiches, *tamalitos* (bite-size tamales), and *anticuchos* (grilled skewered meat).

We will also become acquainted with a wide range of soups containing ingredients from the sea, the Andes, and the Amazon region.

The delicious culture of rice, with its different preparations and textures, as well as recipes with distinct influences, will astound you.

We will discover the flavorsome world of slow cooking and stews, transformed into chili dishes and *seco* stews, and also the world of sautés and dishes cooked over high heat.
Finally, we will enjoy the sweet world of desserts born of the different influences in Peruvian cuisine, and enter the universe of cocktails prepared with our national grape brandy, pisco.
This is the magic of our cuisine. It is a multicolored cuisine of a thousand flavors, which, thanks to its numerous influences, has known how to incorporate techniques, uses, and customs from other countries to give them a Peruvian twist. Our love of raw and marinated food is influenced by Japanese traditions, and our sautéed dishes are the result of Chinese influence. Stews begin with beautiful European-influenced condiments, seasoned with the rhythm and aroma of African-inspired spices, all brought together by the techniques inherent to our ancient cultures, which we continue to respect to this day throughout Peru.

Indeed, to visit Peru is to discover a people proud of its cuisine and happy to enjoy it, but above all, eager to share it so that all can appreciate the secrets hidden in the recipes of this book. You will see that behind each recipe is a long history of ingredients, of human dialogue, of the love of cooking, and respect for the land and our own culture.

This is Peruvian cuisine, which we invite you to discover in this book. We hope that through its pages, you will draw some of the feelings and flavors of Peru into your heart.

Gastón Acurio

PERUVIAN CUISINE

The history of Peruvian cuisine is as rich as its ingredients and nuances are varied and exquisite. You would have to go back 5,000 years to trace its origins and when ingredients such as tubers, cereals, and fruits appeared, ancient dwellers of modern-day Peru domesticated and cultivated them with utmost respect for the environment, in a harmonious dialogue between nature and man.

Ancient Peruvians cultivated potatoes and corn in the Andes, and pumpkins and lima (butter) beans on the coast. They discovered aromatic herbs and the spicy power of chile peppers, as well as the wonderful fruits of the Amazon region. Their nourishment came from fish and mollusks or from llama meat and poultry. Nature was their pantry, providing unsurpassed variety thanks to the country's three regions—the coast, the mountains, and the jungle—as well as the ocean and rivers, and its numerous ecosystems and microclimates.

The Conquest in the sixteenth century, followed by the Viceroyalty, brought many traditions and customs from Spain as well as ingredients, which quickly adapted to these lands. Rice, onions, citrus fruits, wheat, vineyards, olives, pigs, cows, and hens met and mingled with potatoes, hot chiles, and tomatoes, giving birth to culinary fusion.

This gastronomic package was also enriched by the Arab-Moorish influence, which characterized the cuisine of the Viceroyalty. This mixture then gave rise to the great Creole cuisine, infused with African touches introduced by workers who arrived to toil on ranches and farms. A flavorsome repertoire of Creole-Peruvian fusion dishes gradually developed, producing wonderful recipes such as *ají de gallina* (spicy chicken stew), *cau cau* (stew of tripe or chicken and other ingredients), *carapulcra* (pork and potato stew), beans with stew, *escabeche* (marinated dishes), and *anticuchos* (pieces of grilled, skewered meat), all as common today as back then.

However, these have not been the only influences to give Peruvian gastronomy its impressive variety and color. Chinese "coolies" arrived in Peru as migrant workers in the nineteenth century, bringing their customs and recipes with them, and these blended with Peruvian dishes producing a delicious result: *chifa* or Chinese-Peruvian cuisine. They also introduced techniques such as sautéing over a high flame, splashing soy sauce into beef stir-fries, and the tradition of eating white rice with almost everything, which today is oh so Peruvian! *Chifa* cuisine has Chinese roots, but its heart and seasonings are Peruvian and, unsurprisingly, there are more than 5,000 of these restaurants dotted across the country.

Japanese immigrants also arrived from Asia toward the end of the nineteenth century. Working in agriculture and trade, they branched out to cook in taverns and restaurants, introducing the Japanese love of seafood, subtlety of flavors, and care in handling ingredients. These principles enabled them to produce exquisite steamed dishes and other creations that gave rise to what we know today as *nikkei* or Peruvian-Japanese cuisine. Octopus in olive oil is an iconic dish created by Rosita Yimura, a classic in ceviche and seafood restaurants. A more recent but also important influence on Peruvian cuisine was that of the Italian immigrants, particularly those from Genoa. This imprint is evident in well-loved homemade dishes such as green noodles, and recipes such as seafood *muchame* (sun-dried seasoned strips of fish), Lima-style minestrone, and Swiss chard pie, a favorite in Peruvian bakeries.

But the variety in Peruvian cuisine does not end with the fusion of seasonings from distant lands, which were generously accepted and tastefully incorporated. Each region of the country has its own exquisite dishes based on local traditions and ingredients. For example, you have northern cuisine with its delicious fish and shellfish, as well as iconic dishes in which ingredients such as mangrove cockles, loche squash, chiles, and duck or goat take center stage.

In the southern Andes meanwhile, you find stews, soups, and chowders laden with treasures such as shrimp (prawn) and rocoto hot chiles from Arequipa, or corn and potatoes from Cusco, in recipes that have been passed from generation to generation.

The country's central region, in the Andes, also offers excellent cuisine with dishes such as the *pachamanca*—a banquet of meats, tubers, and greens cooked underground with aromatic herbs—which, because of its exquisite taste, has been adopted by other regions.

The jungle, for its part, with its extraordinary Amazonian products, is an adventure for the senses and adds a touch of the exotic to each mouthful of dishes such as *tacacho con cecina* (roasted plantain fritters with dried salted meat), *juanes* (rice and meat wrapped in bijao leaves), or *patarashca* (flame-grilled fish stew packages).

It is impossible to refer to Peruvian gastronomy without mentioning its seafood cuisine. The ceviche restaurant is a national institution and the ideal informal restaurant in which to enjoy good times and excellent cuisine. Here you can enjoy ceviches, *tiraditos* (thinly sliced, marinated raw fish), *chicharrones* (fried pork rind), and succulent rice dishes, to name but a few. Ancient and modern, classic and innovative recipes all coexist in that happy place that is the ceviche restaurant, which can be modest and very traditional, or contemporary and avant-garde, but always very Peruvian.

The 1980s heralded the arrival of the new Peruvian cuisine, which at the time was called "New Andean" cuisine. Promoted by individuals such as Bernardo Roca Rey and Chef Luis "Cucho" La Rosa, it combined ancestral ingredients and culinary techniques with the avant-garde trends of international cuisine. For the first time quinoa, *ulluku* (root vegetable), and *huacatay* (an Andean herb also known as "Peruvian black mint") left home kitchens to shine in all their splendor in contemporary dishes, creating and re-creating culinary offerings based on flavors bursting with tradition and history.

This is Peruvian cuisine, an immense variety of ingredients, textures, and aromas that blend and are enjoyed at tables throughout Peru; a flavorsome fusion that the whole world should discover.

CEVICHE

CEVICHE CLÁSICO
CLASSIC CEVICHE

Serves: 4
Preparation Time: 10 minutes

Always use firm-fleshed white fish, without skin and bones, to prepare classic ceviche. Avoid oily or fatty varieties of fish.

4 × 6-oz (175-g) white fish fillets (such as sole, croaker, or grouper)
2 cloves garlic, very finely chopped
2 teaspoons limo chile, chopped
juice of 20 small lemons
1 teaspoon chopped culantro or cilantro (coriander) leaves
2 or 3 ice cubes
1 red onion, sliced into half-moon crescents
salt and pepper

To serve
1 corncob, cooked and kernels removed
½ sweet potato, boiled and sliced

Cut the fish into ¾-inch/2-cm cubes, place in a bowl, and season with salt and pepper. After 1 minute, add the garlic and limo chile. Mix together well.

Pour over the lemon juice and add the chopped culantro or cilantro (coriander) leaves and ice cubes. Stir and let stand for a few seconds. Add the red onion and remove the ice cubes. Mix together and adjust the seasoning to taste.

Serve in a large shallow bowl with cooked corn kernels and boiled sweet potato slices.

CEVICHE CRIOLLO
CREOLE CEVICHE

Serves: 4
Preparation Time: 12 minutes

You can prepare this ceviche with the most inexpensive types of fish you can find, such as comber, mackerel, horse mackerel, or silverside fish.

1 × 1 lb 9¼-oz (720-g) or 4 × 6-oz (175-g) fillets fish (such as comber, mackerel, or silverside fish)
2 cloves garlic, very finely chopped
2 teaspoons chopped limo chile
juice of 20 small lemons
½ cup (4 fl oz/120 ml) Blended Yellow Chiles (see p. 404)
1 teaspoon chopped culantro or cilantro (coriander) leaves
2 or 3 ice cubes
1 red onion, sliced into half-moon crescents
4 tablespoons cancha (toasted corn), plus extra to garnish (optional)
salt and pepper

To serve
1 corncob, cooked and kernels removed
½ sweet potato, boiled and sliced

Cut the fish into ¾-inch/2-cm cubes, place in a bowl, and season with salt and pepper. After 1 minute, add the garlic and limo chile. Mix together well.

Pour over the lemon juice and add the blended yellow chiles, culantro or cilantro (coriander) leaves, and ice cubes. Stir and let stand for a few seconds. Add the red onion and remove the ice cubes. Add the cancha, mix together, and adjust the seasoning to taste.

Serve in a large shallow bowl with cooked corn kernels and boiled sweet potato slices. You can also add a little extra cancha to garnish, if desired.

Classic Ceviche

CEVICHE MIXTO
MIXED CEVICHE

Serves: 4
Preparation Time: 15 minutes

You can prepare this ceviche with any type of seafood and any type of chile.

5½ oz (160 g) squid, cleaned
1 × 6-oz (175-g) white fish fillet
12 blanched shrimp (prawns)
7 oz (200 g) Cooked Octopus, thinly sliced (see p. 406)
12 scallops, cleaned
2 cloves garlic, very finely chopped
2 teaspoons chopped limo chile
juice of 20 small lemons
1 teaspoon chopped culantro or cilantro (coriander) leaves
2 or 3 ice cubes
1 red onion, sliced into half-moon crescents
salt and pepper

To serve
1 corncob, cooked and kernels removed
½ sweet potato, boiled and cut into 8 slices

Put the squid in boiling water for 40 seconds. Drain and cut in ¼-inch/5-mm rings.

Cut the fish into ¾-inch/2-cm cubes and place in a bowl with the shrimp (prawns), squid, octopus, and scallops. Season with salt and pepper. After 1 minute, add the garlic and limo chile. Mix together well.

Pour over the lemon juice and add the culantro or cilantro (coriander) leaves and ice cubes. Stir and let stand for a few seconds. Add the red onion and remove the ice cubes. Mix together and adjust the seasoning to taste.

Serve in a large shallow bowl with cooked corn kernels and boiled sweet potato slices.

CEVICHE DE CARRETILLA
CARRETILLA CEVICHE

Serves: 4
Preparation Time: 20 minutes
Cooking Time: 10 minutes

8 mussels, cleaned
6 snails
2 × 9-oz (250-g) squid, cleaned
12 silverside fish fillets (or fresh anchovies or fresh sardines), cleaned
12 scallops, cleaned
8 shrimp (prawns), shelled
2 cloves garlic, very finely chopped
2 teaspoons chopped limo chile
1 teaspoon chopped culantro or cilantro (coriander) leaves
juice of 20 small lemons
2 or 3 ice cubes
1 small red onion, chopped
8 sea urchin tongues
salt and pepper

To serve
¼ corncob, cooked and kernels removed
2 tablespoons cancha (toasted corn)

To cook the mussels, place them in their shells in boiling water for 2 minutes. Drain and remove the meat from the shells.

Boil the snails in 8½ cups (68 fl oz/2 liters) water for 3 minutes until tender. Drain and remove from their shells, then chop. Set aside and refrigerate if not used immediately.

Put the squid in boiling water for 40 seconds. Drain and cut in ¼-inch/5-mm rings.

Place the silverside fish fillets, scallops, shrimp (prawns), squid, mussels, and snails in a bowl. Add the garlic, chopped limo chile, and culantro or cilantro (coriander) leaves and season to taste with salt and pepper. Mix together well.

Pour over the lemon juice and add the ice cubes to the mixture to chill. Taste and adjust the seasoning if necessary. Add the red onion and remove the ice cubes. Mix together.

Spoon into dessert bowls or glass bowls and top with the sea urchin tongues. Serve with cooked corn kernels and cancha.

Mixed Ceviche

CEVICHE ANTIGUO
OLD-FASHIONED CEVICHE

Serves: 4
Preparation Time: 15 minutes

You can use bonito, tuna, salmon, or trout to prepare this ceviche.

4 × 6-oz (175-g) bonito fillets (or tuna, salmon, or trout), cleaned
2 cloves garlic, very finely chopped
2 teaspoons chopped limo chile
1 teaspoon chopped culantro or cilantro (coriander) leaves
juice of 20 small lemons
½ cup (4 fl oz/120 ml) Blended Yellow Chiles (see p. 404)
2 or 3 ice cubes
1 red onion, sliced into half-moon crescents
4 tablespoons cancha (toasted corn), plus extra to garnish (optional)
salt and pepper

To serve
1 corncob, cooked and kernels removed
½ sweet potato, boiled and sliced

Cut the bonito fillets into ½-inch/1-cm cubes and place in a bowl. Season with salt and pepper. After 1 minute, add the garlic, limo chile, and culantro or cilantro (coriander) leaves. Mix together well.

Pour over the lemon juice and add the blended chiles, and ice cubes to chill. Taste and adjust the seasoning if necessary. Add the onion and remove the ice cubes. Add the cancha and mix together well.

Serve in a large shallow bowl with cooked corn kernels and boiled sweet potato slices. You can also add a little extra cancha to garnish, if desired.

CEVICHE CHIFA
CHINESE CEVICHE

Serves: 4
Preparation Time: 20 minutes, plus 6 hours standing

More than 10 percent of Peru's population has Chinese ancestry, so a ceviche born of that fusion should be expected.

4 × 6-oz (175-g) white fish fillets (such as sole, croaker, or grouper)
5 teaspoons granulated sugar
1 limo chile, thinly sliced
1 cup (8 fl oz/250 ml) lemon juice, from about 2¼ lb (1 kg) small lemons
8–10 scallions (spring onions), white part only, thinly sliced
4 teaspoons sesame oil
1 tablespoon toasted peanuts
salt

Pickled vegetables
1 × 3½ oz (100 g) turnip, thinly sliced
½ cup (2 oz/50 g) seeded and thinly sliced cucumber
2-inch (5-cm) piece fresh ginger, peeled and thinly sliced
1 carrot, thinly sliced
½ cup (5 oz/150 g) salt
¾ cup (5 oz/150 g) granulated sugar
3 tablespoons white wine vinegar

To garnish
1 tablespoon toasted peanuts
2 tablespoons chopped culantro or cilantro (coriander) leaves
4 wonton wrappers, cut into 1½ × ¼-inch (3.75 cm × 5-mm) strips and fried

For the pickled vegetables, place the turnip, cucumber, ginger, and carrot in a bowl. Add the salt, mix together, and set aside for 5 hours.

After 5 hours, rinse under running water until the vegetables no longer taste salty. Drain well, put in a bowl with the sugar, and stir until the sugar is completely dissolved. Add the vinegar. Set aside for 1 hour to let the pickle flavor develop.

Cut the fish into 1½ × ½ × ¼-inch (3.75-cm × 1-cm x 5-mm) slices and place in a bowl. Add the sugar, limo chile and lemon juice, season with salt and mix together well.

Add the pickled vegetables along with the scallion (spring onion), sesame oil, and the peanuts. Mix together.

Spoon onto a serving plate. Garnish with toasted peanuts, culantro or cilantro (coriander) leaves, and fried wonton strips. Serve.

CEVICHE NIKKEI
JAPANESE-INSPIRED CEVICHE

Serves: 4
Preparation Time: 15 minutes
Cooking Time: 5 minutes

Japanese immigrants arriving in Peru from the end of the nineteenth century have shown us the value of many previously unappreciated marine species, and fostered the rise of Japanese-inspired cuisine.

1½ oz (40 g) fresh yuyo seaweed
1 × 1 lb 8½-oz (700-g) tuna fillet, cut into ¾-inch (2-cm) cubes
1 tablespoon chopped limo chile
½ tablespoon chopped culantro or cilantro (coriander) leaves
2 scallions (spring onions), green part only, chopped
juice of 20 small lemons
½ tablespoon Panca Chili Paste (see p. 406)
1 teaspoon honey
1 teaspoon soy sauce
1 tablespoon sugar-free tamarind juice concentrate
2 teaspoons sesame oil
2 or 3 ice cubes
¾ red onion, sliced into half-moon crescents
½ Japanese cucumber (kyuri), thinly sliced
1 × 2½ oz (65 g) small turnip, thinly sliced
1 nori seaweed sheet, thinly sliced, to garnish
½ avocado, sliced, to serve
salt

Blanch the yuyo seaweed in a pan of boiling water. Set aside.

Place the tuna in a bowl. Season with salt and add the limo chile, culantro or cilantro (coriander) leaves, and chopped scallion (spring onion). Mix together.

In another bowl, mix together the lemon juice, chile paste, honey, soy sauce, tamarind juice, and sesame oil. Pour over the tuna and add the ice cubes to chill. Add the onion, yuyo seaweed, Japanese cucumber, and turnip. Remove the ice and mix together well.

Spoon into a large shallow bowl, garnish with nori seaweed slices, and serve with sliced avocado.

CEVICHE TRUJILLANO
TRUJILLO-STYLE CEVICHE

Serves: 4
Preparation Time: 10 minutes

Don't be afraid to use chile when preparing this ceviche, because it gives it a very particular flavor.

1 × 1 lb 9¼-oz (720-g) croaker or grouper fillet
2 teaspoons chopped mochero chile, plus 1 slice for rubbing
1 teaspoon chopped culantro or cilantro (coriander) leaves
juice of 20 small lemons
2 or 3 ice cubes
1 red onion, sliced into half-moon crescents
¼ small celery stalk, chopped
salt

To serve
½ yucca root (cassava), peeled, boiled, and cut into medium-size pieces
½ sweet potato, boiled and sliced

Cut the fish into 1½ × ½ × ¼-inch (3.75-cm × 1-cm × 5-mm) slices.

Rub the inside of a bowl with the slice of mochero chile so that the chile aroma lingers in the bowl. Discard.

Place the fish in the bowl and season with salt, then add the chopped mochero chile and culantro or cilantro (coriander) leaves. Mix together well. Pour over the lemon juice and add the ice cubes to chill.

Taste and adjust the seasoning if necessary. Remove the ice cubes and add the red onion, celery, and cooked sarandaja beans. Mix together.

Serve in a large shallow bowl with pieces of boiled yucca root (cassava), boiled sweet potato slices, and a few extra sarandaja beans, if desired.

CEVICHE AMAZÓNICO
AMAZONIAN CEVICHE

Serves: 4
Preparation Time: 12 minutes

The Amazon rain forest is one of the great treasures of Peru and South America.

1¾ lb (800 g) white fish fillet
1 tablespoon salt
½ tablespoon pepper
3 oz (80g) cocona fruit, cut into small cubes
1 cup (8 fl oz/250 ml) cocona fruit juice
2 sweet chiles, seeded, membranes removed, and chopped
1 tablespoon charapita chilies, ground to a paste
2 cloves garlic, very finely chopped
2 tablespoons chopped sacha culantro or cilantro (coriander) leaves
juice of 10 small lemons
½ cup (4 fl oz/120 ml) fish broth (stock)
1 red onion, thinly sliced
8 bijao leaves

Cut the fish into ¾-inch/2-cm cubes and place in a bowl. Add a tablespoon salt, a pinch of pepper, the cocona fruit, cocona fruit juice, sweet chiles, charapita chiles, garlic, and culantro or cilantro (coriander) leaves. Mix together thoroughly.

Add the lemon juice to the fish mixture, stir, and set aside for a few minutes. Pour over the broth (stock), add the onion, and mix together. Season with salt and pepper.

Take 2 bijao leaves and lay one over the other in a serving bowl to form a cross. Place a serving of ceviche in the middle and pour some of the marinade over it. Repeat with the remaining ceviche and leaves.

CEVICHE DE CONCHAS NEGRAS
MANGROVE COCKLE CEVICHE

Serves: 4
Preparation Time: 20 minutes

Mangrove cockles, like black clams, are found in Peru's mangrove swamps.

40 mangrove cockles
1 red onion, diced
1 limo chile, plus 4 slices to garnish
4 teaspoons chopped culantro or cilantro (coriander) leaves
2 cloves garlic, very finely chopped
juice of 20 small lemons
2 or 3 ice cubes
salt

To serve
¼ corncob, cooked and kernels removed
2 tablespoons cancha (toasted corn)

Open the mangrove cockles very carefully so as not to waste any of the juices inside. Scrape out the cockle meat, place in a bowl with the juices, and set aside.

Place the onion, chopped limo chile, culantro or cilantro (coriander) leaves, and garlic in a separate bowl. Season with salt. Pour over the lemon juice and mix together well.

Add the cockle meat and juices to the mixture along with the ice cubes to chill. Taste and add more salt if necessary. Remove the ice cubes and mix together well.

Spoon into dessert bowls or glass bowls. Garnish each bowl with a limo chile slice and serve with cooked corn kernels and cancha.

CEVICHE DE ERIZOS
SEA URCHIN CEVICHE

Serves: 4
Preparation Time: 10 minutes

Peru's sea urchins are one of a kind: creamy, delicate, and intensely flavored.

- 1 limo chile, chopped, plus 1 slice for rubbing
- 1½ red onions, diced
- 1 tablespoon chopped culantro or cilantro (coriander) leaves
- 1 clove garlic, very finely chopped
- juice of 12 small lemons
- 32 sea urchin tongues
- 2 or 3 ice cubes
- salt

To serve

- 1 corncob, cooked and kernels removed
- ⅔ cup (5 oz/150 g) cancha (toasted corn)

Rub the inside of a bowl with the limo chile slice so that the chile aroma lingers in the bowl. Discard.

Put the diced onions, chopped limo chile, culantro or cilantro (coriander) leaves, and garlic into the bowl. Season with salt and mix together well. Pour over the lemon juice.

Add the sea urchin tongues and the ice cubes to chill. Taste and add more salt if necessary. Remove the ice cubes.

Spoon into dessert bowls or glass bowls and serve with the cooked corn kernels and cancha.

CEVICHE DE CHAMPIÑONES
BUTTON MUSHROOM CEVICHE

Serves: 4
Preparation Time: 15 minutes

You can make ceviche with button mushrooms or any other type of vegetable. Ceviche is a blank canvas, not just a recipe.

- 1 lb 5 oz (600 g) white button mushrooms, cut into halves
- 1 limo chile, chopped, plus 1 slice for rubbing
- 1 tablespoon chopped culantro or cilantro (coriander) leaves
- 3 tablespoons Blended Yellow Chiles (see p. 404)
- 1 clove garlic, very finely chopped
- juice of 15 small lemons
- 2 or 3 ice cubes
- 1½ red onions, sliced into half-moon crescents
- salt

To serve

- 1 corncob, cooked and kernels removed
- ½ sweet potato, boiled and sliced

Fill a bowl with boiling water and let cool slightly. Fill a second bowl with cold water. Carefully place the mushroom halves into the hot water, let stand for a few seconds, then drop in the cold water to stop the cooking process. Drain and set aside.

Rub the inside of a bowl with the limo chile slice so that the chile aroma lingers in the bowl. Discard.

Add the mushrooms to the bowl and season with salt. Add the chopped limo chile, chopped culantro or cilantro (coriander) leaves, blended chiles, and garlic. Mix together well.

Pour over the lemon juice and add the ice cubes to chill. Taste and add more salt if necessary. Add the onion and remove the ice cubes. Mix together.

Spoon onto a serving plate and serve with cooked corn kernels and boiled sweet potato slices.

Hot Stone Shrimp Ceviche

CEVICHE DE CAMARONES A LA PIEDRA
HOT STONE SHRIMP CEVICHE

Serves: 4
Preparation Time: 8 minutes
Cooking Time: 40 minutes

- 1 yucca root (cassava), peeled
- 4 tablespoons Yellow Chili Paste (see p. 405)
- 1 tablespoon Garlic Paste (see p. 406)
- 1 tablespoon Shrimp Head Paste (see p. 29)
- 4 tablespoons fish broth (stock)
- 1 red onion, thinly sliced
- 40 shrimp (prawns), peeled and deveined, with tails still intact
- juice of 20 small lemons
- 8 limo chile slices
- 1 tablespoon chopped culantro or cilantro (coriander) leaves
- salt and white pepper

Bring a pan of water to a boil, add the yucca root (cassava), and cook for 30 minutes until tender.

Drain and chop into large cubes. Set aside.

Sauté the chili paste, garlic paste, and shrimp head paste in a pan over medium heat. Add the broth (stock), half the onion, and the shrimp (prawns). Bring to a boil, add the lemon juice and chile slices, and season with salt and pepper to taste. Cook for 1 minute. Add the yucca root and chopped culantro or cilantro (coriander).

Serve in a large bowl, sprinkling over the remaining onion.

CEVICHE DE ALMEJAS
CLAM CEVICHE

Serves: 4
Preparation Time: 12 minutes

You can also use cooked octopus and diced squid to prepare this ceviche.

- 32 clams, cleaned
- juice of 20 small lemons
- 2 teaspoons chopped limo chile
- 2 red onions, diced
- 2 or 3 ice cubes
- 1 teaspoon chopped culantro or cilantro (coriander) leaves
- 2 cloves garlic, very finely chopped
- 1 corncob, cooked and kernels removed, to serve
- salt

To garnish
- 2 sprigs culantro or cilantro (coriander) leaves
- 1 limo chile, sliced

Cut the clams into ½-inch/1-cm slices and season with salt. Set aside in a bowl.

In another bowl, mix together the lemon juice with the chopped limo chile, red onions, ice cubes, culantro or cilantro (coriander) leaves, and garlic.

Pour the lemon juice mixture over the clams and mix together well. Taste and add more salt if necessary. Remove the ice cubes.

Spoon into a large shallow bowl, garnish with culantro leaves and slices of limo chile, and serve with cooked corn kernels.

CEVICHE DE TRUCHA
TROUT CEVICHE

Serves: 4
Preparation Time: 12 minutes

Try adding a few artichokes to this ceviche, as is customary in the Peruvian Andes.

4 × 6-oz (175-g) trout fillets, cleaned
1 teaspoon chopped culantro or cilantro (coriander) leaves
2 teaspoons chopped rocoto chile
juice of 20 small lemons
2 or 3 ice cubes
1 red onion, sliced into half-moon crescents
salt

To serve
1 corncob, cooked and kernels removed
½ sweet potato, boiled and sliced

Cut the trout fillets into 1½ × ¾ × ¼-inch/3.75 × 1.5 × 5-mm strips, place in a bowl and season with salt. After 2 minutes, add the chopped culantro or cilantro (coriander) leaves and rocoto chile. Mix together well.

Pour over the lemon juice and add the ice cubes to chill. Taste and add more salt if necessary. Add the onion and remove the ice cubes. Mix together.

Serve in a large shallow bowl with cooked corn kernels and boiled sweet potato slices.

CEVICHE BACHICHE
ITALIAN CEVICHE

Serves: 4
Preparation Time: 12 minutes

Thousands of Genovesi arrived at the Port of Callao with nothing but their dreams and culinary traditions. At first, they were contemptuously referred to as *bachiches*. This ceviche is a tribute to them.

juice of 15 small lemons
1 tablespoon extra-virgin olive oil
2 tablespoons grated Parmesan cheese
4 × 6-oz (175-g) white fish fillets
2 teaspoons chopped limo chile, plus 1 slice for rubbing
1 teaspoon chopped culantro or cilantro (coriander) leaves
½ small celery stalk, chopped
2 or 3 ice cubes
4 tablespoons evaporated milk
1 red onion, sliced into half-moon crescents
salt

To serve
1 corncob, cooked and kernels removed
½ sweet potato, boiled and sliced

Pour the lemon juice and olive oil into a blender. Add the Parmesan cheese and blend together. Transfer to a suitable container and refrigerate until needed.

Cut the fish fillets into 1½ × ¾ × ¼-inch/3.75 × 1.5 × 5-mm slices, cut diagonally.

Rub the inside of a bowl with the limo chile slice so that the chile aroma lingers in the bowl. Discard.

Add the fish to the bowl with the chopped limo chile, culantro or cilantro (coriander) leaves, and chopped celery. Season with salt and mix together well.

Pour over the blended lemon juice mixture and add a few ice cubes to chill. Taste and add more salt if necessary. Stir in the evaporated milk, add the onion and remove the ice cubes.

Serve in a large shallow bowl with cooked corn kernels and boiled sweet potato slices.

CEVICHE DE CAMARONES CRUDOS
RAW SHRIMP CEVICHE

Serves: 4
Preparation Time: 15 minutes

You can use any type of crustacean for this ceviche.

40 shrimp (prawns), peeled and deveined, with tails still intact
2 teaspoons chopped limo chile
1 teaspoon chopped culantro or cilantro (coriander) leaves
juice of 20 small lemons
1½ tablespoons Shrimp Head Paste (see p. 29)
4 tablespoons Rocoto Chili Paste (see p. 407)
1 tablespoon Blended Yellow Chiles (see p. 404)
2 or 3 ice cubes
1 red onion, sliced into half-moon crescents
salt

To serve
1 corncob, cooked and kernels removed
2 potatoes, peeled, boiled, and sliced

Place the shrimp (prawns) in a bowl and season with salt. Add the chopped limo chile and culantro or cilantro (coriander) leaves, and mix together well. Stir in the lemon juice, shrimp head paste, chili paste, and blended chiles.

Add the ice cubes to chill. Taste and add more salt if necessary. Add the red onion and remove the ice cubes. Mix together.

Serve in a large shallow bowl with cooked corn kernels and boiled potato slices.

CELADORES DE AREQUIPA
AREQUIPA-STYLE SHRIMP

Serves: 4
Preparation Time: 18 minutes

24 shrimp (prawns)
juice of 12 small lemons
6 cloves garlic, crushed
3 red onions, cut into wedges
5 tomatoes, cut into wedges
1 rocoto chile, seeded, membrane removed, and thinly sliced
5 tablespoons chicha de jora
4 tablespoons red wine vinegar
4 potatoes, boiled and sliced, to serve
salt and pepper

Peel and devein the shrimp (prawns), leaving the tails on. Remove the meat from the heads, push through a strainer (sieve), and mix with the lemon juice in a bowl.

Place the shrimp on a tray and cover with the shrimp head and lemon juice mixture and crushed garlic. Set aside for 5 minutes.

After 5 minutes, add the onions, tomatoes, and chile. Pour over the chicha de jora and red wine vinegar and season to taste with salt and pepper.

Mix together thoroughly.

Serve on a large plate on a bed of sliced boiled potatoes.

CEVICHE DE CANGREJO
CRAB CEVICHE

Serves: 4
Preparation Time: 15 minutes
Cooking Time: 1 minute

You can use any variety of crab to prepare this ceviche.

8 × 12-oz (350-g) large crabs, cleaned
juice of 20 small lemons
5 tablespoons Rocoto Chili Paste (see p. 407)
2 teaspoons chopped limo chile
1 teaspoon chopped culantro or cilantro (coriander) leaves
1 medium celery stalk, chopped
1½ oz (40 g) fresh yuyo seaweed
1½ cups (12 fl oz/350 ml) Tiger Milk (see p. 409)
2 or 3 ice cubes
1 red onion, thinly sliced
salt

To serve
1 corncob, cooked and kernels removed
2 sweet potatoes, boiled and sliced
4 tablespoons cancha (toasted corn)

Place the clean crabs in a bowl and crush them with a heavy kitchen tool. Extract most of the meat from the shells, setting aside the meat in the head.

In a separate bowl, mix together the lemon juice, chile paste, limo chile, culantro or cilantro (coriander) leaves, celery, and yuyo seaweed. Season to taste with salt.

Pour the lemon juice mixture and the tiger milk over the crab meat and add the ice cubes to chill. Add the reserved crab head meat and mix together well. Taste and add more salt if necessary. Add the red onion and remove the ice cubes.

Serve in a large shallow bowl with cooked corn kernels, boiled sweet potato slices, and cancha.

CEVICHE MIXTO A LA CREMA DE AJÍES
MIXED CEVICHE WITH CHILI CREAM

Serves: 4
Preparation Time: 5 minutes

When preparing this ceviche, the chiles used for the paste should be blanched to be sure that their flavor is preserved, without being too aggressive.

5½ oz (160 g) squid, cleaned
2 × 5½-oz (160-g) white fish fillets
12 shrimp (prawns)
2 octopus tentacles, cooked and thinly sliced
2 teaspoons chopped limo chile
1 teaspoon chopped culantro or cilantro (coriander) leaves
juice of 10 small lemons
4 tablespoons Rocoto Chili Paste (see p. 407)
3 tablespoons Blended Yellow Chiles (see p. 404)
2 or 3 ice cubes
4 tablespoons evaporated milk
1 red onion, sliced into half-moon crescents
salt and white pepper

To serve
1 corncob, cooked and kernels removed
1 sweet potato, boiled and sliced

To cook the squid, place it in boiling water for 40 seconds. Drain and cut in ¼-inch/5-mm rings.

Cut the fish into ¾-inch/1.5-cm cubes and place in a bowl with the shrimp (prawns), octopus, and squid. Season with salt and white pepper. After 1 minute, add the limo chile and culantro or cilantro (coriander) leaves. Mix thoroughly.

In a separate bowl, mix together the lemon juice with the chili paste, blended chiles, and ice cubes. Pour over the seafood mixture and adjust the seasoning to taste. Stir in the evaporated milk, add the onion, and remove the ice cubes.

Serve in a large shallow bowl with cooked corn kernels and boiled sweet potato slices.

CEVICHE DE PATO
DUCK CEVICHE

Serves: 4
Preparation Time: 10 minutes plus 2 hours marinating
Cooking Time: 1 hour 35 minutes

This dish is not really a ceviche, more a delicious citrus stew with an acidity reminiscent of ceviche.

1 × 4½-lb (2-kg) duck, quartered
juice of 2 lemons
1 cup (8 fl oz/250 ml) orange juice
4 tablespoons vegetable oil
8 cloves garlic, very finely chopped
4 tablespoons Mirasol Chili Paste (see p. 405)
3 tablespoons Yellow Chili Paste (see p. 405)
½ teaspoon ground cumin
5 red onions, thinly sliced
2 mochero chiles, seeded, membranes removed, and chopped
1 cup (8 fl oz/250 ml) chicken broth (stock), if needed
2 tablespoons chopped culantro or cilantro (coriander) leaves
½ yucca root (cassava), peeled, boiled, and quartered, to serve
salt and pepper

Put the duck pieces in a bowl, add the lemon and orange juices, and let marinate for approximately 2 hours.

Heat the vegetable oil in a pan, add the garlic and both chili pastes, and sauté for 5 minutes. Add the ground cumin and season with salt and pepper, then add the onions and mochero chiles, and cook, stirring, for a few minutes until the onion has softened.

Add the marinated duck quarters to the pan. Pour over the marinade, cover, and cook over low heat for approximately 1½ hours until the duck is tender. If the liquid runs out, add a little chicken broth (stock).

Once the duck quarters are tender, taste and adjust the seasoning. Sprinkle over the chopped culantro or cilantro (coriander).

Serve hot with a side of boiled yucca root (cassava).

SIVINCHE DE CAMARONES
SHRIMP CEVICHE

Serves: 4
Preparation Time: 25 minutes

This recipe is similar to Peruvian shrimp tartar. *Sivinche* is a different variety of shrimp ceviche from the Arequipa region.

Shrimp Head Paste
24 small shrimp (prawns)
3 garlic cloves
2 tablespoons chicha de jora

2 red onions, diced
1 tomato, skinned, seeded, and diced
1 rocoto chile, seeded, membrane removed, and finely chopped
½ teaspoon chopped parsley leaves
½ teaspoon chopped oregano leaves
½ teaspoon chopped culantro or cilantro (coriander) leaves
½ teaspoon chopped huacatay leaves
½ teaspoon chopped mint leaves
3 tablespoons vegetable oil
1 tablespoon white wine vinegar
salt and pepper

To serve
2 potatoes, peeled, boiled, and chopped, to serve

Clean and devein the shrimp (prawns). Remove the meat from the heads, place in a mortar or batán (Peruvian grinder), and grind with the garlic to form a paste. Season with salt and pepper and pour over the chicha de jora. Set aside.

Finely chop the shrimp tail meat and place in a bowl. Add the diced red onions, tomato, rocoto chile, and shrimp head paste. Mix together thoroughly.

Add the chopped herbs along with the vegetable oil and vinegar. Mix together and season with salt and pepper.

Serve with boiled potatoes.

LECHE DE TIGRE AL ROCOTO EN VASO
ROCOTO CHILE-SPICED TIGER MILK IN A GLASS

Serves: 4
Preparation Time: 25 minutes
Cooking Time: 10 minutes

This tiger milk is also delicious if you add a few drops of pisco (grape brandy).

8 snails
1 × 9-oz (250-g) squid, cleaned
4 large clams
¼ corncob
1 tablespoon chopped red onion
1 teaspoon chopped limo chile
8 silverside fish fillets, cut into thirds
3 oz (85 g) octopus, cooked and chopped
juice of 5 small lemons
½ cup (4 fl oz/120 ml) Rocoto Chili Paste (see p. 407)
3 ice cubes
1 teaspoon chopped culantro or cilantro (coriander) leaves
2 tablespoons cancha (toasted corn)
salt

Tiger milk
1 cup (8 fl oz/250 ml) lemon juice from around 2¼ lb (1 kg) of lemons
¼ cup (3 oz/80 g) fish scraps (trimmings)
½ cup (120 ml/4 fl oz) fish broth (stock)
1 medium celery stalk, chopped
3 ice cubes
½ limo chile, seeded, membrane removed, and chopped
1 teaspoon chopped culantro or cilantro (coriander) leaves
1 small red onion, chopped

Boil the snails in 8½ cups (68 fl oz/2 liters) water until tender. Drain and remove from their shells. Cut into ¼-inch (5-mm) slices.

Put the squid in boiling water for 40 seconds, drain, and chop.

Cook the clams (in their shells) in boiling water for 20 seconds. Remove the meat from the shells and chop into ½-inch/1-cm cubes.

For the tiger milk, put the lemon juice, fish scraps (trimmings), broth (stock), celery, and ice cubes in a blender. Season with salt. Add the limo chile, culantro or cilantro (coriander) leaves, and red onion and blend together. Taste and add more salt if necessary. Strain into a suitable container and refrigerate until needed.

Bring a pan of water to a boil, add the corncob, and cook until tender. Drain and remove the kernels.

Put the red onion and chopped limo chile into a bowl. Add the silverside fish pieces, snails, clams, octopus, and squid. Pour over the lemon juice and season with salt. Mix together well. Add the rocoto chili paste, pour over the refrigerated tiger milk mixture, and add the ice cubes to chill. Add the culantro leaves and taste, adding more salt if necessary.

Divide the cooked corn kernels and cancha between four tall glasses.

Remove the ice cubes from the mixture and pour into the glasses. Serve.

CEVICHE DE CARACOLES
SNAIL CEVICHE

Serves: 4
Preparation Time: 25 minutes
Cooking Time: 5 minutes

Try using land snails (as opposed to sea snails) to prepare this ceviche.

1 lb 9¼ oz (720 g) snails
1 teaspoon chopped culantro or cilantro (coriander) leaves
2 teaspoons chopped rocoto chiles
juice of 15 small lemons
2 or 3 ice cubes
1 red onion, sliced into half-moon crescents
salt

To serve
1 corncob, cooked and kernels removed
3 oz (80 g) cancha (toasted corn)

Boil the snails in 8½ cups (68 fl oz/2 liters) water until tender. Drain and remove from their shells. Set aside and refrigerate if not using immediately.

Cut the snails into quarters and place in a bowl. Season with salt. Add the culantro or cilantro (coriander) leaves and rocoto chiles and mix well.

Pour over the lemon juice and add the ice cubes to chill. Taste and add more salt if necessary. Add the red onion and remove the ice cubes. Mix together. Serve in a large shallow bowl with cooked corn kernels and cancha.

Rocoto Chile-Spiced Tiger Milk in a Glass

CEVICHE PIURANO
PIURA-STYLE CEVICHE

Serves: 4
Preparation Time: 55 minutes, plus overnight soaking
Cooking Time: 45 minutes

Cancha are corn kernels that have been roasted or deep-fried, and are a popular snack in Peru. The sarandaja is a Peruvian bean that can be replaced with any other type of bean you have at home.

- 1½ cups (9 oz/250 g) cooked sarandaja beans
- 11 oz (300 g) yucca root (cassava), peeled
- 1¾ lb (800 g) white fish fillet
- 1½ cups (375 ml/13 fl oz) lemon juice
- 2 red onions, thinly sliced
- 2 limo chiles, seeded, membranes removed, and chopped
- 2 teaspoons chopped culantro or cilantro (coriander) leaves
- 4 lettuce leaves
- 1 tomato, sliced
- 4 tablespoons cancha (toasted corn)

Soak the beans in cold water overnight. Drain and put into a pan with cold water and boil for around 45 minutes until tender. Drain and set aside.

Meanwhile, bring a pan of water to a boil, add the yucca root (cassava), and cook until tender. Drain and chop into large cubes. Set aside.

Cut the fish into ¾-inch/2-cm cubes and place in a bowl. Add the lemon juice, red onions, limo chiles, and chopped culantro or cilantro (coriander) and season with salt and pepper. Mix together thoroughly.

Arrange the lettuce leaves in the center of a large plate and spoon over the ceviche. Surround with the boiled yucca root and sarandaja beans, top with the tomato, and sprinkle over the cancha to finish.

LECHE DE TIGRE AL AJÍ AMARILLO EN VASO
YELLOW CHILE-SPICED TIGER MILK IN A GLASS

Serves: 4
Preparation Time: 25 minutes
Cooking Time: 2 minutes

The yellow chile in this tiger milk adds both flavor and heat and is a staple of Peruvian cuisine.

- 1 × 9-oz (250-g) squid
- 4 large clams
- ¼ corncob
- 1 tablespoon chopped red onion
- 1 teaspoon chopped limo chile
- 8 silverside fish fillets, cut into thirds
- 8 scallops
- 3 oz (85 g) octopus, cooked and chopped
- juice of 8 small lemons
- ½ cup (4 fl oz/120 ml) Blended Yellow Chiles (see p. 404)
- 3 ice cubes
- 1 teaspoon chopped culantro or cilantro (coriander) leaves
- 2 tablespoons cancha (toasted corn)
- salt

Tiger milk

- 1 cup (250 ml/8 fl oz) lemon juice (from around 2¼ lb (1 kg) of small lemons)
- ¼ cup (80 g) fish scraps (trimmings)
- ½ cup (120 ml/4 fl oz) fish broth (stock)
- 1 celery stalk, chopped
- 3 ice cubes
- ½ limo chile, seeded, membrane removed, and chopped
- 1 teaspoon chopped culantro or cilantro (coriander) leaves
- 1 small red onion, chopped

Put the squid in boiling water for 40 seconds, drain, and chop.

Cook the clams (in their shells) in boiling water for 20 seconds. Remove the meat from the shells and chop into ½-inch/1-cm cubes.

For the tiger milk, put the lemon juice, fish scraps (trimmings), broth (stock), celery, and ice cubes into a blender. Season with salt. Add the limo chile, culantro or cilantro (coriander) leaves, and red onion and blend together. Taste and add more salt if necessary. Strain into a container and refrigerate until needed.

Bring a pan of water to a boil, add the corncob, and cook until tender. Drain, remove the kernels, and set aside.

Place the red onion and chile in a bowl. Add the silverside fish fillets, scallops, clams, octopus, and squid. Pour over the lemon juice and season with salt. Mix together well. Add the blended chiles, pour over the refrigerated mixture, and add the ice cubes to chill. Add the culantro leaves and taste.

Divide the cooked corn kernels and cancha between four tall glasses.

Remove the ice cubes from the mixture and pour into the glasses. Serve.

CEVICHE DE MANGO
MANGO CEVICHE

Serves: 4
Preparation Time: 15 minutes, plus 15 minutes standing
Cooking Time: 12 minutes

There are some amazing varieties of mango in Peru. To prepare this dish, choose large mangoes with plenty of firm pulp.

- ½ sweet potato, peeled
- 8 large mangoes, peeled and pits (stones) removed
- 1 small red onion, thinly sliced
- 1 teaspoon chopped culantro or cilantro (coriander) leaves
- 1 teaspoon chopped limo chile
- 1 cup (8 fl oz/250 ml) lemon juice, from around 2¼ lb (1 kg) of small lemons
- 2 or 3 ice cubes
- 2 tablespoons cooked corn kernels
- salt and pepper

Bring a pan of water to a boil, add the sweet potato, and cook until tender. Drain and chop into ¾-inch/2-cm cubes. Set aside.

Chop the mango pulp into ¾-inch/2-cm cubes and set aside in the refrigerator to chill. Submerge the onion in iced water until it becomes crunchy, about 5 minutes.

Tip the mango cubes into a bowl and add the chopped culantro or cilantro (coriander) leaves and chile. Season with salt and mix together thoroughly. Add the lemon juice, the red onion, and a few ice cubes to chill the mixture. Mix together and remove the ice cubes.

To finish, add the boiled, cubed sweet potato and corn kernels. Season to taste with salt and pepper and serve.

CEVICHE DE ALCACHOFA
ARTICHOKE CEVICHE

Serves: 4
Preparation Time: 12 minutes
Cooking Time: 25–45 minutes

This recipe calls for very tender artichoke hearts.

- 16 artichoke hearts
- 1 tablespoon chopped limo chile
- 1 tablespoon chopped culantro or cilantro (coriander) leaves
- ½ teaspoon Garlic Paste (see p. 406)
- juice of 12 small lemons
- 1 red onion, thinly sliced
- 2 or 3 ice cubes
- salt and pepper

Bring a pan of water to a boil, add the artichoke hearts, and cook for 25–45 minutes until tender. Drain and slice into ¼-inch/5-mm slices, then place in a bowl and season with salt and pepper. Add the chopped chile, culantro or cilantro (coriander), and garlic paste and mix together thoroughly.

Pour in the lemon juice and mix thoroughly again, then add the red onion and the ice cubes to chill the mixture for a few minutes. Remove the ice cubes, taste, and season with salt and pepper.

Serve on individual plates.

CHINGUIRITO
DRIED FISH CEVICHE

Serves: 4
Preparation Time: 15 minutes, plus 8 hours 30 minutes soaking
Cooking Time: 45 minutes

If you can't find dried guitarfish, dried salt cod can be used instead, provided it has been soaked and desalinated.

2½ tablespoons cooked sarandaja beans
1 lb 5 oz (600 g) dried guitarfish or dried salt cod
2 cloves garlic, very finely chopped
2 teaspoons chopped culantro or cilantro (coriander) leaves
2 teaspoons chopped mochero chile
juice of 15 small lemons
2 or 3 ice cubes
1 red onion, sliced into half-moon crescents
salt and white pepper

To prepare the beans, soak them in cold water overnight. Drain and put into a pan with cold water. Boil for 45 minutes until tender. Drain.

Put the dried guitarfish or dried salt cod in a bowl of cold water, cover with water, and let stand for 30 minutes to soak, changing the water every 10 minutes.

Drain well, shred it into small pieces, and place in a bowl. Add the chopped garlic, culantro or cilantro (coriander) leaves, and mochero chile and mix together well. Season with salt to taste.

Pour over the lemon juice and add the sarandaja beans. Mix together. Season with salt and white pepper. Add the ice cubes to chill and mix thoroughly.

Taste and add more salt if necessary. Add the red onion and remove the ice cubes. Serve on individual plates.

TIRADITO LA MAR LAQUEADO
SEARED LA MAR TUNA TIRADITO

Serves: 4
Preparation Time: 10 minutes
Cooking Time: 15 minutes

This La Mar tiradito was born in our Lima *cevichería* five years ago. It is now a classic in many other restaurants.

Banana Passion Fruit Juice
1 cup (8 fl oz/250 ml) banana passion fruit or passion fruit juice made from the pulp of 2¼ lb (1 kg) of banana and 1 lb (800 g) passion fruit

2 tablespoons honey
¼-inch/5-mm piece fresh ginger, peeled and finely chopped
1 sprig lemon verbena
3 tablespoons Mayonnaise (see p. 412)
1 tablespoon oyster sauce
1 × 14-oz (400-g) tuna fillet
1 cup (11 oz/300 g) salt
juice of 12 small lemons
1 × 2½ oz (65 g) small turnip, thinly sliced

To garnish
2 teaspoons sesame seeds
2 scallions (spring onions), green part only, chopped

Put the banana passion fruit or passion fruit juice, honey, ginger, and lemon verbena into a pan over medium heat. Cook, stirring, for around 10 minutes or until the liquid has reduced to a syrup. Set aside to cool.

Mix together the mayonnaise and oyster sauce in a bowl, cover with plastic wrap (clingfilm), and refrigerate until needed.

Coat the tuna fillet with the salt, then pierce the fillet with a skewer and place it directly over a naked flame so that a crust forms. Once all sides of the tuna fillet have been exposed to the flame, plunge the fish into iced water to stop the cooking process.

Remove the salt crust from the tuna, dry thoroughly and cut into slices of around 1¼ × ¾ × 1½ inches (3 × 2 × 4 cm). Fan the slices out on a plate or platter and season with salt.

Mix together the lemon juice and cooled passion fruit syrup in a bowl and pour over the tuna slices.

Drizzle lines of oyster mayonnaise across the tuna and place the turnip slices in the center of the plate. Sprinkle sesame seeds and chopped scallion (spring onion) around the edges to garnish.

LECHE DE TIGRE CLÁSICA EN VASO
CLASSIC TIGER MILK IN A GLASS

Serves: 4
Preparation Time: 25 minutes
Cooking Time: 20 minutes

Tiger milk is traditionally used as a marinade for ceviche. Nowadays, it is also served as an aperitif that supposedly has the power to cure hangovers and act as an aphrodisiac.

8 snails
4 mussels
1 × 9-oz (250-g) squid, cleaned
¼ corncob
1 tablespoon chopped red onion
1 teaspoon chopped limo chile
8 silverside fish fillets, cut into thirds
8 scallops, cut in half
4 shrimp (prawns), shelled, cut in half lengthwise
juice of 5 small lemons
3 ice cubes
1 teaspoon chopped culantro or cilantro (coriander) leaves
2 tablespoons cancha (toasted corn), to garnish
salt

Tiger milk
1 cup (8 fl oz/250 ml) lemon juice from around 2¼ lb (1 kg) small lemons
¼ cup (3 oz/80 g) fish scraps (trimmings)
½ cup (4 fl oz/120 ml) fish broth (stock)
1 celery stalk, chopped
3 ice cubes
½ limo chile, seeded, membrane removed, and chopped
1 teaspoon chopped culantro or cilantro (coriander) leaves
1 small red onion, chopped

Boil the snails in 8½ cups (68 fl oz/2 liters) water until tender. Drain and remove from their shells. Cut into ¼-inch/5-mm slices.

Cook the mussels (in their shells) in boiling water for 2 minutes. Remove the meat from the shells. Put the squid in boiling water for 40 seconds, drain, and chop.

For the tiger milk, put the lemon juice, fish scraps (trimmings), broth (stock), celery, and ice cubes into a blender. Season with salt. Add the limo chile, culantro or cilantro (coriander) leaves, and red onion and blend together. Taste and add more salt if necessary. Strain into a suitable container and refrigerate until needed.

Bring a pan of water to a boil, add the corncob, and cook until tender. Drain and remove the kernels. Set aside.

Put the red onion and chopped limo chile into a bowl. Add the silverside fish pieces, scallops, snails, shrimp (prawns), mussels, and squid. Pour over the lemon juice and season with salt. Mix together well. Pour over the refrigerated tiger milk mixture and add the ice cubes to chill. Add the culantro leaves and taste, adding more salt if necessary.

Divide the cooked corn kernels between 4 tall glasses.

Remove the ice cubes from the mixture and pour into the glasses. Sprinkle over the cancha to garnish and serve.

Classic Tiradito

TIRADITO AL ROCOTO
ROCOTO CHILE SPICED TIRADITO

Serves: 4
Preparation Time: 10 minutes
Cooking Time: 12 minutes

When it comes to tiraditos, Peruvians like them hot. Don't be afraid to add spice to feel the heat in this dish.

¼ corncob
14 oz (400 g) white fish fillet (such as sole, croaker, or grouper)
juice of 12 small lemons
2 tablespoons Rocoto Chili Paste (see p. 407)
4 tablespoons evaporated milk
2 ice cubes
salt and white pepper

To garnish
2 teaspoons chopped culantro or cilantro (coriander) leaves
2 teaspoons chopped limo chile

Bring a pan of water to a boil, add the corncob and cook until tender. Drain and remove the kernels. Set aside.

Cut the fish into thin slices of around 1¼ × ¾ × 1½ inches/3 × 2 × 4 cm and fan them out on a plate or platter. Season with salt and white pepper.

Mix together the lemon juice, chili paste, and evaporated milk in a separate bowl. Add the ice cubes to chill, taste, and adjust the seasoning if necessary. Remove the ice cubes.

Pour the lemon and chile dressing over the fish slices and place the cooked corn kernels in the center of the fan.

Garnish with chopped culantro or cilantro (coriander) leaves and limo chile.

TIRADITO CLÁSICO
CLASSIC TIRADITO

Serves: 4
Preparation Time: 8 minutes
Cooking Time: 12 minutes

The tiradito is closely related to ceviche. The characteristic way the fish is cut into thin slices is thought to be influenced by Japanese culinary style, although Italians around the Port of Callao also claim it as their creation.

¼ corncob
14 oz (400 g) white fish fillet (such as sole, croaker, or grouper)
juice of 12 small lemons
salt and white pepper

To garnish
2 teaspoons chopped culantro or cilantro (coriander) leaves
2 teaspoons chopped limo chile

Bring a pan of water to a boil, add the corncob, and cook until tender. Drain and remove the kernels. Set aside.

Cut the fish into thin slices of around 1¼ × ¾ × 1½ inches (3 × 2 × 4 cm) and fan them out on a plate or platter. Season with salt and white pepper and pour over the lemon juice.

Garnish with the cooked corn kernels, chopped culantro or cilantro (coriander) leaves, and limo chile.

TIRADITO DE PULPO DOS OLIVOS DEL CHEF CIRO WATANABE
CIRO WATANABE'S TWO-OLIVE OCTOPUS TIRADITO

Serves: 4
Preparation Time: 12 minutes
Cooking Time: 2–5 minutes

Watanabe is a Peruvian chef of Japanese descent. His people skills and culinary talent bring beautiful dishes like this tiradito to life.

1 tablespoon Black Olive Paste (see p. 408)
4 tablespoons Mayonnaise (see p. 412)
1 tablespoon Green Olive Paste (see p. 408)
2 tablespoons sesame oil
2 tablespoons oyster sauce
juice of 5 small lemons
14 oz (400 g) Cooked Octopus, thinly sliced (see p. 406)
1 teaspoon chopped limo chile
1 teaspoon chopped culantro or cilantro (coriander) leaves
½ teaspoon shichimi togarashi spice mixture
¾ cup (½ oz/15 g) arugula (rocket) leaves
½ cup (½ oz/15 g) watercress
16 gyoza wrappers
1 cup (8 fl oz/250 ml) vegetable oil
salt and pepper

Mix together the black olive paste and half the mayonnaise. Set aside. Repeat with the green olive paste and remaining mayonnaise.

Mix together the sesame oil, oyster sauce, and two-thirds of the lemon juice in a bowl.

Divide the cooked octopus slices into 2 portions and arrange on a plate or platter, leaving a space in the middle. Season with salt and pepper.

Drizzle a line of black olive mayonnaise across one-half of the octopus slices. Sprinkle over the chopped limo chile and culantro or cilantro (coriander) leaves and pour over half the remaining lemon juice.

Drizzle a line of green olive mayonnaise across the other half of the octopus slices. Sprinkle with the shichimi togarashi and pour over the last of the lemon juice.

Put the arugula (rocket) and watercress into a bowl with the sesame and oyster sauce dressing. Mix together well.

Heat the vegetable oil in a saucepan and fry the gyoza wrappers in batches for 1–2 minutes on each side until golden brown. Drain.

Place the salad in the center of the plate and serve the fried gyoza wrappers on the side.

JALADITO DE CACHEMA DEL CHEF HÉCTOR SOLÍS
HÉCTOR SOLÍS' SALT-CURED FISH

Serves: 2
Preparation Time: 5 minutes, plus 20 minutes curing

The Solís family are great worldwide ambassadors of Northern Peruvian cooking. Their heir, Héctor, is also one of the greatest chefs in Peru. His flavorsome creations are nothing short of perfect.

⅔ cup (7 oz/200 g) salt
7 oz (200 g) white fish fillet (such as Peruvian weakfish or croaker)
juice of 6 small lemons
4 yellow chiles, seeded, membrane removed, and chopped

To cure the fish fillet, spread ⅓ cup (3½ oz/100 g) salt on a flat dish. Place the fillet on top and sprinkle another ⅓ cup (3½ oz/100 g) of salt over the fish until it is evenly coated. Let stand for 20 minutes.

Once the fish has been cured, remove the salt. Cut the fish into 1¼ × ¾ × 1½-inch/3 × 2 × 4-cm slices and fan them out on a plate or platter. Pour over the lemon juice, sprinkle over the yellow chiles, and serve.

TIRADITO DE ATÚN Y COCONA DEL CHEF FLAVIO SOLÓRZANO

FLAVIO SOLÓRZANO'S TUNA AND COCONA FRUIT TIRADITO

Serves: 4
Preparation Time: 12 minutes

The Solórzano family have always encouraged a love of Peruvian flavors, even when cooks of my generation still looked to Europe for inspiration. Flavio, a third-generation cook, continues to inspire us today.

1 cup (8 fl oz/250 ml) cocona fruit juice
1 teaspoon Garlic Paste (see p. 406)
1 teaspoon ginger juice made from ⅓ cup (1¼ oz/30 g) pulped fresh ginger
½ small white onion, chopped
1 limo chile, crushed with the back of a knife
1 lb 5 oz (600 g) tuna fillet
½ avocado
30 yucca root (cassava) chips (crisps)
salt and white pepper

To garnish
1 tablespoon culantro or cilantro (coriander) leaves, chopped
1 limo chile, sliced

Mix together the cocona fruit juice, garlic paste, ginger juice, and chopped onion in a bowl. Season with salt and white pepper, add the crushed limo chile, and set aside for a few minutes to let the flavors develop.

Cut the tuna into 1¼ × ¾ × 1½-inch/3 × 2 × 4-cm slices.

Cut the avocado into ½-inch/1-cm cubes, season with salt, and mix together with ½ teaspoon of the cocona mixture in a bowl.

Spoon 2 tablespoons of the cocona mixture onto the center of a plate or platter. Fan the tuna slices out on top and cover with the remaining mixture.

Spoon the avocado cubes onto the center of the plate and pile the cassava chips (crisps) on top. Garnish with culantro or cilantro (coriander) leaves and limo chile slices.

TIRADITOESTILO ORIENTAL DE LA CHEF MARILÚ MADUEÑO

MARILÚ MADUEÑO'S ASIAN-STYLE TIRADITO

Serves: 4
Preparation Time: 12 minutes
Cooking Time: 5 minutes

Huaca Pucllana, run by the amazing Marilú Madueño, is one of the most beautiful restaurants in Lima.

1 lb 5 oz (600 g) tuna fillet
2 tablespoons Yellow Chili Paste (see p. 405)
1-inch (2.5-cm) piece fresh ginger, peeled and grated
1 tablespoon oyster sauce
juice of 5 small lemons
2 tablespoons soy sauce
1 tablespoon sesame oil
1 tablespoon shichimi togarashi spice mixture
salt

Vegetable side salad
1 cup (2½ oz/65 g) snow peas (mangetout)
⅓ carrot, chopped
⅓ red bell pepper, seeded, membrane removed, and chopped
2 tablespoons chopped peanuts
2 tablespoons olive oil

To prepare the vegetable side salad, bring a pan of water to a boil, add the snow peas (mangetout), and cook until tender. Drain, coarsely chop, and put into a bowl with the chopped carrot, bell pepper, and peanuts. Add the olive oil and mix together. Season with salt and set aside.

Cut the tuna into 1¼ × ¾ × 1½-inch/3 × 2 × 4-cm slices.

In a bowl, mix together the yellow chili paste, grated ginger, and oyster sauce with a whisk. Whisk in four-fifths of the lemon juice, the soy sauce, and the sesame oil, then add the shichimi togarashi. Mix together well.

Fan the tuna slices out on a plate or platter, season with salt, and pour over the remaining lemon juice. Spoon over the chile mixture and serve with the vegetable side salad.

TIRADITO AL AJÍ AMARILLO
YELLOW CHILE-SPICED TIRADITO

Serves: 4
Preparation Time: 10 minutes
Cooking Time: 12 minutes

The silverside fish fillets can be replaced with fresh anchovies or fresh sardines.

¼ corncob
48 silverside fish fillets (1 lb/450 g), cleaned
2 teaspoons chopped limo chile
¼ small celery stalk, chopped
4 teaspoons chopped culantro or cilantro (coriander) leaves
juice of 12 small lemons
3 tablespoons Blended Yellow Chiles (see p. 404)
2 ice cubes
salt and white pepper

Bring a pan of water to a boil, add the corncob, and cook until tender. Drain and remove the kernels. Set aside.

Place the silverside fish fillets in a bowl and season with salt and white pepper. Add the chopped limo chile, celery, and half the culantro or cilantro (coriander) leaves. Mix thoroughly to combine the flavors.

In a separate bowl, mix together the lemon juice and blended chiles. Add the ice cubes to chill, taste, and adjust the seasoning if necessary. Remove the ice cubes.

Fan the silverside fish fillets out on a plate or platter. Pour over the lemon and chile dressing and place the cooked corn kernels in the center of the fan.

Garnish with the remaining chopped culantro leaves.

TIRADITO BACHICHE
ITALIAN TIRADITO

Serves: 4
Preparation Time: 10 minutes
Cooking Time: 12 minutes

The Parmesan cheese in this recipe should be added sparingly, following the culinary style adopted by the earliest Italian immigrants in Peru.

¼ corncob
1 cup (250 ml/8 fl oz) lemon juice, plus the juice of 12 small lemons
2¼ oz (60 g) fish scraps (trimmings)
1 tablespoon extra-virgin olive oil
2 tablespoons grated Parmesan cheese
2 × 6-oz (175-g) white fish fillets (such as sole, croaker, or grouper)
4 tablespoons evaporated milk
salt

To garnish
1 teaspoon chopped culantro or cilantro (coriander) leaves
2 teaspoons chopped limo chile

Bring a pan of water to a boil, add the corncob, and cook until tender. Drain and remove the kernels. Set aside.

Put 1 cup (8 fl oz/250 ml) lemon juice into a blender with the fish scraps (trimmings), olive oil, and Parmesan cheese. Blend together, strain, and set aside.

Cut the fish fillets into 1¼ × ¾ × 1½-inch/3 × 2 × 4-cm slices and fan them out on a plate or platter. Season with salt and pour over the remaining lemon juice.

Mix together the lemon and Parmesan mixture with the evaporated milk in a bowl. Taste and add more salt if necessary. Pour this mixture over the fish slices and place the cooked corn kernels in the center of the plate.

Garnish with chopped culantro or cilantro (coriander) leaves and limo chile.

Yellow Chile-Spiced Tiradito

TIRADITO TEMPLANZA DEL RESTAURANTE PESCADOS CAPITALES
TEMPLANZA TUNA TIRADITO FROM THE PESCADOS CAPITALES RESTAURANT

Serves: 4
Preparation Time: 12 minutes
Cooking Time: 12 minutes

The restaurant Pescados Capitales specializes in fish and seafood and is a favorite in Lima.

¾ corncob
1 lb 1 oz (480 g) tuna fillet
3½ oz (100 g) white button mushrooms
8 asparagus spears, blanched
3 tablespoons lemon juice
1 celery stalk, chopped
2 teaspoons chopped culantro or cilantro (coriander) leaves
2 teaspoons chopped limo chile
1 teaspoon ground black pepper
1 cooked sweet potato

Templanza sauce
½ cup (4 fl oz/120 ml) olive oil
1 cup (8 fl oz/250 ml) vegetable oil
1½ eggs
1½ tablespoons mango chutney
1½ tablespoons honey
2 teaspoons oyster sauce
1 teaspoon balsamic vinegar
1 tablespoon orange juice
pinch of ground black pepper

Bring a pan of water to a boil, add the corncob, and cook until tender. Drain and remove the kernels. Set aside.

To prepare the templanza sauce, whisk together all the ingredients in a bowl until you have a smooth, emulsified dressing. Set aside.

Cut the tuna into 1¼ × ¾ × 1½-inch/3 × 2 × 4-cm slices and roll them up. Arrange the tuna rolls on a plate or platter, interspersed with the white button mushrooms and asparagus spears, leaving space in the center of the plate.

Mix together the lemon juice, celery, culantro or cilantro (coriander) leaves, limo chile, and black pepper in a bowl. Pour over the tuna rolls.

Place the glazed sweet potato in the center of the plate and spoon over the cooked corn kernels. Finish by drizzling the sauce over the rolls.

TIRADITO A LA CHALACA DEL CHEF JOSÉ DEL CASTILLO
JOSÉ DEL CASTILLO'S CHALACA-STYLE TIRADITO

Serves: 4
Preparation Time: 12 minutes
Cooking Time: 12 minutes

José del Castillo has inherited the flavors of a family that has been dedicated to Peruvian cooking for decades. His restaurant La Red is a firm favourite in Peru.

2 corncobs
1¾ lb (800 g) Peruvian weakfish fillet or other white fish fillet
2 limo chiles
juice of 15 small lemons
1 clove garlic, crushed
1 tablespoon white wine vinegar
2 red onions, diced
2 tomatoes, skinned, seeded, and chopped
3 tablespoons chopped culantro or cilantro (coriander) leaves
salt and pepper

To serve
3 sweet potatoes, boiled and sliced
2 tablespoons cancha (toasted corn)

Bring a pan of water to a boil, add the corncobs, and cook until tender. Drain and remove the kernels. Set aside.

Cut the fish into 1¼ × ¾ × 1½-inch/3 × 2 × 4-cm slices and fan them out on 4 plates or one large platter. Refrigerate.

Seed, remove the membranes, and chop the limo chiles, keeping a slice of chile aside.

Mix together the lemon juice, crushed garlic, vinegar, and the reserved chile slice in a bowl. Season with salt and pepper and set aside.

In a separate bowl, mix together the onions, chopped limo chile, tomatoes, cooked corn kernels, and culantro or cilantro (coriander) leaves to make a salsa.

Remove the fish from the refrigerator and season with salt and pepper. Pour over the lemon juice mixture, spoon over the salsa, and serve with the sweet potatoes and cancha.

TIRADITO APALTADO DEL CHEF RAFAEL OSTERLING

CHEF RAFAEL OSTERLING'S TIRADITO APALTADO

Serves: 4
Preparation Time: 35 minutes
Cooking Time: 1 hour 25 minutes

Rafael Osterling is one of Peru's greatest chefs. His ceviche restaurant El Mercado created this amazing tiradito that is bursting with flavor.

2 cups (18 fl oz/500 ml) Tiger Milk (see p. 409)
juice of 6 small lemons
½ cup (4 fl oz/120 ml) fish broth (stock)
12 oz (350 g) sole fillet
24 scallops
½ avocado, quartered and thinly sliced
3 tablespoons extra virgin olive oil
3 small sprigs culantro or cilantro (coriander), to garnish
salt

Vegetable cream
½ celery stalk, trimmed and chopped
½ leek, trimmed and chopped
1 onion, chopped
10 cloves garlic
¼-inch (5-mm) piece fresh ginger, peeled and chopped
4 cups (34 fl oz/1 liter) fish broth (stock)

Rocoto chili aioli
1 garlic bulb
1 rocoto chile
1 tablespoon olive oil

Chile condiment
1 limo chile, seeded, membrane removed, and chopped
1 yellow mochero chile, seeded, membrane removed, and chopped
4 finely chopped red onions, soaked in iced water and drained
juice of 3 lemons
2 tablespoons olive oil
1 teaspoon chopped culantro or cilantro (coriander) leaves
salt

For the vegetable cream, place all the ingredients in a pan, bring to a simmer, and cook for 25 minutes until the vegetables are very tender. Let cool, then place in a food processor and blend together until smooth and creamy. Set aside.

To prepare the rocoto chili aioli, clean the garlic bulb and slice off the top and bottom. Place the garlic bulb in a pan with the chile, cover with water, and simmer for about 30 minutes over low heat. Drain and repeat the process. Let cool, then extract the cooked garlic pulp and peel and seed the chile. Blend the garlic and chile together in a food processor with the olive oil until smooth. Strain the mixture and set aside.

For the tiradito, pour the tiger milk and lemon juice into a bowl. Add 2 tablespoons of the vegetable cream, 1 teaspoon of the rocoto chili aioli, and the fish broth (stock). Whisk together thoroughly and refrigerate until needed.

In a separate bowl, prepare the chile condiment by mixing together the limo chile, yellow mochero chile, and chopped onions, and season with salt. Add the lemon juice and olive oil, stir through the chopped culantro or cilantro (coriander) leaves, and mix together thoroughly.

Cut the fish and scallops into ¼-inch/5-mm slices and arrange them on a plate, alternating the fish and scallop slices. Season with salt and pour over the refrigerated tiger milk mixture. Spoon the prepared condiment in a strip down the length of the plate and fan out the avocado slices in the center of the plate.

Drizzle with the extra-virgin olive oil and garnish with the culantro sprigs.

TIRADITO NIKKEI
JAPANESE-INSPIRED TIRADITO

Serves: 4
Preparation Time: 10 minutes

You can also use bonito, salmon, or trout to prepare this tiradito dish.

1 × 14-oz (400-g) tuna fillet
juice of 12 small lemons
½ tablespoon Panca Chili Paste (see p. 406)
1 teaspoon honey
1 teaspoon soy sauce
1 tablespoon sugar-free tamarind juice concentrate
2 teaspoons pickled sushi ginger
2 scallions (spring onions), green part only, chopped
2 teaspoons sesame oil
1 × 2½ oz (65 g) small turnip, thinly sliced
1 nori seaweed sheet, thinly sliced, to garnish
salt and white pepper

Cut the tuna into thin slices of around 1¼ × ¾ × 1½ inches/3 × 2 × 4 cm and fan them out on a plate or platter. Season with salt and white pepper.

Mix together the lemon juice, panca chili paste, honey, soy sauce, and tamarind juice in a bowl. Pour the mixture over the tuna.

Scatter the pickled sushi ginger and scallions (spring onions) over the tuna slices. Drizzle over the sesame oil and place the turnip slices in the center of the plate. Garnish with nori seaweed sheet slices.

TIRADITO A LOS DOS AJÍES
DOUBLE CHILE TIRADITO

Serves: 4
Preparation Time: 8 minutes
Cooking Time: 12 minutes

This tiradito dish should always be prepared with firm-fleshed, skinless, boneless white fish.

1 corncob
2 tablespoons Blended Yellow Chiles (see p. 404)
2 tablespoons Rocoto Chili Paste (see p. 407)
juice of 15 small lemons
4 ice cubes
2 × 6-oz (175-g) white fish fillets (such as sole, croaker, or grouper)
salt and white pepper

Bring a pan of water to a boil, add the corncob, and cook until tender. Drain and remove the kernels. Set aside.

Place the blended chiles in one bowl and the chili paste in another. Divide the lemon juice, reserving 2 tablespoons, evenly between both bowls and season both with salt and white pepper. Add 2 ice cubes to each bowl to chill the mixtures and stir. Remove the ice cubes from both bowls.

Cut the fish fillets into thin slices of around 1¼ × ¾ × 1½ inches (3 × 2 × 4 cm) and fan them out on a plate or platter. Season with salt. Pour over the remaining lemon juice.

Pour the yellow chile mixture over half of the fish fillet slices and the rocoto chili mixture over the other half. Place the cooked corn kernels in the center. Serve.

Japanese-Inspired Tiradito

Serves: 4
Preparation Time: 12 minutes, plus 3 hours chilling
Cooking Time: 2 minutes

Pedro Miguel Schiaffino's passion for the Peruvian Amazon has inspired many other chefs to appreciate this region. His boundless creativity brings magical dishes such as this one to life.

½ oz (20 g) airampo seeds or 2 beets (beetroot)
11 oz (300g) sole fillet
salt and pepper

Banana passion fruit milk
4 tablespoons Banana Passion Fruit Juice (see p. 34)
4 tablespoons Tiger Milk (see p. 409)

Avocado cream
1 ripe avocado, peeled, pitted (stoned), and chopped
2 tablespoons Tiger Milk (see p. 409)
1 tablespoon olive oil

To garnish
1 tablespoon flying fish roe, salmon roe, or caviar
3 cress flowers

TIRADITO TAIDAI DE PESCADO CON JUGO DE TUMBO DEL CHEF PEDRO MIGUEL SCHIAFFINO

CHEF MIGUEL SCHIAFFINO'S TIE-DYE FISH TIRADITO WITH BANANA PASSION FRUIT JUICE

Put the airampo seeds or beets (beetroot) into a pan, cover with 5 tablespoons water, and warm over a medium heat for 2 minutes. Strain into a bowl. Add a 32-inch/80-cm square piece of gauze to the pan to dye it, then remove it from the liquid, squeezing out any excess water. Lay the gauze on a baking sheet and let dry.

Wrap the fish fillet in the dyed gauze, then cover with plastic wrap (clingfilm) and refrigerate for 3 hours.

For the banana passion fruit milk, whisk the banana passion fruit juice with the tiger milk until emulsified. Cover with plastic wrap (clingfilm) and refrigerate.

To make the avocado cream, put the avocado and tiger milk in a blender and blend together, gradually adding the olive oil, until the mixture is creamy. Refrigerate until needed.

Cut the fish fillet into thin slices and season them with salt and pepper. Arrange the slices one on top of the other so that they overlap slightly, then roll them tightly together to form a rosette. Place on a cutting board and pour over the banana passion fruit milk.

Spoon the avocado cream onto the center of a plate and place the fish rosette on top. Garnish with the fish roe and cress flowers.

TIRADITO DE CONCHAS TOMA DE MAR DEL CHEF VIRGILIO MARTÍNEZ
CHEF VIRGILIO MARTÍNEZ'S TOMA DE MAR SCALLOP TIRADITO

Serves: 4
Preparation Time: 15 minutes, plus 12 hours chilling
Cooking Time: 18 minutes

Chef Virgilio Martínez has become a worldwide sensation thanks to his talent, passion, and commitment. His cooking is a box of surprises that never ceases to amaze, and recounts the history of Peru.

- 1 cup (9 oz/250 g) cooked and fried amaranth
- 4 cups (32 fl oz/950 ml) vegetable oil
- 20 large scallops, cleaned
- scant ½ cup (3½ fl oz/100 ml) Tiger Milk (see p. 409)
- 1¼ cups (10 fl oz/300 ml) cocona fruit juice
- ⅔ cup (5 fl oz/150 ml) lemon juice
- scant 1 cup (7 fl oz/200 ml) Banana Passion Fruit Juice (see p. 34)
- 1 tablespoon Yellow Chili Paste (see p. 405)
- pinch of sugar
- starflower calyx, to garnish
- salt

Avocado and seaweed emulsion

- 1 bunch parsley leaves
- 1 cup (8 fl oz/250 ml) vegetable oil
- 2 avocados
- juice of 4 small lemons
- ¾ oz (20g) yuyo seaweed

Boil 3 cups (26 fl oz/700 ml) of water and add the amaranth. Boil for 8 minutes and drain well.

When the amaranth is dry, put the oil in a pan. Heat to 350°F/180°C and fry the amaranth until it is crispy and colored.

Drain, remove, and place on paper towels to absorb the remaining oil. Set aside in a warm place.

For the avocado and seaweed emulsion, bring a pan of water to a boil, add the parsley, and blanch for 1 minute. Remove the parsley from the water, shaking off any excess, and put into a blender with the vegetable oil. Blend together, then strain through a fine-meshed strainer (sieve). Refrigerate overnight.

The following day, peel, pit (stone), and cut the avocado into pieces. Put the avocado into a food processor with the oil and parsley mixture, lemon juice, and yuyo seaweed and blend together until smooth. Set aside.

To make the tiradito, cut the scallops into quarters and coat with the cooked, fried, and crispy amaranth. Set aside.

Mix the tiger milk together with the cocona fruit juice, lemon juice, banana passion fruit juice, chili paste, and sugar. Season with salt and refrigerate for a maximum of 4 hours.

Dot a serving platter with the avocado emulsion, place the amaranth-coated scallop quarters on top, and drizzle over the tiger milk mixture. Garnish with the starflower calyx.

TIRADITO DE PEJERREY CON CONCHAS AL AJÍAMARILLO AHUMADO DEL CHEF MITSUHARU TSUMURA – RESTAURANTE MAIDO
CHEF MITSUHARU TSUMURA'S SILVERSIDE TIRADITO WITH SCALLOPS IN SMOKED YELLOW CHILI SAUCE

Serves: 6
Preparation Time: 30 minutes
Cooking Time: 25 minutes

Chef Micha, as his friends call him, is one of the chefs who are reinventing Peruvian-Japanese cuisine, also known as Nikkei cuisine. His restaurant Maido is a must-try in Lima.

3 scallops
1 scallion (spring onion), sliced diagonally
2 tablespoons red bell pepper, seeded, membrane removed, and thinly sliced
6 silverside fish fillets (2½–2¾ oz/60–70 g each)
1 oz (30 g) tenkatsu (deep-fried tempura batter)
2 nori seaweed sheets cut into thin strips

Tiger milk
8 small lemons
½ cup (4 fl oz/120 ml) ichiban dashi or light fish broth (stock)
¼ clove garlic, peeled and grated
pinch of salt
1 celery stalk
⅛ oz (5 g) white fish, cut into ½-inch (1-cm) cubes

Smoked yellow chili sauce
7 oz (200 g) whole yellow chiles, seeded, membranes removed, and halved
¾ cup (6 fl oz/175 ml) vegetable oil
2 tablespoons finely diced red onion
½ small garlic clove, peeled
pinch of salt
1 teaspoon tamari soy sauce
1 tablespoon rice vinegar
1 small scallion (spring onion), green part only, cut into thin rings

Chile condiment
2 tablespoons diced red onion
¼ limo chile, seeded, membrane removed, and diced
½ teaspoon chopped culantro or cilantro (coriander) leaves
2 teaspoons ponzu sauce

Start by making the tiger milk. Pour the lemon juice and the dashi or fish broth (stock) into a bowl and add the grated garlic and salt. Mix together thoroughly. Crush the celery stalk a little with a rolling pin and add it to the mixture with the fish. Cover with plastic wrap (clingfilm) and refrigerate until needed.

To make the smoked yellow chili sauce, put the chiles into a pan and cover with water. Bring to a boil and simmer for 8 minutes. Drain and let cool, then peel off the skins and set aside.

Heat 2 tablespoons of the vegetable oil in a wok over very high heat. Add the onion, garlic, and parboiled chiles and stir-fry for 2 minutes, then lower the heat and cook slowly for 10 minutes until the onion mixture is very soft. Transfer the mixture to a blender, add the salt, and blend together, gradually adding the tamari soy sauce, rice vinegar, and remaining oil until the mixture is smooth and creamy. Strain into a bowl and let cool, then add the scallion (spring onion) and 2½ tablespoons of the prepared tiger milk. Set aside.

Make the chile condiment by mixing the red onion, limo chile, and culantro or cilantro (coriander) leaves in a small bowl. Add the ponzu sauce and 2 tablespoons of the prepared tiger milk. Set aside.

To make the tiradito, take one scallop and cut lengthwise with a knife, then shape it to form a rectangle. Cut the rectangle in half and repeat the process with the remaining scallops.

Place a scallop half and a little scallion and sliced bell pepper in the center of 1 silverside fillet. Roll up the fillet and repeat the process with the remaining fillets and scallops. Refrigerate.

Spread ½ cup (4 fl oz/120ml) of the smoked yellow chili sauce evenly over the center of a rectangular platter. Arrange the silverside rolls on top and spoon over the chile condiment. Garnish with tenkatsu and nori to finish.

MUCHAME DE ATÚN
TUNA MUCHAME

Serves: 4
Preparation Time: 10 minutes, plus 20 minutes soaking

A derivation of *mojama* or *musciame*, Peruvian *muchame* was originally prepared with a type of dolphin meat, which endangered the species. Fortunately, the use of dolphin has been forbidden for some time and now other marine species such as tuna are used.

- 14 oz (400 g) dried, salted, sun-cured tuna fillet
- juice of 4 small lemons
- 1 tablespoon red wine vinegar
- 4 tablespoons olive oil
- 2 cloves garlic, very finely chopped
- 1 teaspoon dried oregano
- 2 ripe avocados
- 6 tomatoes
- saltine crackers or savory crackers, to serve
- salt and pepper

Cut the tuna into thin slices, put into a bowl, and soak in water for 10 minutes. Change the water and soak for another 10 minutes. Strain and place on a serving platter.

Add a quarter of the lemon juice, the red wine vinegar, olive oil, garlic, and oregano. Season with salt and pepper to taste, mix together thoroughly, and set aside.

Peel, pit (stone), and slice the avocados. Skin, slice, and dress the tomatoes with the remaining lemon juice and a little salt. Arrange the avocado and tomato slices on a separate serving platter.

To serve, place one avocado slice and one tomato slice on a cracker and top with the tuna.

ALMEJAS A LA CHALACA
CLAMS A LA CHALACA

Serves: 4
Preparation Time: 15 minutes
Cooking Time: 15 minutes

This recipe also works well with oysters.

- 1 corncob
- 16 clams, cleaned
- 1½ tomatoes, skinned, seeded, and chopped
- 3 teaspoons chopped limo chile
- 1 red onion, chopped
- 1 clove garlic, very finely chopped
- 1½ teaspoons chopped culantro or cilantro (coriander) leaves
- ½ chopped scallion (spring onion), green part only
- juice of 15 small lemons
- 3 or 4 ice cubes, plus extra for serving
- salt and white pepper

Bring a pan of water to a boil, add the corncob, and cook until tender. Drain and remove the kernels. Set aside.

Clean and wash the clam meat, setting the shells aside. Bring a pan of water to a boil. Add the clams and blanch. Drain and set aside.

To make the chalaca dressing, put the chopped tomatoes, limo chile, red onion, garlic, culantro or cilantro (coriander) leaves, and scallion (spring onion) into a bowl. Season with salt and white pepper and mix together.

Pour over the lemon juice and add the cooked corn kernels and the ice cubes to chill. Mix together well, taste, and add more salt if necessary, then remove the ice.

Return the clams to their shells and pour over the dressing. Serve on a platter on a bed of crushed ice.

CONCHAS A LA CHALACA
SCALLOPS A LA CHALACA

Serves: 4
Preparation Time: 12 minutes
Cooking Time: 12 minutes

The name of this recipe comes from the word *chalaco,* which is the name given to the residents of the Port of Callao, west of Lima.

1 corncob
1 tomato, skinned, seeded, and chopped
2 teaspoons chopped limo chile
1 small red onion, chopped
1 clove garlic, very finely chopped
1 teaspoon chopped culantro or cilantro (coriander) leaves
¼ chopped scallion (spring onion), green part only
juice of 12 small lemons
3 or 4 ice cubes, plus extra for serving
12 scallops in their shells, cleaned
salt

Bring a pan of water to a boil, add the corncob, and cook until tender. Drain and remove the kernels. Set aside.

To make the chalaca dressing, put the chopped tomato, limo chile, red onion, garlic, culantro or cilantro (coriander) leaves, and scallion (spring onion) into a bowl. Season with salt and mix together.

Pour over the lemon juice and add the cooked corn kernels and the ice cubes to chill. Mix together well, taste, and add more salt if necessary, then remove the ice.

Place each clean scallop in a half shell and pour over the dressing. Serve on a platter on a bed of crushed ice.

CHORITOS A LA CHALACA
MUSSELS A LA CHALACA

Serves: 4
Preparation Time: 18 minutes
Cooking Time: 15 minutes

½ corncob
16 mussels, washed
1½ tomatoes, skinned, seeded, and chopped
3 teaspoons chopped limo chile
1 red onion, chopped
1 clove garlic, very finely chopped
1½ teaspoons chopped culantro or cilantro (coriander) leaves
½ scallion (spring onion), green part only, chopped
juice of 12 small lemons
3 or 4 ice cubes, plus extra for serving
salt

Bring a pan of water to a boil, add the corncob and cook until tender. Drain and remove the kernels. Set aside.

Bring a pan of water to a boil. Add the mussels and cook for 3–4 minutes until tender. Drain, remove the meat, and set the shells aside.

To make the chalaca dressing, put the chopped tomato, limo chile, red onion, garlic, culantro or cilantro (coriander) leaves, and scallion (spring onion) into a bowl. Season with salt and mix together.

Pour over the lemon juice, then add the cooked corn kernels and the ice cubes to chill. Mix together well, taste, and add more salt if necessary, then remove the ice.

Return the mussels to their shells and pour over the dressing. Serve on a platter on a bed of crushed ice.

Scallops a la Chalaca

SARSA DE ERIZOS
SEA URCHIN SARSA

Serves: 4
Preparation Time: 10 minutes

Sarsa **is a type of salad typically served in Arequipa, Southern Peru.**

40 sea urchin tongues
juice of 8 small lemons
1 tablespoon Garlic Paste (see p. 406)
½ cup (4 fl oz/120 ml) olive oil
1½ onions, sliced into half-moon crescents
1½ tomatoes, skinned, seeded, and thinly sliced
1 rocoto chile, seeded, membrane removed, and thinly sliced
2 yellow chiles, seeded, membranes removed, and thinly sliced
4 tablespoons white wine vinegar
handful of culantro or cilantro (coriander) leaves, to garnish
salt and pepper

Place the sea urchin tongues in a bowl and season with salt and pepper. Add half the lemon juice, the garlic paste, and half the olive oil and mix together.

In another bowl, add the sliced onions, tomatoes, rocoto chile, and yellow chiles. Season with salt and pepper, add the remaining lemon juice, olive oil, and vinegar, and mix together.

Combine the sea urchin tongues with the onion mixture. Arrange on a large platter, garnish with the culantro or cilantro (coriander) leaves, and serve.

SARSA DE CHANQUES
ABALONE SARSA

Serves: 4
Preparation Time: 12 minutes, plus 20 minutes freezing
Cooking Time: 1 minute

16 abalone (ormers), cleaned, scrubbed, and trimmed
1 tablespoon Garlic Paste (see p. 406)
1 onion, sliced into half-moon crescents
1 rocoto chile, seeded, membrane removed, and thinly sliced
5 tablespoons white wine vinegar
¾ cup (6 fl oz/175 ml) vegetable oil
juice of 4 small lemons
handful of coarsely chopped parsley leaves
salt and pepper

Put the prepared abalone (ormers) in the freezer for 20 minutes, until partially frozen. Remove from the freezer and cut into thin slices with a sharp knife.

Bring a pan of salted water to a boil. Blanch the abalone slices for 15 seconds, then quickly cool in plenty of iced water. Remove from the water, drain, and set aside.

Place the abalone in a bowl, add the garlic paste, and season with salt and pepper. Add the onion and rocoto chile, followed by the vinegar, oil, lemon juice, 5 tablespoons water, and chopped parsley. Mix together well.

Serve piled high in the center of a large platter.

SARSA DE MACHAS
CLAM SARSA

Serves: 4
Preparation Time: 10 minutes

Machas **are pink clams that are unfortunately now endangered in many areas where they used to thrive. You can use white clams for this recipe instead.**

- 24 large machas or other clams, cleaned, meat extracted, and trimmed
- 1 tablespoon Garlic Paste (see p. 406)
- 1 onion, sliced into half-moon crescents
- 1 rocoto chile, seeded, membrane removed, and thinly sliced
- 5 tablespoons white wine vinegar
- ¾ cup (6 fl oz/175 ml) vegetable oil
- juice of 4 small lemons
- handful of huacatay leaves, coarsely chopped
- handful of culantro or cilantro (coriander) leaves, coarsely chopped
- salt and pepper

Place the clam meat in a bowl with the garlic paste and season with salt and pepper. Add the onion and rocoto chile, followed by the vinegar, oil, lemon juice, 5 tablespoons water, and the chopped huacatay and culantro or cilantro (coriander) leaves. Mix together well.
Serve on a plate.

SARSA DE CAMARONES
SHRIMP SARSA

Serves: 4
Preparation Time: 15 minutes
Cooking Time: 20 minutes

This sarsa is a versatile dish that can be prepared with pretty much any seafood or meat.

- ½ corncob
- 2½ oz (65 g) fava (broad) beans
- juice of 12 small lemons
- 1 tablespoon white wine vinegar
- 2 tablespoons vegetable oil
- 1 onion, thinly sliced
- 2 tomatoes, seeded and thinly sliced
- 1 rocoto chile, seeded, membrane removed, and chopped
- 40 shrimp (prawn) tails, cooked
- 1 tablespoon chopped parsley leaves
- ½ tablespoon chopped oregano leaves
- 1½ oz (40 g) queso fresco, cut into cubes
- 8 pitted black olives, chopped
- 4 medium-size potatoes, peeled and boiled, to serve
- salt and pepper

Bring a pan of water to a boil, add the corncob, and cook until tender. Drain and remove the kernels. Set aside. Boil the fava (broad) beans Wuntil tender. Drain, shell, and set aside.

Mix the lemon juice, vinegar, and vegetable oil together in a bowl. Season with salt and pepper and mix together well.

In another bowl, place the onion, tomatoes, fava beans, rocoto chile, shrimp (prawn) tails, and cooked corn kernels. Pour over the lemon juice mixture and mix together.

Add the parsley, oregano, queso fresco, and olives. Mix together well, taste, and add more salt if necessary. Serve with boiled potatoes.

APPETIZERS

PAPA A LA HUANCAÍNA
HUANCAÍNA POTATOES

Serves: 4
Preparation Time: 8 minutes
Cooking Time: 15–20 minutes

The original Huancaína recipe was prepared using a pestle and mortar but nowadays a blender is more commonly used.

4 large yellow potatoes, peeled
2 cups (18 fl oz/500 ml) Huancaína Sauce (see p. 413)

To serve
4 iceburg lettuce leaves

To garnish
2 eggs, hard-boiled and cut into quarters
8 pitted black olives
½ yellow chile, seeded, membrane removed, and thinly sliced (optional)

Bring a pan of water to a boil, add the potatoes, and cook until tender. Drain and cut into ½-inch/1-cm slices. Set aside.

Arrange the potato slices on a serving plate alongside the lettuce leaves. Pour the huancaína sauce over the potatoes and garnish with the hard-boiled egg quarters, olives, and yellow chile slices, if using, and serve with a side of the lettuce.

PAPA A LA HUANCAÍNA A LA ANTIGUA
OLD-FASHIONED HUANCAÍNA POTATOES

Serves: 4
Preparation Time: 8 minutes
Cooking Time: 15–20 minutes

The secret of this Huancaína sauce is to slowly grind all the ingredients in the *batán* (Peruvian grinder) so that they gradually blend and become a cohesive mixture. This old-fashioned Huancaína sauce is characterized by its texture, which you would think had been chopped as you can feel the pieces. It's not a creamy sauce like the regular huancaína.

4 large yellow potatoes
4 iceburg lettuce leaves
2 cups (18 fl oz/500 ml) Old-Fashioned Huancaína Sauce (see p. 412)

To garnish
2 eggs, hard-boiled and cut into quarters
8 pitted black olives
½ yellow chile, seeded, membrane removed, and thinly sliced

Bring a pan of water to a boil, add the potatoes, and cook until tender. Drain and set aside.

Peel and slice the potatoes and arrange them and the lettuce leaves on a serving plate. Pour over the old-fashioned huancaína sauce and garnish with the hard-boiled egg quarters, olives, and yellow chile slices.

Huancaína Potatoes

Ocopa Potatoes

OCOPA
OCOPA POTATOES

Serves: 4
Preparation Time: 5 minutes
Cooking Time: 15–20 minutes

2 potatoes
2 cups (18 fl oz/500 ml) Ocopa Sauce (see p. 415)
1 egg, hard-boiled and cut into quarters, to garnish
4 whole black olives, to garnish

Bring a pan of water to a boil, add the potatoes, and cook until tender. Drain, cut into ½-inch/1-cm slices, and arrange on a serving plate.

Pour over the ocopa sauce and garnish with the hard-boiled egg quarters and olives.

PAPAS CON JAPCHI
POTATOES IN JAPCHI SAUCE

Serves: 4
Preparation Time: 8 minutes
Cooking Time: 15–20 minutes

This is a very simple and extremely flavorsome recipe in which you can replace the suggested chiles with any chiles you have on hand.

16 potatoes, boiled

Sauce
9 oz (250 g) queso fresco
¾ cup (6 fl oz/175 ml) whole (full-fat) milk
4 tablespoons chopped rocoto chiles
2 tablespoons chopped huacatay leaves
salt

Bring a pan of water to a boil, add the potatoes, and cook until tender. Drain and cut into halves. Set aside.

For the sauce, place the queso fresco in a bowl. Mash it into small pieces with a fork, gradually adding the milk to form a sauce. Add the rocoto chile and huacatay leaves and mix together thoroughly. Taste and season with salt if necessary. (If the cheese you are using is very salty, no additional salt will be needed.)

Arrange the potato halves on a serving plate. Cover with the sauce and serve.

ESCRIBANO
POTATO SALAD WITH CHILES

Serves: 4
Preparation Time: 10 minutes
Cooking Time: 15–20 minutes

When preparing this recipe, you can also mash all the ingredients at the table and have some fun.

6 potatoes, peeled
2 tomatoes, skinned, seeded, and diced
6 tablespoons chopped rocoto chiles
1 tablespoon chopped parsley
1½ teaspoons salt
½ teaspoon pepper
½ cup (4 fl oz/120 ml) olive oil
4 tablespoons white wine vinegar

Bring a pan of water to a boil, add the potatoes, and cook until tender. Drain. Chop 5 of the potatoes into 1¾-inch/4.5-cm cubes and put into a bowl. In a separate bowl, add the remaining potato and mash together with a fork, then add the tomatoes, rocoto chiles, and parsley. Mix together well.

Add the salt, pepper, olive oil, and vinegar, mix everything together thoroughly, and serve on a plate.

PAPAS Y HABAS CON LLATÁN
POTATOES AND FAVA BEANS WITH LLATÁN SAUCE

Serves: 4
Preparation Time: 5 minutes
Cooking Time: 15–20 minutes

Llatán is one of the many chili sauces you will find across Peru.

12 potatoes
3 cups (12 oz/350 g) fava (broad) beans in their pods
2 cups (18 fl oz/500 ml) Llatán Sauce (see p. 413), to serve

Bring a pan of water to a boil, add the potatoes, and cook until tender. Drain and cut into halves. Set aside. Boil the fava (broad) beans in their pods until tender. Drain.

Arrange the potato halves on plates with the fava bean pods and serve with the sauce.

CAUSA VEGETARIANA
VEGETARIAN CAUSA POTATOES

Serves: 4
Preparation Time: 15 minutes
Cooking Time: 20–35 minutes

8 yellow potatoes, peeled
½ cup (4 fl oz/120 ml) Yellow Chili Paste (see p. 405)
juice of 8 small lemons
4 tablespoons vegetable oil
⅓ cup (2 oz/50 g) peas
1 small carrot, cubed
½ cup (2 oz/50 g) chopped green beans
½ onion, diced
1 cup (8 oz/225 g) Mayonnaise (see p. 412), plus 3 tablespoons to finish
1 avocado, sliced
2 tomatoes, sliced
2 teaspoons chopped parsley, to garnish
salt

Bring a pan of water to a boil, add the potatoes, and cook until tender. Drain and mash thoroughly until smooth and free of lumps. Put in a bowl, add the chili paste, three-quarters of the lemon juice, and the oil. Season with salt and mix together thoroughly. Set aside.

Boil the peas, carrots, and green beans in water until tender. Drain and mix together in a bowl with the onion, remaining lemon juice, and the mayonnaise. Season with salt and mix together thoroughly.

Place half the potato mixture in a 6 × 4-inch/15- × 10-cm rectangular mold, covering the bottom. Layer by layer, add the avocado, sliced tomatoes, and finally the vegetable filling. Top with the remaining potato mixture, finish with extra mayonnaise, and garnish with chopped parsley. Serve.

CAUSA DE PALLARES
LIMA BEAN CAUSA DISH

Serves: 4
Preparation Time: 12 minutes
Cooking Time: 25 minutes

1 large red bell pepper
1 lb 2 oz (500 g) white fish fillets
1 cup (4 oz/120 g) all-purpose (plain) flour
4 tablespoons vegetable oil, plus extra for deep-frying
6 cups (2¼ lb/1 kg) green lima (butter) beans
juice of 5 small lemons
2 tablespoons Yellow Chili Paste (see p. 405)
½ cup (4 oz/120 g) Mayonnaise (see p. 412)
3 cloves garlic, very finely chopped
1½ cups (13 fl oz/ 375 ml) Creole Sauce (see p. 416)
salt and pepper

Place the red bell pepper over a naked flame, turning, until the skin is entirely blackened. Remove from the fire, peel, seed, and cut into strips. Set aside.

Cut the fish fillets into strips, season with salt and pepper, and coat in flour.

Heat 4 cups (34 fl oz/1 liter) vegetable oil for deep-frying in a large pan or deep fryer to 350°F/180°C, or until a cube of bread browns in 30 seconds. Drop the fish fillets carefully into the hot oil and cook until crispy and golden. Drain well on paper towels and set aside.

Bring a large pan of salted water to a boil, add the green lima (butter) beans, and cook for 10 minutes until tender. Drain well and mash thoroughly, pushing the mashed beans through a strainer (sieve) to break up any lumps.

Tip the mashed lima beans into a bowl withfour-fifths of the lemon juice, the chili paste, and vegetable oil. Season with salt and mix together well.

Put the roasted bell pepper into a blender with the mayonnaise, reserved lemon juice, and garlic and blend together. Season with salt and set aside.

Place the lima bean mixture in the center of a plate or platter. Arrange the fried fish strips over the mixture, pour over the Creole sauce, and spoon the roasted bell pepper mayonnaise around the outside to finish.

SOLTERITO
SOLTERITO SALAD

Serves: 4
Preparation Time: 12 minutes
Cooking Time: 25 minutes

This is a basic solterito recipe but you can add seafood, cooked meat, grains or anything else you fancy.

1 cup (6 oz/175 g) fava (broad) beans
2 potatoes
1 cup (6 oz/175 g) corn kernels
½ red onion, diced
2 tomatoes, skinned, seeded, and diced
½ cup (2 oz/50 g) pitted black olives, halved
6 oz (175 g) queso fresco
1 rocoto chile, seeded, membrane removed, and chopped
1½ teaspoons dried oregano
4 tablespoons white wine vinegar
½ cup (4 fl oz/120 ml) olive oil
1½ teaspoons salt
1 tablespoon chopped parsley

Bring a pan of water to a boil, add the fava (broad) beans, and cook until tender. Drain and set aside. Boil the potatoes until tender, then drain and cut into ½-inch/1-cm cubes. Boil the corn kernels until tender.

In a bowl, mix together the fava beans, onion, tomatoes, olives, queso fresco, potatoes, corn kernels, and chopped rocoto chile. Add the oregano, vinegar, olive oil, and salt. Mix together thoroughly.

Stir through the chopped parsley and serve.

OCOPA DE CAMARONES
SHRIMP OCOPA

Serves: 4
Preparation Time: 10 minutes, plus overnight soaking
Cooking Time: 20–35 minutes

8 yellow potatoes
24 cooked shrimp (prawn) tails
¾ cup (3 oz/80 g) pitted black olives
2 eggs, hard-boiled and cut into quarters
a few huacatay leaves, to garnish

Sauce
5 mirasol chiles, seeded, membranes removed, and soaked overnight
½ cup (4 fl oz/120 ml) vegetable oil, plus extra for frying
½ onion, diced
1 clove garlic
½ cup (2½ oz/65 g) walnuts, toasted and peeled
1 small handful huacatay leaves
1 tablespoon Shrimp Head Paste (see p. 29)
7 oz (200 g) queso fresco, coarsely chopped
1 cup (8 fl oz/250 ml) evaporated milk
3 oz (80 g) sweet animalito cookies
salt and pepper

Bring a pan of water to a boil, add the potatoes, and cook until tender. Drain and set aside.

For the sauce, drain the soaked chiles. Heat a little vegetable oil in a skillet or frying pan and sauté the chiles, onion, and garlic over low heat for a few minutes until softened. Add the walnuts, huacatay leaves, and the shrimp head paste. Cook for a few more minutes. Remove from the heat and let cool.

Put the cooled mixture into a blender with the queso fresco, evaporated milk, animalito cookies, and oil and blend to the consistency of a creamy sauce. Season with salt and pepper to taste.

Slice the boiled yellow potatoes and arrange on plates. Pour over the sauce and top with the shrimp (prawn) tails, black olives, and hard-boiled eggs. Garnish with a few huacatay leaves.

Solterito Salad

Tuna-Stuffed Causa Potato Dish from Lima

CAUSA LIMEÑA RELLENA
TUNA-STUFFED CAUSA POTATO DISH FROM LIMA

Serves: 4
Preparation Time: 15 minutes
Cooking Time: 15–20 minutes

This *causa* can also be stuffed with cooked chicken or just vegetables instead of tuna.

8 yellow potatoes, peeled
½ cup (4 fl oz/120 ml) Yellow Chili Paste (see p. 405)
juice of 6 small lemons
4 tablespoons vegetable oil
1 lb 5 oz (600 g) canned tuna in oil, drained
1 small red onion, finely diced
1 cup (8 oz/225 g) Mayonnaise (see p. 412)
1 avocado, sliced
2 tomatoes, sliced
4 eggs, hard-boiled and sliced
2 teaspoons chopped parsley
salt

Bring a pan of water to a boil, add the potatoes, and cook until tender. Drain and mash thoroughly until smooth and free of lumps. Put into a bowl and add the chili paste, lemon juice, and vegetable oil. Season with salt and mix together thoroughly. Set aside.

In another bowl, put the canned tuna, red onion, and ¾ cup (6 oz/175 g) of the mayonnaise. Mix together thoroughly.

Place half the potato mixture in a 6 × 4-inch/15 × 10-cm rectangular mold, covering the bottom. Layer by layer, add the avocado, sliced tomatoes, sliced eggs, and tuna mixture. Finish with the remaining potato mixture. Top with the remaining mayonnaise and chopped parsley. Serve.

CAUSA AL ROCOTO
ROCOTOCHILE CAUSA POTATO DUMPLINGS

Serves: 4
Preparation Time: 20 minutes
Cooking Time: 18–24 minutes

8 yellow potatoes, peeled
5 tablespoons Rocoto Chili Paste (see p. 407)
4 tablespoons vegetable oil
juice of 8 small lemons
30 shrimp (prawns), peeled and deveined
¼ small red onion, chopped
½ cup (4 oz/120 g) Mayonnaise (see p. 412)
3 tablespoons Avocado Aioli (see p. 68)
4 tablespoons Huancaína Sauce (see p. 413)
10 cherry tomatoes, cut into halves
5 quail eggs, cut into quarters
culantro or cilantro (coriander) leaves, to garnish
salt

Bring a pan of water to a boil, add the potatoes, and cook until tender. Drain and mash thoroughly until smooth and free of lumps. Place the mashed potato in a bowl and add the rocoto chili paste, vegetable oil, and three-quarters of the lemon juice. Season with salt and mix thoroughly until well combined.

Bring a pan of water to a boil, add the shrimp (prawns), and cook for 2 minutes. Drain well, let cool, and finely chop.

Place the chopped shrimp in a bowl. Season with salt to taste and add the red onion, mayonnaise, and remaining lemon juice. Mix together well.

Using your hands, roll a little of the potato mixture into a small ball. Make a hole in the center and fill it with a little of the avocado aioli and shrimp filling. Press a little more potato around the filling to close and repeat with the remaining ingredients, reserving a little of the aioli.

Place the potato balls on a plate or serving platter and spoon the huancaína sauce around the sides. Top with the remaining aioli, cherry tomato halves, and quail egg quarters. Garnish with culantro or cilantro (coriander) leaves.

CAUSA DE CANGREJO
CRAB-STUFFED CAUSA POTATO DISH

Serves: 4
Preparation Time: 10 minutes
Cooking Time: 15–20 minutes

8 yellow potatoes, peeled
½ cup (4 fl oz/120 ml) Yellow Chili Paste (see p. 405)
4 tablespoons vegetable oil
juice of 7 small lemons
7 oz (200g) fresh crab meat
¾ cup (6 oz/175 g) Mayonnaise (see p. 412)
1 avocado, cut into ½-inch (1-cm) cubes
2 eggs, hard-boiled and coarsely chopped
handful of parsley leaves, to garnish (optional)
salt

Bring a pan of water to a boil, add the potatoes, and cook until tender. Drain and mash thoroughly until smooth and free of lumps. Put into a bowl, add the chili paste, oil, and four-fifths of the lemon juice. Season with salt and mix together thoroughly. Set aside.

In another bowl, put the crab meat, ½ cup (4 oz/ 120 g) mayonnaise and the remaining lemon juice and mix together thoroughly.

Spread the potato mixture on a piece of plastic wrap (clingfilm) in a rectangle shape to a thickness of ½ inch/1 cm. Layer the cubed avocado, chopped hard-boiled eggs, and most of the crab mixture on top of the potato mixture, setting a little aside as garnish.

Taking the edges of the plastic wrap, carefully roll the mixture into a thick roll. Remove the plastic wrap and place on a serving platter. Top with the remaining mayonnaise, crab mixture, and the parsley.

CAUSA EN LAPA
MACKEREL-STUFFED CAUSA POTATO DISH

Serves: 4
Preparation Time: 15 minutes
Cooking Time: 30–35 minutes

Causa en lapa is a dish typical of the north of Peru.

9 yellow potatoes, peeled
4 tablespoons Yellow Chili Paste (see p. 405)
juice of 4 small lemons
½ cup (4 fl oz/120 ml) vegetable oil
2 whole dried mackerel, soaked in water overnight
2 tablespoons olive oil
1 tablespoon Garlic Paste (see p. 406)
2 tablespoons Panca Chili Paste (see p. 406)
2 small onions, sliced into half-moon crescents
2 yellow chiles, seeded, membranes removed, and sliced
½ teaspoon dried oregano
4 tablespoons white wine vinegar
½ cup (4 fl oz/120 ml) chicha de jora
¾ cup (3 oz/80 g) pitted black olives
2 eggs, hard-boiled and cut into quarters
1 sweet potato, boiled and sliced
7 oz (200 g) yucca root (cassava), peeled, boiled, and cut into 2 × ¾-inch (5 × 2-cm) strips
4 lettuce leaves
salt and pepper

Bring a pan of water to a boil, add the potatoes, and cook until tender. Drain and mash thoroughly until smooth. Put in a bowl, add the yellow chili paste, lemon juice, and vegetable oil. Season with salt and mix together thoroughly. Set aside.

Preheat a broiler (grill) to high. Cut the soaked mackerel into 2–3 pieces, removing the heads. Place the mackerel pieces under the hot broiler and cook for 1 minute on each side until golden. Remove the flesh from the bones and flake.

Meanwhile, heat the olive oil in a skillet or frying pan, add the garlic and panca chili pastes, and cook for a few minutes, then add the onion, yellow chiles, and dried oregano. Season with salt and pepper, add the white wine vinegar and chicha de jora, and simmer for 10 minutes.

Place half the potato mixture on a serving platter, then add the mackerel and the onion, reserving a small amount of each for the garnish.

Cover with the remaining potato mixture and top with the black olives, boiled eggs, sweet potato, yucca root (cassava), and lettuce leaves. Spoon over the remaining mackerel and onion to finish.

Crab-Stuffed Causa Potato Dish

CAUSA DE CABALLA
MACKEREL-STUFFED CAUSA

Serves: 4
Preparation Time: 15 minutes, plus soaking overnight
Cooking Time: 35–40 minutes

This is yet another delicious causa dish from the north of Peru, born of its rich cultural heritage.

1 lb 5 oz (600 g) dried mackerel, soaked in water overnight
8 potatoes, peeled
½ cup (4 fl oz/120 ml) vegetable oil
juice of 2 small lemons
salt and pepper

Sauce
½ cup (4 fl oz/120 ml) vegetable oil
2 red onions, cut into sixths
2 yellow chiles, seeded, membranes removed, and thinly sliced
6 cloves garlic, very finely chopped
3 tablespoons Panca Chili Paste (see p. 406)
3 tablespoons red wine vinegar
½ cup (4 fl oz/120 ml) fish broth (stock)
juice of 1 lemon

To serve
1 lb 2 oz (500 g) yucca root (cassava), peeled, boiled, and cut into pieces
4 sweet potato slices, boiled
1 cooked corncob, cut into 4 pieces
1 green plantain, boiled and peeled

Bring a large pan of water to a boil. Add the soaked mackerel and cook for 5 minutes. Drain, remove the bones, and cut into pieces. Set aside.

Bring another pan of water to a boil, add the potatoes, and cook until tender. Drain and mash thoroughly until smooth and free of lumps. Put into a bowl, add the vegetable oil and lemon juice, and season with salt and pepper. Mix together well.

For the sauce, heat the oil in a pan over medium heat. Add the onions and chiles and sauté for a few minutes, then add the garlic and panca chili paste. Cook for 1 minute, then add the red wine vinegar and cook for 2 minutes before adding the fish broth (stock) and lemon. Season with salt and pepper. Cook for 2–3 minutes until the onion is soft and the sauce has thickened and reduced.

Place some of the potato mixture on the plates, top with some of the mackerel, and cover with some of the sauce. Serve with the yucca root (cassava), sweet potatoes, corn, and cooked plantain.

CAUSA NIKKEI
JAPANESE-INSPIRED CAUSA POTATO DUMPLINGS

Serves: 4
Preparation Time: 20 minutes
Cooking Time: 15–20 minutes

8 yellow potatoes, peeled
½ cup (4 fl oz/120 ml) Yellow Chili Paste (see p. 405)
juice of 6 small lemons
4 tablespoons vegetable oil
¼ sheet nori seaweed, cut into thin strips
½ cup (4 fl oz/ 120 ml) Huancaína Sauce (see p. 413)
1 teaspoon shichimi togarashi spice mixture
salt

Filling
12 oz (350 g) tuna steak
½ teaspoon shichimi togarashi spice mixture
3 tablespoons Mayonnaise (see p. 412)
4 tablespoons sweet chili sauce
¼ small red onion, chopped
pinch of wasabi powder
2 teaspoons sesame oil
juice of 2 small lemons

Avocado aioli
½ avocado, mashed
1 tablespoon Mayonnaise (see p. 412)
juice of ½ lemon

To prepare the filling, finely chop the tuna steak. Put the chopped tuna in a bowl, add the other filling ingredients, and mix together well. Set aside.

For the aioli, put the ingredients into a blender and blend until smooth. Refrigerate until needed.

Bring a pan of water to a boil, add the potatoes, and cook until tender. Drain and mash thoroughly until smooth and free of lumps.

Place the mashed potato in a bowl and add the chili paste, lemon juice, and vegetable oil. Season with salt and mix together until well combined.

Using your hands, roll a little of the potato mixture into a small ball. Make a hole in the center and fill it with a little of the avocado aioli and tuna filling. Press a little more potato around the filling to seal it and repeat with the remaining ingredients.

Place the potato balls on a plate or serving platter and scatter over the nori seaweed strips. Spoon the huancaína sauce around the sides and sprinkle over the shichimi togarashi to finish.

Mackerel-Stuffed Causa

PULPO AL OLIVO
OCTOPUS IN OLIVE MAYONNAISE

Serves: 4
Preparation Time: 5 minutes

1 lb 1 oz (480 g) Cooked Octopus (see p. 406)
1 cup (8 oz/225 g) Mayonnaise (see p. 412)
½ cup (4 fl oz/120 ml) Black Olive Paste (see p. 408)
1 tablespoon olive oil
1 tablespoon chopped parsley leaves, to garnish

Cut the octopus into slices and arrange on a plate or platter.

Mix the mayonnaise together with the black olive paste in a bowl. Spoon the mayonnaise over the octopus, drizzle over the olive oil, and garnish with chopped parsley.

CAUSA AL OLIVO
OLIVE CAUSA POTATO DUMPLINGS

Serves: 4
Preparation Time: 20 minutes
Cooking Time: 25–30 minutes

1 teaspoon honey
½ cup (4 fl oz/120 ml) Olive Paste (see p. 408)
4 tablespoons Mayonnaise (see p. 412)
1 red bell pepper
8 yellow potatoes, peeled
½ cup (4 fl oz/120 ml) Yellow Chili Paste (see p. 405)
juice of 6 small lemons
½ cup (4 fl oz/120 ml) vegetable oil
14 oz (400 g) octopus, cooked and sliced
fried parsley sprigs, to garnish
salt

Avocado mayonnaise
4 tablespoons Mayonnaise (see p. 412)
½ avocado, chopped

Put the honey, olive paste, and mayonnaise together into a bowl and whisk together well to make a creamy sauce. Set aside.

Place the red bell pepper over a naked flame, turning it, until the skin is entirely blackened. Remove from the fire, peel, seed, and cut into strips. Set aside.

Bring a pan of water to a boil, add the potatoes, and cook until tender. Drain and mash thoroughly until smooth and free of lumps. Place the mashed potato into a bowl and add the chili paste, lemon juice, and half the vegetable oil. Season with salt and mix together well.

For the avocado mayonnaise, put the mayonnaise and avocado into another bowl and whisk together. Using your hands, roll a little of the potato mixture into a small ball. Make a hole in the center and fill it with a little of the avocado filling. Press a little more potato around the filling to seal it and repeat with the remaining ingredients.

Heat the remaining oil in a pan over medium heat, add the octopus slices, and cook until browned. Set aside. Repeat with the red pepper strips.

Top the potato balls with the octopus slices and red pepper strips and spoon the creamy olive sauce around the sides. Garnish with fried parsley.

CAUSA CHIMBOTANA
YELLOW YUCCA ROOT CAUSA DISH

Serves: 4
Preparation Time: 10 minutes, plus 8 hours soaking and 15 minutes standing
Cooking Time: 40 minutes

- 1 lb 5 oz (600 g) dried mackerel, soaked in water overnight
- 4½ lb (2 kg) yellow yucca root (cassava)
- 3 tablespoons vegetable oil
- 3 red onions, cut into wedges
- 2 yellow chiles, seeded, membrane removed, and thinly sliced
- 4 tablespoons Yellow Chili Paste (see p. 405)
- 1 banana leaf
- salt and pepper

Bring a pan of water to a boil. Drain the soaked mackerel, add to the pan, and cook for about 5 minutes until rehydrated and all salt has been removed. Drain and let cool, then cut into pieces.

Boil the yucca root (cassava) in a separate pan in plenty of water until cooked. Remove from the heat, drain, and let cool.

Heat the vegetable oil in a pan over medium heat, add the onions, chiles, and chili paste and sauté for a few minutes until the onion has softened. Season with salt and pepper.

Mix together all the ingredients.

Cut the banana leaf into a 12-inch/30-cm square. Place the cooked yucca root, chopped mackerel, and onion and chili mixture in the center of the leaf. Carefully fold up the banana leaf to wrap up the filling snugly and tie with string to secure. Let stand for 15 minutes. Unwrap to serve.

ESCABECHE NORTEÑO CON CAUSA DE YUCCA
NORTHERN SEA BASS AND YUCCA ROOT ESCABECHE

Serves: 4
Preparation Time: 20 minutes
Cooking Time: 45 minutes

- 1 lb 5 oz (600 g) sea bass fillet, cut into 4 pieces
- 14 oz (400 g) yucca root (cassava), peeled
- 3 yellow chiles, seeded and membranes removed
- 1 cup (8 fl oz/250 ml) vegetable oil
- 1 white onion, diced
- 8 bijao or banana leaves (about 10 inches/25 cm long)
- salt and pepper

Bring a large pan of water to a boil. Season the sea bass pieces with salt and pepper, add to the water, and cook for 4 minutes. Remove with a slotted spoon and drain on paper towels.

Bring another pan of water to a boil, add the yucca root (cassava), and cook until tender. Drain and cut into pieces. Set aside.

Grind the chiles in a batán (Peruvian grinder) or with a pestle and mortar until it is a coarse paste. Heat the oil in a skillet or frying pan over medium heat. Add the ground chile and diced onion and cook for a few minutes until the onion has softened. Season with salt and set aside.

Take 2 bijao leaves and lay one over the other to form a cross. Place a serving of yucca root on top, followed by a piece of fish and a serving of the onion mixture. Carefully fold up the banana leaf to wrap up the filling snugly and tie with string to secure. Repeat the process with the remaining ingredients and banana leaves. Keep warm in a steamer over simmering water until ready to serve.

Transfer to individual plates, cutting the string before serving.

Traditional Bonito Fish Escabeche

ESCABECHE DE BONITO TRADICIONAL
TRADITIONAL BONITO FISH ESCABECHE

Serves: 4
Preparation Time: 12 minutes
Cooking Time: 30–35 minutes

Escabeche is a dish from Lima that the younger generations are starting to forget. The secret is to let the fish sit in the escabeche sauce for a decent amount of time.

1 sweet potato
1 lb 5 oz (600 g) bonito fish fillets, cut into 8 equal pieces
⅓ cup (2 oz/50 g) all-purpose (plain) flour
1½ cups (13 fl oz/375 ml) vegetable oil
1½ red onions, sliced
3 cloves garlic, chopped
2 yellow chiles, seeded, membrane removed, and thinly sliced
2 tablespoons Panca Chili Paste (see p. 406)
1 bay leaf
1 sprig oregano
5 tablespoons white wine vinegar
4 lettuce leaves
salt

To garnish
1 egg, hard-boiled and cut into quarters
8 pitted black olives

Bring a pan of water to a boil. Add the sweet potato and cook until tender. Drain and slice into ¾-inch/1.5-cm slices. Set aside.

Put the fish pieces into a bowl with the flour and mix to coat.

Heat two-thirds of the oil in a skillet or frying pan over medium heat. Add the fillets and cook for 2 minutes on both sides until golden. Set aside.

Heat the remaining oil in another skillet or frying pan, add the onions, garlic, and chiles and sauté for a few minutes, until the onion has softened. Add the chili paste, bay leaf, oregano, and fish fillets, pour over the white wine vinegar, and cook for about 5 minutes. Season with salt, remove from the heat, and let cool.

Arrange the sweet potato slices and lettuce leaves on a serving platter. Lay the bonito fillets over the sweet potato slices, spoon over the sauce, and garnish with the hard-boiled egg quarters and black olives.

ESCABECHE DE GALLINA
CHICKEN ESCABECHE

Serves: 4
Preparation Time: 12 minutes, plus 8 hours chilling
Cooking Time: 2 hours 15 minutes

1 × 3¼-lb (1.5-kg) chicken
½ cup (4 fl oz/120 ml) vegetable oil
2 red onions, cut into sixths
1 yellow chile, seeded, membrane removed, and diced
4 tablespoons Panca Chili Paste (see p. 406)
1 tablespoon Garlic Paste (see p. 406)
1 bay leaf
1 sprig oregano
4 tablespoons red wine vinegar
1 teaspoon salt
1 sweet potato, boiled and peeled, to serve

To garnish
8 black olives
2 eggs, hard-boiled and cut into quarters

Bring a large pan of water to a boil. Add the chicken, reduce to a simmer, and cook for approximately 2 hours until the meat is tender. Remove from the pan and let cool, reserving 4 tablespoons of the cooking water.

Heat half the oil in a skillet or frying pan over medium heat. Add the onions and chile and cook for a few minutes, until the chile has softened. Add the chili paste, garlic, bay leaf, and oregano and pour in the red wine vinegar and reserved cooking water. Bring to a boil, then reduce the heat and simmer until the liquid reduces by half. Set aside.

Remove the chicken legs from the carcass and debone the breast. Add the legs and breasts to the sauce and season with salt. Add the remaining oil, cover, and refrigerate overnight.

Cut the sweet potato into 8 slices and arrange on plates. Serve half a chicken leg and half a breast, cut into 3, on each plate. Cover with the sauce and garnish with the olives and hard-boiled egg quarters.

ESCABECHE DE PATITAS
PIG FEET ESCABECHE

Serves: 4
Preparation Time: 10 minutes, plus 1 hour marinating
Cooking Time: 1 hour 50 minutes

4 pig feet, cleaned
1 bay leaf
1 clove garlic
2 carrots
⅔ cup (2½ oz/65 g) green beans
1 red onion, thinly sliced
4 tablespoons white wine vinegar
1 rocoto chile, seeded, membrane removed and thinly sliced
1 tablespoon chopped parsley leaves
1 tablespoon olive oil
4 potatoes, boiled, to serve
salt and pepper

Place the pig feet in a large pot with the bay leaf, garlic clove, and a pinch of salt and cover with water. Bring to a boil, then reduce the heat and simmer for 1½ hours. Remove from the heat, drain, and let cool, then remove the meat from the bone and coarsely chop.

Bring a pan of water to a boil, add the carrots, and cook until tender. Drain and cut into batons. Boil the beans until tender. Put the carrots and beans into a bowl with the onion and vinegar and let marinate for 1 hour.

After 1 hour, add the chopped meat, chile, parsley, and olive oil to the bowl. Mix together well and season with salt and pepper.

Arrange on a platter and serve with boiled potatoes.

ENSALADA DE PALLARES
LIMA BEAN SALAD

Serves: 4
Preparation Time: 12 minutes, plus 8 hours soaking
Cooking Time: 45 minutes

2¼ cups (1 lb 2 oz/500 g) dried lima (butter) beans
1 yellow chile, seeded, membrane removed, and chopped
2 tomatoes, skinned, seeded, and diced
1 large onion, thinly sliced
¾ cup (3 oz/80 g) pitted black olives, halved
1 teaspoon oregano
juice of 3 small lemons
3 tablespoons olive oil
1 teaspoon white wine vinegar
2 tablespoons chopped parsley
½ avocado, cubed
salt and pepper

To prepare the lima (butter) beans, soak the dried beans in water overnight. Drain and put into a pan of cold water. Over medium heat, boil the beans for 45 minutes until tender. Drain.

Put the lima beans, chile, tomatoes, onion, and olives into a serving bowl. Add the oregano, lemon juice, olive oil, vinegar, and half the chopped parsley, season with salt and pepper, and mix together thoroughly. Gently stir in the avocado so that it keeps its shape.

Sprinkle over the remaining chopped parsley to finish.

Lima Bean Salad

ENSALADA DE CHONTA
FRESH HEART OF PALM SALAD

Serves: 4
Preparation Time: 10 minutes
Cooking Time: 20 minutes

It is quite a sight to see fresh heart of palm being sold in the markets of the Peruvian Amazon.

- 1½ cups (13 fl oz/(375 ml) cocona fruit juice
- 2 tablespoons honey
- 1 bunch culantro or cilantro (coriander) leaves, chopped
- 3 cloves garlic, chopped
- 4 tablespoons vegetable oil
- juice of 4 small lemons
- salt and pepper
- 9 oz (250 g) beef jerky, thinly sliced
- 1 lb 5 oz (600 g) fresh heart of palm, shredded
- 10 whole sweet chiles, seeded, membranes removed and thinly sliced

Place the cocona fruit juice and honey in a pan over medium heat. Bring to a boil, then reduce the heat and simmer for 10 minutes until the liquid reduces by half. Remove from the heat and let cool.

Setting 1 tablespoon aside, place the culantro or cilantro (coriander) in a bowl and add the garlic, oil, and lemon juice. Season with salt and pepper to taste and mix together well. Set aside.

In a skillet or frying pan, pan-fry the beef jerky for 8 minutes in its own fat until crispy. Remove from the heat and let cool, then chop finely.

Place the fresh heart of palm, beef jerky, sweet chiles, and reserved culantro in a bowl. Stir in half the dressing and toss together.

Serve the salad on a platter, drizzling over the remaining dressing.

SARSA DE PATITAS
PIG FEET SARSA

Serves: 4
Preparation Time: 12 minutes
Cooking Time: 1–1 hour 30 minutes

- 4 pig feet
- 1 onion, diced
- 1 rocoto chile, seeded, membrane removed, and thinly sliced
- 2 tomatoes, skinned, seeded, and thinly sliced
- 1 yellow chile, seeded, membrane removed, and thinly sliced
- 1 tablespoon chopped culantro or cilantro (coriander) leaves
- 1 tablespoon chopped parsley
- 3 tablespoons white wine vinegar
- 6 tablespoons vegetable oil
- salt and pepper

Place the pig feet in a large pot and cover with water. Bring to a boil, then reduce the heat and simmer, covered, for 1–1½ hours. Remove from the heat, drain, and let cool, then remove the meat from the bone and coarsely chop.

Place the chopped meat, onion, rocoto chile, tomatoes, yellow chile, culantro or cilantro (coriander) leaves, parsley, vinegar, and oil in a bowl. Season with salt and pepper and mix together thoroughly. Serve.

SARSA DE CRIADILLAS
BULL TESTICLE SARSA

Serves: 6
Preparation Time: 10 minutes
Cooking Time: 10 minutes

12 bull testicles (about 9 oz/250 g)
1 clove garlic
1 red onion, diced
1 tablespoon chopped parsley
juice of 12 small lemons
1 yellow chile, seeded, membrane removed, and thinly sliced
1 rocoto chile, seeded, membrane removed, and thinly sliced
5 tablespoons vegetable oil
salt

Place the bull testicles in a large pot and cover with water. Bring to a boil, then reduce the heat and simmer for 5 minutes. Remove from the heat, drain, and let cool, then cut into medium slices.

Blanch the garlic in hot water for 3 or 4 minutes, drain, and very finely chop.

Place the testicle slices in a bowl and add the garlic, onion, parsley, lemon juice, yellow chile, rocoto chile, and oil. Season to taste with salt and mix together well. Serve on a platter.

SARSA DE SENCAS
BEEF CHEEK SARSA

Serves: 4
Preparation Time: 12 minutes
Cooking Time: 2 hours

1 lb 5 oz (600 g) beef cheeks
5 tablespoon white wine vinegar
⅔ cup (4 fl oz/150 ml) vegetable oil
1 onion, cut into half-moon crescents
1 yellow chile, seeded, membrane removed, and thinly sliced
1 tomato, skinned, seeded, and thinly sliced
2 teaspoons chopped parsley leaves
salt

Bring a large pan of salted water to a boil. Add the beef cheeks, reduce the heat, and simmer for 2 hours until tender. Remove from the heat, drain, reserving a few tablespoons of the cooking liquid, and place in a bowl.

While the beef cheeks are still warm, add the vinegar, reserved cooking liquid, and oil. Season with salt, mix together thoroughly, and let cool.

Once cool, remove the beef cheeks from the bowl and cut into equal bite-size pieces. Return to the bowl, adding the onion, chile, tomato, and parsley. Season with salt to taste and mix together thoroughly. Serve.

Quinoa Solterito

SOLTERITO DE QUINUA
QUINOA SOLTERITO

Serves: 4
Preparation Time: 10 minutes

Quinoa is one of the most nutritious grains cultivated by our ancestors, which we are once again sharing with the world.

- 1⅓ cups (19 oz/250 g) quinoa grains, cooked
- 4 oz (120 g) queso fresco, cubed
- ½ cup (3 oz/80 g) corn kernels, cooked
- ¾ cup (4½ oz/130 g) fava (broad) beans, shelled and boiled
- 1 small onion, diced
- 1 tomato, skinned, seeded, and diced
- 1 rocoto chile, seeded, membrane removed, and chopped
- 1 yellow chile, seeded, membrane removed, and chopped
- 1 tablespoon chopped parsley
- 1 tablespoon chopped huacatay leaves
- ¾ cup (3 oz/80 g) black olives, cut in ½ × 2-inch (1 × 5-cm) strips
- 4 tablespoons white wine vinegar
- 5 tablespoons vegetable oil
- ½ teaspoon dried oregano
- salt and pepper

Place all the ingredients together in a bowl. Mix together well and season with salt and pepper to taste. Serve.

SOLTERITO DE CAMARONES
SHRIMP SOLTERITO

Serves: 4
Preparation Time: 20 minutes
Cooking Time: 35–40 minutes

- 32 shrimp (prawns)
- juice of 8 small lemons
- 2 potatoes
- ⅓ cup (2 oz/50 g) fava (broad) beans
- 1 corncob
- 1 rocoto chile, seeded, membrane removed, and chopped
- 1 red onion, diced
- 4 tablespoons vinegar
- ½ cup (4 fl oz/120 ml) olive oil
- 2 tomatoes, skinned, seeded, and diced
- 6 oz (175 g) queso fresco, cut into cubes
- ½ cup (2 oz/50 g) pitted black olives, chopped
- ½ teaspoon oregano
- 1 tablespoon chopped parsley leaves
- salt and pepper

Clean and devein the shrimp (prawns), separating the tails from the heads. Remove the meat from the heads, push through a strainer (sieve), and mix with the lemon juice in a bowl. Set aside.

Bring a pan of water to a boil, add the potatoes, and cook until tender. Drain and cut into cubes. Boil the fava (broad) beans until tender, drain, and shell. Boil the corncob until tender, drain, and remove the kernels. Set aside.

Cook the shrimp tails in salted boiling water for 2 minutes, remove from the water, and plunge into iced water. Peel the shrimp tails and set aside.

Mix the chile, onion, vinegar, and oil in a bowl and season with salt and pepper. Add the tomatoes, cheese, potatoes, cooked corn, fava beans, olives, and cooked shrimp tails. Mix in the oregano, shrimp, and lemon juice mixture. Taste, adding more salt if necessary. Add the chopped parsley and serve.

SOLTERITO DE CONCHAS
SCALLOP SOLTERITO

Serves: 4
Preparation Time: 15 minutes
Cooking Time: 30–35 minutes

This recipe can also be prepared with clams or mussels.

2 potatoes
⅓ cup (2 oz/50 g) fava (broad) beans
1 corncob
1 rocoto chile, seeded, membrane removed, and chopped
1 medium red onion, diced
4 tablespoons vinegar
½ cup (4 fl oz/120 ml) olive oil
28 scallops
2 tomatoes, skinned, seeded, and diced
6 oz (175 g) queso fresco, cut into cubes
½ cup (2 oz/50 g) pitted black olives, chopped
juice of 8 small lemons
½ teaspoon oregano
1 tablespoon chopped parsley leaves
salt and pepper

Bring a pan of water to a boil, add the potatoes, and cook until tender. Drain and cut into cubes. Boil the fava (broad) beans until tender, drain, and shell. Boil the corncob until tender, drain, and remove the kernels. Set aside.

Mix the chile, onion, vinegar, and olive oil together in a bowl and season with salt and pepper.

Add the scallops, tomatoes, queso fresco, potatoes, corn, fava beans, olives, and lemon juice. Mix together. Add the oregano and chopped parsley, taste, and add more salt if necessary. Serve.

YUQUITAS FRITAS
FRIED YUCCA ROOT BATONS

Serves: 4
Preparation Time: 8 minutes
Cooking Time: 40–45 minutes

2¼ lb (1 kg) yucca root (cassava)
4 cups (34 fl oz/1 liter) vegetable oil
1 cup (8 fl oz/250 ml) Huancaína Sauce (see p. 413), to serve
salt

Peel the yucca root (cassava) and cut into 4-inch/10-cm pieces. Bring a large pan of salted water to a boil, add the yucca root, and cook until tender. Remove from the heat, drain, and let cool.

Once cool, cut the yucca root pieces into ¾ × 3 × ¾-inch/2 × 6 × 2-cm thick batons. Transfer to a suitable container and freeze until needed.

Heat the vegetable oil in a large pan or deep fryer to 350°F/180°C, or until a cube of bread browns in 30 seconds. Drop the frozen yucca-root batons carefully into the hot oil and cook for about 2 minutes, until crispy and golden on the outside and creamy on the inside. Drain well. Season with salt to taste and serve immediately with huancaína sauce.

CHICHARRÓN CUSQUEÑO
CUSCO-STYLE FRIED PORK RIND

Serves: 4
Preparation Time: 10 minutes, plus 8 hours soaking
Cooking Time: 1 hour 15 minutes–1 hour 20 minutes

The difference between the *chicharrón* from Lima and the *chicharrón* from Cusco lies in their accompaniments. The Creole sauce from Cusco calls for a large amount of mint and instead of being served with sweet potato, it is served with cooked hominy grits.

- 1 cup (4½ oz/130 g) dried white hominy grits (corn), soaked in water overnight
- ½ teaspoon anise seeds
- 1 teaspoon granulated sugar
- 1 lb 2 oz (500 g) pork ribs, skin on, cut into pieces
- 1 lb 2 oz (500 g) pork loin, cut into pieces
- 1½ tablespoons Garlic Paste (see p. 406)
- 4 potatoes
- 1 sprig mint, plus 1 small handful of leaves
- 1 large onion, thinly sliced
- juice of 5 small lemons
- 1 teaspoon salt
- ½ cup (4 fl oz/120 ml) Uchucuta Sauce (see p. 417), to serve

Place the soaked hominy grits (corn) in a pan over low heat, cover with water, add the anise seeds and sugar, and cook gently, stirring occasionally, for 35 minutes or until tender.

Meanwhile, trim the fat from the pork rib pieces, setting aside the rind. Place the pork rib and loin pieces in a bowl, rub with the garlic paste, and let stand for 15 minutes.

Bring a pan of water to a boil, add the potatoes, and cook until tender. Drain and cut into ½-inch/1-cm slices. Set aside.

Put a large pan over low heat, add the pork pieces, ½ cup (4 fl oz/120 ml) water, and the mint sprig. Cover and bring to a boil, then reduce the heat and simmer, uncovered, for 20 minutes, stirring, until all the liquid has evaporated. Set aside.

Place the pork rind in another pan and cook over medium heat until the fat has rendered. Add the pork pieces and sauté for 5 minutes until golden brown and crispy. Remove and set aside. Add the potatoes to the pan and sauté over medium heat for 7–10 minutes until golden. Set aside.

Put the onion into a bowl and mix together with the mint leaves, lemon juice, and salt.

Serve the pork pieces with the hominy, the sautéed potatoes, uchucuta sauce, and the mint sauce.

TORREJAS DE CHOCLO
CORN FRITTERS

Serves: 4
Preparation Time: 5 minutes
Cooking Time: 10 minutes

These fritters are delicious served with Huancaína sauce (see page 413).

- 3 cups (26 fl oz/750 ml) liquefied corn from 8¾ lb (4 kg) corn, liquefied without water
- 1 teaspoon granulated sugar
- 3 tablespoons all-purpose (plain) flour
- 4 tablespoons cold sparkling water
- 4 cups (34 fl oz/1 liter) vegetable oil
- 2 cups (18 fl oz/500 ml) Huancaína Sauce (see p. 413), to serve (optional)
- salt and pepper

Pour the liquefied corn into a bowl, add the sugar, and season with salt and pepper. Mix together thoroughly.

Place the flour and cold sparkling water in another bowl. Mix thoroughly with a whisk to form a batter. Pour the batter over the corn mixture, stirring with a wooden spoon to combine. Adjust the seasoning to taste.

Heat the vegetable oil in a large pan or deep fryer to 350°F/180°C, or until a cube of bread browns in 30 seconds. Shape 2 tablespoons of the fritter batter with a spoon, drop carefully into the hot oil, and cook until crispy and golden. Drain well and serve immediately with huancaína sauce, if desired.

TORREJAS DE ATÚN
TUNA PATTIES

Serves: 4
Preparation Time: 15 minutes
Cooking Time: 35–40 minutes

- 3 red bell peppers
- 3 tablespoons all-purpose (plain) flour
- 1 egg
- 7 oz (200 g) canned tuna
- 2 onions, 1 diced and 1 sliced into half-moon crescents
- 2 yellow chiles, seeded, membranes removed, and finely chopped
- 1 cup (8 fl oz/250 ml) vegetable oil, for frying
- juice of 4 small lemons
- 3 tablespoons olive oil
- 3 potatoes, boiled and sliced, to serve
- salt and pepper

Preheat the oven to 350°F/180°C/Gas 4.

Wrap the red bell peppers with aluminum foil, season with 1 teaspoon salt, and roast for 25 minutes. Remove from the oven, peel, seed, and slice.

Place the flour and egg in a bowl. Add ½ cup (4 fl oz/120 ml) water, beat the mixture together with a fork, and season with salt and pepper to taste. Add the canned tuna, diced onions, and yellow chiles to the mixture. Mix together, adjust the seasoning, and set aside.

Heat a little vegetable oil in a skillet or frying pan. Divide the pattie mixture into 8. Using your hands, shape each into a ball, then flatten into a patty shape. Put the patties in the pan and sauté on each side until golden and crispy. Set aside.

Put the roasted peppers and the remaining sliced onion in a bowl. Add the lemon juice and olive oil and season with salt and pepper. Mix together well. Arrange the tuna patties on a plate and serve with the boiled potato slices and onion and pepper salad.

TORREJITAS AREQUIPEÑAS DE VERDURAS
AREQUIPA-STYLE VEGETABLE FRITTERS

Serves: 4
Preparation Time: 12–15 minutes
Cooking Time: 10–15 minutes

If you don't have any huacatay, a generous amount of peppermint or fresh mint can also be used in this recipe.

- 1½ cups (13 fl oz/ 375 ml) liquefied corn, from 5½ lb (2.5 kg) of corn liquefied without water
- 1¾ cups (7 oz/200 g) grated pumpkin flesh
- ⅔ cup (2¾ oz/70 g) grated fig-leaf gourd flesh
- ½ tablespoon chopped quinoa leaves or chopped culantro or cilantro (coriander) leaves
- 1 tablespoon chopped huacatay leaves
- 4 oz (120 g) queso fresco, cubed
- ¼ tablespoon ground cumin
- 2 teaspoons granulated sugar
- ½ cup (2½ oz/65 g) all-purpose (plain) flour
- 3 egg yolks
- 4 cups (34 fl oz/1 liter) vegetable oil
- salt and pepper

Put the corn, pumpkin, fig-leaf gourd, quinoa leaves, huacatay leaves, and queso fresco into a large bowl. Add the cumin and sugar, season with salt and pepper, and mix together well. Set aside.

In another bowl, add the flour and egg yolks with ½ cup (4 fl oz/120 ml) water and mix together thoroughly to form a batter. Pour the batter over the vegetable mixture, stir to combine, and adjust the seasoning as necessary. Shape into round fritters with your hands.

Heat the vegetable oil in a deep fryer or large pot to 350°F/180°C, or until a cube of bread browns in 30 seconds. Drop the fritters carefully into the hot oil and cook until crispy and golden. Drain well and serve immediately.

TORREJITAS DE QUINUA
QUINOA FRITTERS

Serves: 4
Preparation Time: 20 minutes
Cooking Time: 10 minutes

- ¼ zucchini (courgette), grated
- ½ carrot, grated
- ¼ head lettuce, finely shredded
- 1 teaspoon chopped huacatay leaves
- 1 tablespoon chopped parsley leaves
- ¼ small white onion, chopped
- 1½ oz (40 g) queso fresco, grated
- 2 tablespoons evaporated milk
- 1 tablespoon granulated sugar
- 1 tablespoon salt
- 2 tablespoons cooked lentils
- ½ cup (3½ oz/100 g) cooked quinoa grains
- 3 tablespoons cooked lima (butter) beans, mashed
- ½ cooked beet (beetroot), cut into cubes
- 3 tablespoons all-purpose (plain) flour
- 2 eggs, beaten
- 4 tablespoons Panko (Japanese bread crumbs) or fresh bread crumbs
- 2 tablespoons vegetable oil

Mix together the zucchini (courgette), carrot, lettuce, huacatay leaves, parsley leaves, and white onion in a bowl. Add the queso fresco, evaporated milk, and sugar and season with salt. Cover with plastic wrap (clingfilm), transfer to a refrigerator, and chill until needed.

Remove the chilled vegetable mixture from the refrigerator and add the lentils, quinoa, mashed lima (butter) beans, and beet (beetroot). Mix together well.

Take a handful of the mixture and shape into a round hamburger-size patty. Coat the patty in flour, then in the beaten eggs, and finally in the Panko or fresh bread crumbs. Repeat with the remaining mixture.

Heat the vegetable oil in a skillet or frying pan. Add the patties and cook, turning, until crispy on both sides. Remove from the pan and place on paper towels to absorb any excess oil. Serve immediately.

Serves: 4
Preparation Time: 8 minutes, plus 8 hours soaking
Cooking Time: 1 hour 25 minutes

- 1 × 1-lb 2-oz (500-g) pork side (belly)
- 1 cup (11 oz/300 g) salt
- 4 cloves garlic
- 2 bay leaves
- ¼ cup (2 fl oz/50 ml) vegetable oil, plus 4 cups (34 fl oz/1 liter) for deep-frying
- 2 sweet potatoes, cut into ½-inch (1-cm) slices
- 1 cup (8 fl oz/250 ml) Creole Sauce (see p. 416), to serve

CHICHARRÓN LIMEÑO
LIMA-STYLE BACON CHICHARRÓN

Place the pork in a bowl with 6 cups (51 fl oz/1.5 liters) water and the salt. Let soak for 8 hours.

Remove the pork from the water, place in a pan, and cover with water. Add the garlic and bay leaves and simmer over low heat for approximately 1 hour. Remove the bacon from the pan, let cool, and cut into 1½-inch/4-cm square pieces.

Heat 4 tablespoons vegetable oil in a skillet or frying pan. Add the pork pieces and fry until crispy. Set aside.

Heat the vegetable oil for deep-frying in a large pan or deep fryer to 350°F/180°C, or until a cube of bread browns in 30 seconds. Drop the sweet potato slices carefully into the hot oil and fry until golden.

Drain well on paper towels.

Serve the bacon chicharrón on a platter with the fried sweet potato and Creole sauce.

Lima-Style Bacon Chicharrón

CHICHARRÓN DE POLLO
CHICKEN CHICHARRÓN

Serves: 4
Preparation Time: 8 minutes, plus 15 minutes marinating
Cooking Time: 15–20 minutes

This is a recipe that is markedly influenced by China's cultural presence in Peru.

8 chicken thighs, each cut into 4 pieces
1 limo chile
1 teaspoon Worcestershire sauce
1½ cups (13 fl oz/375 ml) lemon juice
2 tablespoons Chinese cinnamon (cassia bark)
2 teaspoons salt
4 cups (34 fl oz/1 liter) vegetable oil
handful of lettuce leaves, washed
pepper

Place the chicken pieces in a bowl. Rub with the limo chile, add the Worcestershire sauce, 4 tablespoon lemon juice, 1 tablespoon of Chinese cinnamon, 1 teaspoon of salt, and a pinch of pepper and let marinate for 10–15 minutes.

Heat the vegetable oil in a large pan or deep fryer to 350°F/180°C, or until a cube of bread browns in 30 seconds. Drop the marinated chicken pieces carefully into the oil and fry for around 10 minutes or until golden. Drain well on paper towels.

Mix the remaining lemon juice and Chinese cinnamon with the remaining salt in a bowl.

Arrange the lettuce leaves on a plate and place the chicken pieces on top. Serve with the lemon and Chinese cinnamon dipping sauce.

CHICHARRÓN DE PESCADO
FISH CHICHARRÓN

Serves: 4
Preparation Time: 8 minutes
Cooking Time: 10–15 minutes

You can serve this fish chicharrón with some tiger milk on the side.

2¼ lb (1 kg) white fish fillets, cut into ¾ x 1½-inch (2 x 3-cm) pieces
6 cloves garlic, very finely chopped
juice of 1 lemon
1¼ cups (5 oz/150 g) all-purpose (plain) flour
4 tablespoons potato starch
4 cups (34 fl oz/1 liter) vegetable oil
salt

To serve
1 cup (8 fl oz/250 ml) Creole Sauce (see p. 416)
1 cup (8 fl oz/250 ml) Tartar Sauce (see p. 412)

Put the fish pieces into a bowl with the chopped garlic and lemon juice. Season with salt and mix together well.

Mix the flour and potato starch together in a separate bowl. Add the fish pieces to the flour mixture and coat evenly.

Heat the vegetable oil in a deep fryer or large pot to 350°F/180°C, or until a cube of bread browns in 30 seconds. Drop the fish pieces carefully into the hot oil and cook for 6–8 minutes until crispy and golden. Drain well and serve immediately with the Creole and tartar sauces.

Chicken Chicharrón

CHICHARRÓN DE CONEJO
RABBIT CHICHARRÓN

Serves: 4
Preparation Time: 20 minutes
Cooking Time: 10 minutes

This *chicharrón* recipe can also be prepared by marinating the rabbit with pureed panca chile, minced garlic, and lemon.

- 2 rabbits, skinned, cleaned, and heads removed
- 8 cups (68 fl oz/2 liters) vegetable oil, for frying
- 2 sweet potatoes, peeled and thinly sliced
- 2 tablespoons chopped parsley, plus 1 sprig
- 6 tablespoons olive oil
- 1 clove garlic
- 2 cups (18 fl oz/500 ml) orange juice
- salt and pepper

Divide each rabbit into 6 neat pieces. Season generously with salt and pepper.

Heat the vegetable oil in a large pan or pot over medium heat. Pan-fry the rabbit pieces until they turn a lovely golden color. Remove from the pan and drain on paper towels. Set aside in a large bowl. Add the sweet potatoes and sauté until crisp, then drain on paper towels. Set aside.

In another bowl, mix together the chopped parsley, olive oil, and whole garlic clove.

Crush the parsley sprig with a fork or pestle in a separate bowl, add the orange juice, and stir to combine.

Slowly drizzle the parsley-infused orange juice over the rabbit pieces and mix together thoroughly. Serve the rabbit with the parsley sauce and fried sweet potato slices.

PEJERREYES ARREBOZADOS
SILVERSIDE FILLETS IN BATTER

Serves: 4
Preparation Time: 5 minutes
Cooking Time: 11–18 minutes

If you can't find silverside, you can prepare this dish with other types of fish such as horse mackerel, Atlantic mackerel, or conger eel.

- ¾ cup (3¼ oz/90 g) cornstarch (cornflour)
- 1 egg
- ½ cup (4 fl oz/120 ml) lager
- ½ cup (4 fl oz/120 ml) sparkling water
- 48 silverside fish fillets (about 1 lb/450 g)
- ⅔ (3 oz/80 g) all-purpose (plain) flour
- 4 cups (34 fl oz/1 liter) vegetable oil
- salt and pepper

To serve
- 1 cup (8 fl oz/250 ml) Creole Sauce (see p. 416)
- ½ cup (4 fl oz/120 ml) Huancaína Sauce (see p. 413)

Put the cornstarch (cornflour), egg, beer, and sparkling water together into a bowl. Season with salt and pepper. Mix together with a whisk to form a batter and place in the refrigerator to chill for 20 minutes.

Season the silverside fillets with salt and pepper to taste. Coat the fillets evenly in the flour and then in the chilled batter.

Heat the vegetable oil in a large pan or deep fryer to 350°F/180°C, or until a cube of bread browns in 30 seconds. Drop the battered silverside fillets carefully into the oil and cook for 6–8 minutes until crispy and golden. Drain well and serve immediately with the creole and huancaína sauces.

HUEVERA FRITA
FRIED FISH ROE

Serves: 4
Preparation Time: 10 minutes
Cooking Time: 11–18 minutes

This dish is one of my all-time favorites. Fried fish roe can be served with Creole sauce and is also delicious with bread.

- 2¼ lb (1 kg) fish roe, cleaned and cut into 2-inch (5-cm) pieces
- 1 teaspoon Garlic Paste (see p. 406)
- juice of 1 lemon
- 1 egg, beaten
- 1 cup (4 oz/120 g) all-purpose (plain) white flour
- 4 tablespoons potato starch
- 4 cups (34 fl oz/1 liter) vegetable oil
- salt and pepper
- 1 cup (8 fl oz/250 ml) Creole Sauce (see p. 416), to serve

Place the fish roe pieces in a bowl, add the garlic paste and lemon juice, and season with salt and pepper. Add the beaten egg and mix together thoroughly.

In a separate bowl, mix the flour with the potato starch. Add the fish roe pieces to the flour mixture and coat evenly.

Heat the vegetable oil in a deep fryer or large pot to 350°F/180°C, or until a cube of bread browns in 30 seconds. Drop the roe pieces carefully into the hot oil and cook for 6–8 minutes until crispy and golden. Drain well and serve immediately with Creole sauce (see page 416), if desired.

JALEA NORTEÑA
NORTHERN-FRIED SEAFOOD AND YUCCA ROOT MEDLEY

Serves: 4
Preparation Time: 18 minutes
Cooking Time: 50–55 minutes

- 14 oz (400 g) yucca root (cassava), peeled
- 12 cloves garlic, very finely chopped
- ½ cup (4 fl oz/120 ml) white wine vinegar
- 2 teaspoons Annatto Oil (see p. 408)
- 1¾ lb (800 g) white fish fillets, cut into strips lengthwise
- 2⅓ cups (11 oz/300 g) all-purpose (plain) flour
- 4 tablespoons potato starch
- 4 cups (34 fl oz/1 liter) vegetable oil
- 1 cup (8 fl oz/250 ml) Creole Sauce (see p. 416)
- 2 tablespoons seeded, membranes removed, and chopped limo chile
- 2 tomatoes, skinned, seeded, and thinly sliced
- ½ cup (4 oz/120 g) cancha
- 2 cups (4 oz/120 g) banana chips
- 4 lemons, cut into slices
- salt and pepper

Bring a pan of water to a boil, add the yucca root (cassava), and cook until tender. Drain and cut into batons. Set aside.

Mix together the garlic, vinegar, and annatto oil in a bowl. Season with salt and pepper to taste, add the fish strips, and let marinate for 2 minutes.

In a separate bowl, mix the flour with the potato starch. Add the marinated fish strips to the flour mixture and coat evenly, shaking off any excess flour.

Heat the vegetable oil in a large pan or deep fryer to 350°F/180°C, or until a cube of bread browns in 30 seconds. Add the yucca-root batons to the oil and fry for 8 minutes until crispy, then remove from the pan and drain on paper towels.

Drop the fish strips carefully into the oil and cook for 6–8 minutes until crispy and golden. Drain well on paper towels and set aside.

Put the Creole sauce, limo chile, and tomatoes into a bowl and mix together.

Place the fried fish in a bowl. Pour over the Creole sauce with tomatoes and mix together thoroughly.

Serve on a platter with the fried yucca root, cancha, banana chips, and slices of lemon.

Lima-Style Fried Seafood and Yucca Root Medley

JALEA LIMEÑA
LIMA-STYLE FRIED SEAFOOD AND YUCCA ROOT MEDLEY

Serves: 4
Preparation Time: 25 minutes
Cooking Time: 1 hour – 1 hour 10 minutes

Use any fresh, flavorsome fish and any type of seafood for this recipe, provided it is very fresh.

- 1 lb 2 oz (500 g) yucca root (cassava), peeled
- 1 corncob
- 14 oz (400 g) fish fillets, cut into ¾ × 1½-inch (2 × 3-cm) pieces
- 12 shrimp (prawns), cleaned
- 12 scallops, cleaned
- 7 oz (200 g) octopus, cooked and cut into pieces
- 4 × 4-oz (120-g) squid, cleaned and cut into rings
- 2 cloves garlic, very finely chopped
- 1 teaspoon soy sauce
- juice of 2 small lemons
- 2⅓ cups (11 oz/300 g) all-purpose (plain) flour
- ½ cup (2½ oz/65 g) potato starch
- 2 eggs, beaten
- 4 cups (34 fl oz/1 liter) vegetable oil, for frying
- 1 cup (8 fl oz/250 ml) Creole Sauce (see p. 416)
- 1½ tomatoes, skinned, seeded, and thinly sliced
- 1 tablespoon limo chile, seeded, membrane removed, and thinly sliced
- 1 cup (8 fl oz/250 ml) Tartar Sauce (see p. 412), to serve
- salt and pepper

To garnish

- 2 cups (4 oz/120 g) banana chips
- 1 cup (8 oz/225 g) cancha (toasted corn)
- 1 small handful of culantro or cilantro (coriander) leaves

Bring a pan of water to a boil, add the yucca root (cassava), and cook until tender. Drain and cut into batons. Boil the corncob until tender, then drain and remove the kernels. Set aside.

Place the fish pieces in a bowl with the shrimp (prawns), scallops, octopus, and squid. Add the chopped garlic, soy sauce, and lemon juice, season with salt and pepper, and mix together well. Set aside.

Mix together the flour and potato starch. Dip the seafood in the beaten egg, drain off any excess, add to the flour mixture, and coat evenly.

Heat the vegetable oil in a large pan or deep fryer to 350°F/180°C, or until a cube of bread browns in 30 seconds. Drop the seafood carefully into the oil and cook for 6–8 minutes until crispy and golden. Drain well on paper towels and set aside.

Add the yucca-root batons to the oil and fry for 8 minutes until crispy, remove from the pan, and drain on paper towels. Arrange the fried seafood and yucca-root batons on a platter with the seafood in the center and the yucca-root batons around the edge.

Mix the Creole sauce with the corn, tomatoes, and limo chile and pour the mixture over the seafood. Top with the banana chips, cancha, and culantro or cilantro (coriander) leaves and serve with tartar sauce.

Serves: 4
Preparation Time: 15 minutes
Cooking Time: 25 minutes

These stuffed chiles taste great served with potato gratin.

4 rocoto chiles
3½ tablespoons granulated sugar
4 American-style cheese slices

Filling
3 tablespoons vegetable oil
1 onion, chopped
3 cloves garlic, chopped
1 tablespoon Panca Chili Paste (see p. 406)
½ cup (2¾ oz/70 g) chopped yellow chiles
1 lb 2 oz (500 g) beef tenderloin (fillet), cubed
1 cup (8 fl oz/250 ml) beef broth (stock)
1 tablespoon finely chopped peanuts
salt and pepper

ROCOTO RELLENO
STUFFED ROCOTO CHILES

Slice the tops off the rocoto chiles. Using a spoon, scrape out the seeds and membranes from inside each chile. Wash well.

Bring a pan of water to a boil, add the chiles, a third of the sugar, and a pinch of salt and blanch for 1 minute. Drain and repeat the process twice. Rinse the chiles under cold water and set aside.

Preheat the oven to 275°F/140°C/Gas Mark 1.

For the filling, heat the oil in a pan over medium heat, add the onion, garlic, chili paste, and yellow chiles and sauté for a few minutes until the onion has softened. Add the cubed beef and cook for a few minutes more, then pour in the broth (stock). Add the peanuts and cook for another 5 minutes. Season with salt and pepper.

Stuff the blanched rocoto chiles with the meat mixture and top each with a cheese slice. Place in an ovenproof dish and cook in the preheated oven for 10 minutes.

Divide the stuffed chiles between plates and serve with a side of potato gratin.

Stuffed Rocoto Chiles

ROCOTO RELLENO DE CAMARONES
SHRIMP-STUFFED ROCOTO CHILES

Serves: 4
Preparation Time: 15 minutes
Cooking Time: 40 minutes

4 rocoto chiles
3½ tablespoons granulated sugar
3 oz (80 g) queso fresco, cut into 4 slices
salt and pepper

Filling
1 cup (5 oz/150 g) fava (broad) beans
4 tablespoons vegetable oil
1 onion, chopped
3 cloves garlic, chopped
2 yellow chiles, seeded, membranes removed, and chopped
1 tablespoon Panca Chili Paste (see p. 406)
1 tablespoon Shrimp Head Paste (see p. 29)
24 shrimp (prawns), peeled and deveined, with tails still intact
2 tablespoons chopped and toasted peanuts
pinch of ground cumin
½ cup (4 fl oz/120 ml) pisco
1 cup (8 fl oz/250 ml) shrimp (prawn) broth (stock)

Slice the tops off the rocoto chiles. Using a spoon, scrape out the seeds and membranes from inside each chile. Wash well.

Bring a pan of water to a boil, add the chiles, a third of the sugar, and a pinch of salt, and blanch for 1 minute. Drain and repeat the process twice. Rinse the chiles under cold water and set aside.

Preheat the oven to 275°F/140°C/Gas Mark 1.

For the filling, bring a pan of water to a boil, add the fava (broad) beans, and cook until tender. Shell and set aside.

Heat the oil in a pan over medium heat. Sauté the onion, garlic, and yellow chiles for a few minutes until the onion has softened. Add the chili paste and shrimp head paste and cook, stirring, for a few more minutes, then add the shrimp (prawn) tails, fava beans, peanuts, and cumin. Season with salt and pepper, pour in the pisco, and let the alcohol evaporate, then add the shrimp broth (stock) and cook for 5–6 minutes. Adjust the seasoning to taste and remove from the heat.

Stuff the blanched rocoto chiles with the shrimp mixture and top with a cheese slice. Place in an ovenproof dish and cook in the preheated oven for 10 minutes.

Divide the stuffed chiles between plates.

SANGRECITA
COOKED CHICKEN BLOOD

Serves: 4
Preparation Time: 10 minutes
Cooking Time: 1 hour–1 hour 5 minutes

The secret of this recipe is to avoid overcooking the blood, which should be creamy.

1 lb 2 oz (550 g) yucca root (cassava), peeled
2 cups (18 fl oz/500 ml) chicken blood
4½ cups (38 fl oz/1.1 liters) vegetable oil
¼ onion, chopped
1 yellow chile, seeded, membrane removed, and chopped
2 cloves garlic, very finely chopped
1 tablespoon Panca Chili Paste (see p. 406)
½ cup (4 fl oz/120 ml) chicken broth (stock)
2 scallions (spring onions), chopped
bunch of mint leaves, chopped
1 cup (8 fl oz/250 ml) Creole Sauce (see p. 416), to serve
salt and pepper

Bring a pan of water to a boil, add the yucca root (cassava), and cook until tender. Drain and cut into batons. Set aside.

Bring a large pan of water to a boil. Pour the blood into the boiling water and cook for 1–2 minutes, until the blood has congealed and solidified. Drain off the water and let cool, then coarsely chop. Set aside.

Heat 4 cups (34 fl oz/1 liter) vegetable oil in a large pan or deep fryer to 350°F/180°C, or until a cube of bread browns in 30 seconds. Drop the yucca-root batons carefully into the oil and cook for 8 minutes until crispy and golden. Drain well on paper towels and set aside.

Heat the remaining oil in a clay pot or pan over medium heat, add the onion, chopped yellow chile, garlic, and chili paste and sauté for 5 minutes until the onions have softened.

Add the cooked chicken blood and chicken broth (stock). Season with salt and pepper to taste. Add the scallions (spring onions) and mint and cook for 10 minutes over medium heat until the broth reduces and thickens.

Arrange the fried yucca-root batons on a serving platter, ladle over the cooked chicken blood mixture, and serve with the Creole sauce.

Corn Pie

PASTEL DE CHOCLO
CORN PIE

Serves: 4
Preparation Time: 12 minutes
Cooking Time: 1 hour–1 hour 5 minutes

It is very important for the corn to be really creamy so that the pie can be eaten with a spoon.

- 1 cup (8 fl oz/250 ml) vegetable oil
- 1 tablespoon Garlic Paste (see p. 406)
- 1 onion, diced
- 14 oz (400 g) beef tenderloin (fillet), cut into ½-inch (1-cm) cubes
- 3 tablespoons chopped pitted black olives
- ½ cup (2½ oz/65 g) raisins, soaked in hot water
- 1 egg, plus 2 hard-boiled and chopped eggs
- 6 corncobs
- ½ cup (4 fl oz/120 ml) Yellow Chili Paste (see p. 405)
- 1 cup (8 fl oz/250 ml) whole (full-fat) milk
- 1 cup (7 oz/200 g) granulated sugar
- 1 tablespoon salt
- 1¾ cups (5 oz/150 g) Parmesan cheese, grated
- 4 parsley sprigs, to garnish (optional)
- pepper

Preheat the oven to 350°F/180°C/Gas Mark 4.

Heat half the oil in a pan and add the garlic paste and two-thirds of the onion. Sauté for 3 minutes until the onion has softened, then add the chopped tenderloin (fillet), olives, raisins, and chopped hard-boiled eggs. Cook for another 4–5 minutes, stirring until the meat has browned all over. Season with salt and pepper to taste. Set aside.

Remove the corn kernels from the cobs, place in a blender, and blend to a puree. Set aside.

Heat the remaining oil in another pan. Add the remaining onion and the chili paste and sauté until the onion is golden, then add the pureed corn and milk. Cook, stirring, for a few minutes until the corn is just cooked. Add the sugar and 1 tablespoon salt, remove from the heat, and pour into a bowl. Add the egg and 4 tablespoons Parmesan cheese and mix together thoroughly with a wooden spoon. Set aside.

Spoon half the corn mixture into a baking dish. Top with the meat filling and cover with the rest of the corn mixture, sprinkling over the remaining Parmesan cheese.

Bake for 40—45 minutes in the preheated oven until it is cooked and golden. Remove from oven and let cool, then remove from the dish and cut into 4 pieces. Serve garnished with sprigs of parsley.

CHIRIMPICO
KID GOAT STEW

Serves: 4
Preparation Time: 12 minutes
Cooking Time: 3 hours 25 minutes

If you can't find kid goat variety meat (offal), you can prepare this dish with lamb or cow variety meat (offal) instead.

9 oz (250 g) kid goat tripe
9 oz (250 g) kid goat lungs
1 tablespoon salt
14 oz (400 g) yucca root (cassava), peeled
9 oz (250 g) kid goat hearts
9 oz (250 g) goats' livers
2 tablespoons vegetable oil
1½ tablespoons Onion Condiment (see p. 404)
9 cloves garlic, very finely chopped
3 tablespoons Yellow Chili Paste (see p. 405)
4 tablespoons chopped culantro or cilantro (coriander) leaves, plus sprigs to garnish
¾ cup (3½ oz/100 g) cubed loche squash
4 tablespoons chicha de jora
1 cup (8 fl oz/250 ml) meat broth (stock)
4 yellow chiles, seeded, membranes removed, and thinly sliced
4 tablespoons chopped mint leaves
pepper

To cook the tripe, wash it thoroughly with cold water, cutting it along the side to wash inside. Boil in water over moderate heat for 2 hours until tender. Drain.

To cook the lungs, put it in a pan with 8½ cups (68 fl oz/2 liters) water, and 1 tablespoon salt. Boil for 45 minutes. Drain.

Meanwhile, bring a pan of water to a boil, add the yucca root (cassava), and cook until tender. Drain and cut into cubes. Set aside.

Wash the lungs and tripe thoroughly with hot water. Once clean, cut into small cubes along with the hearts and livers.

Heat the oil in a pan over medium heat. Add the onion condiment, garlic, and chili paste. Sauté for 2–3 minutes, stirring, then add the kid goat hearts, lungs, livers, and tripe. Season with salt and pepper. Add the chopped culantro, yucca root, squash, chicha de jora, and broth (stock) and simmer over medium heat for 15 minutes until it reduces by a quarter. Stir in the yellow chiles and mint and remove from the heat and serve.

TEQUEÑOS DE LOMO SALTADO
BEEF TENDERLOIN SPRING ROLLS

Serves: 4
Preparation Time: 15 minutes
Cooking Time: 20–25 minutes

7 oz (200 g) beef tenderloin (fillet), cut into ½-inch (1-cm) cubes
2 tablespoons vegetable oil for stir-frying, plus 4 cups (34 fl oz/1 liter) for deep-frying
1 red onion, chopped
1 yellow chile, seeded, membrane removed, and chopped
1 tomato, skinned, seeded, and thinly sliced
6 cloves garlic, very finely chopped
3 tablespoons white wine vinegar
2 tablespoons soy sauce
2 tablespoons oyster sauce
6 scallions (spring onions), green parts only, chopped
2 tablespoons chopped culantro or cilantro (coriander) leaves
20 spring roll wrappers
1 egg, beaten
1 cup (8 fl oz/250 ml) Rocoto Chili Cream (see p. 411), to serve
salt and pepper

Season the beef tenderloin (fillet) with salt and pepper. Heat the vegetable oil in a wok over high heat. Add the cubed beef and cook for a few minutes, stirring, then add the onion, chile and tomato. Cook for 2 minutes before adding the garlic. Stir together thoroughly.

Add the white wine vinegar, soy sauce and oyster sauce. Sauté for a few seconds more, then add the scallions (spring onions) and culantro. Stir together, remove from the heat, and let cool.

Lay the spring roll wrappers on a clean work counter and place 1 tablespoon of filling in the center of each one. Brush the edges with beaten egg and roll up lengthwise into spring rolls.

Heat the oil for deep-frying in a large pan or deep fryer to 350°F/180°C, or until a cube of bread browns in 30 seconds. Drop the spring rolls carefully into the oil and cook for 6–8 minutes until crispy and golden. Drain well on paper towels and serve immediately with the chili cream.

YUCAS RELLENAS
STUFFED YUCCA ROOT BALLS

Serves: 4
Preparation Time: 20 minutes
Cooking Time: 1 hour

Be careful not to let the yucca root (cassava) dry out when it cools. It should be very creamy.

4½ cups (37 fl oz/1.1 liters) vegetable oil
1½ red onions, chopped
6 cloves garlic, very finely chopped
2 yellow chiles, seeded, membranes removed, and chopped
2 teaspoons Panca Chili Paste (see p. 406)
14 oz (400 g) beef (sirloin) steak, coarsely chopped
½ cup (3 oz/80 g) raisins, soaked in water
pinch of dried oregano
pinch of ground cumin
1 cup (8 fl oz/250 ml) beef broth (stock)
2¼ lb (1 kg) yucca root (cassava), peeled
1 egg, hard-boiled and cut into quarters
4 pitted black olives
1 cup (8 fl oz/250 ml) Rocoto Chili Sauce (see p. 417), to serve
2 cups (18 fl oz/500 ml) Creole Sauce (see p. 416), to serve
salt and pepper

Heat ½ cup (4 fl oz/120 ml) oil in a skillet or frying pan over medium heat. Add the red onion, garlic, and yellow chiles and sauté for 3 minutes until the onions have started to soften, then add the chili paste and sauté for a few minutes more until the paste is fragrant and the onions are cooked.

Add the steak, raisins, oregano, and cumin to the pan and season with salt and pepper. Pour in the beef broth (stock) and cook until the stock has evaporated. Remove from the heat and set aside.

Bring a pan of water to a boil, add the yucca root (cassava), and cook until tender. Drain and mash thoroughly until smooth and free of lumps. Divide the mashed yucca root into 4 portions. Spread one portion out on a clean work counter to form a thick layer. Place a boiled egg quarter, an olive, and a little of the steak mixture in the center. Pull the edges of the mashed yucca root together to form an oval-shape ball. Repeat with the remaining ingredients.

Heat the remaining 4 cups (34 fl oz/1 liter) vegetable oil in a large pan or deep fryer to 350°F/180°C, or until a cube of bread browns in 30 seconds. Drop the yucca root balls carefully into the oil and cook for 6 minutes until crispy and golden. Drain well on paper towels and serve immediately with the rocoto sauce and creole sauce.

FRITO TRUJILLANO
FRIED PORK RIBS

Serves: 4
Preparation Time: 5 minutes, plus 12 hours soaking
Cooking Time: 1 hour 15 minutes

***Frito trujillano* is served with cassava on the side instead of potatoes or sweet potatoes, which are served with chicharrón in other parts of Peru.**

1 cup (11 oz/300 g) salt
3¼ lb (1.5 kg) pork ribs
5 cups (2¼ lb/1 kg) lard

To serve
7 oz (200 g) yucca root (cassava), peeled and boiled and cut into ¾ × 2-inch (2 × 5-cm) pieces
1 cup (8 fl oz/250 ml) Creole Sauce (see p. 416)

Pour 4 cups (34 oz/1 liter) water into a bowl. Add the salt and pork ribs and set aside to soak for 12 hours, or overnight.

Once soaked, remove the ribs from the water and drain well.

Put the lard in a large skillet or frying pan over medium heat to melt. Once melted, add the pork ribs to the pan, lower the heat, and cook for 1 hour, turning occasionally, until tender and cooked through. Turn the heat up to high and brown the ribs on all sides, then remove from the pan and drain on paper towels.

Serve on a platter with boiled yucca root (cassava) and creole sauce.

WANTÁN DE MARISCOS CON CREMA DE ROCOTO
SEAFOOD WONTONS WITH ROCOTO CHILI CREAM

Serves: 4
Preparation Time: 15 minutes
Cooking Time: 20–25 minutes

This is another Chinese–Peruvian fusion dish. You can fill the wontons with any ingredients you have on hand.

12 napa (Chinese) cabbage leaves
½ cup (3 oz/80 g) chopped Cooked Octopus (see p. 406)
½ cup (3 oz/80 g) shrimp (prawns), cleaned and chopped
½ cup (3 oz/80 g) chopped squid
2 scallions (spring onions), white part only, chopped
1 teaspoon chopped culantro or cilantro (coriander) leaves
1-inch (2.5-cm) piece of fresh ginger, peeled and grated
½ teaspoon granulated sugar
1 tablespoon sesame oil
salt
1 egg, beaten, plus 1 egg white
16 wonton wrappers
4 cups (34 fl oz/1 liter) vegetable oil
1 cup (8 fl oz/250 ml) Rocoto Chili Cream (see p. 411), to serve

Bring a pan of water to a boil, add the cabbage leaves, and cook until tender. Drain and coarsely chop. Set aside.

Place the octopus, shrimp (prawns), and squid in a bowl. Add the scallions (spring onions), Chinese cabbage, culantro or cilantro (coriander), ginger, sugar, and sesame oil, season with salt, and mix together thoroughly. Add the egg white and mix together again.

Lay the wonton wrappers on a clean work counter. Place a little seafood filling in the center of each wrapper, brush the edges with a little beaten egg, and fold over into a triangle shape, bringing the points of the triangle together to finish.

Heat the vegetable oil in a large pan or deep fryer to 350°F/180°C, or until a cube of bread browns in 30 seconds. Drop the wontons carefully into the oil and cook for 6–8 minutes until crispy and golden. Drain well on paper towels and serve immediately.

YUQUITAS RELLENAS DE QUESO CON SALSA OCOPA
CHEESY YUCCA-ROOT CROQUETTES WITH OCOPA SAUCE

Serves: 4
Preparation Time: 15 minutes
Cooking Time: 35–40 minutes

These cassava croquettes are delicious when they are creamy on the inside and the cheese is not too strong.

2¼ lb (1 kg) yucca root (cassava), peeled
1¾ cups (8 oz/225 g) all-purpose (plain) flour
5¼ oz (150 g) queso fresco, cut into 14 small rectangles
1½ eggs, beaten
4 cups (34 fl oz/1 liter) vegetable oil
1 cup (8 fl oz/250 ml) Ocopa Sauce (see p. 415), to serve
salt and pepper

Bring a large pan of water to a boil, add the yucca root (cassava), and cook for 25 minutes until tender. Remove from the heat, drain, and mash while still hot.

Put the mashed yucca root in a bowl with two thirds of the flour, season with salt and pepper, and mix together thoroughly. Divide the mixture into 14 portions and spread one on the palm of your hand. Place a piece of queso fresco in the center and roll the mixture into a cylinder shape. Repeat with the remaining yucca root and queso fresco.

Coat the yucca-root cylinders in the beaten egg and then in the remaining flour.

Heat the vegetable oil in a large pan or deep fryer to 350°F/180°C, or until a cube of bread browns in 30 seconds. Drop the yucca-root cylinders carefully into the oil and cook for 6 minutes until crispy and golden. Drain well on paper towels and serve immediately with the ocopa sauce.

Seafood Wontons with Rocoto Chili Cream

AJÍ DE HUEVOS
CHILE EGGS

Serves: 4
Preparation Time: 10 minutes
Cooking Time: 40 minutes

Be careful not to overcook the eggs. They should be creamy.

- 3 white bread slices
- 1 cup (8 fl oz/250 ml) whole (full-fat) milk
- 4 potatoes, peeled
- 2 tablespoons vegetable oil
- 1 small red onion, diced
- 1 clove garlic, chopped
- 1½ yellow chiles, seeded, membranes removed, and thinly sliced
- 4 tablespoons Mirasol Chili Paste (see p. 405)
- 2 tablespoons Yellow Chili Paste (see p. 405)
- 2 cups (18 fl oz/500 ml) chicken broth (stock)
- 8 eggs
- pinch of ground oregano
- pinch of ground cumin
- 3 oz (80 g) queso fresco, grated
- salt and pepper

To garnish
- 8 pitted black olives
- 3 oz (80 g) queso fresco, cut into ½-inch (1-cm) cubes

Put the bread and milk into a blender and blend together to form a puree. Set aside.

Bring a pan of water to a boil, add the potatoes, and cook until tender. Drain and set aside.

Heat the oil in a skillet or frying pan over medium heat. Add the onion, garlic, chiles, and chili pastes and sauté for a few minutes until the onions have softened.

Add the broth (stock) and the blended bread and milk mixture and cook for approximately 10 minutes until the mixture has thickened. Add the eggs and cook, stirring continuously, until the eggs have set. Add the oregano and cumin, season with salt and pepper, and sprinkle over the grated queso fresco.

Arrange the potato slices on plates. Spoon over the eggs and top with the olives and queso fresco. Serve immediately.

HUEVOS A LA RABONA
EGGS RABONA

Serves: 4
Preparation Time: 5 minutes, plus 10 minutes standing
Cooking Time: 20 minutes

- 1 small red onion, diced
- 2 tablespoons chopped rocoto chile
- 2 tablespoons chopped yellow chile
- juice of 2 small lemons
- ¾ cup (6 fl oz/175 ml) vegetable oil
- 8 eggs
- 4 country-style bread slices, toasted
- salt and pepper

Mix together the onion, rocoto chile, and yellow chile in a bowl. Add the lemon juice along with 2 tablespoons of the oil and season with salt and pepper. Let stand for 10 minutes.

Heat the remaining oil in a pan over high heat. Add the eggs one at a time, stirring the oil gently so that the whites enclose the yolks. Cook for 2 minutes, (being careful not to overcook them so the yolks remain lovely and juicy), then remove the eggs with a slotted spoon.

Place a slice of toasted country-style bread on each plate, top with 2 eggs, and spoon over the onion and chile salsa to finish.

TORTILLA DE RAYA
SKATE TORTILLA

Serves: 4
Preparation Time: 10 minutes, plus 12 hours soaking
Cooking Time: 15 minutes

Dry salt cod can also be used to prepare this tortilla, provided it has been soaked to desalinate the fish.

2¼ lb (1 kg) dried skate or salt cod
½ cup (4 fl oz/120 ml) vegetable oil
12 eggs
1 small onion, chopped
2 limo chiles, skinned, membranes removed, and chopped
2 tablespoons chopped culantro or cilantro (coriander) leaves
1 cup (8 fl oz/250 ml) Creole Sauce (see p. 416), to serve
salt and pepper

Put the dried skate into a bowl, cover with water, and let soak for 12 hours, or overnight, changing the water occasionally. Once soaked, remove the skate from the water and drain well. Shred the skate meat and set aside.

Heat half the oil in a skillet or frying pan over medium heat, add the shredded skate, and fry for a few minutes, stirring, until browned. Remove from the heat and let cool.

Beat the eggs together in a bowl and add the onion, chiles, culantro or cilantro (coriander), and skate. Season and mix together thoroughly.

Heat the remaining oil in a nonstick pan over medium heat. Pour the egg mixture into the pan and cook for 4 minutes until the tortilla has set and is brown on the bottom but still juicy on the inside. Turn over carefully and cook for another minute, then turn out onto a plate and serve with the creole sauce.

TORTILLA DE HUEVERA
FISH ROE TORTILLA

Serves: 4
Preparation Time: 5 minutes
Cooking Time: 8–10 minutes

The fish roe and eggs should be very fresh for this recipe.

2¼ lb (1 kg) fish roe
12 eggs
3 tablespoons vegetable oil
2 cups (18 fl oz/500 ml) Creole Sauce (see p. 416), to serve
salt

Rinse the fish roe thoroughly, then press through a fine strainer (sieve).

Beat the eggs together in a bowl and season with salt. Add the fish roe and mix together thoroughly.

Heat the oil in a nonstick skillet or frying pan over medium heat. Pour the egg mixture into the pan and cook for 6–8 minutes until the tortilla has set and is brown on the bottom but still juicy on the inside. Turn over very carefully and cook for another minute, then turn out onto a plate and serve with the creole sauce.

HUEVOS CON SALCHICHA DE HUACHO
EGGS WITH HUACHO SAUSAGE

Serves: 4
Preparation Time: 5 minutes
Cooking Time: 8 minutes

This egg dish calls for Huacho sausages, a spicy, bright orange Peruvian sausage, though you can use any type of fresh spicy sausage.

4 Huacho sausages or other spicy sausages
4 tablespoons vegetable oil
½ onion, finely diced
2 tablespoons finely chopped yellow chile
12 eggs, beaten
salt and pepper

Slice the Huacho sausages lengthwise down the middle and remove the skins.

Heat the oil in a pan over medium heat. Crumble in the sausage meat and cook for 2 minutes, stirring, until cooked through, then add the onion and yellow chile.

Cook for another minute before adding the eggs. Season with salt and pepper and continue to cook, stirring, until the eggs have just set. Serve immediately.

CARACOLES AL SILLAO
SNAILS IN SOY SAUCE

Serves: 4
Preparation Time: 20 minutes, plus 24 hours freezing and 1 hour defrosting
Cooking Time: 2 hours 15 minutes

You can also use octopus or shellfish to prepare this dish, adjusting the cooking times accordingly.

24 sea snails
5 tablespoons packed brown sugar
1 cup (8 fl oz/250 ml) soy sauce
¼-inch (5-mm) piece of fresh ginger, peeled and sliced
½ cup (4 fl oz/120 ml) pisco
1 teaspoon salt

Without removing them from their shells, wash the snails under running water until any sand or dirt has been removed. Once clean, place the snails in a suitable container and freeze them for 24 hours, so that the fibers tauten and crack.

Defrost the snails for around 1 hour before cooking.

Place the brown sugar, soy sauce, 102 fl oz/3 liters water, ginger, pisco, and salt in a large pan. Bring to a boil and cook for 10 minutes. Add the snails in their shells, reduce the heat, and simmer gently over low heat for 2 hours, or until the liquid has reduced and the snails are very tender.

Remove the snails from the pan using a slotted spoon, reserving the cooking liquid. Extract, clean, and trim the snail meat before returning it to the shells. Serve the snails on a plate either hot or cold, covered in the reserved cooking liquid.

Eggs with 'Huacho' Sausage

STREET FOOD

ANTICUCHO DE CORAZÓN DE RES
BEEF HEART ANTICUCHO

Serves: 4
Preparation Time: 12 minutes, plus 3 hours marinating
Cooking Time: 35–40 minutes

1 × 4-lb (1.75-kg) beef heart
2 white potatoes
3 cups (26 fl oz/750 ml) Anticuchera Sauce (see p. 403)
½ cup (4½ oz/130 g) Rocoto Chili Paste (see p. 407)
1 scallion (spring onion), chopped
1 tablespoon salt

To serve
2 corncobs, cooked and halved
4 corn husks

Coarsely chop the beef heart into around 24 even pieces about ½-inch/1-cm thick.

Bring a pan of water to a boil, add the potatoes, and cook until tender. Drain and cut into ½-inch /1-cm slices. Set aside.

Place the heart pieces in the anticuchera sauce and let marinate for 3 hours in the refrigerator. Assemble the anticuchos by sliding 3 pieces of heart onto each skewer. Repeat the process until you've used up all the pieces. Mix the chili paste with the scallion (spring onion) and salt in a bowl.

Cook the anticuchos in a very hot ridged grill pan for 2 minutes on each side, basting, until medium rare, being careful not to overcook them so that they are still succulent. Set aside.

Place the boiled potatoes in the grill pan and cook for a few minutes until browned.

Place 2 of the anticuchos in the center of each corn husk and serve immediately with the sliced potatoes, halved corncobs, and chili sauce mixture.

ANTICUCHO DE CORAZÓN DE POLLO
CHICKEN HEART ANTICUCHO

Serves: 4
Preparation Time: 10 minutes, plus 2 hours marinating
Cooking Time: 35–40 minutes

If you cook the chicken hearts so that they are medium well done they will be delicious.

2¼ lb (1 kg) chicken hearts
3 cups (26 fl oz/750 ml) Anticuchera Sauce (see p. 403)
2 potatoes
1 cup (8 fl oz/250 ml) Yellow Chili Paste (see p. 405)
2 scallions (spring onions), green part only, chopped
juice of 1 lemon
salt and pepper

To serve
2 corncobs, cooked and halved
4 corn husks

Place the chicken hearts in the anticuchera sauce and let marinate for 2 hours in the refrigerator.

Bring a pan of water to a boil, add the potatoes, and cook until tender. Drain and cut into ½-inch /1-cm slices. Set aside.

Slide the chicken hearts onto skewers.

Mix the yellow chili paste and scallions (spring onions) in a bowl with the lemon juice and season with salt and pepper.

Cook the anticuchos in a very hot ridged grill pan for until cooked and browned for 2 minutes on each side until browned, basting with the marinade and being careful not to overcook them so that they are still succulent. Set aside.

Place the boiled potatoes in the grill pan and cook for a few minutes until browned.

Place 2 of the anticuchos in the center of each corn husk and serve immediately with the sliced potatoes, halved corncobs, and chili sauce mixture.

Beef Heart Anticucho

ANTICUCHO DE HÍGADO DE POLLO
CHICKEN LIVER ANTICUCHO

Serves: 4
Preparation Time: 10 minutes, plus 3 hours marinating
Cooking Time: 35–40 minutes

- 1 lb 9 oz (725 g) chicken livers
- 3 cups (26 fl oz/750 ml) Anticuchera Sauce (see p. 403)
- 2 white potatoes
- ½ cup (4½ oz/130 g) Rocoto Chili Paste (see p. 407)
- 1 scallion (spring onion), chopped
- salt and pepper

To serve

- 2 corncobs, cooked and halved
- 4 corn husks

Place the chicken livers in the anticuchera sauce and let marinate for 3 hours.

Bring a pan of water to a boil, add the potatoes, and cook until tender. Drain and cut into ½-inch /1-cm slices. Set aside.

Slide the chicken livers onto skewers.

Mix the chili paste with the scallion (spring onion) in a bowl and season with salt and pepper.

Cook the anticuchos in a very hot ridged grill pan for 1 minute on each side until browned, being careful not to overcook them so that they are still succulent. Set aside.

Place the boiled potato slices in the grill pan and brown for a few minutes.

Place 2 of the anticuchos in the center of each corn husk and serve immediately with the sliced potatoes, halved corncobs, and chili sauce mixture.

ANTICUCHO DE LOMO
BEEF TENDERLOIN ANTICUCHO

Serves: 4
Preparation Time: 10 minutes, plus 3 hours marinating
Cooking Time: 35–40 minutes

- 1 lb 5 oz (600 g) beef tenderloin (fillet), trimmed
- 2 white potatoes
- 3 cups (26 fl oz/750 ml) Anticuchera Sauce (see p. 403)
- ½ cup (4½ oz/130 g) Rocoto Chili Paste (see p. 407)
- 1 tablespoon chopped scallion (spring onion)
- salt and pepper

To serve

- 2 corncobs, cooked and halved
- 4 corn husks

Cut the beef tenderloin (fillet) into 1½ x 2 x ½-inch / 3 × 4 × 1-cm pieces.

Bring a pan of water to a boil, add the potatoes, and cook until tender. Drain and cut into ½-inch /1-cm slices. Set aside.

Place the beef pieces in the anticuchera sauce and let marinate for 3 hours in the refrigerator. Slide the beef pieces onto anticucho or kebab skewers.

In a separate bowl, mix the chili paste with the scallion (spring onion) and season with salt and pepper.

Cook the anticuchos in a very hot ridged grill pan until cooked and browned on each side until browned, being careful not to overcook them so that they are still succulent. Set aside.

Place the boiled potato slices in the grill pan and brown for a few minutes.

Place 2 of the anticuchos in the center of each corn husk and serve immediately with the sliced potatoes, halved corncobs, and chili sauce mixture on the side.

Chicken Liver Anticucho

Fish Anticucho

112

ANTICUCHO DE PESCADO
FISH ANTICUCHO

Serves: 4
Preparation Time: 10 minute, plus 3 hours marinating
Cooking Time: 35–40 minutes

14 oz (400 g) swordfish or other firm white fish fillets
2 white potatoes
3 cups (26 fl oz/750 ml) Anticuchera Sauce (see p. 403)
½ cup (4½ oz/130 g) Rocoto Chili Paste (see p. 407)
1 scallion (spring onion), chopped
salt and pepper

To serve
2 corncobs, cooked with kernels removed
4 corn husks

Cut the fish into around 16 even pieces.

Bring a pan of water to a boil, add the potatoes, and cook until tender. Drain and cut into ½-inch /1-cm slices. Set aside.

Place the fish pieces in the anticuchera sauce and let marinate for 3 hours. Slide the fish pieces onto anticucho or kebab skewers.

In a separate bowl, mix the chili paste with the scallion (spring onion) and season with salt and pepper.

Cook the anticuchos in a very hot ridged grill pan for 2 minutes on each side, being careful not to overcook them so that they are still succulent. Set aside.

Place the boiled potato slices in the grill pan and brown for a few minutes.

Place 2 of the anticuchos in the center of each corn husk and serve immediately with the sliced potatoes, corn, and chili sauce mixture.

ANTICUCHO DE POLLO
CHICKEN ANTICUCHO

Serves: 4
Preparation Time: 10 minutes, plus 3 hours marinating
Cooking Time: 35–40 minutes

1 lb 5 oz (600 g) skin-on chicken thighs
2 white potatoes
3 cups (26 fl oz/750 ml) Anticuchera Sauce (see p. 403)
½ cup (4½ oz/130 g) Rocoto Chili Paste (see p. 407)
1 scallion (spring onion), chopped
salt and pepper

To serve
2 corncobs, cooked and halved
4 corn husks

Cut the chicken thighs into 1½ x ¾inch/3 × 2-cm pieces.

Bring a pan of water to a boil, add the potatoes, and cook until tender. Drain and cut into ½-inch /1-cm slices. Set aside.

Place the chicken pieces in the anticuchera sauce and let marinate for 3 hours. Slide the chicken pieces onto anticucho or kebab skewers.

In a separate bowl, mix the rocoto chili paste with the scallion (spring onion) and season with salt and pepper.

Cook the anticuchos in a very hot ridged grill pan for 2 minutes on each side until browned, being careful not to overcook them so that they are still succulent, basting continuously. Set aside.

Place the boiled potato slices in the grill pan and brown for a few minutes.

Place 2 of the anticuchos in the center of each corn husk and serve immediately with the sliced potatoes, halved corncobs, and chili sauce mixture.

PANCITA CON CHONCHOLÍ
GRILLED BEEF TRIPE AND INTESTINE

Serves: 4
Preparation Time: 8 minutes, plus 3 hours marinating
Cooking Time: 2 hours 10 minutes

To prepare this dish, the tripe and intestines should be cooked very slowly so that you end up with a confit.

- 1 lb 2 oz (500 g) beef tripe, cleaned
- 1 lb 2 oz (500 g) beef small intestines, cleaned
- 3 cups (26 fl oz/750 ml) Anticuchera Sauce (see p. 403)
- 4 corn husks

To serve

- 2 potatoes, boiled and cut into ½-inch (1-cm) slices
- 1 cup (8 fl oz/250 ml) Carretilla Sauce (see p. 415)

Bring a large pot or pan of water to a boil. Add the tripe and intestines and boil for 2 hours until cooked. Remove from the heat, drain, and chop into 1½ x ¾-inch/3 × 2-cm pieces.

Place the tripe and intestine cubes in the anticuchera sauce and let marinate for 3 hours in the refrigerator.

Heat a ridged grill pan to very hot, add the meat, and cook for 4 minutes on each side until brown.

Place a portion of the meat in the center of each corn husk and serve immediately with sliced boiled potatoes and carretilla sauce.

PANQUITAS ANTICUCHERAS
VARIETY MEATS ON CORN HUSKS

Serves: 4
Preparation Time: 12 minutes, plus 3 hours marinating
Cooking Time: 2 hours 30 minutes

- 2 corncobs
- 9 oz (250 g) beef tripe, cleaned
- 9 oz (250 g) beef small intestines, cleaned
- 9 oz (250 g) beef heart, chopped
- 9 oz (250 g) chicken livers
- 4 cups (34 fl oz/1 liter) Anticuchera Sauce (see p. 403)
- 2 tablespoons butter
- 2 teaspoons chopped parsley
- 8 corn husks
- 1 cup (8 fl oz/250 ml) Carretilla Sauce (see p. 415), to serve

Bring a pan of water to a boil, add the corncobs, and cook until tender. Drain and remove the kernels. Set aside.

Bring another large pot or pan of water to a boil. Add the tripe and intestines and boil for 2 hours until cooked. Remove from the heat, drain, and chop into ¾-inch/2-cm cubes.

Place the tripe and intestine cubes, chopped heart, and chicken livers in the anticuchera sauce and let marinate for 3 hours in the refrigerator.

Heat a ridged grill pan to very hot, add the meat, and cook for 5 minutes on each side until brown, being careful not to overcook it so that it remains succulent. Set aside.

Heat the butter in a skillet or frying pan over medium heat. Add the corn kernels and sauté for a few minutes until golden, then add the chopped parsley and stir together well. Remove from the heat.

To serve, place 2 corn husks on each plate and top with the sautéed corn, tripe and intestine cubes, chopped heart, and chicken livers. Serve with carretilla sauce.

TAMAL LIMEÑO
LIMA-STYLE TAMALES

Serves: 4
Preparation Time: 20 minutes, plus 2–3 hours soaking
Cooking Time: 1 hour 30 minutes

It is important for cooked tamales to have a creamy texture. They can be served with Creole sauce.

2 cups (11 oz/300 g) hominy (dried corn)
½ cup (3½ oz/100 g) lard
½ red onion, chopped
1 teaspoon Garlic Paste (see p. 406)
2 tablespoons chopped yellow chiles
2 tablespoons Annatto Oil (see p. 408)
2 tablespoons vegetable oil
7 oz (200 g) cooked chicken breast
16 banana leaves, well rinsed
8 black olives
1 cup (8 fl oz/250 ml) Creole Sauce (see p. 416), to serve
salt and pepper

Soak the hominy (dried corn) in water for 2–3 hours. Strain and pass through a hand mill.

Melt the lard in a skillet or frying pan. Add the onion, garlic paste, chiles, and annatto oil and cook over medium heat until the onion is golden. Add the ground hominy, stir in 2 cups (18 fl oz/500 ml) water, and season generously with salt and pepper.

Continue to cook over low heat, stirring with a wooden spoon, until the mixture has thickened and the bottom of the pan can be seen when the spoon is dragged across it. Remove from the heat and set aside.

Heat the vegetable oil in a skillet or frying pan and brown the chicken on both sides. Remove from the heat and cut into 1½-inch/3-cm pieces. Season with salt and pepper and set aside.

Use 8 banana leaves to assemble the tamales. Place a serving of the hominy mixture in the center of each leaf. Spread the mixture out toward the edges and top with a portion of the cooked chicken and an olive. Carefully fold up the banana leaf to wrap up the filling snugly and tie with string to secure. Repeat the process with the remaining ingredients and banana leaves.

Cover the bottom of a pan with the remaining banana leaves and place the tamales on top. Cover with water and let simmer for 1 hour.

Remove the loose banana leaves and tamales from the pan. Place a banana leaf on each plate and top with an unwrapped tamale. Serve with Creole sauce.

TAMALITO VERDE
GREEN TAMALES

Serves: 4
Preparation Time: 20 minutes
Cooking Time: 1 hour 20 minutes

Once the tamales are ready, you can drizzle them with the juices of any stew. They will taste delicious.

- 8 corncobs
- handful of culantro or cilantro (coriander) leaves
- ½ cup (3½ oz/100 g) lard
- 2 tablespoons Yellow Chili Paste (see p. 405)
- 1 tablespoon Onion Condiment (see p. 404)
- ½ teaspoon ground cumin
- salt and pepper
- 42 corn husks
- 1 cup (8 fl oz/250 ml) Creole Sauce (see p. 416), to serve

Remove the kernels from the corncobs, reserving the cobs, and put in a blender with the culantro or cilantro (coriander) leaves. Blend together to form a coarse paste.

Put the lard into a pan over medium heat to melt. Once melted, add the chili paste, onion condiment, and cumin and season with salt and pepper. Cook for 5 minutes until the onions are cooked and the chili paste is fragrant. Add the blended kernels to the pan and continue to cook, stirring, for 10 minutes or until the mixture thickens slightly. Set aside. Place a serving of the corn mixture in the center of 2 overlapping corn husks. Carefully fold up the edges to wrap up the filling snugly and tie with string to secure. Repeat the process with the remaining corn mixture and husks to make 16 tamales.

Cover the bottom of a pan with the remaining 10 corn husks and place the tamales on top. Fill the pan halfway with water and simmer for 1 hour.

Remove the tamales from the pan, unwrap, and serve with Creole sauce.

HUMITA DE MAÍZ
CORN HUMITAS

Serves: 4
Preparation Time: 15 minutes
Cooking Time: 40 minutes

Try this recipe out with different types of cheese. Humitas taste good with all varieties.

- 8 corncobs
- 1 cup (8 fl oz/250 ml) whole (full-fat) milk
- 1 cup (7 oz/200 g) lard
- 24 corn husks
- 4 oz (120 g) queso fresco, cut into 8 pieces
- salt and pepper

Remove the corn kernels from the cobs and place in a blender with the milk. Blend to a puree. Season with salt and pepper and set aside.

Melt the lard in a pan over medium heat. Pour the corn mixture into the pan, lower the heat, and cook, stirring, until the corn starts to thicken. Remove from the heat.

Use the corn husks to assemble the humitas. Place a portion of the mixture into the middle of 2 overlapping corn husks. Place a piece of cheese in the center, carefully wrap up the sides, and tie with string to make one humita. Repeat the process with to make 8 humitas.

Cover the bottom of a pan with the remaining corn husks. Place the humitas on top and fill the pan halfway with water. Cook on low heat for 30 minutes with the lid on. Remove the humitas from the corn husks to serve.

TAMALITO DE CHOCLO NORTEÑO
NORTHERN-STYLE CORN TAMALES

Serves: 4
Preparation Time: 15 minutes
Cooking Time: 1 hour 20 minutes

These tamales can be stuffed with chicken, pork, or seafood, and served with Creole sauce.

4 cups (1 lb 5 oz/600 g) corn kernels
½ cup (4 fl oz/120 ml) vegetable oil
7 oz (200 g) pork meat, such as neck or ribs, cut into coarse chunks
1 cup (7 oz/200 g) lard
1 small red onion, chopped
1 teaspoon Garlic Paste (see p. 406)
2 tablespoons chopped yellow chiles
2 tablespoons Annatto Oil (see p. 408)
16 banana leaves, well rinsed
1 cup (8 fl oz/250 ml) Creole Sauce (see p. 416), to serve
salt and pepper

Grind the corn in a hand mill.

Heat the oil in the pan, add the pork, and cook until brown all over. Season with salt and pepper and set aside.

Melt the lard in a pan. Add the onion, garlic paste, yellow chiles, and annatto oil and sauté over medium heat until the onion is golden. Add the ground corn, stir in 2 cups (18 fl oz/500 ml) water, and season generously with salt and pepper. Cook on low heat until the mixture has thickened and the bottom of the pan can be seen when a wooden spoon is dragged across it. Remove from the heat and set aside.

Use 8 banana leaves to assemble the tamales. Place a serving of the corn mixture in the center of each leaf. Spread the mixture out toward the edges and top with the cooked pork pieces. Cover with a little more corn mixture and carefully fold up the banana leaf to wrap up the filling snugly. Tie with string to secure.

Cover the bottom of a pan with the remaining banana leaves and place the tamales on top. Cover with water and let simmer for 1 hour.

Remove the loose tamales and banana leaves from the pan. Place a banana leaf on each plate and top with 2 unwrapped tamales. Serve with Creole sauce.

Serves: 4
Preparation Time: 20 minutes, plus 24 hours soaking
Cooking Time: 1 hour 10 minutes

This dish can also be made with salt cod, provided it has been soaked and desalted first. Sacha culantro can be replaced with culantro or cilantro (coriander).

- 1 lb 2 oz (500 g) dried salted paiche (Amazonian fish) or salt cod
- 2¼ lb (1 kg) yucca root (cassava), peeled and grated
- ½ cup (3½ oz/100 g) lard
- 1 onion, chopped
- 2 tablespoons ground turmeric
- ½ cup (4 fl oz/120 ml) Blended Sacha Culantro (see p. 407) or culantro or cilantro (coriander)
- 4 eggs, plus 2 hard-boiled and halved
- 8 bijao leaves
- 4 pitted black olives
- 1 cup (8 fl oz/250 ml) Cocona and Chili Salsa (see p. 409), to serve
- salt

JUANE DE YUCCA
AMAZONIAN YUCCA ROOT TAMALES

Put the paiche into a bowl, cover with water, and let soak for 24 hours, changing the water 2 times.

Bring a large pan of water to a boil. Drain the soaked paiche, add to the pan, and cook for about 5 minutes until rehydrated and all the salt has been removed. Drain and let cool, then cut into 4 pieces.

Wrap the grated yucca root (cassava) in a clean towel into a ball and squeeze to remove any excess juice.

Put the lard into a large skillet or frying pan over medium heat to melt. Once melted, add the onion and turmeric and sauté for a few minutes, until the onion has softened. Season with salt. Add the blended sacha culantro or cilantro (coriander) and cook for a few minutes until some of the liquid evaporates. Add the grated yucca root and continue to cook for 8 minutes, stirring occasionally, until the mixture thickens. Remove from the heat.

Beat the eggs together and add to the yucca root mixture. Mix together well and divide into 4 portions.

Lightly roast the bijao leaves directly over a gas flame for a few seconds to give a smoky scent and make them more flexible. Take 2 bijao leaves and place one over the other to form a cross. Place a portion of the yucca root mixture, 1 piece of paiche, half a boiled egg, and 1 olive in the middle. Carefully fold up the edges to wrap up the filling snugly and tie with string to secure. Repeat the process with the remaining bijao leaves and ingredients.

Bring a large pan of water to a boil. Add the tamales to the water, reduce the heat, and simmer for 40 minutes.

Remove the tamales from the pan, unwrap, and serve with the cocona and chili salsa.

JUANE
AMAZONIAN RICE TAMALES

Serves: 4
Preparation Time: 20 minutes
Cooking Time: 1 hour 40 minutes

You can make these *juanes* with salted fish, pork, or beef casserole filling.

- 4 tablespoons lard
- 1 × 3¼-lb (1.5-kg) chicken, quartered
- 1 tablespoon Onion Condiment (see p. 404)
- 6 cloves garlic, very finely chopped
- 1 teaspoon ground or mashed fresh turmeric
- 3 tablespoons Yellow Chili Paste (see p. 405)
- 2 tablespoons chopped sacha culantro or cilantro (coriander) leaves
- 6 cups (51 fl oz/1.5 liters) chicken broth (stock)
- 2 cups (14 oz/400 g) rice
- 1 cup (2¾ oz/70 g) sweet chiles, seeded, membranes removed, and chopped
- 4 eggs, plus 2 hard-boiled and halved
- 7 oz (200 g) yucca root (cassava), peeled and grated
- 2 tablespoons vegetable oil
- 8 bijao leaves
- 4 pitted black olives
- salt and pepper

Put the lard into a pan over medium heat to melt. Once melted, add the chicken quarters and brown all over. Remove from the pan and set aside.

Add the onion condiment, garlic, turmeric, and chili paste to the pan and cook for a few minutes, stirring. Return the chicken pieces to the pan with the culantro or cilantro (coriander) leaves, pour over the broth (stock), and season with salt and pepper. Let simmer for 45 minutes, until the chicken is tender. Remove the chicken pieces from the pan and set aside.

Add the rice and sweet chiles to the pan and simmer for another 15 minutes until the rice is cooked. Set aside.

Beat the eggs together in a bowl. Add the grated yucca root (cassava), cooked rice, and vegetable oil, season with salt and pepper, and mix together thoroughly. Divide the mixture into 4 portions.

Take 2 bijao leaves and place one over the other to form a cross. Place 1 portion of rice, 1 piece of chicken, half a boiled egg, and 1 olive in the middle. Carefully fold up the edges to wrap up the filling snugly and tie with string to secure. Repeat the process with the remaining bijao leaves and ingredients.

Put the tamales in a steamer and cook for 30 minutes. Unwrap and serve.

Stuffed Potatoes

PAPA RELLENA
STUFFED POTATOES

Serves: 4
Preparation Time: 25 minutes
Cooking Time: 40–50 minutes, plus 2–3 hours standing

It used to be a common sight to see stuffed potatoes arranged in straw baskets being sold on the streets.

- 9 (about 2¼ lb/1 kg) potatoes, peeled
- ½ cup (4 fl oz/120 ml) vegetable oil, plus 4 cups (34 fl oz/1 liter) for deep-frying
- 2 onions, chopped
- 3 cloves garlic, chopped
- 2 tablespoons Panca Chili Paste (see p. 406)
- 2–3 yellow chiles, seeded, membranes removed, and chopped
- ½ cup (4 fl oz/120 ml) chicken broth (stock)
- 1 lb 2 oz (500 g) beef tenderloin (fillet), cut into ½-inch (1-cm) cubes
- 8 pitted black olives
- 2 eggs, hard-boiled and cut into quarters
- salt and pepper

To serve

- 1 cup (8 fl oz/250 ml) Creole Sauce (see p. 416), to serve
- ½ red onion, finely sliced
- ½ yellow chile, finely sliced

Bring a pan of water to a boil, add the potatoes, and cook until tender. Drain and mash thoroughly until smooth and free of lumps, put in a bowl, and season with salt and pepper to taste. Set aside for 2–3 hours in a cool place.

Heat ½ cup (4 fl oz/120 ml) of the vegetable oil in a skillet or frying pan, add the onions, garlic, chili paste, and chiles and sauté over medium heat for 4–5 minutes, stirring, until the onion has softened. Pour in the broth (stock), add the tenderloin (fillet) cubes, and mix together thoroughly. Continue to cook for a few minutes until the beef is cooked. Season with salt and pepper to taste. Set aside.

To make the stuffed potatoes, knead and shape the cooled mashed potato into 8 oval balls, about 3 × 2 inches/7.5 × 5 cm. Flatten the balls and place a portion of the beef filling, an olive, and a boiled egg quarter in the center of each. Close the mashed potato around the filling and reshape into ovals.

Heat the vegetable oil for deep-frying in a large pan or deep fryer to 350°F/180°C, or until a cube of bread browns in 30 seconds. Drop the stuffed potatoes carefully into the hot oil and cook for 8 minutes or until crispy and golden. Drain well and serve immediately with creole sauce, onion, and chile on the side.

CHOCLO CON QUESO
CHEESY CORN ON THE COB

Serves: 4
Preparation Time: 8 minutes
Cooking Time: 10 minutes

This is a simple dish that we love, especially during corn season in the Andes.

- 4 choclo corncobs
- juice of 2 lemons
- 4 oz (120 g) queso fresco
- 2 tablespoons whole (full-fat) milk
- 2 tablespoons chopped rocoto chiles
- 2 tablespoons chopped huacatay leaves

Bring a pan of water to a boil, add the corncobs and cook for around 5 minutes until the corn is tender. Remove the pan from the heat, add the lemon juice to the water, and set aside.

Place the queso fresco in a bowl and mash with a fork. Add the milk a little at a time, continuing to mash, until thoroughly mixed, then stir in the rocoto chiles and huacatay leaves.

Place the corncobs on a plate and pour over the cheese mixture to finish.

SÁNGUCHE DE PESCADO FRITO
FRIED FISH SANDWICH

Serves: 4
Preparation Time: 15 minutes
Cooking Time: 16 minutes

You can also use other types of fish, such as horse mackerel, Pacific bonito, Atlantic mackerel, or red snapper to make these sandwiches.

4 silverside fish fillets, fresh anchovies, or fresh sardines, about 1 lb (450 g)
juice of 1 lemon
2 eggs, beaten
⅓ cup (2 oz/50 g) all-purpose (plain) flour
4 cups (34 fl oz/1 liter) vegetable oil
4 French bread rolls or any crusty rolls
1 cup (8 fl oz/250 ml) Mayonnaise (see p. 412) or Tartar Sauce (see p. 412)
4 iceberg lettuce leaves
1 cup (8 fl oz/250 ml) Creole Sauce (see p. 416)
salt and pepper

Place the silverside fillets in a bowl, add the lemon juice, and season with salt and pepper. Mix together thoroughly.

Dip the fillets in the beaten egg and coat evenly with the flour.

Heat the vegetable oil in a large pan or deep fryer to 350°F/180°C, or until a cube of bread browns in 30 seconds. Drop the fish fillets carefully into the hot oil and cook for 6 minutes or until crispy and golden. Drain well on paper towels.

Slice the bread rolls lengthwise down the middle and fill the sandwiches with the mayonnaise or tartar sauce, lettuce leaves, silverside fillets, and Creole sauce. Serve.

SÁNGUCHE DE PAVO
TURKEY SANDWICH

Serves: 4
Preparation Time: 8 minutes, plus 8 hours marinating
Cooking Time: 1 hour 30 minutes

If you're able to roast a whole turkey, you can make these sandwiches with meat from both the legs and breast for an even better flavor.

½ tablespoon Panca Chili Paste (see p. 406)
¼ clove garlic, very finely chopped
4 tablespoons cola
1 tablespoon white wine vinegar
½ tablespoon soy sauce
2¼-lb (1-kg) turkey breast
4 French bread rolls or any crusty rolls
4 tablespoons Mayonnaise (see p. 412)
4 lettuce leaves
1 cup (8 fl oz/250 ml) Creole Sauce (see p. 416)
salt and pepper

Put the chili paste in a bowl together with the garlic, cola, white wine vinegar, and soy sauce. Season with salt and pepper and mix together well. Add the turkey breast to the bowl and let marinate overnight in the refrigerator.

Preheat the oven to 300°F/150°C/Gas Mark 2. Remove the turkey breast from the marinade, transfer to a roasting pan, and cook in the preheated oven for 1½ hours, until golden and cooked through.

Remove from the oven. Carve the turkey breast into thick slices and let cool.

Slice the bread rolls lengthwise down the middle and fill with mayonnaise, lettuce leaves, turkey slices, and Creole sauce. Serve.

PAPA RELLENA DE MARISCOS
SEAFOOD-STUFFED POTATOES

Serves: 4
Preparation Time: 30 minutes
Cooking Time: 50–60 minutes, plus 2–3 hours standing

These stuffed potatoes, a twist on the original recipe, can be prepared with any seafood you may have to hand.

9 (about 2¼ lb/1 kg) white potatoes, peeled
½ cup (3 oz/80 g) peas
½ cup (4 fl oz/120 ml) vegetable oil, plus 4 cups (34 fl oz/1 liter) for deep-frying
2 onions, chopped
1 clove garlic, chopped
2 tablespoons Panca Chili Paste (see p. 406)
2–3 yellow chiles, seeded, membranes removed, and chopped
8 scallops, cleaned
8 uncooked small shrimp (prawns), peeled and deveined
4 oz (120 g) octopus, cleaned, cooked, and chopped (see p. 406)
½ cup (4 fl oz/120 ml) fish broth (stock)
1 tablespoon chopped culantro or cilantro (coriander) leaves
8 pitted black olives
2 eggs, hard-boiled and cut into quarters
1 cup (8 fl oz/250 ml) Creole Sauce (see p. 416), to serve
salt and pepper

Bring a pan of water to a boil, add the potatoes, and cook until tender. Drain and mash thoroughly until smooth and free of lumps, put in a bowl, and season with salt and pepper to taste. Set aside for 2–3 hours in a cool place.

Boil the peas until tender, drain, and set aside.

Heat ½ cup (4 fl oz/120 ml) oil in a skillet or frying pan, add the onions, garlic, chili paste, and chiles and sauté over medium heat for 4–5 minutes, stirring, until the onion has softened. Add the seafood and peas and season with salt and pepper to taste.

Pour in the broth (stock) and cook for 12 minutes, until the seafood is cooked and the liquid has reduced. Add the chopped culantro or cilantro (coriander) and set aside.

To make the stuffed potatoes, knead and shape the cooled mashed potato into 8 medium balls.

Flatten the balls and place a portion of the seafood filling, an olive, and a boiled egg quarter in the center of each. Close the mashed potato around the filling and shape into ovals.

Heat the vegetable oil for deep-frying in a large pan or deep fryer to 350°F/180°C, or until a cube of bread browns in 30 seconds. Drop the stuffed potatoes carefully into the hot oil and cook for 8 minutes or until crispy and golden. Drain well and serve immediately with creole sauce.

SÁNGUCHE DE CHICHARRÓN
PORK CRACKLING SANDWICH

Serves: 4
Preparation Time: 5 minutes, plus soaking overnight
Cooking Time: 1 hour 30 minutes

These sandwiches can also be made with country bread, ciabatta, or baguette. They all work wonderfully.

1 × 4½-lb (2-kg) pork side (belly)
1 cup (11 oz/300 g) salt
5 cups (2¼ lb/1 kg) lard
4 cloves garlic
2 sweet potatoes, sliced
4 cups (34 fl oz/1 liter) vegetable oil
4 French bread rolls or any crusty rolls
1 cup (8 fl oz/250 ml) Creole Sauce (see p. 416)

To serve
¼ red onion, thinly sliced
½ red chile, thinly sliced
handful cilantro (coriander), leaves picked

Put the pork side (belly) in a large bowl with the salt, cover with water, and let soak for 8 hours, or overnight. Once soaked, remove the pork from the water and rinse well. Drain and cut into 2 × 1¾-inch/5 × 4-cm pieces.

Put the lard into a large skillet or frying pan over medium heat to melt. Once melted, add the whole garlic cloves and pork pieces, lower the heat, and cook gently for 45 minutes, stirring occasionally. Turn up the heat and cook for another 25 minutes, until the meat has browned and the fat is crisp and golden. Set aside.

Heat the vegetable oil in a large pan or deep fryer to 350°F/180°C, or until a cube of bread browns in 30 seconds. Drop the sweet potato slices carefully into the hot oil and cook for 5 minutes, or until crispy and golden. Drain well on paper towels.

Slice the bread rolls lengthwise down the middle and fill with the fried sweet potato slices, pork pieces, and Creole sauce, onion, chile, and cilantro (coriander). Serve.

SÁNGUCHE DE LECHÓN
PORK SANDWICH

Serves: 8
Preparation Time: 8 minutes, plus 4 hours marinating
Cooking Time: 2 hours

You can also use pork shoulder, rib, or loin to prepare these sandwiches.

1 tablespoon vegetable oil
½ cup (4 fl oz/120 ml) Panca Chili Paste (see p. 406)
5 cloves garlic, very finely chopped
2½ teaspoons dried oregano
2½ teaspoons ground cumin
salt and pepper
1 × 5½-lb (2.5-kg) boned pork leg
1 cup (8 fl oz/250 ml) white wine
8 French bread rolls or any crusty rolls
2 cups (18 fl oz/500 ml) Creole Sauce (see p. 416)

Put the oil in a bowl with the chili paste, garlic, oregano, and cumin. Season with salt and pepper and mix together well.

Wash and dry the pork leg thoroughly. Coat the leg with the chili mixture and set aside to marinate for 4 hours.

Preheat the oven to 300°F/150°C/Gas Mark 2.

Transfer the pork leg to a roasting pan. Pour over ½ cup (4 fl oz/120 ml) water and cook in the preheated oven for 1 hour. Mix the white wine with 1 cup (8 fl oz/250 ml) water, pour over the pork, and continue to cook for another hour until golden and cooked through.

Remove the pork from the oven and let cool. Carve the meat into thick slices and set aside.

Slice the bread rolls lengthwise down the middle and fill with the pork slices and Creole sauce. Serve.

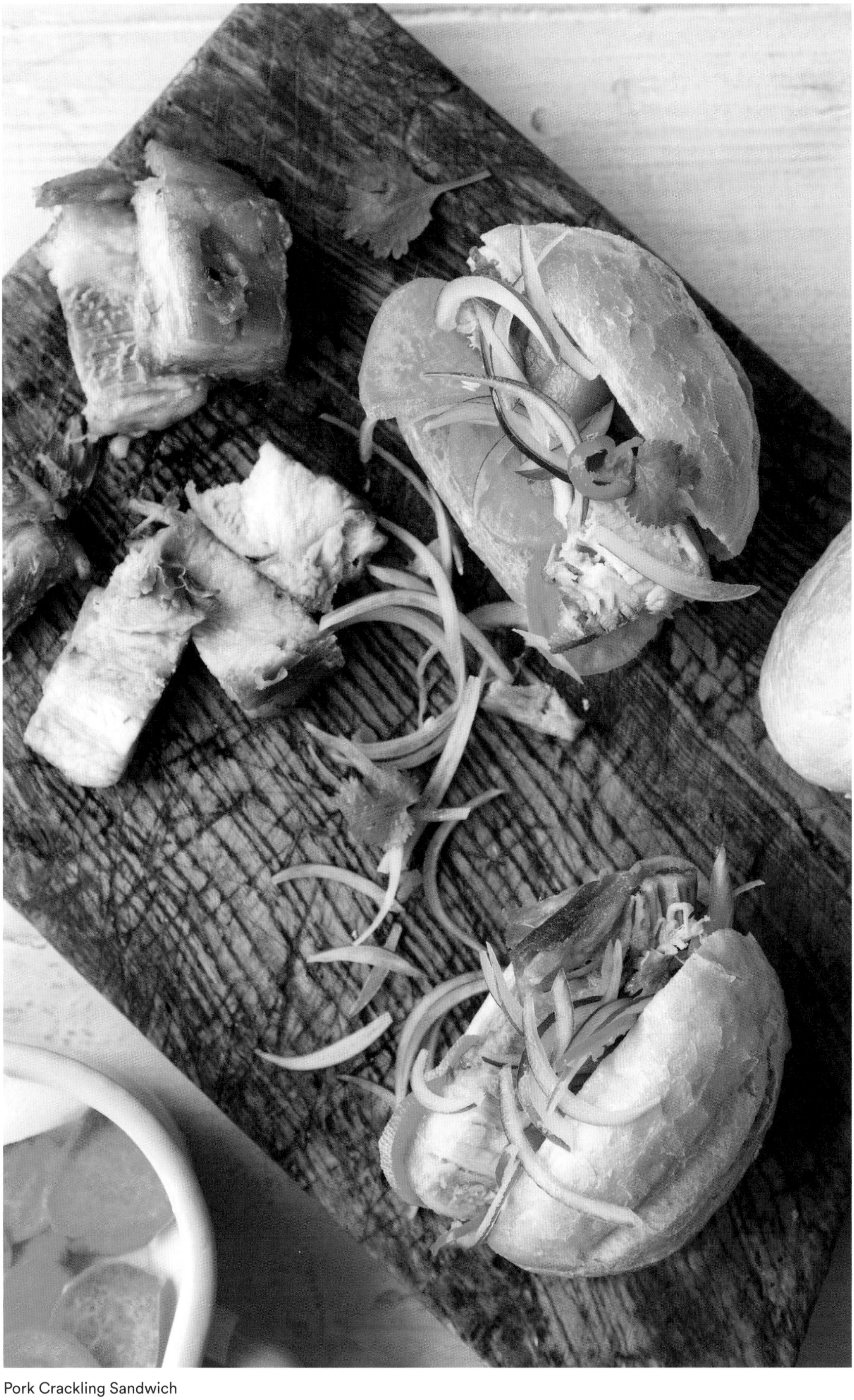

Pork Crackling Sandwich

SÁNGUCHE DE ASADO
POT-ROAST BEEF SANDWICH

Serves: 8
Preparation Time: 10 minutes, plus 10 minutes soaking
Cooking Time: 1 hour

The filling for these sandwiches is a juicy slow-cooked casserole instead of a roast.

1 × 2¼-lb (1-kg) bottom round roast or rump roast (silverside)
1 tablespoon salt
1½ teaspoons pepper
½ cup (4 fl oz/120 ml) vegetable oil
2 celery stalks, chopped
1 leek, trimmed and chopped
2 carrots, chopped
1 red onion, chopped
3 cloves garlic
1½ tomatoes, skinned, seeded, and grated
1 bay leaf
½ oz (15 g) dried mushrooms, soaked in warm water for 10 minutes
4 tablespoons Panca Chili Paste (see p. 406)
1 cup (8 fl oz/250 ml) red wine
8½ cups (68 fl oz/2 liters) beef broth (stock)
8 French bread rolls or any crusty rolls
1 cup (8 fl oz/250 ml) Creole Sauce (see p. 416), to serve

Season the beef with the salt and pepper.

Heat the oil in a Dutch oven (casserole dish) over medium heat. Add the beef and brown on all sides. Remove from the pan and set aside.

Add the celery, leek, carrots, onion, garlic, tomatoes, bay leaf, and soaked mushrooms to the pan and sauté for 5 minutes until the onion has softened. Add the chili paste and cook for a few minutes more, then return the beef to the pan. Pour in the red wine and cook for a few minutes until the alcohol has evaporated, then pour in the broth (stock). Season with salt and pepper to taste and let cook, covered, over low heat for 45 minutes, until the meat is soft and tender.

Remove the beef from the pan, transfer to a board, and let cool slightly. Carve into thick slices.

Put the vegetables from the pan into a blender and blend together, then strain into a bowl to make a smooth sauce. Place the beef slices in the sauce and mix together well.

Warm the bread rolls and slice lengthwise down the middle. Fill the sandwiches with the sauce-covered beef slices and top with the Creole sauce. Serve.

SÁNGUCHE DE HUEVERA FRITA
FRIED FISH ROE SANDWICH

Serves: 4
Preparation Time: 5 minutes
Cooking Time: 15 minutes

These traditional sandwiches used to be very popular but are less widely available nowadays, other than in the Port of Callao (Lima).

2¼ lb (1 kg) fish roe, washed
1 clove garlic, chopped
juice of 1 lemon
1 cup (4 oz/120 g) all-purpose (plain) flour
1 teaspoon chopped parsley leaves
4 cups (34 fl oz/1 liter) vegetable oil
4 French bread rolls or any crusty rolls
4 tablespoons Mayonnaise (see p. 412)
2 cups (18 fl oz/500 ml) Creole Sauce (see p. 416)
salt and pepper

Cut the fish roe in half lengthwise, as if opening a book, then cut into 4 even pieces. Place in a bowl with the garlic and lemon juice and season with salt and pepper. Mix together well and leave for 2 minutes.

Mix the flour and parsley together in a separate bowl, add the fish roe pieces, and coat evenly.

Heat the vegetable oil in a large pan or deep fryer to 350°F/180°C, or until a cube of bread browns in 30 seconds. Drop the fish roe pieces carefully into the hot oil and cook until crispy and golden on the outside but still juicy on the inside. Drain well on paper towels.

Slice the bread rolls lengthwise down the middle and fill the sandwiches with the fried fish roe, mayonnaise, and Creole sauce. Serve.

PAN CON RELLENO
PERUVIAN BLOOD SAUSAGE SANDWICH

Serves: 4
Preparation Time: 5 minutes
Cooking Time: 10 minutes

Relleno is typical Peruvian blood sausage (black pudding) that can be replaced with any type of blood sausage.

4 tablespoons vegetable oil, plus extra for frying
1 yellow chile, seeded, membrane removed, and chopped
1¾ lb (800 g) pork relleno or other blood sausage (black pudding), sliced
1 teaspoon granulated sugar
1 tablespoon chopped mint
2 sweet potatoes, peeled and sliced
4 small baguettes
salt and pepper

Heat the oil in a skillet or frying pan, add the yellow chile, and sauté briefly until softened. Add the pork relleno, sugar, and mint and season with salt and pepper. Cook on low heat until the flavors blend. Set aside and keep warm.

Sauté the sweet potato slices in a separate pan in plenty of oil until crisp. Set aside.

Cut the baguettes in half lengthwise and fill with the sweet potato slices and relleno mixture. Serve.

EMPANADA SERRANITA DE QUESO, HUACATAY Y ROCOTO
CHEESE, HUACATAY, AND ROCOTO CHILE EMPANADAS

Serves: 4
Preparation Time: 25 minutes, plus 10 minutes chilling
Cooking Time: 25 minutes

You can try this recipe with different types of cheese and replace the huacatay with mint. The empanadas will still taste delicious.

Filling
1 red onion, finely sliced
12 oz (350 g) mantecoso cheese, grated
1–2 rocoto chiles, seeded, membranes removed, and chopped
2 tablespoons chopped huacatay leaves

Pastry dough
1 tablespoon granulated sugar
1 teaspoon salt
1½ oz (40 g) margarine, cut into cubes plus extra for greasing
1½ oz (40 g) vegetable shortening, cut into cubes
1 cup (4 oz/120 g) all-purpose (plain) flour, plus extra for dusting

Extras
1 egg, beaten
confectioners' (icing) sugar, for dusting

For the filling, cook the onion in vegetable oil over very low heat until caramelized. Once cooked and soft, remove and set aside to cool.

Place the mantecoso cheese, chiles, huacatay, and caramelized onion in a bowl. Mix together thoroughly and set aside.

To make the pastry dough, dissolve the sugar and salt in 3 tablespoons of water. Set aside.

Using your hands, combine the margarine and vegetable shortening together in a bowl, gradually adding the flour and pouring in the sugar and salt mixture to form a dough. Cover with plastic wrap (clingfilm) and refrigerate for 10 minutes.

Preheat the oven to 350°F/180°C/Gas Mark 4. Prepare a baking sheet by lightly greasing it.

Remove the dough from the refrigerator, divide into 4 pieces, and shape into balls. Roll each ball out on a floured surface with a rolling pin into a circle about ¼-inch/5-mm thick. Place a quarter of the cheese filling in the center of each pastry circle. Brush the edges with beaten egg, fold the pastry over the filling, and crimp down the edges to seal.

Place the empanadas on the prepared baking sheet.

Bake in the preheated oven for 15 minutes until golden. Remove and dust with confectioners' (icing) sugar to finish. Serve warm.

Beef Empanadas

EMPANADA DE CARNE
BEEF EMPANADAS

Serves: 4
Preparation Time: 25 minutes, plus 10 minutes chilling
Cooking Time: 30 minutes

The secret of this recipe is to chop the beef instead of grinding it.

Filling
3 tablespoons vegetable oil
1 onion, chopped
2 yellow chiles, seeded, membrane removed, and chopped
6 cloves garlic, very finely chopped
14 oz (400 g) beef, chopped into ½-inch (1-cm) cubes
½ teaspoon ground cumin
1 cup (8 fl oz/250 ml) beef broth (stock)
salt and pepper

Pastry
1 tablespoon granulated sugar
1 teaspoon salt
1½ oz (40 g) margarine, cut in cubes, plus extra for greasing
1½ oz (40 g) vegetable shortening, cut in cubes
1 cup (4 oz/120 g) all-purpose (plain) flour, plus extra for dusting

Extras
1 egg, beaten
confectioners' (icing) sugar, for dusting
lime wedges, to serve

To make the filling, heat the oil in a skillet or frying pan over medium heat. Add the onion and chiles and sauté for a few minutes until just brown, then add the garlic, beef, and cumin. Season with salt and pepper, pour over the beef broth (stock), and let cook for a few minutes until the liquid has reduced and the filling is cooked but not dry. Taste and adjust the seasoning if necessary. Set aside.

To make the pastry dough, dissolve the sugar and salt in 3 tablespoons of water. Set aside.

Using your hands, combine the margarine and vegetable shortening together in a bowl, gradually adding the flour and pouring in the sugar and salt mixture to form a dough. Cover with plastic wrap (clingfilm) and refrigerate for 10 minutes.

Preheat the oven to 350°F/180°C/Gas Mark 4. Prepare a baking sheet by lightly greasing and setting aside.

Remove the dough from the refrigerator, divide into 4 pieces, and shape into balls. Roll each ball out on a floured surface with a rolling pin into a circle about ¼-inch/5-mm thick. Place a quarter of the beef filling in the center of each pastry circle. Brush the edges with beaten egg, fold the pastry over the filling, and crimp down the edges to seal.

Place the empanadas on the prepared baking sheet. Bake in the preheated oven for 15 minutes, until golden. Remove and dust with confectioners' (icing) sugar to finish. Serve hot or cold with lime wedges.

EMPANADA DE AJÍ DE GALLINA
SPICY CREAMED CHICKEN EMPANADAS

Serves: 4
Preparation Time: 25 minutes, plus 5 minutes soaking and 10 minutes chilling
Cooking Time: 25 minutes

Any Peruvian stew can be used as a filling for these empanadas.

Filling
2 bread slices, crusts removed
½ cup (4 fl oz/120 ml) milk
3 tablespoons vegetable oil
1 onion, diced
1 clove garlic, crushed
6 tablespoons Blended Yellow Chiles (see p. 404) or Yellow Chili Paste (see p. 405)
1 cup (8 fl oz/250 ml) chicken broth (stock)
1 cup (8 fl oz/250 ml) evaporated milk
1½ cups (7 oz/200 g) shredded cooked chicken breast
2 tablespoons grated Parmesan cheese
3 tablespoons chopped pecans or walnuts
pinch of grated nutmeg
salt and pepper

Pastry dough
1 tablespoon granulated sugar
1 teaspoon salt
1½ oz (40 g) margarine, cut into cubes, plus extra for greasing
1½ oz (40 g) vegetable shortening, cut into cubes
1 cup (4 oz/120 g) all-purpose (plain) flour, plus extra for dusting

Extras
1 egg, beaten
confectioners' (icing) sugar, for dusting

To make the filling, soak the bread slices in the milk for 5 minutes and blend in a blender.

Heat the oil in a skillet or frying pan over medium heat. Add the onion, garlic, and chiles and sauté for a few minutes, until the onion has softened. Add the soaked bread, stirring continuously, then pour in the broth (stock) and evaporated milk. Add the shredded chicken, Parmesan cheese, pecans or walnuts, and nutmeg and season with salt and pepper to taste. Cook, stirring, for 2 minutes. Set aside.

To make the pastry dough, dissolve the sugar and salt in 3 tablespoons water. Set aside.

Using your hands, combine the margarine and vegetable shortening together in a bowl, gradually adding the flour and pouring in the sugar and salt mixture to form a dough. Cover with plastic wrap (clingfilm) and refrigerate for 10 minutes.

Preheat the oven to 350°F/180°C/Gas Mark 4. Prepare a baking sheet by lightly greasing it.

Remove the dough from the refrigerator, divide into 4 pieces, and shape into balls. Roll each ball out on a floured surface with a rolling pin into a circle about ¼-inch/5-mm thick. Place a quarter of the spicy creamed chicken filling in the center of each pastry circle. Brush the edges with beaten egg, fold the pastry over the filling, and crimp down the edges to seal.

Place the empanadas on the prepared baking sheet. Bake in the preheated oven for 15 minutes, until golden. Remove and dust with confectioners' (icing) sugar to finish. Serve warm.

EMPANADA DE PICANTE DE CARNE
SPICY BEEF EMPANADAS

Serves: 4
Preparation Time: 25 minutes, plus 10 minutes chilling
Cooking Time: 1 hour 20 minutes–1 hour 25 minutes

Be careful not to overcook the potatoes used for the filling. If overcooked, they will break and absorb all the juice.

2 potatoes
½ cup (4 fl oz/120 ml) vegetable oil
1 onion, diced
12 cloves garlic, very finely chopped
2 tablespoons Panca Chili Paste (see p. 406)
1 tablespoon Mirasol Chili Paste (see p. 405)
2 cups (18 fl oz/500 ml) beef broth (stock)
11 oz (300 g) boneless beef chuck or beef round (stewing beef)
1 bay leaf
½ carrot, diced
1/8 cup (1 oz/25 g) peas
salt and pepper

Pastry dough
1 tablespoon granulated sugar
1 teaspoon salt
1½ oz (40 g) margarine, cut into cubes, plus extra for greasing
1½ oz (40 g) vegetable shortening, cut into cubes
1 cup (4 oz/120 g) all-purpose (plain) flour, plus extra for dusting

Extras
1 egg, beaten
confectioners' (icing) sugar, for dusting

Bring a pan of water to a boil, add the potatoes, and cook until tender. Drain and cut into ½-inch/1-cm cubes. Set aside.

Heat the oil in a pan over medium heat. Add the diced onion, garlic, and chili pastes. Sauté for 5–10 minutes until the onion has softened and browned. Season with salt and pepper.

Add the broth (stock), beef, and bay leaf and cook for 45 minutes, stirring occasionally, until the meat is tender. Add the carrot, peas, and potatoes and cook for another 10 minutes, until the carrot and peas are tender but the potatoes still retain their shape. Taste and adjust the seasoning as necessary. Set aside.

To make the pastry dough, dissolve the sugar and salt in 3 tablespoons water. Set aside.

Using your hands, combine the margarine and vegetable shortening together in a bowl, gradually adding the flour and pouring in the sugar and salt mixture to form a dough. Cover and refrigerate for 10 minutes.

Preheat the oven to 350°F/180°C/Gas Mark 4. Prepare a baking sheet by lightly greasing it.

Remove the dough from the refrigerator, divide into 4 pieces, and shape into balls. Roll each ball out on a floured surface with a rolling pin into a circle about ¼-inch/5-mm thick. Place a quarter of the spicy beef filling in the center of each pastry circle. Brush the edges with beaten egg, fold the pastry over the filling, and crimp down the edges to seal.

Place the empanadas on the prepared baking sheet. Bake in the preheated oven for 15 minutes, until golden. Remove and dust with confectioners' (icing) sugar to finish. Serve hot or warm.

Serves: 4
Preparation Time: 12 minutes
Cooking Time: 10 minutes

These sandwiches are part of the new wave of Peruvian recipes that have emerged in the last few years.

14 oz (400 g) beef tenderloin (fillet)
6 tablespoons vegetable oil
1 small red onion, thinly sliced
1 yellow chile, seeded, membrane removed, and thinly sliced
2 cloves garlic, finely chopped
1 tomato, cut into wedges
4 teaspoons chopped culantro or cilantro (coriander) leaves
2 scallions (spring onions), chopped
4 French bread rolls or any crusty rolls
5 oz (150 g) Mantecoso cheese
½ cup (4 fl oz/120 ml) Chicken Condiment (see p. 410)
salt

Sauce
3 tablespoons white wine vinegar
1 tablespoon soy sauce
4 tablespoons oyster sauce

SÁNGUCHE DE LOMO SALTADO Y QUESO
CHEESY STIR-FRIED BEEF SANDWICH

For the stir-fried beef sauce, mix the vinegar, soy sauce, and oyster sauce in a bowl. Set aside.

Cut the beef into ¾ x ½-inch/1.5 × 1-cm strips and season with salt. Heat the oil in a wok over high heat. Once the oil is nice and hot, add the beef and sauté for 1–2 minutes until browned but still tender. Set aside.

Add the red onion, yellow chile, garlic, and sauce to the wok and sauté for 1–2 minutes. Return the beef to the wok, followed by the tomato, culantro or cilantro (coriander) leaves, and scallions (spring onions). Taste and add more salt if necessary. Remove from the heat and set aside.

Slice the bread rolls lengthwise down the middle and fill with the stir-fried beef mixture, Mantecoso cheese, and chicken condiment. Serve.

Cheesy Stir-Fried Beef Sandwich

EMPANADA DE MARISCOS
SEAFOOD PASTRIES

Serves: 4
Preparation Time: 30 minutes, plus 5 minutes chilling
Cooking Time: 30 minutes

When preparing these empanadas, you can also add a little milk to the filling for a creamier texture.

Filling

- 1 red bell pepper
- 8 shrimp (prawns), peeled and deveined
- 8 scallops
- 1 × 9 oz (250 g) small octopus, cooked and chopped (see p. 406)
- ½ cup (4 fl oz/120 ml) vegetable oil
- 2 onions, chopped
- 1 clove garlic, chopped
- 2 tablespoons Panca Chili Paste (see p. 406)
- 1 yellow chile, chopped
- 4 tablespoons fish broth (stock)
- 1 tablespoon chopped culantro or cilantro (coriander) leaves
- 2 eggs, hard-boiled and cut into halves
- 8 pitted black olives
- salt and pepper

Pastry dough

- 2 tablespoons granulated sugar
- 1 teaspoon salt
- 3 tablespoons margarine, plus extra for greasing
- 3 tablespoons vegetable shortening
- ¾ cup (3 oz/80 g) all-purpose (plain) flour, plus extra for dusting

Extras

- 1 egg, beaten

Place the red bell pepper over a naked flame, turning, until the skin is entirely blackened. Remove from the fire, peel, seed, and coarsely chop. Set aside and reserve half for another use.

Thoroughly wash the shrimp (prawns), scallops, and octopus. Drain.

Heat the oil in a pan over medium heat. Add the onions, garlic, chili paste, and chiles. Cook for 4–5 minutes until the onion has softened.

Add the seafood and chopped roasted peppers. Season with salt and pepper to taste. Add the broth (stock) and cook until the liquid reduces, then add the chopped culantro or cilantro (coriander) leaves. Set aside.

To make the pastry dough, dissolve the sugar and salt in 3 tablespoons water. Set aside.

Using your hands, combine the margarine and vegetable shortening together in a bowl, gradually adding the flour and pouring in the sugar and salt mixture to form a dough. Cover with plastic wrap (clingfilm) and refrigerate for 10–15 minutes.

Preheat the oven to 350°F/180°C/Gas Mark 4. Prepare a baking sheet by lightly greasing it.

Remove the dough from the refrigerator, divide into 4 pieces, and shape into balls. Roll each ball out on a floured surface with a rolling pin into a circle about ¼-inch/5-mm thick. Place a quarter of the seafood mixture, half a boiled egg, and 2 olives in the center of each pastry circle. Brush the edges with beaten egg, fold the pastry over the filling, and crimp down the edges to seal.

Place the empanadas on the prepared baking sheet and bake in the preheated oven for 15 minutes, until golden. Remove from the oven and serve.

PASTEL DE ACELGA
SWISS CHARD PIE

Serves: 4–6
Preparation Time: 30 minutes
Cooking Time: 1 hour 10 minutes

This dish can also be prepared with spinach instead of Swiss chard.

8¾ lb (4 kg) Swiss chard
4 tablespoons oil
5 oz (150 g) ham, cut into cubes
2 tablespoons Onion Condiment (see p. 404)
¾ cup (7 oz/200 g) white (béchamel) sauce, store-bought or homemade
½ cup (4 fl oz/120 ml) whole (full-fat) milk
½ cup (2 oz/50 g) grated Parmesan cheese
7 eggs
salt and pepper

Pastry dough
5 tablespoons vegetable shortening
1½ cups (11 oz/300 g) margarine
4 cups (1 lb 2 oz/500 g) all-purpose (plain) flour
scant ½ cup (3½ fl oz/100 ml) whole (full-fat) milk
2 egg yolks

Wash the Swiss chard leaves and put them, wet, in a pan. Cook, covered, for 5 minutes, drain well, and chop finely.

Heat the oil in a skillet or frying pan over medium heat. Add the ham and sauté for 2 minutes, then add the onion condiment and cook, stirring, for another minute. Add the Swiss chard, mix together thoroughly, and season with salt and pepper. Remove from the heat and let cool.

Once cooled, transfer the mixture to a bowl. Add the white (béchamel) sauce, milk, and grated Parmesan cheese. Mix together thoroughly and set aside.

To make the pastry dough, combine the vegetable shortening, and margarine in a bowl. Gradually add the flour, tip onto a clean surface, and, using your hands, knead together with the milk and 1 egg yolk to form a dough. Cover the dough with plastic wrap (clingfilm) and set aside in the refrigerator for 30 minutes.

Preheat the oven to 325°F/160°C/Gas Mark 3.

Halve the rested dough and roll each half out into a sheet large enough to cover a 12-inch/30-cm loose-bottom round tart or quiche pan.

Line the pan with 1 pastry sheet. Spoon in half the Swiss chard filling. Use your hands to make 7 wells in the filling and crack a whole egg into each.

Cover with the remaining filling. Use the other pastry sheet to cover the pie and crimp down the edges to seal.

Mix the remaining egg yolk with 1 teaspoon water in a small bowl and brush over the pastry top. Bake in the preheated oven for 1 hour until golden. Remove from the pan. Serve hot or cold.

SOUPS, BROTHS & CHOWDERS

CALDO DE CHOROS
MUSSEL BROTH

Serves: 4
Preparation Time: 10 minutes
Cooking Time: 25 minutes

As a child, I used to love going to the market to enjoy some mussel broth. Fall (autumn) can be a tough season in Lima, but a shot of mussel broth makes it all worthwhile.

- 1 tablespoon olive oil
- ½ red onion, finely chopped
- 1 clove garlic, chopped
- ¼-inch (5-mm) piece fresh ginger, peeled and chopped
- 1 tablespoon Yellow Chili Paste (see p. 405)
- 48 mussels, cleaned, in their shells
- 4 tablespoons white wine
- 4 cups (34 fl oz/1 liter) vegetable broth (stock)
- 1 tablespoon chopped culantro or cilantro (coriander)
- 1 limo chile, seeded, membrane removed, and chopped
- 2 small lemons
- salt

Heat the olive oil in a large pan over low heat, add the onion, garlic, ginger, and chili paste and sauté for 5 minutes until the onion has softened.

Add the mussels and pour over the white wine and vegetable broth (stock). Cover and bring to a simmer. Cook for 15 minutes until the mussels have opened and cooked through.

Season to taste with salt and stir through the chopped culantro or cilantro (coriander) and limo chile to finish. Ladle the broth into large shallow bowls, drizzle over the lemon juice, and serve.

CALDO VERDE
GREEN BROTH

Serves: 4
Preparation Time: 10 minutes
Cooking Time: 20 minutes

The lovely aromatic herbs in this dish turn it a beautiful shade of green, hence the name. You can use any of your favorite local herbs to prepare it.

- 1 tablespoon vegetable oil
- 1 red onion, finely chopped
- 6 cloves garlic, very finely chopped
- 1 tablespoon Mirasol Chili Paste (see p. 405)
- 4 cups (34 fl oz/1 liter) vegetable broth (stock)
- 4 white potatoes, peeled and cut into ¾-inch (2-cm) chunks
- 2½ oz (65 g) queso fresco, grated
- ½ tablespoon each of chopped parsley, wormseed, mint, and huacatay leaves, plus extra to garnish
- 4 eggs
- salt and pepper

Heat the olive oil in a large pan over low heat, add the onion, garlic, and chili paste and sauté for 5 minutes until the onion softens.

Pour over the vegetable broth (stock) and add the potato chunks. Simmer over medium heat for 10 minutes until the potato chunks are cooked. Stir in the queso fresco and season to taste with salt and pepper.

Add the parsley, wormseed, mint, and huacatay leaves and simmer over medium heat for another 2 minutes, then stir in the beaten eggs and continue stirring for 1 minute. Remove from the heat.

Ladle the soup into large shallow bowls and garnish with a few more chopped fresh herbs. Serve.

Mussel Broth

Serves: 6
Preparation Time: 20 minutes, plus overnight soaking
Cooking Time: 4 hours 50 minutes

The seven different types of meat used in this recipe can be substituted with any type of meat you can find at your trusted local market.

½ cup (3½ oz/100 g) dried chickpeas
3 × 5-oz (150-g) dried lamb tongues
14 oz (400 g) beef marrow bone in 12 pieces
2¼ lb (1 kg) beef brisket, cut into 4 chunks
8 cloves garlic, crushed
1 red onions, halved
1 sprig oregano
½ chicken (2¼ lb/1 kg), cut into 8 pieces
4 × 5-oz (150-g) boneless lamb loin (steaks), halved
½ young turkey (6 oz/180 g) hen, cut into pieces
7 oz (200 g) bacon
6 white chuño (freeze-dried potatoes)
14 oz (400 g) yucca root (cassava), peeled and cut into 2-inch (5-cm) chunks
2 cups (400 g/14 oz) Peruvian-Style Cooked White Rice (see p. 178), to serve
salt and pepper

Mint Creole Sauce
1 red onion, finely chopped
2 yellow chiles, seeded, membranes removed, and chopped
handful of spearmint leaves
juice of 2 small lemons

CALDO DE SIETE CARNES
SEVEN-MEAT BROTH

Put the chickpeas into a large bowl, cover with water, and let soak overnight. Drain and set aside.

The next day, place the dried lamb tongues in a bowl of water, cover with water, and let soak for at least 6 hours before draining.

Place the beef marrow bone, beef brisket, soaked and drained lamb tongues, garlic, onion halves, oregano sprig, a little salt, and 204 fl oz/6 liters water together in a large pan. Simmer over low heat for 4 hours until the meat is tender.

When the meat has cooked for 3 hours, add the soaked and drained chickpeas.

Remove the meats from the pan once tender and set the meats, chickpeas, and cooking liquid aside separately. Cut up the tongues and beef brisket into ¾ x ¾-inch (2 × 2-cm pieces).

Put the cooking liquid in a pan, bring to a boil, and add the chicken, lamb, turkey, and bacon. Cook for 40 minutes until the chicken and turkey are beginning to separate from the bone. Add a little salt, the white chuño (freeze-dried potatoes) and yucca root (cassava) chunks, and cook for 8 minutes, then add the beef brisket, lamb tongue chunks, and cooked chickpeas. Adjust the seasoning to taste.

For the mint creole sauce, mix together all the ingredients in a bowl. Season with salt and pepper.

Serve the broth in large shallow bowls with Peruvian-style cooked white rice and the mint Creole sauce.

CALDO DE CABEZA
LAMB HEAD BROTH

Serves: 4
Preparation Time: 25 minutes, plus overnight soaking
Cooking Time: 2 hours 35 minutes

Peruvians consider this lamb head broth to be one of the best remedies for a bad hangover. Each mouthful is infused with flavor.

- 1¼ cups (7 oz/200 g) hominy (dried corn), soaked overnight
- 1 × 3¼ lb (1.5 kg) lamb or sheep head, cleaned and cut into 4 pieces
- 2 red onions
- 4 cloves garlic
- 2 large celery stalks, chopped
- 1 bay leaf
- 1 mirasol chile, lightly roasted over a gas flame, seeded, membrane removed, and sliced
- 2 sprigs parsley
- 4 sprigs mint or wormseed
- 4 yellow potatoes, cut in half
- 2 sprigs mint, chopped
- 2 rocoto chiles, seeded, membranes removed, and chopped
- 1 scallion (spring onion), chopped
- juice of 2 small lemons
- salt and pepper

To cook the hominy (dried corn), put it into a pan with water (1 part hominy, 2 parts water), and boil over medium heat for about 35 minutes or until tender. Drain and set aside.

Place the lamb pieces in a large pan, cover with 204 fl oz/6 liters water, and bring to a boil over medium heat, skimming off any impurities that float to the surface with a slotted spoon. Add the onions, garlic, celery, bay leaf, mirasol chile, parsley, and mint, reduce the heat to a simmer, and cook for 2 hours until the lamb is tender. Add the potatoes and simmer for another 8 minutes until cooked, then add the cooked hominy. Simmer for another 5 minutes.

Season to taste and stir through the chopped mint, rocoto chiles, and scallion (spring onion) to finish. Ladle the soup into large shallow bowls and drizzle over the lemon juice. Serve.

CALDO DE GALLINA
CHICKEN BROTH

Serves: 4
Preparation Time: 20 minutes
Cooking Time: 2 hours 35 minutes

A true Peruvian chicken broth should always be served with a dash of lemon, some scallion (spring onion), and chopped chiles, or rocoto. Otherwise, it's simply not a Peruvian broth.

- 2 × 6¾-lb (3-kg) black silkie chickens, cleaned and cut into 8 pieces
- 2 red onions
- 4 cloves garlic
- 2-inch (5-cm) piece fresh ginger, peeled and chopped
- 2 large celery stalks, chopped
- 1⅓ cups (6 oz/175 g) ¾-inch (2-cm) squash cubes
- 1 leek, chopped
- 4 yellow potatoes, peeled and cut into chunks
- 1 lb 2 oz (500 g) spaghetti
- ½ tablespoon ground oregano
- 4 hard-boiled eggs
- juice of 2 small lemons
- salt and pepper

To garnish
- 1 scallion (spring onion), chopped
- 2 rocoto chiles, seeded, membranes removed, and chopped

Place the chicken pieces in a large pan, cover with 272 fl oz/8 liters water, and bring to a boil over medium heat, skimming off any impurities or froth that float to the surface with a slotted spoon.

Add the onions, garlic, ginger, celery, squash, leek, yellow potatoes, and a little salt and cook for about 1 hour until the chicken is tender.

Add the spaghetti and the oregano and continue to simmer for about 10 minutes until the pasta is al dente and the yellow potatoes have dissolved into the broth. Remove the pan from the heat and season to taste with salt and pepper.

Divide the hard-boiled eggs among bowls, ladle over the broth, and drizzle over the lemon juice. Garnish with chopped scallion (spring onion) and rocoto chiles.

Fish Chowder

CHUPE DE PESCADO
FISH CHOWDER

Serves: 4
Preparation Time: 10 minutes
Cooking Time: 30–35 minutes

Fish chowder is increasingly hard to find in restaurants—a great shame because it's one the tastiest types of soup made in Lima.

- 1 tablespoon vegetable oil, plus extra for deep-frying
- 4 × 3½-oz (100-g) white fish fillets
- ½ cup (2½ oz/65 g) all-purpose (plain) flour
- 1 red onion, finely chopped
- 6 cloves garlic, very finely chopped
- 4 tablespoons Yellow Chili Paste (see p. 405)
- 8½ cups (68 fl oz/2 liters) fish broth (stock)
- 4 yellow potatoes, boiled
- ⅓ cups (1½ oz/40 g) fava (broad) beans, blanched for 1 minute and peeled
- 3 tablespoons corn kernels
- 4 eggs
- 25 g (1 oz) queso fresco serrano, chopped
- 4 tablespoons whole (full-fat) milk
- 1 tablespoon chopped culantro or cilantro (coriander), to garnish
- salt and pepper

Fill a large pan or deep fryer halfway with vegetable oil and heat to 350°F/180°C, or until a cube of bread browns in 30 seconds. Season the fish fillets with salt and pepper and coat in the flour, then drop carefully into the hot oil and cook until crispy and golden. Drain well on paper towels.

Heat 1 tablespoon oil in a pan over low heat, add the onion and garlic, and sauté for 5 minutes until the onion softens. Add the chili paste and cook for another 2–3 minutes.

Pour over the fish broth (stock), bring to a gentle simmer, and add the boiled potatoes, fava (broad) beans, and corn kernels. Cook for 8 minutes until the corn kernels are tender, then season with salt and pepper.

Carefully crack the eggs into the pan and poach for 3–4 minutes. Stir in the cheese and milk and adjust the seasoning to taste.

Ladle the chowder into large shallow bowls, topping each with a fried fish fillet. Garnish with chopped culantro or cilantro (coriander) and serve.

CHUPE DE HABAS
FAVA BEAN CHOWDER

Serves: 4
Preparation Time: 10 minutes
Cooking Time: 25 minutes

This is perhaps the most humble of all the Peruvian chowders, but it is tasty nonetheless. It is inexpensive to prepare and goes a long way, so is definitely worth trying.

- 2 tablespoons olive oil
- 2 red onions, very finely chopped
- 3 cloves garlic, very finely chopped
- 1 tomato, skinned, seeded, and grated
- 4 tablespoons Panca Chili Paste (see p. 406)
- 2 sprigs mint
- 3 sprigs oregano
- ⅔ cup (3½ oz/100 g) corn kernels
- 4 potatoes, peeled
- 4 cups (1 lb 5 oz/600 g) fava (broad) beans, blanched in boiling water and peeled
- 2⅔ cups (12 oz/350 g) ½-inch (1-cm) squash cubes
- 1 cup (8 fl oz/250 ml) whole (full-fat) milk
- 2½ oz (65 g) queso fresco serrano, cubed
- dried oregano, to garnish
- salt and pepper

Heat the olive oil in a pan over low heat, add the onions and garlic, and sauté for a few minutes until the onions start to soften. Add the tomato and Panca chili paste and cook for another 5 minutes, stirring until fragrant.

Season with salt and pepper and add the mint, oregano sprigs, corn kernels, and potatoes. Pour in 136 fl oz/4 liters of water to cover the ingredients, cover the pan, and simmer over low heat for 8 minutes until the potatoes are just tender.

Add the fava (broad) beans and squash and simmer for another 6 minutes, until all the vegetables are cooked. Stir in the milk and cheese and adjust the seasoning to taste.

Ladle the soup into large shallow bowls and sprinkle over the dried oregano to garnish.

CHUPE DE LANGOSTINOS
SHRIMP CHOWDER

Serves: 4
Preparation Time: 20 minutes
Cooking Time: 1 hours 30 minutes

Of all the Peruvian soups and chowders, this shrimp (prawn) chowder is undoubtedly the most refined and lauded. Take your time, cook it slowly, and you will be delighted by the results.

20 uncooked large shrimp (prawns)
4 tablespoons olive oil
4 red onions, chopped
6 cloves garlic, very finely chopped
5 tomatoes, skinned, seeded, and grated
6 tablespoons Panca Chili Paste (see p. 406)
3 sprigs fresh oregano
1 corncob, sliced into ¾-inch (2-cm) slices
1⅓ cups (6 oz/175 g) squash, cut into ½-inch (1-cm) cubes
1 cup (5 oz/150 g) fava (broad) beans
4 potatoes, cut in half
½ cup (3 oz/80 g) white long-grain rice
4 cabbage leaves
40 uncooked shrimp (prawns), peeled and deveined with tails detached
½ cup (100 g) queso fresco, cut into ½-inch (1-cm) cubes
1 cup (8 fl oz/250 ml) whole (full-fat) milk
2 teaspoons ground oregano
salt and pepper

To garnish
4 poached eggs
8 sprigs huacatay, to garnish
4 slices fried country bread

Preheat the oven to 400°F/200°C/Gas Mark 6.

Clean and peel the large shrimp (prawns), place the shells in the preheated oven, and cook for 6 minutes until golden and crispy. Set aside.

Heat 2 tablespoons olive oil in a pan over low heat, add half the chopped onions and garlic, and sauté for 2–3 minutes until the onions start to soften. Add two thirds of the grated tomatoes and 4 tablespoons of the chili paste and cook, stirring, for 5 minutes until fragrant.

Season with salt and pepper, add the oregano sprigs and golden shrimp shells, and cover with 204 fl oz/6 liters water. Bring to a simmer and cook for 1 hour over medium heat. Remove from the heat, then crush the shrimp shells, slightly with a large wooden spoon on a board to bring out the flavors. Strain the broth and set aside.

In a separate pan, heat 2 tablespoons olive oil over low heat and sauté the remaining onion for a few minutes. Add the rest of the tomatoes and chili paste and let cook for 5 minutes. Pour the reserved shrimp broth into the pan. Add the sliced corncob, squash, fava (broad) beans, potatoes, rice, and cabbage leaves and cook for 2 minutes until the vegetables are tender and the rice is cooked.

Add the whole large shrimp and cook for 1 minute, then stir in the shrimp tails, cheese, and milk and cook for another minute until the shrimp are cooked. Add the oregano and season with salt and pepper.

Serve the shrimp chowder in large shallow bowls, topping each with a poached egg, a few sprigs of fresh huacatay, and a little fried country bread to garnish.

Shrimp Chowder

CHUPE DE QUINUA
QUINOA CHOWDER

Serves: 4
Preparation Time: 11 minutes
Cooking Time: 22–24 minutes

This is a chowder recipe that has reintroduced quinoa to Peruvians who previously never ate it. Nowadays, Andean quinoa is highly prized in markets all over the world.

1 tablespoon oil
1 red onion, finely chopped
1 tablespoon Garlic Paste (see p. 406)
4 tablespoons Yellow Chili Paste (see p. 405)
8½ cups (68 fl oz/2 liters) vegetable broth (stock)
½ cup (3 oz/80 g) multicolored quinoa grains, washed
⅓ cup (1½ oz/40 g) fava (broad) beans, blanched for 1 minute and peeled
½ tablespoon chopped huacatay leaves, plus extra to garnish
25 g (1 oz) queso fresco serrano, chopped, plus extra to garnish
½ rocoto chile, slices
4 tablespoons whole (full-fat) milk
salt and pepper

To serve
4 yellow or native Peruvian potatoes, boiled
4 soft-boiled eggs
4 country bread slices, toasted

Heat the oil in a pan over low heat, add onion and garlic paste, and sauté for 5 minutes until the onion is soft. Add the yellow chili paste and cook for 6–8 minutes until fragrant.

Pour over the vegetable broth (stock), add the quinoa, and bring to a simmer. Cook for 8 minutes over medium heat, then stir in the fava (broad) beans and huacatay leaves and cook for another 2 minutes or until the quinoa grains have split.

Stir in the queso fresco, rocoto chile slices, and milk and season with salt and pepper to taste.

Ladle the chowder into large shallow bowls and serve with the potatoes, eggs, and toasted country bread slices. Garnish with a few huacatay leaves and a little extra cheese.

CHUPE DE VIERNES
FRIDAY CHOWDER

Serves: 4
Preparation Time: 11 minutes
Cooking Time: 15 minutes

Peruvian cuisine is, above all, the sum of its delicious regional dishes. Each town and region has its own repertoire of recipes based on local products and culture, like this delicious Friday chowder.

2 tablespoons olive oil
2 red onions, chopped
3 cloves garlic, very finely chopped
1 tomato, skinned, seeded, and grated
4 tablespoons Mirasol Chili Paste (see p. 405)
1 teaspoon turmeric
2 sprigs huacatay
8½ cups (68 fl oz/2 liters) vegetable broth (stock)
⅓ cup (1½ oz/40 g) fava (broad) beans, blanched
in boiling water for 1 minute, peeled
14 oz (400 g) angel hair pasta
1 cup (8 fl oz/250 ml) whole (full-fat) milk
3 oz (80 g) queso fresco, cut into small strips
salt and pepper

To garnish
4 poached eggs
dried oregano

Heat the olive oil in a pan over low heat, add the onions and garlic and sauté for 2–3 minutes until the onions start to soften. Add the tomato andcchili paste and cook, stirring, for another 5 minutes until it is fragrant.

Season with salt and pepper and stir in the turmeric and huacatay sprigs. Pour over the vegetable broth (stock), add the fava (broad) beans, and bring to a simmer. Continue to cook over low heat for 2 minutes.

Snap the angel hair pasta in half, add to the pan, and simmer for 2–3 minutes until cooked. Stir in the milk and cheese and adjust the seasoning to taste.

Ladle the soup into large shallow bowls, top with the poached eggs, and sprinkle with dried oregano. Serve.

CHAIRO
CHAIRO SOUP

Serves: 4
Preparation Time: 15 minutes, plus overnight soaking
Cooking Time: 1 hour 30 minutes

The city of Arequipa is one that loves soup and this *chairo* soup is one of its best. The secret is to carefully balance the ingredients so that each contributes its own unique flavor without overpowering the others.

- 1¼ cups (7 oz/200 g) hominy (dried corn), soaked overnight
- 4 white chuño (freeze-dried potatoes), soaked overnight
- 1 lb 2 oz (500 g) beef brisket
- 9 oz (250 g) lamb intestines, cleaned
- 7 oz (200 g) lamb ribs
- 2 tablespoons vegetable oil
- ½ red onion, chopped
- 4 cloves garlic, chopped
- 2 tablespoons Panca Chili Paste (see p. 406)
- 4 tablespoons multicolored quinoa, washed
- 1 teaspoon dried oregano
- 4 teaspoons salt
- 1 teaspoon cumin
- 1 teaspoon ground pepper
- ½ cup (3 oz/80 g) fava (broad) beans
- 2 white potatoes, boiled and cut into cubes
- 1 teaspoon chopped mint leaves
- ½ rocoto chile, sliced

To cook the hominy (dried corn), put it into a pan with water (1 part hominy, 2 parts water) and boil over medium heat for about 35 minutes or until tender. Drain and set aside.

Drain the chuño and cut into ¾-inch/2-cm chunks.

Place the beef brisket, lamb intestines, and lamb ribs in a large pan and cover with 272 fl oz/8 liters of water. Bring to a simmer and cook for 1 hour, or until the meats are tender. Drain and reserve the cooking liquid.

Cut the beef brisket and lamb into ¾-inch/2-cm chunks. Chop the intestines into 1-inch/2.5-cm cylinders.

In a separate pan, heat the oil over low heat, add the onion, garlic, and chili paste and sauté for 5 minutes until the onion starts to soften and the mix is fragrant. Pour over the reserved cooking liquid and add the chunks of meat.

Bring to a boil, then reduce to a simmer. Stir in the hominy, rehydrated chopped chuños, quinoa, cumin, and oregano, season with the salt and pepper, and cook for 7–8 minutes until it is cooked.

Add the fava (broad) beans, potato cubes, mint, and rocoto chile slices. Cook another 5 minutes until they are cooked through. Ladle the soup into large shallow bowls. Serve.

CHUPE DE TUBÉRCULOS
TUBER CHOWDER

Serves: 4
Preparation Time: 10 minutes
Cooking Time: 18 minutes

Try this recipe out with any local varieties of tubers and chiles. You will not be disappointed.

2 tablespoons olive oil
1 red onion, finely chopped
3 cloves garlic, very finely chopped
4 tablespoons Panca Chili Paste (see p. 406)
2 tablespoons Yellow Chili Paste (see p. 405)
2 sprigs huacatay
1 sprig oregano
2 yellow potatoes, cut into 1-inch (2.5-cm) cubes
8½ cups (68 fl oz/2 liters) vegetable broth (stock)
6 ullukus, cut into ¼-inch (5-mm) strips
4 mashuas, unpeeled, cut into ¾-inch (2-cm) chunks
4 ocas, unpeeled, sliced
1 cup (8 fl oz/250 ml) whole (full-fat) milk
3½ oz (100 g) diced queso fresco
4 country bread slices, toasted
1 teaspoon dried oregano, to garnish
salt and pepper

Heat the olive oil in a pan over low heat, add the onion and garlic, and sauté for 2–3 minutes until the onion has started to soften. Add the chili pastes and cook, stirring, for 5 minutes until fragrant.

Season with salt and pepper and add the huacatay and oregano sprigs, potato chunks, and vegetable broth (stock). Bring to a simmer and let cook over low heat for 4 minutes until the potatoes are just tender.

Add the ullukus, mashuas, and ocas and simmer for another 4 minutes until the tubers are cooked. Stir in the milk and cheese and adjust the seasoning to taste.

Arrange the toasted country bread slices in large shallow bowls, ladle over the soup, and sprinkle with dried oregano. Serve.

CHAQUE DE TRIPAS
LAMB INTESTINE CHAQUE SOUP

Serves: 4
Preparation Time: 15 minutes, plus overnight soaking
Cooking Time: 3 hours

I first tried this soup when I was a boy, eating out at a restaurant in Arequipa with my father. I discovered that intestines and squash are a match made in heaven.

1 cup (7 oz/200 g) wheat berries, soaked overnight
2¼ lb (1 kg) lamb or beef intestines, cleaned
1 bay leaf
1 onion, cut into quarters
2 garlic cloves
2 tablespoons olive oil
2 red onions, very finely chopped
3 cloves garlic, very finely chopped
4 tablespoons Panca Chili Paste (see p. 406)
2 sprigs mint, chopped
3 sprigs oregano
4½ lb (2 kg) beef brisket
4 potatoes, peeled and halved
1 cup (5 oz/150 g) fava (broad) beans
1⅓ cups (6 oz/175 g) 1-inch (2.5-cm) squash cubes
8 cabbage leaves
8 turnip leaves
salt and pepper

To garnish
1 rocoto chiles, seeded, membrane removed, and chopped
2 tablespoons chopped mint leaves

Cook the wheat berries in a pan of lightly salted boiling water for about 30 minutes. Drain and set aside.

To cook the intestines, boil it in water with the bay leaf, quartered onions, and whole garlic for 2 hours over medium heat until tender. Cut into 2-inch (5-cm) pieces.

Heat the olive oil in a pan over low heat, add the red onions and chopped garlic and sauté for 2–3 minutes until the onions start to soften. Add the chili paste and cook for another 5 minutes until it is fragrant.

Season with salt and pepper. Add the mint, oregano sprig, and beef brisket and cover with 204 fl oz/6 liters water. Simmer over low heat for 40 minutes until the meat is tender.

Add the potatoes and simmer for another 6 minutes until just tender, then add the intestines, fava (broad) beans, squash, cooked wheat berries, cabbage leaves, and turnip leaves. Simmer over medium heat for another 5 minutes.

Adjust the seasoning to taste, then ladle the soup into large shallow bowls. Garnish with chopped rocoto chiles and chopped mint. Serve.

MENESTRÓN MARINO
SEAFOOD MINESTRONE

Serves: 4
Preparation Time: 25 minutes, plus overnight soaking
Cooking Time: 3 hours 30 minutes

Lima is a coastal city, so it's not surprising that most of its traditional dishes contain seafood and fish, or that dishes that traditionally don't contain seafood have a seafood version, such as this minestrone.

4 limpets
4 tablespoons canary beans
8 mussels
8½ cups (68 fl oz/2 liters) mussel or fish broth (stock)
2 oz (50 g) yucca root (cassava), peeled and cut into 4 pieces
4 potatoes, cut into ¾-inch (1.5-cm) cubes
1 carrot, diced
1⅓ cups (6 oz/175 g) ¾-inch (2-cm) cubes macre squash
1 × 3½ oz (100 g) turnip, cut into ¾-inch (1.5-cm) cubes
⅓ cup (2 oz/50 g) canned lima (butter) beans
1 corncob, sliced in 1¼-inch (3-cm) slices
5 oz (150 g) penne pasta
12 cooked shrimp (prawns)
2 × 7-oz (200-g) squid, cleaned and cut into rings
8 large clams
12 scallops
½ tablespoon grated Parmesan cheese, to garnish
salt and pepper

Lima-style pesto
2 tablespoons vegetable oil
¼ red onion, chopped
2 cloves garlic
1¾ cups (2¾ oz/70 g) basil leaves
1½ cups (1½ oz/40 g) spinach leaves
6 whole walnuts, shelled
40 g (1½ oz) queso fresco, coarsley chopped
3 tablespoons grated Parmesan cheese
2 tablespoons olive oil
4 teaspoons salt

Clean the limpets and cook in 4 cups (34 fl oz /1 liter) water for 3 hours until tender. Drain, remove the shells, and chop the flesh. Refrigerate until needed.

Soak the beans in generous 2 cups (17 fl oz /500 ml) water overnight. Drain, put in a pan with 2 cups (17 fl oz /500 ml) water, and cook for 35 minutes until tender. Drain and set aside.

Clean the mussels and cook them in their shells in boiling water for 2 minutes or until they are open. Remove the meat from the shells and set aside.

Prepare the Lima-style pesto. Heat the vegetable oil in a pan over low heat, add the onion and garlic, and sauté for 4 minutes until the onion starts to soften. Add the basil and spinach leaves and cook for another 2 minutes. Remove from the heat, let cool, and put in a food processor with the walnuts, queso fresco, Parmesan cheese, olive oil, and salt. Blend the ingredients together to a smooth paste. Set aside.

For the minestrone, pour the mussel broth (stock) into a pan and place over the heat, adding the yucca root (cassava), potatoes, beans, carrot, squash, turnip, and lima (butter) beans. Bring to a simmer and cook for 10 minutes until the vegetables are tender. Add the sliced corncob and penne pasta and cook for another 8 minutes until the pasta is cooked.

Stir through the cooked limpets and shrimp, then add the squid, clams, scallops, and mussels and cook for 1 minute until the seafood have cooked. Finally, add the Lima-style pesto and mix everything together well. Season with salt and pepper to taste.

Ladle the soup into large shallow bowls and garnish with Parmesan cheese. Serve.

CHUPE BLANCO DE PESCADO
FISH CHOWDER

Serves: 4
Preparation Time: 15 minutes
Cooking Time: 40 minutes

If you ever make it to Lima, you must try the small family-run restaurants of the Port of Callao. They serve the most delicious fish chowders.

- 2 tablespoons olive oil
- 2 red onions, very finely chopped
- 6 cloves garlic, very finely chopped
- 1 teaspoon ground cumin
- 3 tablespoons Yellow Chili Paste (see p. 405)
- 1 sprig oregano
- 1 corncob, cut into 1¼-inch (3-cm) slices
- 2 yellow potatoes, halved
- 8½ cups (68 fl oz/2 liters) fish broth (stock)
- ½ cup (3 oz/80 g) fava (broad) beans
- ⅔ cup (3 oz/80 g) chopped squash
- 2¾ oz (70 g) cabbage, chopped
- 2¼ lb (1 kg) white croaker, grouper, or conger eel, cleaned and cut into 10 pieces
- 4 tablespoons whole (full-fat) milk
- ½ cup (3½ oz/100 g) Peruvian-style Cooked White Rice (see p. 178)
- salt and pepper

Heat the olive oil in a pan over low heat, add the onions and garlic, and sauté for a few minutes until the onions have softened. Season with salt and pepper to taste, stir in the cumin and chili paste, and cook, stirring, for 5 minutes until fragrant.

Add the oregano, corncob slices, and potatoes and pour over the fish broth (stock). Bring to a simmer, add the fava (broad) beans, chopped squash, and cabbage, and cook for 10 minutes, until the potatoes are just tender.

Add the fish, cover the pan, and cook for 8 minutes until the fish is almost cooked. Add the milk and rice and cook for another 2–3 minutes. Adjust the seasoning to taste.

Ladle the chowder into large shallow bowls. Serve.

Fish Chowder

CHILCANO DE PESCADO
FISH CHILCANO SOUP

Serves: 4
Preparation Time: 12 minutes
Cooking Time: 1 hour 35 minutes

The simplicity of this dish is inspiring and not to be confused with the pisco-based cocktail also known as *chilcano*. This is a fish soup that is as simple as it is delicious.

1 × 2½ lb (1.2 kg) croaker, grouper, or sole carcass (including the head), washed
2 red onions, cut in half
4 cloves garlic
2 celery stalks, halved
2 parsley stems, leaves removed
4 yellow potatoes, cut into ½-inch (1-cm) cubes
1 lb 5 oz (600 g) fish fillet, cut into ¾-inch (2-cm) cubes
½ scallion (spring onion), chopped
1 rocoto chile, seeded, membrane removed, and chopped
1 tablespoon chopped culantro or cilantro (coriander) leaves, plus extra to garnish
juice of 2 small lemons
salt and pepper

Place the fish carcass in a pan and cover with 170 fl oz/5 liters water. Bring to a boil, skimming off any impurities that float to the surface with a slotted spoon. Reduce the heat to a simmer, add the onions, garlic, celery, and parsley stems, and let cook for 1 hour.

Strain the cooking liquid into another pan and simmer for about 25 minutes until it reduces by a quarter of its original volume. Add the potato cubes and cook for another 6 minutes until just tender.

Add the fish cubes, scallion (spring onion), rocoto chile, and culantro or cilantro (coriander) and season to taste with salt and pepper. Cook together for 1 minute.

Ladle the soup into large shallow bowls, drizzle over the lemon juice, and garnish with culantro leaves. Serve.

CHUPÍN DE MARISCOS
SEAFOOD CHUPÍN SOUP

Serves: 4
Preparation Time: 30 minutes
Cooking Time: 3 hours 20 minutes

***Chupín* is perhaps a derivation of the Genovesi dish *cioppino*, an Italian fish soup. It is a dish beloved of the residents of Callao, the Peruvian port where Genovesi fishermen settled a century and a half ago, bringing many of their customs.**

11 oz (300 g) limpets in their shell
2 tablespoons olive oil
2 red onions, finely chopped
pinch of cumin
2 tomatoes, skinned, seeded, and grated
4 tablespoons Panca Chili Paste (see p. 406)
1 sprig oregano
2 yellow potatoes, cut into ½-inch (1-cm) cubes
8½ cups (68 fl oz/2 liters) fish broth (stock)
½ cup (3 oz/80 g) fava (broad) beans
⅓ cup (1½ oz/40 g) squash, cut into ½-inch (1-cm) chunks
12 small scallops, cleaned
6 shrimp (prawns), peeled and deveined
2 × 7-oz (200-g) squid, cleaned and cut into rings
4 oz (120 g) Cooked Octopus (see p. 406)
7 oz (200 g) croaker, grouper, or conger eel, cleaned and cut into 1-inch (2.5-cm) pieces
½ cup (4 fl oz/120 ml) whole (full-fat) milk
salt and pepper

Clean the limpets and cook them in 4 cups (34 fl oz/1 liter) water for 3 hours until they are tender. Remove the shells, chop the flesh, and refrigerate until needed.

Heat the olive oil in a pan over low heat, add the onion and cumin, season with salt and pepper, and sauté for 2–3 minutes until the onion softens.

Stir in the grated tomatoes and chili paste and cook, stirring, for 5 minutes until the mixture is fragrant.

Add the oregano sprig, potatoes, and fish broth (stock), bring to a simmer, and cook for 5 minutes over low heat. Add the fava (broad) beans, squash, scallops, shrimp (prawns), squid, limpets, octopus, and fish. Simmer for 1 minute, then stir in the milk and simmer for another 2 minutes until the fish and seafood are cooked through. Season to taste with salt and pepper.

Ladle the soup into large shallow bowls. Serve.

INCHICAPI
CHICKEN INCHICAPI

Serves: 4
Preparation Time: 15 minutes
Cooking Time: 1 hour 15 minutes

This is a delicious and complete soup or stew that is infused with exotic jungle flavors and textures.

- 2 × 3½ lb (1.8 kg) young chickens
- 7 oz (200 g) yucca root (cassava), peeled and cut into 4 large pieces
- 2 tablespoons vegetable oil
- ½ red onion, chopped
- 6 cloves garlic, very finely chopped
- 1 teaspoon turmeric
- ½ cup (3 oz/80 g) yellow cornmeal (polenta)
- ½ cup (2½ oz/65 g) ground peanuts
- 1 tablespoon chopped oregano leaves
- 1 cup (7 oz/200 g) Cocona and Chili Salsa (see p. 409)
- salt and pepper

For the inchicapi, cut the chicken into 8 pieces and place in a pan with the yucca root (cassava). Cover with 170 fl oz/5 liters water, place over medium heat, and bring to a simmer. Let cook for 35 minutes, or until the yucca root disintegrates completely. Remove the chicken pieces from the pan and strain the broth. Set aside.

In a separate pan, heat the oil over low heat, add the onion, garlic, and turmeric and sauté for 5 minutes until the onion has softened. Add the strained chicken broth, bring to a boil, and sprinkle over the cornmeal (polenta) and ground peanuts, stirring continuously with a wooden spoon.

Season with salt and pepper, add the oregano, and cook over medium heat for 30 minutes until the broth has thickened and reduced and the flavors have melded together. Add the chicken pieces, taste, and adjust the seasoning if necessary.

Ladle the broth into large shallow bowls and serve accompanied by cocona salsa.

LAWA DE CHOCLO
BLENDED CORN LAWA

Serves: 4
Preparation Time: 10 minutes
Cooking Time: 15 minutes

This is a dish my grandmother, from Cusco, used to make every Sunday, just like her mother and her mother before that. Traditional Cusco cuisine at its best.

- 2⅓ cups (11 oz/350 g) corn kernels
- 2 tablespoons vegetable oil
- ½ white onion, finely chopped
- 1 clove garlic, chopped
- 4 white potatoes, cut into ¾-inch (1.5-cm) cubes
- 2 sprigs huacatay
- 1 cup (5 oz/150 g) fava (broad) beans
- 5 oz (150 g) queso fresco, cut into ½-inch (1-cm) cubes
- 2 eggs, beaten
- salt

Put the corn kernels into a food processor with 4 tablespoons water and blend together to form a smooth paste. Set aside.

Heat the oil in a pan over low heat, add the onion and garlic, and sauté for 2–3 minutes until the onion starts to soften, being careful not to let the onion brown.

Pour over 6¼ cups (51 fl oz/1.5 liters) water, add the potatoes, huacatay sprigs, and blended corn, and bring to a simmer. Cook for 10 minutes over medium heat, stirring continuously, until reduced by a quarter.

Add the fava (broad) beans, queso fresco, and eggs and bring to a gentle boil. Cook for 1 minute until the eggs have just cooked. Season with salt.

Ladle the soup into large shallow bowls. Serve.

Lima-Style Minestrone

MENESTRÓN
PERUVIAN-STYLE MINESTRONE

Serves: 4
Preparation Time: 20 minutes, plus 8 hours soaking
Cooking Time: 1 hour 30 minutes

The Italian community brought minestrone soup to Peru. The two cultures gradually fused and the recipe took on Peruvian flavors, from which a new Italian-Peruvian soup was born.

- 1 × 4½-lb (2-kg) beef brisket, cut into 4 pieces
- 2 oz (50 g) yucca root (cassava), peeled and cut into 4 pieces
- 4 potatoes, cut into ½-inch (1-cm) cubes
- 4 tablespoons canary beans, soaked overnight
- 2 carrots, diced
- 1⅓ cups (6 oz/175 g) ¾-inch (1.5-cm) macre squash cubes
- 1 × 3½ oz (100 g) turnip, sliced
- ⅓ cup (2 oz/50 g) canned Lima (butter) beans, drained
- 1 corncob, sliced into 1¼-inch (3-cm) slices
- 5 oz (150 g) penne or rigatoni pasta
- 8 medium cabbage leaves
- 4 oz (120 g) cubed queso fresco, to garnish
- salt and pepper

Lima-style pesto

- 2 tablespoons vegetable oil
- ¼ red onion, chopped
- 2 cloves garlic, crushed
- 1¾ cups (2¾ oz/70 g) basil leaves
- 1½ cups (1½ oz/40 g) spinach leaves
- 6 whole walnuts, shelled
- 40 g (1½ oz) queso fresco, coarsely chopped
- 3 tablespoons grated Parmesan cheese
- 2 tablespoons olive oil
- 4 teaspoons salt

Start by preparing the Lima-style pesto. Heat the vegetable oil in a pan over low heat, add the onion and garlic, and sauté for 6 minutes until the onion starts to soften. Add the basil leaves and spinach and cook for another 2 minutes. Remove from the heat, let cool, and put into a food processor with the walnuts, queso fresco, Parmesan cheese, olive oil, and salt. Blend the ingredients together to a smooth paste. Set aside.

Add the brisket pieces to a pan, sprinkle over a little salt, and cover with 136 fl oz/4 liters water. Bring to a simmer and cook over medium heat for 1 hour, stirring occasionally, until the beef is almost done. Add the yucca root (cassava), potatoes, beans, carrots, squash, turnip, and lima (butter) beans and continue to simmer for 8 minutes until the vegetables are tender.

Add the corncob slices and pasta and cook, stirring, for 6 minutes. Add the cabbage leaves and cook for another 2–3 minutes until the pasta is cooked and the cabbage leaves are tender, then add the Lima-style pesto and mix everything together. Adjust the seasoning to taste with salt and pepper.

Ladle the soup into large shallow bowls and garnish with queso fresco. Serve.

CONCENTRADO DE CANGREJOS
CRAB IN SPICY BROTH

Serves: 4
Preparation Time: 10 minutes
Cooking Time: 20 minutes

There is a restaurant in Lima that serves a perfect version of this dish. It is a small family-run place in the lovely district of Barranco called MiPerú, and their crab in spicy broth (stock) is beyond delicious.

2 tablespoons olive oil
1 red onion, very finely chopped
3 cloves garlic, very finely chopped
1 teaspoon ground cumin
1 tomato, skinned, seeded, and grated
4 tablespoons Panca Chili Paste (see p. 406)
6 × 12-oz (350-g) stone crabs, cleaned and cut in half
4 slices from ½ rocoto chile, to garnish
juice of 2 small lemons, to serve
salt and pepper

Heat the olive oil in a pan over low heat, add the onion and garlic, and sauté for 8 minutes until the onion starts to soften. Season with salt and pepper to taste. Add the cumin, tomato, and chili paste and cook for another 6 minutes until fragrant.

Next, add the crabs and enough water to cover them. Cover the pan and cook over low heat for 5 minutes until the crab meat is cooked, then taste and adjust the seasoning.

Ladle the broth (stock) into large shallow bowls, topping each with a crab and rocoto chile slice to garnish. Drizzle with lemon juice and serve.

PARIHUELA NIKKEI
JAPANESE-INSPIRED SEAFOOD SOUP

Serves: 4
Preparation Time: 40 minutes
Cooking Time: 20 minutes

This Japanese-inspired *parihuela*, as indicated by the name, is a soup that combines Peruvian and Japanese flavors. It is where the fishermen of Japan meet those of the Port of Callao (Lima).

2 tablespoons oil
2 onions, finely chopped
3 cloves garlic, chopped
1-inch (2.5-cm) piece fresh ginger, peeled and chopped
4 tomatoes, peeled, seeded, and grated
2 tablespoons Panca Chili Paste (see p. 406)
1 teaspoon hondashi seasoning
4 × 11-oz (300-g) stone crabs, cleaned and cut in half
12 mussels, cleaned
4 cups (34 fl oz/1 liter) fish broth (stock)
4 tablespoons white wine
12 shrimp (prawns), peeled and deveined
4 × 7-oz (200-g) squid, cleaned and cut into rings
12 scallops, cleaned
14 oz (400 g) fish fillet (such as Peruvian grunt, grouper, or croaker), cut into 8 pieces
¼ cup (1 oz/25 g) rehydrated wakame
1 tablespoon soy sauce
1 scallion (spring onion), chopped
½ cup (1 oz/25 g) chopped culantro or cilantro (coriander) leaves, to garnish
juice of 2 small lemons
salt and pepper

Heat the oil in a large pan over medium heat, add the onions, garlic, and ginger, and sauté for 3 minutes until the onions have started to soften. Add the grated tomatoes and chili paste and cook for another 2–3 minutes until fragrant. Stir in the hondashi seasoning and season with salt and pepper.

Add the crab halves and mussels to the pan and cook for 1 minute, then pour over the fish broth (stock) and white wine and bring to a boil. Add the shrimp (prawns), squid, scallops, and fish pieces and cook for a few minutes until the fish is cooked through.

Stir through the wakame, soy sauce, and scallion (spring onion) to finish. Ladle into large shallow bowls, garnish with the culantro or cilantro (coriander) leaves, drizzle with lemon juice, and serve.

Crab in Spicy Broth

Serves: 4
Preparation Time: 40 minutes
Cooking Time: 25 minutes

A really good *parihuela* should have a strong seafood taste. The most famous versions of this dish are those that combine rock fish with shellfish, but a *parihuela* made with crustaceans is also surprisingly delicious.

4 × 2-oz (50-g) lobster tails, cleaned
2 tablespoons oil
3 onions, 2 finely chopped and 1 very thinly sliced
3 cloves garlic, chopped
1-inch (2.5-cm) piece fresh ginger, peeled and chopped
6 tomatoes, 4 peeled, seeded, and grated and 2 thinly sliced
2 tablespoons Panca Chili Paste (see p. 406)
pinch of ground cumin
4 × 11-oz (300-g) stone crabs, cleaned and cut in half
4 tablespoons white wine
4 cups (34 fl oz/1 liter) fish broth (stock)
7 oz (200 g) yucca root (cassava), peeled and chopped into 4 pieces
16 large shrimp (prawns)
12 small shrimp (prawns)
1 tablespoon cornstarch (cornflour)
4 tablespoons chopped yuyo seaweed
culantro or cilantro (coriander) leaves, to garnish
juice of 4 small lemons
salt and pepper

PARIHUELA DE CRUSTÁCEOS
CRUSTACEAN SOUP

Extract the lobster tail meat from the shells and set both aside.

Heat the oil in a large pan over medium heat, add the chopped onions, garlic, and ginger and sauté for 3 minutes until the onions start to soften. Add the grated tomatoes and chili paste and cook the ingredients for another 2–3 minutes until fragrant. Stir in the cumin and season with salt and pepper to taste.

Add the crab halves to the pan, along with the lobster shells, and cook for 4 minutes. Pour over the white wine and fish broth (stock), bring to a simmer, and cook for 10 minutes. Add the lobster tail meat and yucca root (cassava) to the pan and cook for another 2 minutes, then add the large and small shrimp (prawns).

Stir in the sliced onion and tomatoes and cook for a few minutes. Dissolve the cornstarch (cornflour) in a little water, add to the pan, and cook, stirring, until thickened slightly. Stir in the chopped yuyo seaweed to finish.

Ladle into large shallow bowls, garnish with the culantro or cilantro (coriander) leaves, and drizzle with lemon juice. Serve.

PATASCA
VEAL SHANK AND TRIPE SOUP

Serves: 4
Preparation Time: 25, plus overnight soaking
Cooking Time: 1 hour 55 minutes

In the Andes, this dish is undoubtedly a party dish. The combination of meats, juices, and natural gelatin from its ingredients have rightly earned it the reputation of being a cure-all dish.

- 1⅓ cups (8 oz/225 g) hominy (dried corn), soaked overnight
- 1 × 2½-lb (1.3-kg) veal shank
- 11 oz (300 g) veal tripe, cleaned
- 1 sprig mint
- 2 tablespoons vegetable oil
- 1 red onion, chopped
- 2 cloves garlic, chopped
- 1 tomato, peeled, seeded, and chopped
- 2 tablespoons Panca Chili Paste (see p. 406)
- 1 tablespoon chopped fresh oregano
- 1 tablespoon chopped culantro or cilantro (coriander)
- 4 white potatoes, cut into ¾-inch (1.5-cm) cubes
- salt and pepper

To garnish

- ½ scallion (spring onion), chopped
- ½ rocoto chile, seeded, membrane removed, and chopped
- 4 tablespoons chopped mint

To cook the hominy (dried corn), put it in a pan with water (1 part hominy, 2 parts water) and boil over medium heat for about 35 minutes or until tender. Drain and set aside.

Place the veal shank and tripe in a large pan with 136 fl oz/4 liters water or enough to cover them. Bring to the boil, reduce to a simmer, and cook for 1 hour until the meat is tender.

Add the hominy and mint and season with salt. When the hominy is cooked and so tender the grain breaks, remove the pan from the heat. Strain and set aside the cooking liquid and hominy and let the veal shank and tripe cool. Once cool, remove the veal meat from the bone and cut into 1¼-inch/3-cm cubes along with the tripe.

Heat the oil in a separate pan over low heat, add the chopped onion, garlic, and tomato, and sauté for 5 minutes until the onion starts to soften. Add the chili paste, season with salt and pepper, and cook for another 2–3 minutes until fragrant.

Add the chopped meats to the pan along with the chopped oregano and culantro or cilantro (coriander). Pour over the reserved meat cooking liquid and stir in the cooked hominy and potatoes. Bring to a simmer and cook over medium heat for 10 minutes. Adjust the seasoning to taste.

Ladle the soup into large shallow bowls and garnish with chopped scallion (spring onion), rocoto chile, and mint. Serve.

Serves: 4
Preparation Time: 30 minutes, plus overnight soaking
Cooking Time: 2 hours 10 minutes

Tacna, a Peruvian city that borders Chile, produces some heart-warming regional dishes such as corn pie, Tacna-style chile, and this version of patasca, which is a powerful and delicious dish due to the variety of ingredients used.

- 2 cups (11 oz/300 g) hominy (dried corn), soaked overnight
- 11 oz (300 g) cooked beef tripe, cut into 1½-inch (4-cm) long strips
- 5 oz (150 g) cooked lamb tripe, cut into 1½-inch (4-cm) long strips
- 2¼ lb (1 kg) lamb ribs
- 1 × 8¾-lb (4-kg) pig head, cleaned and cut in half
- 4 × 11-oz (300-g) lamb feet, cleaned
- 11 oz (300 g) bacon
- 10 cloves garlic, 4 whole and 6 very finely chopped
- 3 onions, 1 whole and 2 finely chopped
- 2 bay leaves
- 1 celery stalk
- 1 leek, cut in half
- 2 sprigs oregano
- 1 tablespoon peppercorns
- 3 tablespoons vegetable oil
- 4 tablespoons Panca Chili Paste (see p. 406)
- pinch of ground cumin
- 2 sprigs mint, chopped, plus extra leaves to garnish
- salt and pepper

PATASCA TACNEÑA
TACNA-STYLE MEAT SOUP

To cook the hominy (dried corn), put it into a pan with water (1 part hominy, 2 parts water) and boil over medium heat for about 35 minutes or until tender. Drain and set aside.

Remove the fat from the beef and lamb tripe, place the meat in a pan, and cover with water. Cook for 40 minutes or until tender. Drain and set aside.

Place the lamb ribs, pig head halves, lamb feet, bacon, whole garlic cloves, whole onion, bay leaves, celery, leek, 1 oregano sprig, and peppercorns in a large pan. Cover with 170 fl oz /5 liters water, bring to a simmer, and cook over low heat for 1 hour, until the meats are tender.

Remove the meats from the pan and leave to cool. Strain and reserve the cooking liquid. Once cool, cut the meat into 1½-inch/4-cm chunks and set aside.

Heat the oil in a separate pan over medium heat, add the chopped onions and garlic, and sauté for 2–3 minutes. Add the chili paste, cumin, chopped mint, and remaining oregano sprig, season with salt and pepper, and cook for 8 minutes.

Pour over the meat cooking liquid and add the chopped meats, tripe strips, and hominy. Bring to a simmer and cook for 4 minutes.

Ladle the soup into large shallow bowls and garnish with mint leaves. Serve.

PEBRE DE LOMOS
LAMB AND BEEF LOIN SOUP

Serves: 4
Preparation Time: 20 minutes, plus 8 hours soaking
Cooking Time: 1 hour 10 minutes

It is said that the city of Arequipa has a soup for each day of the week, which is undoubtedly true. This *pebre de lomos* is one of the delicious traditional soups of which the families of Arequipa are so proud.

1 cup (7 oz/200 g) dried chickpeas
1 lb 2 oz (500 g) lamb loin
1 lb 2 oz (500 g) beef tenderloin (fillet)
10 cloves garlic, 4 left whole and 6 very finely chopped
3 onions, 1 whole and 2 finely chopped
2 bay leaves
1 celery stalk
1 leek, cut in half
2 sprigs oregano
1 tablespoon peppercorns
2 tablespoons vegetable oil
4 tablespoons Yellow Chili Paste (see p. 405)
2 sprigs mint, chopped, plus extra leaves to garnish
salt and pepper

Soak the chickpeas in water overnight. Drain, put into a pan, and cover with cold water. Boil for 35 minutes or until tender. Drain and set aside.

Place the lamb loin, beef tenderloin (fillet), whole garlic cloves, whole onion, bay leaves, celery, leek, oregano sprig, and peppercorns in a large pan. Cover with 102 fl oz/3 liters water, bring to a simmer, and cook over low heat for 20 minutes, until the meats are cooked.

Remove the meats from the pan and let cool. Strain and reserve the cooking liquid. Once cool, cut the meat into 1½-inch/4-cm chunks and set aside.

Put the chickpeas into a food processor with about 4 tablespoons of the strained cooking liquid and blend together until smooth. Set aside.

Heat the oil in a separate pan over medium heat, add the chopped onions and garlic, and sauté for 2–3 minutes until the onions start to soften. Add the chili paste, chopped mint, and the remaining oregano sprig, season with salt and pepper, and cook for 8 minutes.

Pour over the meat-cooking liquid, add the chopped meat and blended chickpeas, and cook for 4 minutes until thick.

Ladle the soup into large shallow bowls and garnish with mint leaves. Serve.

Seafood Soup

SHÁMBAR
MEAT AND PEARL BARLEY SOUP

Serves: 4
Preparation Time: 10 minutes, plus overnight soaking
Cooking Time: 2 hours

My aunt is from Trujillo, my mother is from Trujillo, my sisters are from Trujillo, and this shámbar recipe is from Trujillo. I only got to try this dish out, however, as a teenager, probably because it is so labor-intensive.

2 cups (14 oz/400 g) pearl barley
¾ cup (5 oz/150 g) dried peas
1 cup (5 oz/150 g) dried fava (broad) beans
1 cup (7 oz/200 g) white or light brown beans
11 oz (300 g) beef flank steak, cut into 1½-inch (4-cm) chunks
11 oz (300 g) pork (with rind), cut into 1½-inch (4-cm) chunks
11 oz (300 g) serrano ham or smoked ham, cut into 1½-inch (4-cm) chunks
4 tablespoons vegetable oil
2 red onions, chopped
4 cloves garlic, chopped
2 tablespoons Panca Chili Paste (see p. 406)
1 tablespoon Mirasol Chili Paste (see p. 405)
1 teaspoon ground cumin
salt and pepper

To garnish
1 cup (7 oz/200 g) cancha (toasted corn)
2 sprigs culantro or cilantro (coriander), leaves removed

Put the pearl barley, dried peas, dried fava (broad) beans, and white or light brown beans in separate bowls, cover each with water, and let soak overnight.

The following day, drain the water from all the bowls and place all the soaked ingredients in a pan. Cover with 204 fl oz/6 liters water, bring to a simmer, and cook for 1 hour or until the grains are just tender.

Add the beef flank steak, pork, and ham to the pan and continue to cook for 30 minutes, stirring occasionally, until the meats are cooked and tender.

Meanwhile, heat the oil in a separate pan over low heat, add the onion and garlic, and sauté for 2–3 minutes until the onion softens. Add the chili pastes and cook for another 3 minutes until fragrant. Stir in the cumin and season with salt and pepper to taste.

Add the sautéed mixture to the simmering meat pan and let cook over low heat for 30 minutes until cooked and the flavors have melded together.

Ladle the soup into large shallow bowls, garnish with cancha (toasted corn) and culantro or cilantro (coriander) leaves, and serve.

PARIHUELA
SEAFOOD SOUP

Serves: 4
Preparation Time: 40 minutes
Cooking Time: 12 minutes

***Parihuela* is the most popular seafood soup in Peru. If you visit Lima and go to a ceviche restaurant, whether in fall (autumn) or winter, you will inevitably find *parihuela* on the menu.**

2 tablespoons vegetable oil
2 onions, finely chopped
3 cloves garlic, chopped
1-inch (2.5-cm) piece fresh ginger, peeled and chopped
4 tomatoes, skinned, seeded, and grated
2 tablespoons Panca Chili Paste (see p. 406)
pinch of ground cumin
4 × 12-oz (350-g) crabs, cleaned and cut in half
12 mussels, cleaned
8½ cups (68 fl oz/2 liters) fish broth (stock)
12 shrimp (prawns), peeled and deveined
4×7-oz (200-g) squid, cleaned and cut into rings
12 scallops, cleaned
14 oz (400 g) fish fillet (such as Peruvian grunt, grouper, or croaker), cut into 8
1 tablespoon cornstarch (cornflour)
4 tablespoons chopped yuyo seaweed
½ cup (1 oz/25 g) chopped culantro or cilantro (coriander) leaves, to garnish
juice of 4 small lemons, to serve
salt and pepper

Heat the oil in a large pan over medium heat, add the onions, garlic, and ginger, and sauté for 3 minutes until the onions have started to soften. Add the grated tomatoes and chili paste and cook for another 2–3 minutes until fragrant. Season with salt and pepper.

Add the cumin, crab halves, and mussels and cook for 1 minute, then pour over the fish broth (stock) and bring to a boil. Add the shrimp (prawns), squid, scallops, and fish pieces and simmer for 2–3 minutes until the seafood is cooked.

Dissolve the cornstarch (cornflour) in a little water, add to the pan, and cook, stirring, until thickened slightly. Stir in the chopped yuyo seaweed to finish.

Ladle into large shallow bowls, garnish with the culantro or cilantro (coriander) leaves, drizzle with lemon juice, and serve.

PARIHUELA DE PESCADOS DE ROCA
ROCK FISH SOUP

Serves: 4
Preparation Time: 40 minutes
Cooking Time: 20 minutes

This is a dish that should come with a danger sign. The concentration of flavors produced by the rock fish will have you sweating for hours after eating it—a burst of energy like you've never experienced before.

- 2 tablespoons oil
- 4 onions, 2 very finely chopped and 2 very thinly sliced
- 6 cloves garlic, very finely chopped
- 1-inch (2.5-cm) piece fresh ginger, peeled and chopped
- 4 tomatoes, peeled, seeded, and grated
- 2 tablespoons Panca Chili Paste (see p. 406)
- pinch of ground cumin
- salt and pepper
- 4 tablespoons white wine
- 4 cups (34 fl oz/1 liter) fish broth (stock)
- 1 × 1 lb 5-oz (600-g) angler fish, cleaned and gutted
- 1 × 1 lb 5-oz (600-g) comber, cleaned, gutted, and cut into 8 pieces
- 1 × 1 lb 5-oz (600-g) suckermouth catfish, cleaned, gutted, and cut into 8 pieces
- 1 × 1 lb 5-oz (600-g) Peruvian blenny, cleaned, gutted and cut into 8 pieces
- ½ yellow chile, seeded, membrane removed, and thinly sliced
- 4 tablespoons chopped yuyo seaweed
- handful of culantro or cilantro (coriander) leaves
- 4 slices from 1 rocoto chile
- 1 tablespoon cornstarch (cornflour)
- juice of 4 small lemons

To garnish

- ½ cup (1 oz/25 g) culantro or cilantro (coriander) leaves
- 4 tablespoons chopped yuyo seaweed

Heat the oil in a large pan over medium heat, add the chopped onion, garlic, and ginger, and sauté for 3 minutes until the onion has started to soften. Add the tomatoes and chili paste and cook for another 2–3 minutes until fragrant. Stir in the cumin and season with salt and pepper to taste.

Pour in the white wine and fish broth (stock), then add the angler fish, comber, suckermouth catfish, and Peruvian blenny. Bring to a simmer and cook for 2 minutes until the liquid has reduced. Stir in the sliced onions and yellow chile, cover the pan, and cook over low heat for 8 minutes until the fish is almost done. Add the chopped yuyo seaweed, culantro or cilantro (coriander) leaves, and rocoto chile slices and cook for another minute.

Dissolve the cornstarch (cornflour) in a little water, add to the pan, and cook, stirring, until thickened slightly.

Transfer the fish to a soup tureen and ladle over the soup. Pour over the lemon juice and garnish with more culantro leaves and chopped yuyo seaweed.

SOPA A LA CRIOLLA
CREOLE SOUP

Serves: 4
Preparation Time: 10 minutes
Cooking Time: 20 minutes

This is a soup from Lima that everyone loves as soon as they try it. The al dente angel hair pasta, the egg, the meat, and the chile all contribute to a tasty and heart-warming soup.

4 tablespoons vegetable oil
2 red onions, finely chopped
4 cloves garlic, chopped
4 tomatoes, finely chopped
2 tablespoons Panca Chili Paste (see p. 406)
7 oz (200 g) beef tenderloin (fillet), cut into ¾-inch (2-cm) chunks
1 teaspoon dried oregano
8½ cups (68 fl oz/2 liters) beef broth (stock)
9 oz (250 g) angel hair pasta
4 tablespoons evaporated milk
salt and pepper

To garnish
4 poached eggs
1 cup (1 oz/25 g) croûtons or fried bread cubes
1 yellow chile, roasted and thinly sliced
1 tablespoon chopped culantro or cilantro (coriander) leaves

Heat the oil in a pan over medium heat, add the onions, garlic, and tomatoes, and sauté for 5 minutes until the onions have softened. Add the chili paste and cook, stirring, for another 5 minutes until fragrant.

Add the beef tenderloin (fillet) and oregano, season with salt and pepper, and cook, stirring, for 1 minute. Pour in the beef broth (stock) and bring to a boil, then add the angel hair pasta and cook for 4 minutes until the pasta is cooked. Stir in the evaporated milk, taste, and adjust the seasoning if necessary.

Ladle the soup into large shallow bowls, topping each with a poached egg, a few croutons, some roasted chile slices, and chopped culantro or cilantro (coriander) leaves to garnish. Serve.

SOPA DE NOVIOS
LOVERS' SOUP

Serves: 4
Preparation Time: 30 minutes, plus 10 minutes soaking
Cooking Time: 1 hour 15 minutes

When it comes to preparing any substantial soup that is almost a stew, the most important thing is patience and a willingness to let the ingredients cook to perfection and absorb all the flavors.

4 French bread rolls or any crusty rolls
5 cups (40 fl oz/1.2 liters) chicken broth (stock)
1 teaspoon Annatto Oil (see p. 408)
½ red onion, chopped
4 cloves garlic, chopped
2 tomatoes, peeled, seeded, and chopped
2 tablespoons Panca Chili Paste (see p. 406)
1 teaspoon oregano powder
11 oz (300 g) chicken gizzards, cleaned
14 oz (400 g) boneless chicken, cut into 8 pieces
11 oz (300 g) chicken livers, cleaned
4 tablespoons chicha de jora
9 oz (250 g) linguine or any long, thin pasta
4 tablespoons raisins
⅓ cup (1½ oz/40 g) chopped black olives
1 teaspoon chopped culantro or cilantro (coriander) leaves
salt and pepper

Break the bread rolls into ¾-inch/2-cm chunks, place in a bowl, and cover with the chicken broth (stock). Let the bread pieces soak for 10 minutes, then remove from the broth and squeeze to remove any excess liquid. Set the bread and broth aside.

Heat the annatto oil in a pan, add the onion, chopped garlic, tomatoes, and chili paste, and sauté for 6 minutes until the onion is soft and the chili paste fragrant. Stir in the oregano and season.

Add the chicken gizzards and the soaked bread and cook, stirring, for 20 minutes until slightly browned. Add the boneless chicken and cook for 4 minutes. Add the livers and cook for another 4 minutes. Pour over the chicha de jora and bring to a simmer, then add the reserved broth and simmer for 30 minutes over medium heat until the bread and meat are tender.

Add the linguine to the pan and cook for another 10 minutes, then stir in the raisins and olives. Adjust the seasoning to taste and stir in the chopped culantro or cilantro (coriander) leaves to finish.

Ladle the soup into large shallow bowls and serve.

Serves: 4
Preparation Time: 15 minutes, plus overnight soaking
Cooking Time: 3 hours

This bean soup, which is increasingly difficult to find in the restaurants and homes of Lima, is definitely one to try. It is a tasty, homely, and filling dish.

1 × 12-oz (350-g) pig ear
7 oz (200 g) dried mutton or beef
7 oz (200 g) pork side (belly)
3 red onions, 1 whole and 2 finely chopped
1 celery stalk
1 leek, cut in half
2 bay leaves
1 tablespoon peppercorns
4 tablespoons olive oil
6 cloves garlic, very finely chopped
2 tablespoons Mirasol Chili Paste (see p. 405)
2½ cups (1 lb 5 oz/600 g) canary beans, soaked overnight
4 oz (120 g) penne or rigatoni pasta
1 teaspoon chopped parsley
salt and pepper

SOPA DE FREJOLES
BEAN SOUP

Place the pig ear, dried mutton or beef, and pork in a pan with the whole onions, celery, leek, bay leaves, and peppercorns. Add enough water to cover the ingredients and simmer over medium heat for 2 hours until the meat is cooked.

Remove the meats from the pan and let cool. Strain and reserve the cooking liquid. Once cool, cut the meats into 1¼-inch/3-cm pieces and set aside.

Heat 3 tablespoons olive oil in a separate pan over low heat, add the chopped onions and garlic, and sauté for 4 minutes until the onions start to soften. Season with salt and pepper, add the chili paste, and cook for another 5 minutes until fragrant.

Drain the beans and add to the pan with the reserved cooking liquid. Let cook over medium heat for 30–40 minutes until the beans are tender.

Remove one third of the beans from the pan with a little cooking liquid, put into a food processor, and blend together until smooth. Return to the pan and stir together well.

Add the penne or rigatoni and cook for 8–10 minutes until the pasta is cooked. Stir through the cooked meats, remaining olive oil, and chopped parsley.

Ladle the soup into large shallow bowls and serve.

SOPA HUACHANA
HUACHANA SOUP

Serves: 4
Preparation Time: 20 minutes
Cooking Time: 1 hour 50 minutes

Huacho is a city in the north of Peru that has beautiful fertile land and a large expanse of sea that together produce wonderful ingredients and recipes. This Huachana soup is one of them.

2¼ lb (1 kg) turkey, cut into 8 pieces
2¼ lb (1 kg) chicken, cut into 8 pieces
3 red onions, 1 whole and 2 finely chopped
10 cloves garlic, 4 left whole and 6 very finely chopped
1 celery stalk
2 tablespoons vegetable oil
1 teaspoon Annatto Oil (see p. 408)
2 Huacho sausages, chopped
3 tomatoes, skinned, seeded, and grated
4 tablespoons Yellow Chili Paste (see p. 405)
1 tablespoon dried oregano
4 turkey or chicken livers, cleaned
2 apples, peeled, cored, and chopped
3 bananas, chopped
4 baguette slices
salt and pepper

To garnish
2 hard-boiled eggs, halved
handful culantro or cilantro (coriander) leaves

Place the turkey and chicken pieces in a large pan, cover with water, and bring to a boil. Add the whole onion, whole garlic cloves, and celery and let cook for 1½ hours until the turkey and chicken are tender, skimming off any sediment that floats to the surface during cooking with a slotted spoon. Remove from the heat, drain, and set the cooked poultry and cooking liquid aside.

Heat the vegetable oil in a pan with the annatto oil over low heat, add the chopped onions and garlic and sauté for 2–3 minutes until the onions start to soften. Season with salt and pepper to taste.

Add the Huacho sausages and cook for 2 minutes, stirring, until slightly browned. Stir in the grated tomatoes and chili paste and cook for another 5 minutes until the chili paste has thickened slightly and is fragrant.

Stir in the oregano, season with salt and pepper, and add the reserved cooking liquid, turkey livers, apples, and bananas. Bring to a simmer and cook until the fruit is beginning to break down and the livers are cooked.

Add the cooked turkey and chicken to the pan along with the baguette slices and adjust to taste. Continue to simmer for 8 minutes until the bread disintegrates.

Ladle the soup into large shallow bowls, garnish with hard-boiled egg halves and culantro or cilantro (coriander) leaves, and serve.

SOPA TEÓLOGA
THEOLOGIAN'S SOUP

Serves: 4
Preparation Time: 12 minutes
Cooking Time: 1 hour 45 minutes

This is an exquisite, almost heavenly soup that we really should resurrect to prevent it disappearing from the repertoire of Peruvian cuisine.

1 × 4½ lb (2 kg) chicken, plus the giblets of 2 chickens
14 oz (400 g) beef brisket
4 red onions, 2 whole and 2 finely chopped
1 leek, cut in half
1 bay leaf
2 celery stalks
4 sprigs parsley
1 carrot, chopped
2 tablespoons vegetable oil
6 cloves garlic, very finely chopped
⅓ cup (1½ oz/40 g) peeled almonds
2 stale French bread rolls or any crusty rolls, broken into ¾-inch (2-cm) chunks
2 tablespoons Yellow Chili Paste (see p. 405)
1 tablespoon Mirasol Chili Paste (see p. 405)
1 tablespoon dried oregano
salt and pepper

To garnish
4 hard-boiled eggs, chopped
1 tablespoon chopped parsley
4 tablespoons chopped black olives

Place the chicken, giblets, and beef brisket in a pan and cover with water. Add the whole onions, leek, bay leaf, celery, parsley, and carrot and bring to a boil. Reduce to a simmer and cook for 1½ hours until the chicken is tender, skimming off any sediment that floats to the surface with a slotted spoon.

Remove the meats from the pan and let cool. Strain and reserve the cooking liquid. Once cool, shred the chicken and set aside. Cut the beef brisket into 1½-inch/4-cm chunks and set aside.

Heat the vegetable oil in a pan over low heat, add the chopped onions and garlic, and sauté for 2–3 minutes until the onions have started to soften. Add the almonds and bread roll chunks and season with salt and pepper. Sauté for another 2–3 minutes, then add the chili pastes and continue to cook, stirring, for 8 minutes until the chili pastes have thickened slightly and are fragrant.

Add the dried oregano, reserved cooking liquid, giblets, beef brisket, and shredded chicken and cook, stirring, for a few more minutes until the meat and stock are warmed through.

Ladle the soup into large shallow bowls and garnish with hard-boiled eggs, chopped parsley, and black olives. Serve.

SOPA A LA MINUTA
QUICK CREOLE SOUP

Serves: 4
Preparation Time: 8 minutes
Cooking Time: 15 minutes

This is a quicker, simpler but equally tasty version of Creole soup.

3 tablespoons olive oil
2 red onions, very finely chopped
6 cloves garlic, very finely chopped
pinch of ground cumin
2 tomatoes, skinned, seeded, and grated
1 tablespoon tomato paste
2 tablespoons Panca Chili Paste (see p. 406)
1 tablespoon dried oregano
4 cups (34 fl oz/1 liter) beef broth (stock)
1 lb 5 oz (600 g) beef tenderloin (fillet), cut into ½-inch (1-cm) chunks
1 lb 2 oz (500 g) angel hair pasta
salt and pepper

Heat the olive oil in a pan over low heat, add the onions and garlic, and sauté for 2–3 minutes. Stir in the cumin and season with salt and pepper to taste.

Add the grated tomatoes, tomato paste, and chili paste and cook for another 5 minutes until fragrant. Adjust the seasoning to taste and add the oregano and beef broth (stock). Bring to a simmer over low heat, add the angel hair pasta, and cook for 2 minutes. Add the chopped beef tenderloin (fillet) and cook for another 1 minute. Taste and adjust the seasoning, if necessary.

Ladle the soup into large shallow bowls and serve.

SOPA WANTÁN
WONTON SOUP

Serves: 4
Preparation Time: 15 minutes
Cooking Time: 45 minutes

This soup would appear to be a Chinese dish but any Chinese person would no doubt disagree. There are subtle differences, influenced by the gradual integration of Chinese flavors and cuisine into Peruvian culture.

- ½-inch (1-cm) piece fresh ginger, peeled
- 9 oz (250 g) brown chicken meat, finely chopped
- 3½ oz (100 g) pork shoulder, finely chopped
- 1 scallion (spring onion), chopped
- pinch of granulated sugar
- 1 teaspoon sesame oil
- 24 wonton wrappers
- beaten egg white or water, for sealing the wontons
- 8½ cups (68 fl oz/2 liters) chicken broth (stock)
- 1 yellow potato, peeled and cut into 1½-inch (4-cm) cubes
- ¼ cup (1½ oz/40 g) 1½-inch (4-cm) cubes squash
- 1 cup (3 oz/80 g) chopped napa (Chinese) cabbage
- 1 cup (3 oz/80 g) chopped Chinese greens (leaves)
- 1 cup (2½ oz/65 g) snow peas (mangetout)
- salt

Chop half the ginger and place in a bowl with the chicken, pork, and half the chopped scallion (spring onion). Season with salt, add the sugar and sesame oil, and mix together well.

Arrange the wonton wrappers on a clean work surface and place a tablespoon of the filling in the center of each one. Shape the wontons by folding them in half to close them and then joining the tips, sealing with a little egg white or water.

Crush the remaining ginger and add to a pan with the chicken broth (stock), potato, and squash. Bring to a simmer and cook over medium heat for 35 minutes until the potato and squash disintegrate.

Strain the broth (stock) and return it to the heat in the pan. Bring to a simmer, then add the wontons, napa (Chinese) cabbage, Chinese greens (leaves), and snow peas (mangetout) and cook for 6 minutes until the wontons are done. Stir through the remaining chopped scallion and adjust the seasoning to taste.

Ladle the soup into bowls and serve.

THIMPO PUNEÑO
LAMB AND FREEZE-DRIED POTATO SOUP

Serves: 4
Preparation Time: 8 minutes, plus 8 hours soaking
Cooking Time: 1 hour 50 minutes

Peru, the country of potatoes, not only produces innumerable fresh potatoes but also semidry and dehydrated potatoes that take on a whole new flavor and add a different taste to dishes. Black and white *chuño* are two examples of these.

- 4½ lb (2 kg) lamb ribs or lamb shoulder, cut into 1¼-inch (4-cm) chunks
- 4 celery stalks
- 1 leek, cut in half
- 1 turnip, sliced
- 1½ red onions, 1 whole and ½ chopped
- 2 tablespoons vegetable oil
- 2 cloves garlic, very finely chopped
- pinch of ground cumin
- 1 cup (3½ oz/100 g) soaked black chuño, soaked for 4 hours
- 1 cup (3½ oz/100 g) white chuño, soaked for 4 hours
- 2 yellow potatoes, cut into ¾-inch (1.5-cm) cubes
- 2 cups (14 oz/400 g) Peruvian-style Cooked White Rice (see p. 178), to serve
- salt and pepper

Place the lamb in a pan with the celery, leek, turnip, and whole onion, and cover with water. Simmer over medium heat for 1½ hours, until the lamb is tender. Set aside.

Heat the oil in a pan over low heat, add the chopped onion and garlic, and sauté over low heat for 5 minutes until nicely caramelized. Stir in the cumin and season with salt and pepper to taste, then add to the broth (stock) pan with the chuño and yellow potatoes. Bring to a simmer and cook for 15 minutes until the potatoes are tender. Adjust the seasoning to taste.

Ladle the soup into large shallow bowls and serve alongside Peruvian-style cooked white rice.

SUDADO DE MERO
GROUPER FILLET SUDADO

Serves: 4
Preparation Time: 10 minutes
Cooking Time: 15 minutes

Grouper is known to be a very gelatinous fish but it works really well in this *sudado*. Chefs tend to be cautious about using it because it is not a variety of fish that abounds in our seas, so we use it sparingly.

- 2 tablespoons vegetable oil
- 2 red onions, thinly sliced
- 4 tomatoes, thinly sliced
- 1 cup (8 fl oz/250 ml) chicha de jora or white wine
- 1 cup (8 fl oz/250 ml) fish broth (stock)
- 1 × 1¾-lb (800-g) grouper fillet, cut into 4 pieces
- 1 yellow chile, seeded, membrane removed, and thinly sliced
- 7 oz (200 g) yucca root (cassava), peeled, cooked, and cut into 4 sticks
- 2 sprigs culantro or cilantro (coriander), plus extra leaves to garnish
- juice of 2 small lemons
- salt and pepper

Heat the vegetable oil in a pan, add the sliced onions and tomatoes, and sauté for 2 minutes until the onions start to soften.

Pour over the chicha de jora and fish broth (stock) and bring to a boil. Add the grouper pieces, sliced yellow chile, cooked yucca root (cassava), and culantro or cilantro (coriander) sprigs, cover the pan, and simmer for 8–10 minutes until the fish is cooked through. Season to taste with salt and pepper.

Ladle into large shallow bowls and drizzle over the lemon juice. Scatter over the culantro leaves to garnish. Serve.

SUDADO DE RAYA
SKATE FILLET SUDADO

Serves: 4
Preparation Time: 15 minutes
Cooking Time: 25 minutes

Skate is the perfect fish for this recipe. You can also add a splash of red wine to the *sudado* to make it even more delicious.

- 1 tablespoon vegetable oil
- 2 cloves garlic, very finely chopped
- 2 tablespoons Panca Chili Paste (see p. 406)
- ½ cup (4 fl oz/120 ml) white wine
- 4¼ cups (34 fl oz/1 liter) fish broth (stock)
- 1 limo chile, sliced
- 4 onions, thinly sliced
- 1 bay leaf
- 3 tomatoes, skinned, seeded, and thinly sliced
- 1 × 2¼-lb (1-kg) skate fillet, cleaned and cut into 4 pieces
- 2 tablespoons chopped culantro or cilantro (coriander), to garnish
- salt

Heat the vegetable oil in a large pan over medium heat, add the garlic, and sauté for 1 minute. Add the chili paste and cook, stirring, for another 4 minutes until thickened and fragrant.

Pour the white wine into the pan, bring to a simmer, and cook for 3 minutes until reduced, then add the fish broth (stock) and limo chile slices. Season with salt and simmer for another 3 minutes over medium heat until the stock has reduced slightly and the flavors have melded together.

Add the onions, bay leaf, and tomatoes and let cook for 5 minutes until the onions are cooked and slightly crunchy. Place the skate pieces in the pan, cover, and cook for about 8 minutes. Remove from the heat.

Ladle the soup into large shallow bowls, garnish with chopped culantro or cilantro (coriander), and serve.

Grouper Fillet Sudado

SUDADO DE LANGOSTINOS
SHRIMP SUDADO

Serves: 4
Preparation Time: 10 minutes
Cooking Time: 4 minutes

You can also prepare this *sudado* with lobster, shrimp (prawns), or crab—it will be just as delicious.

44 shrimp (prawns), cleaned and shells left intact
3 onions, thinly sliced
1 teaspoon Garlic Paste (see p. 406)
1 yellow chile, thinly sliced
½ cup (4 fl oz/120 ml) white wine
1 cup (8 fl oz/250 ml) fish broth (stock)
3 tablespoons Yellow Chili Paste (see p. 405)
2 tomatoes, cut into thick strips
4 sprigs culantro or cilantro (coriander)
salt and pepper

Place the shrimp (prawns) in a large pan with the onions, garlic paste, and sliced yellow chile. Season with salt and pepper and cook for 2 minutes over medium heat.

Pour over the white wine and fish broth (stock), then add the yellow chili paste and tomatoes. Cover the pan and cook for 2 minutes until the shrimp are cooked through. Adjust the seasoning to taste with salt and pepper.

Arrange the shrimp in a serving bowl and garnish with the culantro or cilantro (coriander) sprigs. Serve.

SUDADO DE PESCADOS DE ROCA
MIXED ROCK FISH SUDADO

Serves: 4
Preparation Time: 10 minutes
Cooking Time: 30 minutes

A rock fish *sudado* will always be a delicacy and you can try it out with local rock fish, which will be just as flavorsome as those listed in this recipe.

7 oz (200 g) comber fillet
7 oz (200 g) suckermouth catfish fillet
7 oz (200 g) Peruvian blenny fillet
7 oz (200 g) angler fish fillet
1 tablespoon vegetable oil
1 clove garlic, chopped
½ cup (4 fl oz/120 ml) Yellow Chili Paste (see p. 405)
½ cup (4 fl oz/120 ml) chicha de jora
4 cups (34 fl oz/1 liter) fish broth (stock)
1 limo chile, sliced
4 onions, thinly sliced
5 tomatoes, skinned, seeded, and thinly sliced
2 tablespoons chopped culantro or cilantro (coriander), to garnish
salt

Season the fish fillets with salt and set aside.

Heat the vegetable oil in a large pan over medium heat, add the garlic, and sauté for 1 minute until cooked. Add the chili paste and cook, stirring, for another 5 minutes until fragrant.

Pour the chicha de jora into the pan, bring to a simmer, and cook for 3 minutes until reduced, then add the fish broth (stock) and Limo chile slices. Season with salt and simmer for another 3 minutes over medium heat until the stock has reduced slightly and the flavors have melded together.

Add the onions and tomatoes and cook for 5 minutes until the onions are cooked and slightly crunchy. Place the fish fillets in the pan, cover, and let cook over medium heat for about 8 minutes. Remove from the heat.

Ladle the soup into large shallow bowls, garnish with chopped culantro or cilantro (coriander), and serve.

Shrimp Sudado

FISH SUDADO

Serves: 4
Preparation Time: 15 minutes
Cooking Time: 35 minutes

This is a wonderful Peruvian-Chinese dish that can be prepared with any local gelatinous rock fish.

4 teaspoons vegetable oil
⅓ cup (1 oz/25 g) chopped broccoli
1 asparagus spear, chopped
1-inch (2.5-cm) piece fresh ginger, peeled and chopped
1¾ cups (12 oz/350 g) steamed white rice
pinch of granulated sugar
4 tablespoons sesame oil
2 egg whites
2 cups (18 fl oz/500 ml) chicken broth (stock)
2 tablespoons soy sauce
¾ oz (20 g) rehydrated dried shiitake mushrooms, soaked in water for 20 minutes and cut in half
4 baby napa (Chinese) cabbage, cut in half
2 × 1¾-lb (800-g) angler fish, cleaned
1 scallion (spring onion), thinly sliced
handful of culantro or cilantro (coriander) leaves
salt

PEJESAPO SUDADO CHIFA
PERUVIAN-CHINESE ANGLER

Heat 3 teaspoons vegetable oil in a wok, skillet, or frying pan over medium heat. Add the chopped broccoli, asparagus, and 1 teaspoon of the chopped ginger and stir-fry for 1 minute. Add the white rice and stir-fry for another 5 minutes until the rice becomes slightly crispy. Stir in the sugar and half the sesame oil and season with salt. Set the pan aside.

Whisk the egg whites in a bowl. Heat 1 teaspoon vegetable oil in a separate nonstick skillet or frying pan and add the egg whites. Cook for 2 minutes, then flip over and cook for another 2 minutes. Remove from the heat and cut the egg-white omelet into pieces.

Add the omelet to the wok or skillet containing the rice and mix together well. Keep warm.

Pour the chicken broth (stock) into a large shallow pan and add the soy sauce, shiitake mushrooms, and remaining chopped ginger. Bring to a simmer and cook over medium heat for 5 minutes. Add the napa (Chinese) cabbage halves and cook for another 2–3 minutes until the cabbage is tender.

Season the angler fish with salt and very carefully place them in the pan. Cover and cook for 12 minutes until the fish are cooked through.

Transfer the angler fish and vegetables to a serving platter and top with the sliced scallion (spring onion) and culantro or cilantro (coriander) leaves. Heat the remaining 2 tablespoons sesame oil and drizzle over the vegetables. Serve with the vegetable-fried rice.

TIMPUSCA
HEARTY MIXED MEAT AND VEGETABLE SOUP

Serves: 4
Preparation Time: 15 minutes, plus 4 hours 30 minutes soaking
Cooking Time: 1 hour 30 minutes

The combination of seaweed or lake algae and Andean garden produce is delicious and commonly seen in dishes like this tasty *timpusca*.

½ cup (3 oz/80 g) wheat berries
1 tablespoon salt
1 cup (3½ oz/100 g) black chuño (freeze-dried potato), soaked
3½ oz (100 g) cocha yuyo seaweed
1 lb 2 oz (500 g) beef brisket
7 oz (200 g) dried mutton, beef jerky, or dried beef
8 × 2-oz (50-g) lamb loins
2 × 5-oz (150-g) lamb tongues, cleaned
2 celery stalks
1 leek, cut in half
1 turnip, sliced
1½ red onions, 1 whole and ½ chopped
2 tablespoons olive oil
2 cloves garlic, very finely chopped
pinch of ground cumin
2 yellow potatoes, cut into cubes
1 sprig mint
4 pears, cut into ¾-inch (2-cm) cubes
⅓ cup (1½ oz/40 g) fava (broad) beans in their pods, cut lengthwise in half
1 tablespoon chopped parsley, to garnish
salt and pepper

Soak the wheat berries overnight in 4¼ cups (34 fl oz/1 liter) water. Drain and put into a pan with cold water and 1 tablespoon salt. Bring to a boil and cook for 30 minutes. Drain and set aside.

Soak the black chuño in cold water for 4 hours and drain.

Put the cocha yuyo seaweed in a bowl, cover with water, and let soak for at least 1 hour. Drain and set aside.

Place the beef brisket, dried mutton, lamb loins and tongues, celery, leek, turnip, and whole onion in a pan. Cover with water, bring to a simmer, and cook over medium heat for 45 minutes until the meats are tender.

Strain and set the various meats and cooking liquid aside. Cut the meat into 1¼-inch/4-cm chunks.

Heat the olive oil in a separate pan over low heat, add the chopped onion and garlic, and sauté for 5 minutes until the onion has started to soften. Stir in the cumin and season with salt and pepper. Add the potatoes, chuño, cooked wheat berries, and mint and cook for 10 minutes.

Add the pears, fava (broad) beans, soaked cocha yuyo seaweed, and cooked meat chunks and cook for 2 minutes. Adjust the seasoning to taste.

Spoon into large shallow bowls and garnish with chopped parsley. Serve.

JUGOSO CHIMBOTANO
JUICY PAN-COOKED PERUVIAN GRUNT FILLETS

Serves: 4
Preparation Time: 5 minutes
Cooking Time: 18 minutes

This is a simple dish that is quick to make. It is a proud creation of the cuisine of the thriving city of Chimbote.

2 tablespoons vegetable oil
6 cloves garlic, very finely chopped
pinch of ground cumin
3 tablespoons Panca Chili Paste (see p. 406)
1 tablespoon Yellow Chili Paste (see p. 405)
4 × 7-oz (200-g) Peruvian grunt fillets, skin on ½ cup (4 fl oz/120 ml) chicha de jora
2 tomatoes, thinly sliced
1 red onion, thinly sliced
handful of culantro or cilantro (coriander) leaves
juice of 2 small lemons
Peruvian-style Cooked White Rice (see p. 178), to serve
salt and pepper

Heat the oil in a pan over low heat, add the garlic, and sauté for 5 minutes. Season with salt and pepper, stir in the cumin and chili pastes, and cook for another 2–3 minutes until the pastes have thickened slightly and are fragrant.

Add the fish fillets, chicha de jora, tomatoes, and onion. Cover the pan and cook for 8 minutes, or until the fish fillets are done. Stir through the culantro or cilantro (coriander) leaves to finish.

Ladle into large shallow bowls and drizzle over the lemon juice. Serve with Peruvian-style cooked white rice.

RICE, STIR-FRIES & TACU TACUS

ARROZ BLANCO GRANEADO
PERUVIAN-STYLE COOKED WHITE RICE

Serves: 6
Preparation Time: 5 minutes
Cooking Time: 20–25 minutes

We eat white rice with almost everything in Lima and it is rare not to see a large pan of cooked white rice in the kitchen at home.

3 tablespoons vegetable oil
4 cloves garlic, finely chopped
2 cups (14 oz/400 g) white long-grain rice
3 tablespoons salt

Heat 2 tablespoons of the vegetable oil in a pan over medium heat, add the garlic, and fry for 2 minutes until softened but not browned.

Pour over 3½ cups (23 fl oz/850 ml) water and bring to a boil. Add the rice and salt to the pan and stir together. Reduce the heat to its lowest setting, cover and cook for 10–15 minutes.

Remove from the heat, drizzle over the remaining tablespoon vegetable oil, and stir together with a fork. Re-cover the pan and let stand for 2 minutes until the rice has achieved the desired consistency. The rice should be cooked but not too soft or sticky, and the grains should separate easily.

ARROZ CON MARISCOS
SEAFOOD RICE

Serves: 4
Preparation Time: 8 minutes
Cooking Time: 10 minutes

There is a very precise method to follow when preparing this recipe. Cooked rice should be used instead of uncooked rice, in the way that Chinese fried rice dishes are prepared, but this has a distinctive Peruvian flavor.

6 mussels, cleaned
2 tablespoons olive oil, plus extra for drizzling
3 tablespoons Panca Chili, Garlic, and Onion Condiment (see p. 403)
1 tablespoon Yellow Chili Paste (see p. 405)
1 teaspoon turmeric
6 cups (2½ lb/1.2 g) Peruvian-Style Cooked White Rice (see p. 178)

1 cup (8 fl oz/250 ml) mussel broth (stock)
2 cups (18 fl oz/500 ml) fish broth (stock)
4 limpets, chopped
12 shrimp (prawns), peeled and deveined
12 scallops
8 clams
4 × 7-oz (200-g) squid, cleaned and cut into rings
1 tablespoon chopped culantro or cilantro (coriander) leaves
salt and pepper

Cook the mussels in their shells in boiling water for 2 minutes. Let cool slightly, then remove the meat from the shells. Set aside.

Heat the olive oil in a large wok, skillet, or frying pan over medium heat, add the chili, garlic, and onion condiment and chili paste and sauté for 2–3 minutes until the paste has thickened slightly and is fragrant. Add the turmeric and cooked white rice and season with salt and pepper. Mix together well.

Gradually pour over the mussel and fish broths (stocks), then add the limpets and shrimp (prawns), followed by the scallops, mussels, clams, and squid. Cook over high heat for 3 minutes, stirring, until the flavors meld together and the seafood is cooked. Be careful not to let it burn.

Stir through the chopped culantro or cilantro (coriander) leaves, then spoon into large shallow bowls and drizzle with olive oil to finish. Serve.

Seafood Rice

ARROZ CON CARNE
RICE WITH BEEF

Serves: 4
Preparation Time: 15 minutes
Cooking Time: 1 hour 30 minutes

We often used to have this dish at home when we were kids. Then, one day, it disappeared off the menu, never to return. Use beef brisket for a distinctive taste.

½ cup (4 fl oz/120 ml) plus 2 tablespoons vegetable oil
2¼ lb (1 kg) beef brisket, cut into 1¼-inch (3-cm) chunks
1 red onion, chopped
4 cloves garlic, chopped
2 tablespoons Yellow Chili Paste (see p. 405)
4 tablespoons Mirasol Chili Paste (see p. 405)
3½ cups (23 fl oz/850 ml) vegetable broth (stock)
3 cups (1 lb 5 oz/600 g) white long-grain rice
⅓ cup (1½ oz/40 g) peas
1 cup (3 oz/80 g) chopped cabbage
½ red bell pepper, seeded, membrane removed, and diced
1 carrot, diced
1 teaspoon chopped mint leaves
salt and pepper
olive oil, for drizzling

Heat the vegetable oil in a pan. Season the beef chunks with salt, add to the pan, and brown on all sides. Remove the beef chunks and set aside.

In a separate pan, heat 2 tablespoons vegetable oil over medium heat, add the onion and garlic, and sauté for 4 minutes until the onion is softened and translucent. Add the chili pastes and cook for another 6 minutes until the pastes have thickened and are fragrant. Season with salt and pepper.

Stir in the beef and pour over the vegetable broth (stock). Bring to a simmer and cook over medium heat for 30–40 minutes until the meat is tender. Add the rice, peas, cabbage, bell pepper, and carrot to the pan, and adjust the seasoning to taste. Cover and cook for another 25 minutes until the rice is fluffy and the grains have separated.

Spoon onto plates, scatter over the chopped mint leaves, and drizzle with the olive oil. Serve.

ARROZ CON CONCHAS NEGRAS
RICE WITH MANGROVE COCKLES

Serves: 4
Preparation Time: 30 minutes
Cooking Time: 12–15 minutes

If you can't find mangrove cockles at your local market, which is likely, you can prepare this dish with clams and add a few drops of squid ink to the rice.

½ cup (3 oz/80 g) peas
52 mangrove cockles
2 tablespoons vegetable oil
1 red onion, finely chopped
6 cloves garlic, finely chopped
2 yellow chiles, seeded, membrane removed, and chopped
4 tablespoons Yellow Chili Paste (see p. 405)
4 tablespoons white wine
1 green bell pepper, seeded, membrane removed, and diced
6 cups (2½ lb/1.2 kg) Peruvian-Style Cooked White Rice (see p. 178)
½ cup (4 fl oz/120 ml) fish broth (stock), plus extra if necessary
2 sprigs culantro or cilantro (coriander), plus 1 tablespoon chopped leaves
1 tablespoon Tiger Milk (see p. 409)
olive oil, to drizzle
salt and pepper

Put the peas into a pan of boiling salted water and cook for 1½ minutes. Drain and cool in a bowl of ice water. Drain again and set aside.

Open up the mangrove cockles with a sharp knife, reserving the liquid from 40. Remove the meat from all but 4 cockles. Set aside.

Heat the olive oil in a large skillet or frying pan over low heat, add the onion, garlic, and yellow chile, and sauté for 2–3 minutes until the onion starts to soften. Add the chili paste and cook for another 2–3 minutes until the paste thickens and is fragrant, then add the white wine, bell pepper and reserved mangrove cockle liquid. Season with salt and pepper, bring to a simmer, and cook for 2–3 minutes until the alcohol has evaporated.

Stir in the rice and gradually pour over the fish broth (stock), then add the peas and mangrove cockle meat. Add more broth if necessary to ensure that the rice is juicy. Cook for 2 minutes, stirring, until cooked.

Stir through the tiger milk, culantro or cilantro (coriander) sprigs and leaves, spoon into large shallow bowls and drizzle with olive oil. Decorate with the 4 whole cockles.

ARROZ CON PATO A LA LIMEÑA
LIMA-STYLE RICE WITH DUCK

Serves: 4
Preparation Time: 10 minutes
Cooking Time: 2 hours 10 minutes–2 hours 15 minutes

Unlike Northern-style rice with duck, the rice in this dish has a vibrant green color because the culantro or cilantro (coriander) is blended rather than chopped.

- 1 cup (8 fl oz/250 ml) plus 4 tablespoons vegetable oil
- 1 × 4½-lb (2-kg) duck, cut into 8 pieces
- 4 cloves garlic, chopped
- 1 red onion, chopped
- 4 tablespoons Yellow Chili Paste (see p. 405)
- 3 cups (26 fl oz/750 ml) Blended Culantro (see p. 407)
- 1 cup (8 fl oz/250 ml) stout
- 6¼ cups (51 fl oz/1.5 liters) chicken broth (stock)
- 4⅓ cups (1¾ lb/800 g) white long-grain rice
- 1¼ cups (6 oz/175 g) peas
- 1 yellow chile, seeded, membrane removed, and thinly sliced
- 1 cup (8 fl oz/250 ml) Creole Sauce (see p. 416), to serve
- salt

Pour 1 cup (8 fl oz/250 ml) vegetable oil into a pan and heat. Season the duck pieces with salt, add to the pan, and brown on all sides over medium heat. Remove the duck pieces from the pan and set aside.

Add the garlic and onion to the same pan and cook, stirring, for 2–3 minutes until the onion has softened and is translucent. Add the chili paste and blended culantro and cook for another 2–3 minutes until the chili paste has thickened and is fragrant.

Pour the stout into the pan, bring to a simmer, and cook for 2 minutes until the alcohol has evaporated, then add the chicken broth (stock) and bring to a boil. Taste and add more salt if necessary.

Place the duck pieces in the pan, reduce the heat and simmer for about 1½ hours until the meat is tender. Remove the duck and cooking juices from the pan and keep warm. Separate the cooking juices, blend them in a food processor, and drizzle them over the duck to make sure it does not dry out.

Heat the remaining 4 tablespoons oil in the pan over medium heat, add the rice, and lightly fry for 2 minutes, stirring gently with a fork. Add the peas and chiles, pour over the duck cooking juices, and cook, covered, for 20–25 minutes until the rice is fluffy and the grains have separated.

Spoon the rice onto plates and top with the duck pieces. Serve with Creole sauce.

ARROZ CON POLLO
RICE WITH CHICKEN

Serves: 4
Preparation Time: 10 minutes
Cooking Time: 1 hour

This is a homely dish that is served on a weekly basis in homes across Lima. It can also be prepared with duck, pigeon, or pork side (belly).

- 1 cup (8 fl oz/250 ml) vegetable oil
- 1 × 4-lb/1.8-kg whole chicken, cut into 8 pieces
- 4 cloves garlic, chopped
- 1 red onion, chopped
- 2 tablespoons Yellow Chili Paste (see p. 405)
- 3 cups (26 fl oz/750 ml) Blended Culantro (see p. 407)
- 6¼ cups (51 fl oz/1.5 liters) chicken broth (stock)
- 4⅓ cups (1¾ lb/800 g) white long-grain rice
- ½ cup (3 oz/80 g) peas
- 1 carrot, diced
- 1 yellow chile, seeded, membrane removed, and thinly sliced
- ½ red bell pepper, seeded, membrane removed, and thinly sliced
- 2 sprigs culantro or cilantro (coriander), to garnish
- 2 cups (18 fl oz/500 ml) Creole Sauce (see p. 416), to serve (optional)
- salt

Heat the oil in a pan over medium heat. Season the chicken pieces with salt, add to the pan, and brown on all sides. Remove the chicken pieces from the pan and set aside.

Add the garlic and onion to the same pan and cook, stirring, for 4 minutes until the onion has softened and is translucent. Add the chili paste and blended culantro and cook for another 2–3 minutes until the mixture has thickened slightly and is fragrant, then pour over the chicken broth (stock). Bring to a boil, taste, and add more salt if necessary. Place the chicken pieces in the pan and cook for 20 minutes over medium heat until the chicken is cooked through. Remove the chicken and the cooking juices from the pan and keep warm.

Add the rice, peas, carrot, chiles and bell pepper to the pan and continue to cook for 20 minutes until the rice is done—not too soft or sticky. The grains should separate easily.

Spoon the rice onto a serving platter and top with the chicken pieces and reserved cooking juices. Garnish with the culantro or cilantro (coriander) sprigs and serve with Creole sauce, if desired.

ARROZ CON LANGOSTINOS
RICE WITH SHRIMP

Serves: 4
Preparation Time: 15 minutes
Cooking Time: 20–25 minutes

You can try this dish out with *gambas*, (shrimp/prawns), or lobster—all versions will be equally delicious and interesting.

- ½ cup (3 oz/80 g) fava (broad) beans
- 2 tablespoons vegetable oil
- 2 red onions, finely chopped
- 5 cloves garlic, chopped
- 1 cup (8 fl oz/250 ml) Yellow Chili Paste (see p. 405)
- ½ cup (4 fl oz/120 ml) Mirasol Chili Paste (see p. 405)
- 1 red bell pepper, seeded, membrane removed, and diced
- 1 teaspoon ground cumin
- 2 teaspoons dried oregano
- 6 cups (2½ lb/1.2 kg) Peruvian-Style Cooked White Rice (see p. 178)
- 1½ cups (13 fl oz/375 ml) shrimp (prawn) broth (stock)
- 40 small shrimp (prawns), peeled and deveined, with tails still intact
- 2½ oz (65 g) queso fresco, cubed
- 1 sprig culantro or cilantro (coriander)
- 1 sprig huacatay
- salt and pepper

Put the fava (broad) beans into a pan of salted boiling water. Cook for 1½ minutes, drain, and let cool in a bowl of ice water. Drain and set aside.

Heat the oil in a pan over low heat, add the onions and garlic, and sauté for 2–3 minutes until the onions have softened and are translucent. Season with salt and pepper.

Add the chili pastes and continue to cook, stirring, for 2–3 minutes until the chili pastes have thickened slightly and are fragrant. Add the diced bell pepper, cumin, and oregano and cook for another 2–3 minutes until the pepper softens, then stir in the cooked white rice and pour over the shrimp (prawn) broth (stock). Bring to a boil and simmer for 2–3 minutes, then add the shrimp tails, fava beans, and cheese, and mix together well. Cook for another 3–4 minutes over high heat.

Stir through the culantro or cilantro (coriander) and huacatay sprigs to finish and spoon onto plates.

Rice with Shrimp

Northern-Style Rice with Duck

ARROZ CON PATO A LA NORTEÑA
NORTHERN-STYLE RICE WITH DUCK

Serves: 4
Preparation Time: 10 minutes
Cooking Time: 2 hours 25 minutes–2 hours 30 minutes

This is a wonderful dish that Peruvians love to cook and enjoy. It is quite labor-intensive but worth the effort.

1 cup (8 fl oz/250 ml) vegetable oil, plus 4 tablespoons
1 × 4½-lb (2-kg) duck, cut into 8 pieces
4 cloves garlic, chopped
1 red onion, chopped
4 tablespoons Yellow Chili Paste (see p. 405)
2¼ cups (7 oz/200 g) grated loche squash
1 bunch culantro or cilantro (coriander) leaves, chopped
1 cup (8 fl oz/250 ml) stout
6¼ cups (51 fl oz/1.5 liters) chicken broth (stock)
4⅓ cups (1¾ lb/800 g) white long-grain rice
6 oz (175 g) peas
1 yellow chile, seeded, membrane removed, and thinly sliced
½ red bell pepper, seeded, membrane removed, and thinly sliced
2 cups (18 fl oz/500 ml) Creole Sauce (see p. 416), to serve
salt

Pour 1 cup (8 fl oz/250 ml) vegetable oil into a pan and heat. Season the duck pieces with salt, add to the pan, and brown on all sides over medium heat. Remove the duck pieces from the pan and set aside.

Add the garlic and onion to the same pan and cook, stirring, for 4 minutes until the onion has softened and is translucent. Add the grated squash and cook for 2 minutes, then add chili paste and cook for another 6 minutes until the paste has thickened and is fragrant. Add half the chopped culantro or cilantro (coriander) and cook, stirring, for another 2–3 minutes.

Pour the stout into the pan, bring to a simmer, and cook for 2 minutes until the alcohol has evaporated, then add the chicken broth (stock) and bring to a boil. Taste and add more salt if necessary.

Place the duck pieces in the pan and cook over medium heat for about 1½ hours until the meat is tender. Remove the duck and the cooking juices from the pan and keep warm. Separate the cooking juice, blend in a food processor, and drizzle over the duck to make sure it does not dry out.

Heat the remaining 4 tablespoons oil in the pan over medium heat, add the rice, and lightly fry, stirring gently with a fork, for 2 minutes. Add the peas, chile, and bell pepper, pour over the duck cooking juices, and cook for 20–25 minutes, covered, until the rice is fluffy and the grains have separated.

Spoon the rice onto plates, top with the duck pieces, and garnish with the remaining chopped culantro leaves. Serve with Creole sauce.

ARROZ CON CHANCHO
RICE WITH PORK

Serves: 4
Preparation Time: 10 minutes
Cooking Time: 1 hour 15 minutes

This is a dish that used to appear regularly on the tables of Peruvian homes. It is a rice dish in which the cabbage and other vegetables absorb the juices in an absolutely sumptuous way.

⅔ cup (5 fl oz/150 ml) vegetable oil, plus 2 tablespoons for drizzling
2¼ lb (1 kg) pork, cut into 1¼-inch (3-cm) chunks
1 red onion, chopped
4 cloves garlic, chopped
3 tablespoons Panca Chili Paste (see p. 406)
1 tablespoon Mirasol Chili Paste (see p. 405)
1 teaspoon turmeric
3½ cups (23 fl oz/850 ml) vegetable broth (stock)
3 cups (1 lb 5 oz/600 g) white long-grain rice
⅓ cup (1½ oz/40 g) peas
1 cup (3 oz/80 g) chopped cabbage
1 carrot, diced
½ red bell pepper, seeded, membrane removed, and thinly sliced
1 yellow chile, seeded, membrane removed, and thinly sliced
1 tablespoon chopped culantro or cilantro (coriander) leaves
salt and pepper

Heat ½ cup (4 fl oz/120 ml) vegetable oil in a pan over medium heat. Season the pork chunks with salt, add to the pan, and brown on all sides. Remove the pork from the pan and set aside.

In a separate pan, heat the remaining 2 tablespoons of oil over medium heat, add the onion and garlic, and sauté for 4 minutes until the onion is softened and translucent. Add the chili pastes and cook for another 6 minutes until the pastes have thickened slightly and are fragrant, then stir in the turmeric and season with salt and pepper.

Stir in the pork and pour over the vegetable broth (stock). Bring to a simmer and cook over medium heat for 20 minutes until the meat is tender. Add the rice, peas, cabbage, and carrot to the pan, cover, and cook for another 30 minutes until the rice is fluffy and the grains have separated. Stir in the bell pepper and yellow chile to finish.

Spoon onto plates, scatter over the chopped culantro or cilantro (coriander) leaves, and drizzle with the vegetable oil. Serve.

Rice with Pork

Serves: 4
Preparation Time: 15 minutes
Cooking Time: 20 minutes, plus 10 minutes soaking

This is a dish that can be underwhelming when badly prepared, but unforgettable when expertly prepared. The secret is to use chopped, not ground (mince), beef.

3 tablespoons golden raisins
4 tablespoons olive oil
1¾ lb (800g) beef tenderloin (fillet), coarsely chopped
2 red onions, finely chopped
6 cloves garlic, finely chopped
2 tomatoes, skinned, seeded, and grated
3 tablespoons Panca Chili Paste (see p. 406)
1 sprig oregano, leaves removed
1 tablespoon almond meal (ground almonds)
10 black olives, chopped
4 hard-boiled eggs, chopped
2 tablespoons chopped parsley, plus extra to garnish
½ cup (4 fl oz/120 ml) beef or vegetable broth (stock)
5 cups (2¼ lb/1 kg) Peruvian-Style Cooked White Rice (see p. 178)
salt and pepper

ARROZ TAPADO
LAYERED RICE AND BEEF STEW

Soak the golden raisins in 4 tablespoons warm water for 10 minutes then drain and set aside.

Heat 2 tablespoons olive oil in a pan over high heat. Season the chopped beef with salt and pepper, add to the pan, and brown on all sides. Remove from the pan and set aside.

Heat 2 tablespoons olive oil in a Dutch oven (casserole dish) over low heat, add the onions and garlic, and sauté for 4 minutes until the onions are soft and translucent. Add the grated tomatoes and chili paste and cook, stirring, for another 2–3 minutes until the mixture has thickened slightly and is fragrant, then stir in the oregano, browned meat, raisins, almond meal (ground almonds), and olives. Cook for 1 minute, then gently stir in the egg and parsley, and pour over the beef or vegetable broth (stock). Mix everything together well.

Spoon half the cooked rice in an even layer over the bottom of a deep round dish or 4 large ramekins. Cover with the stew and finish with the remaining rice, pressing the layered ingredients down to compact them.

Carefully flip the dish or ramekins onto a serving platter or individual plates, releasing the ingredients to form a tower. Garnish with a little extra chopped parsley and serve.

ARROZ CHAUFA
CHAUFA FRIED RICE

Serves: 4
Preparation Time: 15 minutes
Cooking Time: 15 minutes

This is a dish that will come to the rescue whenever you need it to. It's quick, easy, and heart-warming—anyone can make a delicious Chaufa fried rice at home.

3 tablespoons vegetable oil
6 eggs, beaten
14 oz (400 g) skinless chicken legs or breasts, cut into ½ x 1¼-inch (1 × 3-cm) strips
¼-inch (5-mm) piece fresh ginger, peeled and chopped
1 clove garlic, chopped
6 cups (2¼ lb/1.2 kg) Peruvian-Style Cooked White Rice (see p. 178)
½ red bell pepper, seeded, membrane removed, and diced
4 tablespoons soy sauce
pinch of granulated sugar
¾ cup (1½ oz/40 g) chopped scallion (spring onion), green part only
½ teaspoon sesame oil
salt

Heat 1 tablespoon vegetable oil in a large skillet or wok over medium heat, add the beaten eggs, and cook for 2 minutes. Flip over and cook for 2 minutes on the other side. Once cooked, remove the omelet from the pan, chop into pieces, and set aside.

Season the chicken pieces with salt, add to the pan, and sauté over high heat for 6 minutes until cooked and juicy. Remove from the pan and set aside.

Wipe the pan clean with paper towels and heat 2 tablespoons vegetable oil over medium heat. Add the chopped ginger and garlic and cook, stirring, for a few seconds, then add the rice and bell pepper and stir-fry for another 2–3 minutes.

Add the chicken pieces and soy sauce and stir. Add the omelet pieces and sugar, season with salt, and stir-fry for 1 minute. Add the chopped scallion (spring onion) and sesame oil and mix together thoroughly.

ARROZ CON CONCHAS
RICE WITH SCALLOPS

Serves: 4
Preparation Time: 10 minutes
Cooking Time: 10–15 minutes

The secret of this rice dish is to be sure that the scallops are juicy and retain their seafood flavor, which is achieved by cooking them quickly over high heat.

2 tablespoons vegetable oil
1 red onion, finely chopped
6 cloves garlic, finely chopped
2 yellow chiles, seeded and chopped
4 tablespoons Yellow Chili Paste (see p. 405)
½ cup (4 fl oz/120 ml) chicha de jora or white wine
6 cups (2½ lb/1.2 kg) Peruvian-Style Cooked White Rice (see p. 178)
½ cup (4 fl oz/120 ml) mussel broth (stock)
½ cup (4 fl oz/120 ml) fish broth (stock)
½ cup (3 oz/80 g) fava (broad) beans
48 × 1-oz/25-g scallops
2 sprigs culantro or cilantro (coriander), plus 1 tablespoon chopped leaves
salt and pepper
olive oil, for drizzling

Heat the vegetable oil in a large skillet or frying pan over low heat, add the onion, garlic, and chiles and cook, stirring, for 2–3 minutes until the onion starts to soften. Add the chili paste and cook for another 2–3 minutes, stirring, until the paste has thickened and is fragrant.

Pour over the chicha de jora or white wine, bring to a simmer, and cook over medium heat for 2–3 minutes until the alcohol has evaporated. Stir in the cooked white rice and season with salt and pepper. Pour over the mussel and fish broths (stocks). Add the fava (broad) beans and scallops, bring to a simmer, and cook for 2–3 minutes or until the beans are tender and the scallops are cooked through.

Stir through the culantro or cilantro (coriander) sprigs and chopped leaves, then spoon into large shallow bowls. Drizzle with olive oil to finish. Serve.

ARROZ CHAUFA AEROPUERTO
AIRPORT-STYLE CHAUFA FRIED RICE

Serves: 4
Preparation Time: 10 minutes
Cooking Time: 25 minutes

This dish is an "airport-style" dish as everything and anything lands on it. It is a rice dish that has gradually won over Peruvians and people all over the world, being the most popular dish in our Chicago restaurant.

- 2 cups (18 fl oz/500 ml) vegetable oil
- 7 oz (200 g) Chinese egg noodles
- 14 oz (400 g) skinless chicken legs or breasts, cut into 20 g boneless chunks
- ¼-inch (5-mm) piece fresh ginger, peeled and chopped
- 1 clove garlic, chopped
- ½ red bell pepper, seeded, membrane removed, and thinly sliced
- ⅔ cup (1½ oz/40 g) snow peas (mangetout), thinly sliced
- 5 cups (2¼ lb/1 kg) Peruvian-Style Cooked White Rice (see p. 178)
- 2 tablespoons oyster sauce
- 1 tablespoon soy sauce
- pinch of granulated sugar
- 2 scallions (spring onions), green part only, chopped
- ½ teaspoon sesame oil
- salt

Heat 2 cups (18 fl oz/500 ml) vegetable oil to 350°F/180°C in a large pan or deep fryer, add the noodles, and deep-fry until golden and crispy. Remove and let drain on paper towels.

Heat 2 tablespoons vegetable oil in a large skillet or wok until very hot. Season the chicken with salt, add to the pan, and sauté over high heat for 6 minutes until cooked and juicy. Remove and set aside.

Wipe the pan clean with paper towels and heat 2 tablespoons vegetable oil over medium heat. Add the chopped ginger and garlic and cook, stirring, for a few seconds, then add the bell pepper, snow peas (mangetout), cooked white rice, oyster sauce, and soy sauce. Stir-fry for another 2–3 minutes.

Add the chicken pieces, stir-fried Chinese noodles and sugar, season with salt, and stir-fry for 1 minute. Add the chopped scallion (spring onion) and sesame oil and mix together thoroughly. Spoon onto a platter and serve.

ARROZ CHAUFA A LO POBRE
POOR MAN'S CHAUFA FRIED RICE

Serves: 4
Preparation Time: 12 minutes
Cooking Time: 12–14 minutes

A dish is known as a "poor man's dish" in Peru when it is garnished with fried eggs and bananas. This turns *Chaufa* fried rice into a complete meal.

- 4 tablespoons vegetable oil
- 4 bananas, sliced in half lengthwise
- 14 oz (400 g) skinless chicken legs or breasts, cut into 1¼-inch (3-cm) boneless chunks
- ¼-inch (5-mm) piece fresh ginger, peeled and chopped
- 1 clove garlic, chopped
- 6 cups (2½ lb/1.2 kg) Peruvian-Style Cooked White Rice (see p. 178)
- ½ red bell pepper, seeded, membrane removed, and diced
- ½ teaspoon soy sauce
- pinch of granulated sugar
- 2 scallions (spring onions), green part only, chopped
- ½ teaspoon sesame oil
- salt

To serve
- 8 fried eggs
- 2 tablespoons vegetable oil

Heat a little vegetable oil in a skillet or frying pan over medium heat, add the banana halves, and cook for 1 minute on each side until browned. Set aside.

Season the chicken with salt, add to the same pan, and sauté over high heat for 5 minutes until cooked and juicy. Remove from the pan and set aside.

Wipe the pan clean with paper towels and heat 2 tablespoons vegetable oil over medium heat. Add the ginger and garlic, and cook, stirring, for a few seconds, then add the rice and bell pepper and stir-fry for another 2–3 minutes.

Add the browned chicken, soy sauce, and sugar, season with salt, and stir-fry for 1 minute. Add the chopped scallion (spring onion) and sesame oil and mix together thoroughly.

Spoon the rice onto a platter, top with the fried eggs, halved bananas, and serve.

Airport-Style Chaufa Fried Rice

ARROZ CHAUFA CHARAPA
AMAZONIAN CHAUFA FRIED RICE

Serves: 4
Preparation Time: 12 minutes
Cooking Time: 15 minutes

Pope John Paul II came to the Peruvian Amazon and declared in his speech that the Pope was a *charapa*, a word that is affectionately used to describe inhabitants of the Peruvian Amazon.

4 tablespoons vegetable oil
6 eggs, beaten
7 oz (200 g) skinless chicken legs or breasts, cut into 1¼-inch (3-cm) boneless chunks
¼-inch (5-mm) piece fresh ginger, peeled and chopped
1 clove garlic, chopped
1 teaspoon turmeric
2 oz/50 g Amazonian chorizo, chopped
2 oz/50 g smoked beef or pork, chopped
6 cups (1½ lb/1.2 kg) Peruvian-Style Cooked White Rice (see p. 178)
½ red bell pepper, seeded, membrane removed, and diced
pinch of granulated sugar
2 scallions (spring onions), green part only, chopped
1 tablespoon chopped sacha culantro or cilantro (coriander) leaves
½ teaspoon sesame oil
salt

Heat 2 tablespoons vegetable oil in a large skillet or wok, add the beaten eggs, and cook for 2 minutes. Flip over and cook for 2 minutes on the other side. Once cooked, remove the omelet from the pan, chop into pieces, and set aside.

Season the chicken pieces with salt, add to the same pan, and sauté over high heat for 6 minutes until cooked and juicy. Remove from the pan and set aside.

Wipe the pan clean with paper towels and heat 2 tablespoons vegetable oil over medium heat. Add the chopped ginger, garlic, turmeric, chorizo, and smoked beef and cook, stirring, for a few seconds, then add the cooked white rice and bell pepper and stir-fry for another 2–3 minutes.

Add the chicken pieces, omelet pieces, and sugar, season with salt, and stir-fry for 1 minute. Add the chopped scallion (spring onion), sacha culantro or cilantro (coriander) leaves, and sesame oil and mix together thoroughly. Spoon onto a platter and serve.

ARROZ BACHICHE
BACHICHE RICE

Serves: 4
Preparation Time: 8 minutes
Cooking Time: 8–10 minutes

This rice dish shows how Peruvian cuisine has been influenced by Italian cuisine, because *bachiche* was the derogatory name given to early Italian immigrants. We are now redefining this word, which was previously used to describe those who arrived in our country with very little but their dreams and limited resources.

2 tablespoons olive oil, plus extra for drizzling
3 tablespoons Yellow Chili, Garlic, and Onion Condiment (see p. 402)
1 tablespoon Yellow Chili Paste (see p. 405)
1 green bell pepper, seeded, membrane removed, and diced
2 tablespoons white wine
6 cups (2½ lb/1.2 kg) Peruvian-Style Cooked White Rice (see p. 178)
2 tablespoons squid ink
½ cup (4 fl oz/120 ml) fish broth (stock)
½ cup (4 fl oz/120 ml) mussel broth (stock)
12 squid, sliced into rings
½ cup (1½ oz/40 g) grated Parmesan cheese
1 tablespoon chopped parsley leaves
1 sprig culantro or cilantro (coriander)
salt and pepper

Heat the olive oil in a large skillet or wok over medium heat and cook the chili, garlic, and onion condiment and chili paste, stirring, for 2–3 minutes until the mix has thickened slightly and is fragrant. Add the bell pepper and cook for another 2–3 minutes. Season with salt and pepper to taste, then stir in the white wine, cooked white rice, squid ink, and ¾ cup (6 fl oz/175 ml) of each of the broths (stocks). Mix together well.

Add the squid rings, bring to a simmer and cook for 2 minutes, then add the remaining broth. Continue to cook, stirring, for 1 minute until the flavors meld. Stir in the Parmesan cheese and chopped parsley leaves and cilantro (coriander) sprig to finish.

Spoon into large shallow bowls and drizzle over a little extra olive oil. Serve.

ARROZ ARVEJADO
RICE WITH BLENDED PEAS

Serves: 4
Preparation Time: 10 minutes
Cooking Time: 20 minutes

This rice goes well with *sudado* dishes—it is a light and flavorsome side dish.

12 oz (350 g) peas in the pods
2 tablespoons olive oil
2 red onions, finely chopped
6 cloves garlic, finely chopped
3 cups (1 lb 5 oz/600 g) white long-grain rice
salt and pepper

Shell the peas, put them in a pan, and cover with water. Bring to a boil and cook for 3 minutes until tender. Drain, then put three-quarters of the peas in a food processor and blend briefly to a coarse paste. Set aside.

Heat the olive oil in a Dutch oven (casserole dish) over low heat, add the onions and garlic, and sauté for 4 minutes until the onions have softened. Season with salt and pepper, add the blended peas, and cook for another 2 minutes until the ingredients have melded together.

Add the rice to the pan, pour over 3 cups (26 fl oz / 750 ml) water, and bring to a simmer. Cook over low heat for 6 minutes until the rice is fluffy and the grains have separated. Stir through the remaining peas and serve.

ARROZ CHAUFA DE MARISCOS
SEAFOOD CHAUFA FRIED RICE

Serves: 4
Preparation Time: 20 minutes
Cooking Time: 10 minutes

You can try this dish out with any seafood from your local area or market. Don't hesitate to adapt it to your world because it will be tasty no matter what.

4 tablespoons vegetable oil
8 eggs, beaten
12 shrimp (prawns), peeled and deveined
12 scallops
3 oz/80 g Cooked Octopus (see p. 406)
2 × 7-oz (200-g) squid, cleaned and cut into rings
1 red bell pepper, seeded, membrane removed, and diced
⅔ cup (1½ oz/40 g) snow peas (mangetout), sliced into thirds
½ cup (1½ oz/40 g) broccoli, chopped
pinch of granulated sugar
2 tablespoons oyster sauce
1 cup (8 fl oz/250 ml) chicken broth (stock)
2 tablespoons soy sauce
¼-inch (5-mm) piece fresh ginger, peeled and chopped
1 clove garlic, chopped
6 cups (2½ lb/1.2 kg) Peruvian-Style Cooked White Rice (see p. 178)
2 tablespoons bean sprouts
2 scallions (spring onions), green part only, chopped
½ teaspoon sesame oil
salt

Heat 2 tablespoons vegetable oil in a large skillet or wok, add the beaten eggs, and cook for 2 minutes. Flip over and cook for 2 minutes on the other side. Once cooked, remove the omelet from the pan and set aside.

Season the shrimp (prawns) and scallops with salt, add to the same pan, and sauté over high heat for a few seconds until the shrimp are colored. Add the octopus and squid and sauté for another 40 seconds, then add the bell pepper, snow peas (mangetout), and broccoli and sauté for 1 minute.

Stir in the sugar, oyster sauce, chicken broth (stock), and half the soy sauce and adjust the seasoning to taste. Remove from the pan, set aside, and keep warm.

Wipe the pan clean with paper towels, add 2 tablespoons vegetable oil, and heat for 1 minute. Add the chopped ginger and garlic and cook, stirring, for a few seconds, then add the cooked white rice and stir-fry for 30 seconds to 1 minute until the rice is lightly browned. Add the bean sprouts and remaining soy sauce and stir through the scallion (spring onions), and sesame oil to finish. Mix together well.

Spoon the rice onto a serving platter and top with the omelet and sautéed seafood mixture. Serve.

Quinoa Chaufa

CHAUFA DE QUINUA
QUINOA CHAUFA

Serves: 4
Preparation Time: 10 minutes
Cooking Time: 10 minutes

This is an easy dish to prepare, which can also be made with just one type of quinoa—whatever type you can find locally.

1⅓ cups (9 oz/250g) cooked white quinoa
1⅓ cups (9 oz/250g) cooked red quinoa
1⅓ cups (9 oz/250g) cooked black quinoa
3 tablespoons vegetable oil
6 eggs, beaten
¼-inch (5-mm) piece fresh ginger, peeled and chopped
1 clove garlic, chopped
3 oz (80 g) asparagus, chopped
3 oz (80 g) broccoli, chopped
½ red or green bell pepper, seeded, membrane removed, and diced
pinch of granulated sugar
2 scallions (spring onions), green part only, chopped
½ teaspoon sesame oil
salt

Put the white, red, and black quinoa together in a bowl and mix together well. Set aside.

Heat 2 tablespoons vegetable oil in a large skillet or wok, add the beaten eggs and cook for 2 minutes. Flip over and cook for 2 minutes on the other side. Once cooked, remove the omelet from the pan, chop into pieces and set aside.

Wipe the pan clean with paper towels and add 1 tablespoon vegetable oil. Add the chopped ginger and garlic and cook, stirring, for a few seconds, then add the asparagus, broccoli, and bell pepper and stir-fry for another 2–3 minutes.

Add the quinoa, omelet pieces, and sugar, season with salt, and stir-fry for 1 minute. Add the chopped scallion (spring onion) and sesame oil and mix together thoroughly. Spoon onto a platter and serve.

ARROZ CON CHOCLO
PERUVIAN CORN RICE

Serves: 4
Preparation Time: 10 minutes
Cooking Time: 35–40 minutes

I used to love eating freshly prepared Peruvian corn rice at home. It's almost addictive and tempting to eat it straight from the pan!

1 corncob
pinch of sugar
2 tablespoons olive oil
4 cloves garlic, chopped
3 cups (1 lb 5 oz/600 g) white long-grain rice
1 tablespoon butter
salt

Put the corncob in a pan with cold water and a pinch of salt and sugar. Bring to a boil and boil until tender. Drain, let cool slightly, and remove the kernels. Set aside.

Heat the olive oil in a Dutch oven (casserole dish) over low heat, add the garlic, and sauté for 4 minutes until the garlic has softened but not browned.

Add 3½ cups (23 fl oz/850 ml) water, bring to a boil and add the rice and corn. Season with salt and stir together, then cover and cook over very low heat for 10–15 minutes until the rice is cooked but not too soft or sticky. The grains should separate easily.

Remove from the heat, add the butter and stir together with a fork. Re-cover the pan and let stand for 2 minutes, until the rice has achieved the desired consistency and is not too soft. Serve.

Serves: 6
Preparation Time: 10 minutes
Cooking Time: 30–40 minutes

This simple and delicious rice dish goes perfectly with any Peruvian stew.

1 corncob
pinch of sugar
2 tablespoons olive oil
1 small red onion, finely chopped
6 cloves garlic, finely chopped
1 tablespoon turmeric
1 tablespoon Yellow Chili Paste (see p. 405)
3 cups (1 lb 5 oz/600 g) white long-grain rice
6 oz (175 g) peas
2 carrots, diced
1 tablespoon butter
1 tablespoon chopped parsley
salt and pepper

ARROZ A LA JARDINERA
RICE A LA JARDINERA

Put the corncob in a pan with cold water and a pinch of salt and sugar. Bring to a boil and cook until tender. Drain, let cool slightly, and remove the kernels. Set aside.

Heat the olive oil in a Dutch oven (casserole dish) over low heat, add the onion and garlic, and sauté for 4 minutes until the onion has softened but not browned. Add the turmeric and chili paste, season with salt and pepper, and cook for another 8 minutes until the paste has thickened slightly and is fragrant.

Add 3½ cups (23 fl oz/850 ml) water, bring to a boil and add the rice, corn, peas, and carrots. Season with salt and stir together, then cover and cook over very low heat for 10–15 minutes until the rice is cooked but not too soft or sticky. The grains should separate easily.

Remove from the heat, add the butter, and stir together with a fork. Re-cover the pan and let stand for 2 minutes until the rice has achieved the desired consistency and is not too soft. Stir through the chopped parsley and serve.

AGUADITO DE CHOROS
MUSSEL AGUADITO SOUP

Serves: 4
Preparation Time: 25 minutes
Cooking Time: 1 hour

This is one of my favorite dishes, which also happens to be a superb hangover cure.

1 corncob
pinch of sugar
2 yellow potatoes
6 oz (175 g) peas, shelled
2 carrots, cut into ¼-inch (5-mm) cubes
1½ cups (13 fl oz/375 ml) white wine
1 celery stalk, chopped
24 large mussels, cleaned
½ cup (4 fl oz/120 ml) vegetable oil
1 red onion, chopped
4 cloves garlic, chopped
4 tablespoons Yellow Chili Paste (see p. 405)
½ cup (4 fl oz/120 ml) Blended Culantro (see p. 407)
½ cup (4 fl oz/120 ml) beer (lager)
8½ cups (68 fl oz/2 liters) fish broth (stock)
4 cups (1¾ lb/800 g) Peruvian-Style Cooked White Rice (see p. 178)
2 yellow chiles, seeded, membrane removed, and sliced
salt and pepper

Put the corncob in a pan with cold water and a pinch of salt and sugar. Bring to a boil and cook until tender. Drain, let cool slightly, and remove the kernels. Set aside.

Put the potatoes in a pan with cold water. Bring to a boil and cook for 15–20 minutes. Drain and peel, then set aside.

Put the peas in a pan with cold water, and bring to a boil. Cook for 1½ minutes until tender, then drain and set aside.

Put the carrots in a pan with cold water. Bring to a boil and cook for 5–7 minutes. Drain and dice, then set aside.

Pour the white wine into a pan. Add the chopped celery and mussels, cover, and cook over medium heat for 8 minutes until the mussels have opened but remain juicy. Remove from the heat.

Strain the mussel cooking liquid into a bowl, remove the mussels from their shells, and add to the liquid. Set aside.

Heat the vegetable oil in a separate pan over medium heat, add the onion and garlic, and sauté for 3 minutes until the onion is slightly caramelized. Add the chili paste and cook for another 6 minutes, until the mixture has separated and appears to curdle.

Stir in the blended culantro and cook for 4 minutes. Pour the beer (lager) into a pan, bring to a simmer over low heat, and cook for 2 minutes until the alcohol has evaporated. Add 1 cup (8 fl oz/250 ml) of the mussel cooking liquid and the fish broth (stock) and simmer for another 8 minutes until the liquid has reduced by a third, then stir in the cooked rice, peas, carrots, corn, and yellow potatoes. Season to taste with salt and pepper and simmer for another 12 minutes over medium heat until the flavors have melded together.

Stir in the yellow chile and reserved mussels and cook for a final 2 minutes, then spoon into large shallow bowls. Serve.

Serves: 4
Preparation Time: 15 minutes
Cooking Time: 1 hour 55 minutes

This *aguadito* soup can also be prepared with pigeon, chicken, or guinea fowl.

2 yellow potatoes
⅓ cup (3 oz/80 g) peas
½ carrot, cut into ¼-inch (5-mm) cubes
½ cup (4 fl oz/120 ml) vegetable oil
2¼ lb (1 kg) turkey meat, cut into 1¼-inch (3-cm) chunks
2 red onions, finely chopped
9 cloves garlic, finely chopped
pinch of ground cumin
6 tablespoons Yellow Chili Paste (see p. 405)
3 tablespoons Mirasol Chili Paste (see p. 405)
3 sprigs culantro or cilantro (coriander)
¼ cup (2 fl oz/50 ml) beer
¼ cup (2 fl oz/50 ml) chicha de jora
4 cups (34 fl oz/1 liter) chicken broth (stock)
¼ cup (2 fl oz/50 ml) Blended Culantro (see p. 407)
4 cups (1¾ lb/800 g) Peruvian-Style Cooked White Rice (see p. 178)
juice of 2 small lemons
salt and pepper

AGUADITO DE PAVITA
TURKEY AGUADITO SOUP

Put the potatoes in a pan with cold water. Bring to a boil and cook for 15–20 minutes. Drain and peel then cut into ½-inch/1-cm cubes. Set aside.

Put the peas in a pan with cold water and bring to a boil. Cook for 1½ minutes until tender, then drain and set aside.

Put the carrots in a pan with cold water. Bring to a boil and cook for 5–7 minutes, until tender. Drain and set aside.

Pour the vegetable oil, reserving 4 tablespoons, into a pan over high heat. Season the turkey pieces with salt and pepper, add to the pan, and brown on all sides. Remove the turkey pieces from the pan and set aside.

Heat 2 tablespoons oil in a separate pan, add two-thirds of the onion and two-thirds of the chopped garlic, and sauté for 2–3 minutes over low heat until the onion softens. Stir in the cumin, season with salt and pepper, and cook, stirring, for another 2–3 minutes, then add 4 tablespoons yellow chili paste and 2 tablespoons of mirasol chili paste. Continue to cook for a few minutes over medium heat until the mixture has thickened slightly and is fragrant.

Add the browned turkey pieces and 2 culantro or cilantro (coriander) sprigs to the pan, pour the beer, chicha de jora, and chicken broth (stock) into the pan, and bring to a simmer. Cook for 1 hour over low heat, or until the turkey is tender. Remove the turkey pieces from the pan, setting both the meat and the cooking juices aside.

In another pan, heat the remaining vegetable oil over medium heat, add the remaining garlic, and onion and cook, stirring, for 3 minutes. Add the remaining chili pastes, reduce the heat to low and continue to cook until the mixture has separated and appears to curdle.

Stir in the blended culantro and cook for 4 minutes. Stir in the cooked rice, peas, carrot, and potatoes and cook for a final 2–3 minutes over medium heat until the flavors have melded together.

Stir the turkey pieces, remaining culantro sprig, and lemon juice into the soup and season with salt. Spoon into large shallow bowls and serve.

AGUADITO DE PATO
DUCK AGUADITO SOUP

Serves: 4
Preparation Time: 15 minutes
Cooking Time: 2 hours 30 minutes

You can use any type of squash to prepare this lovely, fortifying dish.

2 yellow potatoes
½ cup (4 fl oz/120 ml) vegetable oil
1 × 5 ½-lb (2.5-kg) duck, cut into 8 pieces
2 red onions, finely chopped
9 cloves garlic, finely chopped
3½ oz (100 g) loche squash, grated
pinch of ground cumin
6 tablespoons Yellow Chili Paste (see p. 405)
3 tablespoons Mirasol Chili Paste (see p. 405)
2 sprigs culantro or cilantro (coriander)
¼ cup (2 fl oz/50 ml) beer
¼ cup (2 fl oz/50 ml) chicha de jora
4 cups (34 fl oz/1 liter) chicken or duck broth (stock)
¼ cup (2 fl oz/50 ml) Blended Culantro (see p. 407)
4 cups (1¾ lb/800 g) Peruvian-Style Cooked White Rice (see p. 178)
⅓ cup (3 oz80 g) peas
juice of 3 bitter oranges
salt and pepper

Put the potatoes in a pan with cold water. Bring to a boil and cook for 15–20 minutes. Drain, peel and cut in ¾-inch/1.5-cm cubes. Set aside.

Pour the vegetable oil, reserving 4 tablespoons, into a pan over high heat. Season the duck pieces with salt, add to the pan, and brown on all sides. Remove the duck pieces from the pan and set aside.

Heat 2 tablespoons oil in a separate pan, add two-thirds of the onion, two-thirds of the chopped garlic, and the loche squash, and sauté for 2–3 minutes over low heat until the onion starts to soften. Stir in the cumin, season with salt and pepper, and cook, stirring, for another 2–3 minutes, then add 4 tablespoons yellow chili paste and 2 tablespoons mirasol chili paste. Continue to cook the ingredients for a few minutes over medium heat until the mixture has thickened slightly and is fragrant.

Add the browned duck pieces and culantro or cilantro (coriander) sprigs to the pan, pour the beer, chicha de jora, and chicken or duck broth (stock) into the pan, and bring to a simmer. Cook for 1½ hours, or until the duck is tender. Let cool, then remove the duck meat from the bones, setting aside the meat and the duck cooking juices.

In another pan, heat the remaining vegetable oil over medium heat, add the remaining garlic and onion, and cook, stirring, for 3 minutes. Add the remaining chili pastes, reduce the heat to low, and continue to cook for 8 minutes until the mixture separates and appears to curdle.

Stir in the blended culantro and cook for 4 minutes until slightly reduced. Stir in the cooked rice, peas, and potatoes and cook for a final 2–3 minutes over medium heat until the flavors have melded together.

Stir the duck meat and orange juice into the soup and season with salt. Spoon into large shallow bowls and serve.

AGUADITO DE MARISCOS
SEAFOOD AGUADITO SOUP

Serves: 4
Preparation Time: 30 minutes
Cooking Time: 1 hour

You will need to use the freshest seafood you can find at your local market to prepare this dish.

1 corncob
pinch of sugar
2 yellow potatoes
2 carrots, cut into ¼-inch (5-mm) cubes
12 mussels, cleaned
½ cup (4 fl oz/120 ml) vegetable oil
4 cloves garlic, chopped
1 red onion, chopped
4 tablespoons Yellow Chili Paste (see p. 405)
½ cup (4 fl oz/120 ml) Blended Culantro (see p. 407)
½ cup (4 fl oz/120 ml) white wine
8½ cups (68 fl oz/2 liters) fish broth (stock)
4 cups (1¾ lb/800 g) Peruvian-Style Cooked White Rice (see p. 178)
⅔ cup (6 oz/175 g) peas
2 yellow chiles, seeded, membrane removed, and sliced
12 shrimp (prawns) peeled and deveined
4 limpets, cooked and chopped
4 × 7-oz (200-g) squid, cleaned and cut into rings
12 scallops
8 clams, cut into 3 pieces
¼ cup (3 oz/80 g) Cooked Octopus (see p. 406)
salt and pepper

Put the corncob in a pan with cold water and a pinch salt and sugar. Bring to a boil and cook until tender. Drain, let cool slightly, and remove the kernels. Set aside.

Put the potatoes in a pan with cold water. Bring to a boil and cook for 15–20 minutes. Drain, peel, and cut in ½-inch/1-cm cubes. Set aside.

Put the carrots in a pan with cold water. Bring to a boil and cook for 5–7 minutes. Drain and dice, then set aside.

Cook the mussels in their shells in boiling water for 2 minutes. Let cool slightly, then remove the meat from the shells. Set aside.

Heat the vegetable oil in a pan over medium heat, add the garlic and onion, and sauté for 3 minutes until the onion is lightly caramelized. Add the chili paste, reduce the heat to low, and continue to cook for 8 minutes until the mixture has separated and appears to curdle.

Stir in the blended culantro and cook for 4 minutes until reduced slightly. Pour in the white wine, bring to a simmer, and cook for 2 minutes until the alcohol has evaporated. Add the fish broth (stock) and simmer for 8 minutes, then stir in the cooked rice, peas, carrots, corn, and yellow potatoes. Season to taste with salt and pepper and simmer for 12 minutes over medium heat until the flavors have melded together.

Stir in the yellow chiles, shrimp (prawns), limpets, squid, scallops, and clams and cook for another 2 minutes until the seafood is cooked, then add the cooked octopus and mussels. Adjust the seasoning to taste and mix everything together well. Spoon into large shallow bowls and serve.

Seafood Aguadito Soup

Serves: 4
Preparation Time: 15 minutes
Cooking Time: 1 hour

You can prepare this dish with any type of fish, provided it is very fresh.

½ corncob
pinch of sugar
2 yellow potatoes
1 carrot
½ cup (4 fl oz/120 ml) vegetable oil
4 cloves garlic, chopped
1 red onion, chopped
4 tablespoons Yellow Chili Paste (see p. 405)
½ cup (4 fl oz/120 ml) Blended Culantro (see p. 407)
½ cup (4 fl oz/120 ml) white wine
8½ cups (68 fl oz/2 liters) fish broth (stock)
4 cups (1¾ lb/800 g) Peruvian-Style Cooked White Rice (see p. 178)
6 oz (175 g) peas
2 yellow chiles, seeded, membrane removed, and sliced
1 bell pepper, seeded, membrane removed, and thinly sliced
1¾ lb (800 g) grouper fillets, cut into 2-oz (50-g) chunks
2 sprigs culantro or cilantro (coriander)
3 small lemons, juiced
salt and pepper

AGUADITO DE MERO
GROUPER AGUADITO SOUP

Put the corncob in a pan with cold water and a pinch of salt and sugar. Bring to a boil and cook until tender. Drain, let cool slightly, and remove the kernels. Set aside.

Put the potatoes in a pan with cold water. Bring to a boil and cook for 15–20 minutes. Drain and peel, then cut into ½-inch/1-cm cubes. Set aside.

Cut the carrot into ¼-inch/5-mm cubes and put in a pan with cold water. Bring to a boil and cook for 5–7 minutes, until tender. Drain and set aside.

Heat the vegetable oil in a pan over medium heat, add the garlic and onion, and sauté for 3 minutes until the onion is lightly caramelized. Add the chili paste, reduce the heat to low, and continue to cook for 2–3 minutes until the mixture has separated and appears to curdle.

Stir in the blended culantro and cook for 4 minutes until reduced slightly. Pour in the white wine, bring to a simmer, and cook for 2 minutes until the alcohol has evaporated. Add the fish broth (stock) and simmer for 8 minutes, then stir in the cooked rice, peas, carrot, corn, and yellow potatoes. Season to taste with salt and pepper and simmer for 12 minutes over medium heat until the flavors have melded together.

Stir in the yellow chiles, bell pepper, and fish pieces. Cover and cook for another 2–3 minutes until the fish is cooked through, then add the culantro or cilantro (coriander) sprigs and lemon juice. Spoon into large shallow bowls and serve.

AGUADITO DE PEJESAPO CON CANGREJO
ANGLER FISH AND CRAB AGUADITO SOUP

Serves: 4
Preparation Time: 15 minutes
Cooking Time: 45 minutes

You should use rockfish and rock crab to prepare this dish. They will infuse it with intense and memorable flavors.

- 4 × 1-lb/450-g crabs
- ½ corncob
- pinch of sugar
- 2 yellow potatoes
- 1 carrot
- 3 tablespoons olive oil
- 4 cloves garlic, chopped
- 1 red onion, chopped
- 4 tablespoons Yellow Chili Paste (see p. 405)
- ½ cup (4 fl oz/120 ml) Blended Culantro (see p. 407)
- ½ cup (4 fl oz/120 ml) white wine
- 8½ cups (68 fl oz/2 liters) fish broth (stock)
- 4 cups (1¾ lb/800 g) Peruvian-Style Cooked White Rice (see p. 178)
- 6 oz (175 g) peas
- 2 yellow chiles, seeded, membrane removed, and sliced
- 1 bell pepper, seeded, membrane removed, and thinly sliced
- 2 × 3½-oz (100-g) angler fish fillets
- 2 sprigs culantro or cilantro (coriander)
- ¼ cup (2½ oz/65 g) crab meat
- 4 rocoto chile slices
- juice of 3 small lemons
- salt and pepper

Lightly smash the crabs with a meat mallet or other heavy kitchen tool, to break the shells. Set aside.

Put the corncob in a pan with cold water and a pinch of salt and sugar. Bring to a boil and cook until tender. Drain, let cool slightly, and remove the kernels. Set aside.

Put the potatoes in a pan with cold water. Bring to a boil and cook for 15–20 minutes. Drain and peel then cut into ½-inch/1-cm cubes. Set aside.

Cut the carrots into ¼-inch/5-mm cubes and put in a pan with cold water. Bring to a boil and cook for 5–7 minutes, until tender. Drain and set aside.

Heat the olive oil in a pan over medium heat, add the garlic and onion, and sauté for 3 minutes until the onion is translucent. Add the chili paste, reduce the heat to low, and continue to cook for 2–3 minutes until the mixture has separated and appears to curdle.

Stir in the blended culantro and cook for about 4 minutes, then add the crabs, white wine, and fish broth (stock). Bring to a simmer and cook for 2–3 minutes until the alcohol has evaporated, then stir in the cooked rice, peas, carrots, corn, and yellow potatoes. Season to taste with salt and pepper and simmer for 6 minutes over medium heat until the flavors have melded together.

Stir in the yellow chiles and bell pepper and carefully place the fish fillets in the pan. Cover and cook for 6 minutes, until the fish is cooked through. Add the culantro or cilantro (coriander), crab meat, rocoto chile, and lemon juice and mix together well. Spoon into large shallow bowls and serve.

Chicken Aguadito Soup

AGUADITO DE POLLO
CHICKEN AGUADITO SOUP

Serves: 4
Preparation Time: 10 minutes
Cooking Time: 1 hour 30 minutes

This is a dish that is often served at Peruvian weddings and celebrations, right at the end of the evening. It means you go to bed with a big smile on your face.

- 2 yellow potatoes, boiled and cut into chunks
- 3 oz (80 g) peas
- ½ carrot, diced
- 1 cup (8 fl oz/250 ml) vegetable oil
- 1 × 3½-lb (1.6-kg) chicken, cut into 8 pieces
- 2 red onions, finely chopped
- 9 cloves garlic, finely chopped
- pinch of ground cumin
- 6 tablespoons Yellow Chili Paste (see p. 405)
- 3 tablespoons Mirasol Chili Paste (see p. 405)
- 5 sprigs culantro or cilantro (coriander)
- 4 cups (34 fl oz/1 liter) chicken broth (stock)
- ¼ cup (2 fl oz/50 ml) Blended Culantro (see p. 407)
- 4 cups (1¾ lb/800 g) Peruvian-Style Cooked White Rice (see p. 178)
- juice of 3 small lemons
- salt and pepper

Put the potatoes in a pan with cold water. Bring to a boil and cook for 15–20 minutes. Drain and peel then cut into ¾-inch/1.5-cm cubes. Set aside.

Put the peas in a pan of salted boiling water and cook for 1½ minutes. Drain and cool in a bowl of ice water. Drain again and set aside.

Cut the carrots into ¼-inch/5-mm cubes and put in a pan with cold water. Bring to a boil and cook for 5–7 minutes, until tender. Drain and set aside.

Pour the vegetable oil, reserving 4 tablespoons, into a pan over high heat. Season the chicken pieces with salt, add to the pan, and brown on all sides. Remove the chicken pieces from the pan and set aside.

Heat 2 tablespoons oil in a separate pan, add two-thirds of the onion and two-thirds of the chopped garlic, and sauté for 2–3 minutes, over low heat until the onion starts to soften. Stir in the cumin, season with salt and pepper, and cook, stirring, for another 2–3 minutes, then add 4 tablespoons of the yellow chili paste and 2 tablespoons of mirasol chili paste. Continue to cook for a few minutes over medium heat until the mix has thickened slightly and is fragrant.

Add the browned chicken pieces and 3 culantro or cilantro (coriander) sprigs to the pan, pour in the chicken broth (stock), and bring to a simmer. Let cook for 30 minutes over low heat, or until the chicken is tender. Remove the chicken pieces from the pan, setting both the meat and the cooking juices aside.

In another pan, heat the remaining vegetable oil over medium heat, add the remaining garlic and onion, and cook, stirring, for 3 minutes. Add the remaining chili pastes, reduce the heat to low, and continue to cook for 8 minutes until the mixture has separated and appears to curdle. Stir in the blended culantro and cook for 4 minutes. Stir in the cooked rice, peas, carrot, and potatoes and cook for a final 2–3 minutes over medium heat until the flavors have melded together.

Stir the chicken pieces, remaining culantro sprigs, and lemon juice into the soup and season with salt. Spoon into large shallow bowls and serve.

TACU TACU A LO POBRE
POOR MAN'S TACU TACU

Serves: 4
Preparation Time: 25 minutes, plus overnight soaking
Cooking Time: 55 minutes

***Tacu tacu* is a typical Peruvian recipe that originated as a way to use up leftover rice and beans. The rice is mixed with cooked, seasoned canary beans, and then fried in a skillet to make a large patty. This is a generous dish that can be shared by several people. The secret is to ensure that the *tacu tacu* has a lovely outer crust.**

1 lb (450 g) any dried beans apart from fava (broad) beans, soaked overnight
4 tablespoons olive oil
2 tablespoons Yellow Chili, Garlic, and Onion Condiment (see p. 402)
1 tablespoon Yellow Chili Paste (see p. 405)
2 cups (14 oz/400 g) Peruvian-Style Cooked White Rice (see p. 178)
½ cup (4 fl oz/120 ml) chicken broth (stock)
pinch of ground cumin
1¾ lb (800g) beef tenderloin, cut into 4 pieces
½ cup (2½ oz/(65 g) all-purpose (plain) flour
2 eggs, beaten
7 oz (200 g) dried bread crumbs
1 cup (8 fl oz/250 ml) vegetable oil
salt and pepper

To serve
4 fried eggs
8 small bananas, sliced in half lengthwise
1 red onion, finely sliced
¼ red chile, finely sliced
2 sprigs culantro or cilantro (coriander)
1 cup (8 fl oz/250 ml) Creole Sauce (see p. 416), to serve

Drain the beans and put in a pan with cold water. Bring to a boil and cook for at least 35 minutes, until tender. Drain. Keep one-sixth of the cooked beans whole. Blend the remaining cooked beans in a food processor. Set aside.

Heat 3 tablespoons olive oil in a pan over low heat, add the chili, garlic, and onion condiment and chili paste, and cook, stirring, for 1 minute until the paste has thickened slightly and is fragrant.

Add the whole beans, blended beans and cooked rice to the pan and mix together well. Cook for 2–3 minutes, gradually pouring in the chicken broth (stock). Add the cumin and season with salt and pepper, then cook for another 3 minutes until the mixture has thickened and reduced. Remove from the heat.

To form the tacu tacus, spoon the mixture onto a clean work surface and divide it into 4 portions, shaping each into a 6 × 8-inch/15 × 20-cm rectangle.

Heat the remaining olive oil in a large skillet or frying pan over medium heat. Add the tacu tacus and cook for 4 minutes on each side until browned. Set aside and keep warm.

Next, flatten the beef tenderloin (fillet) pieces with a meat tenderizer. Season the pieces with salt and pepper, coat them in the flour, then the beaten egg, and finally the bread crumbs.

Heat the vegetable oil in a non-stick skillet or frying pan, add the breaded beef pieces, and cook for 4 minutes on each side until browned. Drain on paper towels.

Divide the tacu tacus between plates, top with the breaded beef, and serve with fried eggs, fried banana halves, sliced onion, chile, and culantro or cilantro (coriander) leaves, and Creole sauce.

Poor Man's Tacu Tacu

TACU TACU MONTADO
TOPPED TACU TACU

Serves: 4
Preparation Time: 15 minutes, plus overnight soaking
Cooking Time: 55 minutes

The term "topped" refers to a dish that comes with a fried egg on top, which makes it juicy and delicious.

- 1 lb (450 g) any dried beans apart from fava (broad) beans, soaked overnight
- 5 tablespoons olive oil
- 2 tablespoons Yellow Chili, Garlic, and Onion Condiment (see p. 402)
- 1 tablespoon Yellow Chili Paste (see p. 405)
- 2 cups (14 oz/400 g) Peruvian-Style Cooked White Rice (see p. 178)
- ½ cup (4 fl oz/120 ml) chicken broth (stock)
- pinch of ground cumin
- salt and pepper

To serve

- 4 fried eggs
- 1 cup (8 fl oz/250 ml) Creole Sauce (see p. 416)

Drain the beans and put in a pan with cold water. Bring to a boil and cook for at least 35 minutes, until tender. Drain. Keep one-sixth of the cooked beans whole. Blend the remaining cooked beans in a food processor. Set aside.

Heat 4 tablespoons olive oil in a pan over low heat, add the chili, garlic, and onion condiment and chili paste and cook, stirring, for 1 minute until the paste has thickened slightly and is fragrant.

Add the whole beans, blended beans, and cooked rice to the pan and mix together well. Cook for 2–3 minutes, gradually pouring in the chicken broth (stock). Add the cumin and season with salt and pepper, then cook for another 3 minutes until the mixture has thickened and reduced. Remove from the heat.

To form the tacu tacus, spoon the mixture onto a clean work surface and divide it into 4 portions, shaping each into a 6 × 8-inch/15 × 20-cm rectangle.

Heat the remaining olive oil in a large skillet or frying pan over medium heat. Add the tacu tacus and cook for 4 minutes on each side until browned.

Divide the tacu tacus between plates, top each one with a fried egg, and serve with Creole sauce.

TACU TACU A LA CHORRILLANA
CHORRILLANA TACU TACU

Serves: 4
Preparation Time: 20 minutes, plus overnight soaking
Cooking Time: 1 hour

***Chorrillana* sauce gets its name from Chorrillos, the Lima fishing district. It is often served with fish but also goes well with meat, and is juicy and colorful.**

1 lb (450 g) any dried beans apart from fava (broad) beans, soaked overnight
5 tablespoons olive oil
2 tablespoons Yellow Chili, Garlic, and Onion Condiment (see p. 402)
1 tablespoon Yellow Chili Paste (see p. 405)
2 cups (14 oz/400 g) Peruvian-Style Cooked White Rice (see p. 178)
½ cup (4 fl oz/120 ml) chicken broth (stock)
pinch of ground cumin
4 sprigs culantro or cilantro (coriander), to garnish
salt

Sauce
2 tablespoons vegetable oil
1 large red onion, thinly sliced
4 tomatoes, skinned, seeded, and thickly sliced
¼ cup yellow chiles, seeded, membrane removed, and thinly sliced
4 tablespoons white vinegar
1 tablespoon Yellow Chili Paste (see p. 405)
2 tablespoons Panca Chili, Garlic, and Onion Condiment (see p. 403)
1 cup (8 fl oz/250 ml) vegetable broth (stock)
1 tablespoon unsalted butter
2 tablespoons chopped culantro or cilantro (coriander) leaves
salt and pepper

Drain the beans and put in a pan with cold water. Bring to a boil and cook for at least 35 minutes, until tender. Drain. Keep one-sixth of the cooked beans whole. Blend the remaining cooked beans in a food processor. Set aside.

Heat 4 tablespoons olive oil in a pan over low heat, add the chili, garlic, and onion condiment and chili paste and cook, stirring, for 1 minute until the paste has thickened slightly and is fragrant.

Add the whole beans, blended beans, and cooked rice to the pan and mix together well. Cook for 2–3 minutes, gradually pouring in the chicken broth (stock). Add the cumin and season with salt, then cook for another 3 minutes until the mixture has thickened and reduced. Remove from the heat.

To form the tacu tacus, spoon the mixture onto a clean work surface and divide it into 4 portions, shaping each into a 6 × 8-inch/15 × 20-cm rectangle.

Heat the remaining 1 tablespoon of olive oil in a large skillet or frying pan over medium heat. Add the tacu tacus and cook for 4 minutes on each side until browned. Set aside and keep warm.

For the sauce, heat the vegetable oil in a skillet or frying pan over medium heat. Add the onion, tomatoes, and sliced yellow chiles and cook for 2 minutes. Add the vinegar, chili paste, and chili, garlic, and onion condiment, cook for 1 minute, and mix together well. Pour in the vegetable broth (stock), bring to a simmer, and cook until the liquid has reduced by a quarter.

Stir the butter and chopped culantro or cilantro (coriander) leaves into the sauce and adjust the seasoning to taste with salt and pepper.

Divide the tacu tacus between plates, and spoon the sauce over them. Garnish with culantro or cilantro (coriander) leaves and serve.

Tacu Tacu with Spicy Shrimp

TACU TACU CON PICANTE DE CAMARONES
TACU TACU WITH SPICY SHRIMP

Serves: 4
Preparation Time: 25 minutes, plus overnight soaking
Cooking Time: 1 hour 10 minutes

This is a party dish that can also be prepared with shellfish or fish.

1 lb (450 g) any dried beans apart from fava (broad) beans, soaked overnight
3 tablespoons olive oil
2 tablespoons Yellow Chili, Garlic, and Onion Condiment (see p. 402)
1 tablespoon Yellow Chili Paste (see p. 405)
2 cups (14 oz/400 g) Peruvian-Style Cooked White Rice (see p. 178)
½ cup (4 fl oz/120 ml) chicken broth (stock)
pinch of ground cumin
4 sprigs huacatay, to garnish
salt and pepper

Shrimp (prawns)
2 tablespoons olive oil
1 tablespoon Yellow Chili, Garlic, and Onion Condiment (see p. 402)
pinch of ground cumin
2 tomatoes, skinned, seeded, and grated
2 tablespoons Yellow Chili Paste (see p. 405)
1 tablespoon pisco
½ cup (4 fl oz/120 ml) evaporated milk
4 slices bread
1 sprig oregano
2 cups (18 fl oz/500 ml) shrimp (prawn) broth (stock)
¼ cup (1 oz/25 g) walnuts, ground in a food processor or grinder
4 whole shrimp (prawns)
44 shrimp (prawns), peeled and deveined, with tails still intact
salt and pepper

Drain the beans and put in a pan with cold water. Bring to a boil and cook for at least 35 minutes, until tender. Drain. Keep one-sixth of the cooked beans whole. Blend the remaining cooked beans in a food processor. Set aside.

For the shrimp (prawns), heat the olive oil in a pan over medium heat, add the chili, garlic, and onion condiment and cook for 2 minutes until the paste has thickened slightly and is fragrant. Stir in the cumin, grated tomato, and chili paste, season with salt and pepper, and cook, stirring, for 2–3 minutes until the paste has thickened slightly and is fragrant. Add the pisco and cook for 2 minutes until the alcohol has evaporated.

Put the evaporated milk and bread in a food processor and blend together. Add the blended mixture to the pan along with the oregano sprig and cook over medium heat for 4 minutes, gradually pouring in the shrimp (prawn) broth (stock).

Add the ground walnuts and the whole shrimp and mix together well. Cover and cook for 2 minutes, then add the shrimp tails and cook for another 1 minute until the shrimp tails are almost cooked. Adjust the seasoning and set aside. Keep warm.

To prepare the tacu tacus, heat 2 tablespoons olive oil in a pan over low heat, add the chili, garlic, and onion condiment and chili paste and cook, stirring, for 4 minutes until the paste has thickened slightly and is fragrant.

Add the whole beans, blended beans, and cooked rice to the pan and mix together well. Cook for 2–3 minutes, gradually pouring in the chicken broth (stock). Add the cumin and season with salt, then cook for another 3 minutes until the mixture has thickened and reduced. Remove from the heat.

To form the tacu tacus, spoon the mixture onto a clean work surface and divide it into 4 portions, shaping each into a 6 × 8-inch/15 × 20-cm rectangle.

Heat the remaining olive oil in a large skillet or frying pan over medium heat. Add the tacu tacus and cook for 4 minutes on each side until browned.

Divide the tacu tacus between plates and spoon over the spicy shrimp mixture over them, ensuring there is 1 whole shrimp on each plate. Garnish with huacatay sprigs. Serve.

Serves: 4
Preparation Time: 15 minutes, plus overnight soaking
Cooking Time: 55 minutes

This dish is known as a "macho" dish because it is not for the faint-hearted. It is loaded with seafood and served with a very spicy sauce.

- 1 lb (450 g) any dried beans apart from fava (broad) beans, soaked overnight
- 4 tablespoons olive oil
- 2 tablespoons Yellow Chili, Garlic, and Onion Condiment (see p. 402)
- 1 tablespoon Yellow Chili Paste (see p. 405)
- 2 cups (14 oz/400 g) Peruvian-Style Cooked White Rice (see p. 178)
- ½ cup (4 fl oz/120 ml) chicken broth (stock)
- pinch of ground cumin
- salt

Sauce
- 2 tablespoons olive oil
- 2 tablespoons Yellow Chili Paste (see p. 405)
- 1 tablespoon Rocoto Chili Paste (see p. 407)
- 12 shrimp (prawns), peeled and deveined
- ¼ cup (3 oz/80 g) Cooked Octopus, chopped (see p. 406)
- 4 × 7-oz/200-g squid, cleaned and cut into rings
- 16 scallops
- 12 clams
- 1 cup (8 fl oz/250 ml) fish broth (stock)
- ¼ cup (2 fl oz/50 ml) evaporated milk
- salt and pepper

TACU TACU A LO MACHO
MACHO TACU TACU

Drain the beans and put in a pan with cold water. Bring to a boil and cook for at least 35 minutes, until tender. Drain. Keep one-sixth of the cooked beans whole. Blend the remaining cooked beans in a food processor. Set aside.

Heat 3 tablespoons olive oil in a pan over low heat, add the chili, garlic, and onion condiment and chili paste and cook, stirring, for 1 minute until the paste has thickened slightly and is fragrant.

Add the whole beans, blended beans, and cooked rice to the pan and mix together well. Cook for 2–3 minutes, gradually pouring in the chicken broth (stock). Add the cumin and season with salt, then cook for another 3 minutes until the mixture has thickened and reduced. Remove from the heat.

To form the tacu tacus, spoon the mixture onto a clean work surface and divide it into 4 portions, shaping each into a 6 × 8-inch/15 × 20-cm rectangle.

Heat the remaining olive oil in a large skillet or frying pan over medium heat. Add the tacu tacus and cook for 4 minutes on each side until browned. Set aside and keep warm.

For the sauce, heat the olive oil in a pan over medium heat, add the chili pastes and cook, stirring, for 2–3 minutes until the pastes have thickened and are fragrant. Add the shrimp (prawns) and octopus, followed by the squid, scallops, and clams, and cook for 1 minute. Pour in the fish broth and evaporated milk and cook until slightly reduced. Season with salt and pepper to finish.

Divide the tacu tacus between plates and spoon the sauce over them. Serve.

TACU TACU RELLENO DE SECO
STEW-FILLED TACU TACU

To prepare the stew filling, heat the vegetable oil in a pan over high heat. Season the beef pieces with salt and pepper, add to the pan, and brown on all sides. Remove the beef pieces from the pan and set aside.

Add the onion, garlic, chili paste, and cumin to the same pan and season with salt and pepper. Cook for 10 minutes over medium heat until the onion is translucent and the paste has thickened and is fragrant. Return the meat pieces to the pan, pour in the vegetable broth (stock), and bring to a simmer. Let cook over medium heat for 15 minutes, then stir through the blended culantro. Adjust the seasoning to taste and cook for 1 hour until the meat is tender. Set aside.

For the tacu tacus, drain the soaked beans and place them in a pan with the onion, garlic cloves, carrot, bay leaves, bacon, peppercorns, and a little salt. Cover with 6 cups (46 fl oz/1.4 liters) water, bring to a simmer and cook over medium heat for 35 minutes until the beans are tender. Drain and reserve the cooking liquid.

Put half the beans in a food processor with a small amount of the cooking liquid and blend together until smooth. Set aside along with the whole beans.

Heat 3 tablespoons olive oil in a pan over low heat, add the chili, garlic, and onion condiment and chili paste and cook for 1 minute until the mixture has thickened slightly and is fragrant. Add the blended beans, the reserved whole beans, and cooked rice and cook for 2–3 minutes, gradually pouring in the chicken broth (stock) and reserved bean cooking liquid. Add a pinch of cumin, season with salt, and cook for another 3 minutes until mixture has thickened and reduced. Remove from the heat.

To form the tacu tacus, spoon the mixture onto a clean work surface and divide it into 8 portions. In a medium non-stick pan, heat 1 tablespoon olive oil, add 1 portion of the mixture and make a circle ¾-inch/1.5-cm thick, covering the surface of the pan and spoon 4 tablespoons of the stew on top. Cover with another portion of mixture to form a round tacu tacu and leave to cook for 4 minutes until browned on the bottom, then carefully flip over and cook for another 4 minutes. Repeat the process until you have 4 stew-filled tacu tacu parcels.

Serve on plates with Creole sauce, cubed avocado, and sliced radishes, and top with any leftover stew.

Serves: 4
Preparation Time: 25 minutes, plus overnight soaking
Cooking Time: 2 hours 20 minutes,

The mixture of the stew and the tacu tacu is what makes this dish delicious and gives it a juicy and creamy texture.

2 cups (13 oz/370 g) canary beans, soaked overnight
1 onion, cut in half
4 cloves garlic
1 carrot, thickly sliced
2 bay leaves
7 oz (200 g) bacon
1 tablespoon peppercorns
4 tablespoons olive oil
2 tablespoons Yellow Chili, Garlic, and Onion Condiment (see p. 402)
1 tablespoon Yellow Chili Paste (see p. 405)
2 cups (14 oz/400 g) Peruvian-Style Cooked White Rice (see p. 178)
¼ cup (2 fl oz/50 ml) chicken broth (stock)
pinch of ground cumin
salt and pepper

Stew filling
½ cup (4 fl oz/120 ml) vegetable oil
2¼ lb (1 kg) beef (beef shank, brisket, or thick flank), cut into ¾-inch (2-cm) chunks
4 red onions, finely chopped
12 cloves garlic, finely chopped
1 tablespoon Yellow Chili Paste (see p. 405)
pinch of ground cumin
4 cups (34 fl oz/1 liter) vegetable broth (stock)
½ cup (4 fl oz/120 ml) Blended Culantro (see p. 407)
salt and pepper

To serve
1 cup (8 fl oz/250 ml) Creole Sauce (see p. 416)
½ avocado, cut into cubes
1 oz (25 g) radishes, thinly sliced

TACU TACU RELLENO AMAZÓNICO
AMAZONIAN STUFFED TACU TACU

Serves: 4
Preparation Time: 20 minutes, plus overnight soaking
Cooking Time: 2 hours 20 minutes

A tacu tacu infused with jungle flavors is both delicious and unusual.

2 cups (13 oz/370 g) canary beans, soaked overnight
1 onion, cut in half
4 cloves garlic
1 carrot, thickly sliced
2 bay leaves
7 oz (200 g) bacon
1 tablespoon peppercorns
4 tablespoons olive oil
2 tablespoons Yellow Chili, Garlic, and Onion Condiment (see p. 402)
1 tablespoon Yellow Chili Paste (see p. 405)
2 cups (14 oz/400 g) Peruvian-Style Cooked White Rice (see p. 178)
¼ cup (2 fl oz/50 ml) chicken broth (stock)
pinch of ground cumin
¾ cup (6 fl oz/175 ml) Cocona and Chili Salsa (see p. 409), to serve
salt and pepper

Filling
½ cup (4 fl oz/120 ml) vegetable oil
2¼ lb (1 kg) beef (beef shank, brisket, or thick flank), cut into ¾-inch (2-cm) chunks
2 red onions, finely chopped
12 cloves garlic, finely chopped
4 charapita chiles, chopped
3 tablespoons Yellow Chili Paste (see p. 405)
pinch of ground cumin
4 cups (34 fl oz/1 liter) vegetable broth (stock)
handful of sacha culantro or cilantro (coriander) leaves
salt and pepper

To prepare the filling, heat the vegetable oil in a pan over high heat. Season the beef pieces with salt and pepper, add to the pan, and brown on all sides. Remove the beef pieces from the pan and set aside.

Add the onion, garlic, and chiles to the same pan and cook for 3 minutes over medium heat until the onion starts to soften. Add the chili paste and cumin, season with salt and pepper, and cook for another 10 minutes until the onion has started to caramelize and the chili paste has thickened and is fragrant. Return the meat pieces to the pan, pour in the vegetable broth (stock), and bring to a simmer. Cook over medium heat for 15 minutes then stir through the sacha culantro leaves. Adjust the seasoning to taste and cook for 1 hour until the meat is tender. Set aside.

For the tacu tacus, drain the soaked beans and place them in a pan with the onion, garlic cloves, carrot, bay leaves, bacon, peppercorns, and a little salt. Cover with 6 cups (46 fl oz/1.4 liters) water, bring to a simmer over medium heat, and cook for 35 minutes until the beans are tender. Drain and reserve the cooking liquid.

Put half the beans in a food processor with a small amount of the cooking liquid and blend together until smooth. Set aside along with the whole beans.

Heat 3 tablespoons olive oil in a pan over low heat, add the chili, garlic, and onion condiment and chili paste and cook for 1 minute until the mixture has thickened slightly and is fragrant. Add the blended beans, the reserved whole beans, and cooked rice and cook for 2–3 minutes, gradually pouring in the chicken broth (stock) and reserved bean cooking liquid. Add a pinch of cumin, season with salt, and cook for another 3 minutes until the mixture has thickened and reduced. Remove from the heat.

To form the tacu tacus, spoon the mixture onto a clean work surface and divide it into 8 portions. In a medium non-stick pan, heat 1 tablespoon of olive oil, add 1 portion of the mixture and make a circle ¾-inch/1.5-cm thick, covering the surface of the pan. Spoon 4 tablespoons of the stew on top. Cover with another portion of the mixture to form a round tacu tacu and cook for 4 minutes until browned on the bottom, then carefully flip over and cook for another 4 minutes. Repeat the process until you have 4 stew-filled tacu tacu parcels.

Serve on plates with cocona and chili salsa and top with any leftover stew.

TACU TACU DE FREJOLES NEGROS ESCABECHADOS
BLACK BEAN TACU TACU IN ESCABECHE SAUCE

Serves: 4
Preparation Time: 20 minutes, plus overnight soaking
Cooking Time: 1 hour 10 minutes

My mother used to make black beans in *escabeche* sauce at home, so it was only a matter of time before this delicious memory was turned into a tacu tacu recipe.

- 1 lb (450 g) any dried beans apart from fava (broad) beans, soaked overnight
- 4 tablespoons olive oil
- 2 tablespoons Yellow Chili, Garlic, and Onion Condiment (see p. 402)
- 1 tablespoon Yellow Chili Paste (see p. 405)
- 2 cups (14 oz/400 g) Peruvian-Style Cooked White Rice (see p. 178)
- ¼ cup (2 fl oz/50 ml) chicken broth (stock)
- pinch of ground cumin
- salt and pepper

Sauce
- 2 tablespoons olive oil
- 2 red onions, thickly sliced
- 2 cloves garlic, finely chopped
- 1 yellow chile, seeded, membrane removed, and sliced
- 1 tablespoon Panca Chili Paste (see p. 406)
- ½ tablespoon Yellow Chili Paste (see p. 405)
- 1 bay leaf
- 1 teaspoon dried oregano
- 6 tablespoons white vinegar
- 2 teaspoons honey
- salt and pepper

Drain the beans and put in a pan with cold water. Bring to a boil and cook for at least 35 minutes, until tender. Drain. Keep one-sixth of the cooked beans whole. Blend the remaining cooked beans in a food processor. Set aside.

For the sauce, heat the olive oil in a skillet or frying pan over medium heat, add the red onion, garlic, and yellow chile, and cook, stirring, for 4 minutes until the onion softens. Add the chili pastes, bay leaf, and oregano, cook for 8 minutes, then add the vinegar and honey and cook for 1 minute. Season with salt and pepper and set aside.

To prepare the tacu tacus, heat 3 tablespoons olive oil in a pan over low heat, add the chili, garlic, and onion condiment and chili paste and cook, stirring, for 1 minute until fragrant.

Add the whole beans, blended beans, and cooked rice to the pan and mix together well. Cook for 2–3 minutes, gradually pouring in the chicken broth (stock). Add the cumin and season with salt, then cook for another 3 minutes, until the mixture is thickened and reduced. Remove from the heat.

To form the tacu tacus, spoon the mixture onto a clean work surface and divide it into 4 portions, shaping each into a 6 × 8-inch/15 × 20-cm rectangle.

Heat the remaining olive oil in a large skillet or frying pan over medium heat. Add the tacu tacus and cook for 4 minutes on each side until browned.

Divide the tacu tacus between plates and spoon the sauce over them. Serve.

TACU TACU DE PALLARES
LIMA BEAN TACU TACU

Serves: 4
Preparation Time: 15 minutes, plus overnight soaking
Cooking Time: 50 minutes

The lima (butter) beans in this dish can be replaced with lentils, chickpeas, fava (broad) beans, or any other local variety of bean.

2 cups (14 oz/400 g) lima (butter) beans, soaked overnight
1 onion, cut in half
4 cloves garlic
1 carrot, thickly sliced
2 bay leaves
7 oz (200 g) bacon
1 tablespoon peppercorns
4 tablespoons olive oil
2 tablespoons Yellow Chili, Garlic, and Onion Condiment (see p. 402)
1 tablespoon Yellow Chili Paste (see p. 405)
2 cups (14 oz/400 g) Peruvian-Style Cooked White Rice (see p. 178)
¼ cup (2 fl oz/50 ml) chicken broth (stock)
pinch of ground cumin
1 cup (8 fl oz/250 ml) Creole Sauce, to serve (see p. 416)
salt

Drain the soaked beans and place them in a pan with the onion, garlic cloves, carrot, bay leaves, bacon, peppercorns, and a little salt. Cover with 4¼ cups (34 fl oz/1 liter) water, bring to a simmer and cook over medium heat for 35 minutes until the beans are tender. Drain, reserving the cooking liquid.

Put half the beans in a food processor with a small amount of the cooking liquid and blend together until smooth. Set aside along with the whole beans.

Heat 3 tablespoons olive oil in a pan over low heat, add the chili, garlic, and onion condiment and chili paste and cook for 1 minute until the mixture has thickened slightly and is fragrant. Add the blended beans, the reserved whole beans, and cooked rice and cook for 2–3 minutes, gradually pouring in the chicken broth (stock) and reserved bean cooking liquid. Add a pinch of cumin, season with salt, and cook for another 3 minutes until the mixture has thickened and reduced. Remove from the heat.

To form the tacu tacus, spoon the mixture onto a clean work surface and divide it into 4 portions, shaping each into a 6 × 8-inch/15 × 20-cm rectangle.

Heat the remaining olive oil in a large skillet or frying pan over medium heat. Add the tacu tacus and cook for 4 minutes on each side until browned.

Divide the tacu tacus between plates and serve with Creole sauce.

TACU TACU DE LENTEJAS CON PESCADO
LENTIL TACU TACU WITH FISH

Serves: 4
Preparation Time: 15 minutes, plus overnight soaking
Cooking Time: 1 hour minutes

This is a very homey and nutritious way to eat tacu tacus. It is also the way many fishermen like to enjoy them.

¼ cup (2 fl oz/60 ml) vegetable oil
4 × 7-oz (200-g) croaker fillets
2 cups (1 lb/450 g) black lentils, soaked overnight
1 onion, cut in half
4 cloves garlic
1 carrot, thickly sliced
2 bay leaves
7 oz (200 g) bacon
7 oz (200 g) pork jowls (cheeks)
1 tablespoon peppercorns
4 tablespoons olive oil
2 tablespoons Yellow Chili, Garlic, and Onion Condiment (see p. 402)
1 tablespoon Yellow Chili Paste (see p. 405)
2 cups (14 oz/400 g) Peruvian-Style Cooked White Rice (see p. 178)
¼ cup (2 fl oz/50 ml) chicken broth (stock)
pinch of ground cumin
salt and pepper

To serve
4 fried eggs
1 cup (8 fl oz/250 ml) Creole Sauce (see p. 416)

Heat 4 tablespoons vegetable oil in a pan over high heat. Season the fish fillets with salt and pepper, add to the pan and brown on all sides. Remove the fish from the pan, set aside and keep warm.

Drain the soaked lentils and place them in a pan with the onion, garlic cloves, carrot, bay leaves, bacon, pork jowls (cheeks), peppercorns, and a little salt. Cover with 4¼ cups (34 fl oz/1 liter) water, bring to a simmer, and cook over medium heat for 35 minutes until the lentils are tender. Drain and reserve the cooking liquid.

Put half the lentils in a food processor with a small amount of the cooking liquid and blend together. Set aside along with the whole lentils.

To prepare the tacu tacus, heat 3 tablespoons olive oil in a pan over low heat, add the chili, garlic, and onion condiment and chili paste, and cook for 1 minute until the mixture has thickened slightly and is fragrant. Add the blended lentils, the reserved whole lentils, and cooked rice and cook for 2–3 minutes, gradually pouring in the chicken broth (stock) and reserved lentil cooking liquid. Add a pinch of cumin, season with salt, and cook for another 3 minutes until the mixture is thickened and reduced. Remove from the heat.

To form the tacu tacus, spoon the mixture onto a clean work surface and divide it into 4 portions, shaping each into a 6 × 8-inch/15 × 20-cm rectangle.

Heat the remaining olive oil in a large skillet or frying pan over medium heat. Add the tacu tacus and cook for 4 minutes on each side until browned.

Divide the tacu tacus between plates and top with the fish fillets. Serve with fried eggs and Creole sauce.

Serves: 4
Preparation Time: 20 minutes, plus overnight soaking
Cooking Time: 1 hour 5 minutes

The tacu tacu in this recipe blends with *nikkei* sauce for a very typical Peruvian-Japanese flavor.

1 lb (450 g) any dried beans apart from fava (broad) beans, soaked overnight
4 tablespoons olive oil
2 tablespoons Yellow Chili, Garlic, and Onion Condiment (see p. 402)
1 tablespoon Yellow Chili Paste (see p. 405)
2 cups (14 oz/400 g) Peruvian-Style Cooked White Rice (see p. 178)
pinch of ground cumin
salt and pepper

Sauce
½ tablespoon Panca Chili, Garlic, and Onion Condiment (see p. 403)
5 tablespoons white miso paste
3 tablespoons mirin
1 teaspoon soy sauce
1 tablespoon sake
2 tablespoons granulated sugar
¼ cup (2 fl oz/50 ml) vegetable broth (stock)
14 shrimp (prawns), peeled and deveined
2 limpets, chopped
4 × 7-oz (200-g) squid, cut into rings
12 scallops, cleaned
4 tablespoons chicken broth (stock)
salt and pepper

TACU TACU NIKKEI
JAPANESE-INSPIRED TACU TACU

Drain the beans and put in a pan with cold water. Bring to a boil and cook for at least 35 minutes, until tender. Drain. Keep one-sixth of the cooked beans whole. Blend the remaining cooked beans in a food processor. Set aside.

To prepare the sauce, put the chili, garlic, and onion condiment and white miso paste in a pan over low heat. Add the mirin, soy sauce, sake, sugar, and vegetable broth (stock), bring to a gentle simmer, and cook for 10 minutes, until the sugar has dissolved and the alcohol has evaporated.

Season the shellfish with salt and pepper. Heat the olive oil in a skillet or frying pan, add the shrimp (prawns), limpets, squid, and scallops, and sauté for 2 minutes until cooked through. Add the shellfish to the pan with the sauce and mix together well. Adjust the seasoning to taste, set aside, and keep warm.

To prepare the tacu tacus, heat 3 tablespoons olive oil in a pan over low heat, add the chili, garlic, and onion condiment and chili paste and cook, stirring, for 1 minute until the paste has thickened slightly and is fragrant.

Add the whole beans, blended beans, and cooked rice to the pan and mix together well. Cook for 2–3 minutes, gradually pouring in the chicken broth (stock). Add the cumin and season with salt, then cook for another 3 minutes until the mixture has thickened and reduced. Remove from the heat.

To form the tacu tacus, spoon the mixture onto a clean work surface and divide it into 4 portions, shaping each into a 6 × 8-inch/15 × 20-cm rectangle.

Heat the remaining olive oil in a large skillet or frying pan over medium heat. Add the tacu tacus and cook for 4 minutes on each side until browned.

Divide the tacu tacus between plates and spoon the shellfish sauce over them. Serve.

Japanese-Inspired Tacu Tacu

TACU CHAUFA
CHINESE-STYLE TACU

Serves: 4
Preparation Time: 30 minutes, plus overnight soaking and 5 hours chilling
Cooking Time: 4 hours

This dish was created by our friend Mitsuharu "Micha" Tsumura in his early days as a chef and is now a firm favorite.

1 lb (450 g) any dried beans apart from fava (broad) beans, soaked overnight
4 tablespoons olive oil
2 tablespoons Yellow Chili, Garlic, and Onion Condiment (see p. 402)
1 tablespoon Yellow Chili Paste (see p. 405)
2 cups (14 oz/400 g) Chaufa Fried Rice (see p. 189)
½ cup (4 fl oz/120 ml) chicken broth (stock)
pinch of ground cumin
1 cup (8 fl oz/250 ml) Creole Sauce, (see p. 416) to serve
salt

Pork side (belly)
1 cup (8 fl oz/250 ml) vegetable oil
1 × 3¼-lb (1.6-kg) boned pork side (belly)
1-inch (2.5-cm) piece fresh ginger, peeled and coarsely chopped
1 tablespoon mirin
1 tablespoon sake
4 cloves garlic
¼ cup (2 fl oz/50 ml) tamari soy sauce
3 tablespoons soy sauce
5 oz (150 g) granulated sugar
salt

Drain the beans and put in a pan with cold water. Bring to a boil and cook for at least 35 minutes, until tender. Drain. Keep one-sixth of the cooked beans whole. Blend the remaining cooked beans in a food processor. Set aside.

To prepare the pork side (belly), heat the vegetable oil, reserving 2 tablespoons, in a large skillet or frying pan over high heat. Season the pork with salt, add to the pan, and brown on both sides.

Remove the browned meat from the pan and place in pot. Pour in 204 fl oz/6 liters, water and add the ginger, mirin, sake, and garlic. Bring to a simmer and cook for 2 hours over low heat, then add the tamari soy sauce and regular soy sauce. Cook for another hour until the pork side is tender. Remove from the heat, drain, and set the pork side and cooking liquid aside separately.

Sandwich the pork between two metal sheets and refrigerate for 5 hours until firm and solid. Once solid, cut the cooked pork into 3-oz (80-g) cubes. Brown again in a pan with 2 tablespoons vegetable oil and set aside, keeping warm.

Pour the reserved cooking liquid into a pan, add the sugar, and bring to a simmer. Cook for 6 minutes, until the sugar is dissolved and the sauce has thickened slightly. Set aside and keep warm.

To prepare the tacu tacus, heat 3 tablespoons olive oil in a pan over low heat, add the chili, garlic, and onion condiment and chili paste, and cook for 1 minute until the mixture has thickened slightly and is fragrant. Add the blended beans, the whole beans, and fried rice, and cook for 2–3 minutes, gradually pouring in the chicken broth (stock). Add a pinch of cumin, season with salt, and cook for another 3 minutes until the mixture is thickened and reduced. Remove from the heat.

To form the tacu tacus, spoon the mixture onto a clean work surface and divide it into 4 portions, shaping each into a 6 × 8-inch/15 × 20-cm rectangle.

Heat the remaining olive oil in a large skillet or frying pan over medium heat. Add the tacu tacus and cook for 4 minutes on each side until browned.

Divide the tacu tacus between plates and top with the cubed pork and reduced sauce. Serve with Creole sauce on the side.

TACU CAUCHE
TACU CAKES WITH SEAFOOD CAUCHE

Serves: 4
Preparation Time: 20 minutes, plus overnight soaking
Cooking Time: 1 hour 5 minutes

Cauche is a classic and truly delicious Arequipan dish. When served with tacu tacu, it's even better.

Tacu tacu
3 cups (1 lb 3 oz/525 g) lima (butter) beans, soaked overnight
3 tablespoons olive oil
3 tablespoons Yellow Chili, Garlic, and Onion Condiment (see p. 402)
1 tablespoon Yellow Chili Paste (see p. 405)
2 cups (14 oz/400 g) Peruvian-Style Cooked White Rice (see p. 178)
½ cup (4 fl oz/120 ml) chicken broth (stock)
pinch of ground cumin
salt and pepper

Seafood cauche
2 tablespoons vegetable oil
12 scallops
12 shrimp (prawns)
12 small shrimp
4 x 7-oz (200-g) squid, cleaned and cut into rings
juice of 2 small lemons
4 red onions, thickly sliced
1 tomato, skinned, seeded, and thickly sliced
3 tablespoons Panca Chili, Garlic, and Onion Condiment (see p. 403)
½ cup (4 fl oz/120 ml) vegetable broth (stock)
1 sprig huacatay, plus extra to garnish
pinch of ground cumin
9 oz (250 g) queso fresco, cubed
¼ cup (2 fl oz/50 ml) evaporated milk
1 rocoto chile, seeded, membrane removed, and diced
½ oz (15 g) butter
salt and pepper

Soak the lima (butter) beans in water overnight. Drain. Put in a pan with cold water and boil for 45 minutes over medium heat until tender. Drain. Put in food processor and blend to a smooth paste.

For the tacu tacus, heat 2 tablespoons olive oil in a pan over low heat, add the chili, garlic, and onion condiment and chili paste, and cook, stirring, for 1 minute until the onion is transparent and the mixture is fragrant.

Add the blended beans and rice and cook for 2–3 minutes, gradually pouring in the chicken broth (stock). Add the cumin and season with salt and pepper, then cook for another 3 minutes until the mixture has cooked and thickened a little. Remove from the heat.

To form the tacu tacus, spoon the mixture onto a clean work surface and divide it into 4 portions, shaping each into a rectangle about ¾-inch /2-cm thick.

Heat the remaining olive oil in a large skillet or frying pan. Add the tacu tacus and cook over a moderate heat for 3–4 minutes on each side until a golden and crispy crust forms. Keep hot until served.

To make the cauche, heat 1 tablespoon vegetable oil in a skillet or frying pan. Season the scallops, regular and small shrimp (prawns), and squid rings with salt and pepper, pour over the lemon juice and add to the pan. Sauté over medium heat for 1 minute until it is cooked, then remove from the pan and set aside.

Add the remaining vegetable oil to the pan along with the onion and tomato and cook, stirring, for 3 minutes until the onion has browned. Season with salt and pepper, add the chili, garlic, and onion condiment, and sauté for another 1 minute until it is cooked. Pour in the vegetable broth (stock), add in the huacatay sprig, and leave for 1 minute before adding the seafood.

Stir in the cumin and sautéed seafood and adjust the seasoning to taste. Add the cubed queso fresco, evaporated milk, and chopped rocoto chile, then add the butter and stir well.

Divide the tacu tacus among plates. Ladle over the cauche and garnish with extra sprigs of huacatay to finish. Serve.

STEWS, CHILIES & ROASTS

Chicken Chili

AJÍ DE GALLINA
CHICKEN CHILI

Serves: 4
Preparation Time: 20 minutes
Cooking Time: 20 minutes

The chili here is not a spice, but the main ingredient of this stew, and the creamy mixture that is ají de gallina is the centerpiece of this dish. It is one of Lima's most beloved stews.

- 2 tablespoons vegetable oil
- 2 red onions, finely chopped
- 5 cloves garlic, chopped
- 1 oz (25 g) shelled pecans or almonds, chopped
- 1 cup (8 fl oz/250 ml) Yellow Chili Paste (see p. 405)
- ½ cup (4 fl oz/120 ml) Mirasol Chili Paste (see p. 405)
- 1 teaspoon ground cumin
- 2 teaspoons dried oregano
- 8 white bread slices
- ½ cup (4 fl oz/120 ml) whole (full-fat) milk, plus extra if necessary
- 1½ cups (13 fl oz/375 ml) chicken broth (stock), plus extra if necessary
- 1 × 1-lb (450 g) cooked chicken breast, shredded
- ¾ oz (20 g) Parmesan cheese
- 2 white potatoes
- 2 cups (14 oz/400 g) Peruvian-Style Cooked White Rice (see p. 178), to serve
- salt and pepper

To garnish

- 4 pitted black olives (optional)
- 1 egg, hard-boiled and cut into quarters
- 1 sprig curly parsley

Heat the oil in a pan over low heat, add the onion and garlic, and sauté for a few minutes, until the onion has softened. Add the chopped pecans or almonds and chili pastes. Season with salt and pepper.

Add the cumin and oregano and continue to cook, stirring, for a few minutes, then remove from the heat and set aside.

Put the bread in a bowl, cover with the milk, and let soak for 5 minutes, then put in a blender with the onion and pecan mixture. Blend together well.

Pour the blended mixture into a pan over medium heat and add the broth (stock), shredded chicken breast, and Parmesan cheese. Taste and adjust the seasoning if necessary. Cook for 8 minutes until it is creamy. If the chili starts to dry out during the cooking process, add a little more broth or milk.

Meanwhile, bring a pan of water to a boil, add the potatoes, and cook until tender. Drain and cut into slices.

Arrange the sliced boiled potatoes on a serving platter and ladle over the chicken chili. Garnish with the olives, hard-boiled egg quarters, and curly parsley and serve with rice.

AJÍ DE LACAYOTE
FIG-LEAF GOURD CHILI

Serves: 4
Preparation Time: 15 minutes
Cooking Time: 35 minutes

This chili can also be prepared with any type of pumpkin, vegetable, or tuber. It is certainly not limited to fig-leaf gourd.

- 2 fig-leaf gourds or pumpkins
- 2 tablespoons vegetable oil
- 2 red onions, chopped
- 4 cloves garlic, finely chopped
- ½ cup (4 fl oz/120 ml) Yellow Chili Paste (see p. 405)
- ½ cup (4 fl oz/120 ml) Mirasol Chili Paste (see p. 405)
- 1 teaspoon ground cumin
- 1 sprig huacatay
- 5 oz (150 g) fava (broad) beans
- 2 white potatoes, peeled
- 4 corncobs
- 2½ oz (65 g) butter
- 1 oz (25 g) all-purpose (plain) flour
- 1½ cups (13 fl oz/375 ml) vegetable broth (stock), plus extra if necessary
- 1 cup (8 fl oz/250 ml) evaporated milk
- 2½ oz (65 g) mantecoso cheese, cut into ½-inch (1-cm) cubes
- salt and pepper

Peel the fig-leaf gourds and remove the seeds. Cut the flesh into ½-inch/1-cm slices and blanch in boiling water for 10 minutes. Drain and set aside. Heat the oil in a pan over medium heat, add the onion and garlic, and sauté for a few minutes, until the onion has softened. Add the chili pastes and season with salt and pepper. Add the cumin and huacatay, reduce the heat and continue to cook, stirring, for 8 minutes until the paste is fragrant. Remove from the heat and set aside.

Meanwhile, bring a pan of water to a boil, add the fava (broad) beans and cook until tender. Drain, peel, and set aside. Repeat with the potatoes and corncobs, removing the kernels from the cobs once cooked.

Melt the butter in a skillet or frying pan and add the blanched fig-leaf gourd, flour, vegetable broth (stock), and evaporated milk. Cook, stirring continuously, until a creamy mixture forms, then add the mantecoso cheese and onion and chile mixture. Finally, add the cooked fava (broad) beans and corn kernels. Cook for 10 minutes until the chili thickens. If the chili starts to dry out during the cooking process, add a little more vegetable broth.

Slice the boiled potatoes and arrange in large shallow bowls. Pour over the chili and serve.

AJIACO DE CAMARONES
POTATO AND CHILE STEW WITH SHRIMP

Serves: 4
Preparation Time: 25 minutes
Cooking Time: 55 minutes

1 lb (450 g) white potatoes, peeled
3 oz (80 g) lima (butter) beans
2 tablespoons vegetable oil
3 cloves garlic, chopped
1 red onion, finely chopped
2 tablespoons Panca Chili Paste (see p. 406)
1 sprig huacatay
3 cups (26½ fl oz/750 ml) vegetable broth (stock)
¼ cup (2 fl oz/50 ml) whole (full-fat) milk
2½ oz (65 g) queso fresco, cut into ½-inch (1-cm) cubes
salt and pepper

Shrimp (prawns)
1 tablespoon vegetable oil
¼ red onion, finely chopped
1 clove garlic, chopped
1 tablespoon Yellow Chili Paste (see p. 405)
40 medium shrimp (prawns), peeled and deveined, with tails still intact
juice of 1 small lemon

To garnish
2½ oz (65 g) queso fresco, grated
1 tablespoon chopped huacatay leaves
½ yellow chile, seeded, membrane removed, and thinly sliced

Bring a pan of water to a boil, add the potatoes, and cook until tender. Drain and cut into ½-inch/1-cm cubes. Boil the lima (butter) beans until tender. Set aside.

For the stew, heat the oil in a pan over low heat. Add the garlic and onion and sauté for a few minutes, until the onion has softened. Add the panca chili paste, season with salt and pepper, and continue to cook, stirring, for 8 minutes until fragrant.

Add the cubed boiled potatoes, huacatay sprig, and broth (stock), and simmer for about 10 minutes, until the mixture has thickened and reduced. Add the cooked lima beans, milk, and cubed queso fresco, and cook for another 2 minutes. Taste and adjust the seasoning if necessary, then remove from the heat.

For the shrimp (prawns), put the oil, onion, and garlic in a skillet or frying pan with the yellow chili paste and cook for 8 minutes, stirring. Add the shrimp and lemon juice and cook for 2–3 minutes until the shrimp are cooked through.

Ladle the stew into large shallow bowls and top with the shrimp and their juices. Garnish with the grated queso fresco, chopped huacatay leaves, and sliced yellow chiles.

AJIACO DE CARNE
BEEF BRISKET AND POTATO STEW

Serves: 4
Preparation Time: 20 minutes
Cooking Time: 1 hour 25 minutes

This dish was created when Andean families were more affluent and added meat to the traditional potato stew.

3 tablespoons vegetable oil
1 red onion, finely chopped
3 cloves garlic, chopped
2 tablespoons Panca Chili Paste (see p. 406)
1 tablespoon Yellow Chili Paste (see p. 405)
1 lb 2 oz (500 g) beef brisket, cut into 1-inch (2.5-cm) cubes
3 cups (26½ fl oz/750 ml) vegetable broth (stock)
1 lb 5 oz (600 g) white potatoes, peeled and cut into ½-inch (1-cm) cubes
1 sprig huacatay
1 cup (8 fl oz/250 ml) whole (full-fat) milk
2½ oz (65 g) queso fresco, cut into ½-inch (1-cm) cubes
salt and pepper

To garnish
2½ oz (65 g) queso fresco, grated
1 tablespoon chopped huacatay leaves
½ yellow chile, seeded, membrane removed, and thinly sliced

Heat the oil in a pan over low heat, add the onion and garlic, and sauté for a few minutes, until the onion has softened. Add the chili pastes, season with salt and pepper, and continue to cook, stirring, for 8 minutes until fragrant.

Add the cubed brisket and broth (stock) and simmer for 1 hour, until the meat is tender. Add the potatoes and huacatay sprig and cook for another 10 minutes over low heat, until the potatoes are cooked. Stir in the milk and cubed queso fresco and cook for another 2 minutes.

Ladle the beef and potato stew into large shallow bowls and garnish with the grated queso fresco, chopped huacatay leaves, and sliced yellow chiles.

AJÍ DE LANGOSTINOS
SHRIMP CHILI

Serves: 4
Preparation Time: 15 minutes
Cooking Time: 20 minutes, plus 5 minutes soaking

Shrimp (prawn) chili is a derivation of chicken chili and can also be prepared with shrimp or crab and lobster. Either option will work beautifully.

- 2 tablespoons vegetable oil
- 2 red onions, finely chopped
- 5 cloves garlic, chopped
- 1 cup (8 fl oz/250 ml) Yellow Chili Paste (see p. 405)
- ½ cup (4 fl oz/120 ml) Mirasol Chili Paste (see p. 405)
- 1 teaspoon ground cumin
- 2 teaspoons dried oregano
- 8 white bread slices
- ½ cup (4 fl oz/120 ml) whole (full-fat) milk, plus extra if necessary
- 1½ cups (13 fl oz/375 ml) shrimp (prawn) broth (stock), plus extra if necessary
- 48 medium shrimp (prawns), peeled and deveined
- ¾ oz (20 g) Parmesan cheese
- 2 white potatoes
- 2 cups (14 oz/400 g) Peruvian-Style Cooked White Rice to serve (see p. 178)
- salt and pepper

To garnish

- 4 pitted black olives
- 1 egg, hard-boiled and cut into quarters
- handful of huacatay leaves

Heat the oil in a pan over low heat, add the onion and garlic, and sauté for a few minutes, until the onion has softened. Add the chili pastes and season with salt and pepper.

Add the cumin and oregano and continue to cook, stirring, for 8 minutes until the paste has thickened and become fragrant, then remove from the heat and set aside.

Put the bread in a bowl, cover with the milk, and let soak for 5 minutes, then put in a blender with the onion and chile mixture. Blend together well.

Pour the blended mixture into a pan over medium heat and add the shrimp (prawn) broth (stock). Simmer for 5 minutes until the mixture has thickened and become creamy. Add the shrimp and Parmesan cheese. Taste and adjust the seasoning if necessary. Simmer for 1 minute until the shrimp have cooked. If the chili starts to dry out during the cooking process, add a little more broth or milk.

Meanwhile, bring a pan of water to a boil, add the potatoes, and cook until tender. Drain and cut into slices.

Arrange the sliced boiled potatoes on a serving platter and ladle over the shrimp chili. Garnish with the olives, hard-boiled egg quarters, and huacatay leaves and serve with rice.

ADOBO CUSQUEÑO
CUSCO-STYLE PORK ADOBO

Serves: 4
Preparation Time: 15 minutes, plus 12 hours marinating
Cooking Time: 1 hour 40 minutes

There is hardly any difference between this dish and the Arequipa-style pork adobo, although residents of Cusco and Arequipa would no doubt disagree and have lengthy debates on which one is tastier.

- 1 × 2¼-lb (1-kg) pork shoulder
- ½ tablespoon Garlic Paste (see p. 406)
- 4 tablespoons Panca Chili Paste (see p. 406)
- 1 teaspoon ground cumin
- 5 cups (42¼ fl oz/1.25 liters) chicha de jora
- 3 red onions, chopped
- 1 tablespoon fresh oregano
- ¼ teaspoon allspice
- 1½ oz (40 g) bizcocho, crumbled
- 2 slices rocoto chile
- ¼ cup (2 fl oz/50 ml) red wine
- 5 oz (150 g) steamed chuñoblanco, to serve
- salt and pepper

Cut the pork into equal-size 2 × 1½-inch/3 × 2-cm pieces, and place in a bowl. Add the garlic and chili pastes, ground cumin, chicha de jora, and onion. Season with salt and pepper and mix together well. Cover with plastic wrap (clingfilm), put in the refrigerator, and marinate for 12 hours.

Once marinated, put the meat and marinade into a pot or large pan with the oregano and allspice. Season with salt and simmer gently for 1½ hours, covered, until the meat is tender and cooked through. Add the bizcocho, rocoto chile slices, and red wine and cook for a few more minutes.

Ladle the stew into large shallow bowls and serve with steamed chuñoblanco.

Shrimp Chili

ADOBO
PORK ADOBO

Serves: 4
Preparation Time: 15 minutes, plus 12 hours marinating
Cooking Time: 1 hour 40 minutes

1 × 2¼-lb (1-kg) pork shoulder
½ tablespoon Garlic Paste (see p. 406)
4 tablespoons Panca Chili Paste (see p. 406)
¼ cup (2 fl oz/50 ml) red wine vinegar
4 cups (34 fl oz/1 liter) chicha de jora
3 red onions, 1 grated and 2 sliced
1 tablespoon fresh oregano
¼ teaspoon allspice
1 rocoto chile
4 sprigs oregano, leaves picked, to garnish
bread, to serve
salt and pepper

Cut the pork into equal-size 1½ x 1-inch/3 × 2-cm pieces and place in a bowl. Add the garlic and chili pastes, red wine vinegar, chicha de jora, and grated onion. Season with salt and pepper and mix together well. Cover with plastic wrap (clingfilm), put in the refrigerator, and marinate for 12 hours.

Once marinated, put the meat and marinade into a pot or large pan with the oregano and allspice. Season with salt and simmer gently for 1½ hours, covered, until the meat is tender and cooked through. Add the sliced red onions, cook for 5 minutes, then add the whole rocoto chile and cook for another 5 minutes, until the stew has a soupy consistency.

Remove the rocoto chile and ladle the stew into large shallow bowls. Garnish with oregano leaves and serve with bread.

ADOBO DE PATITAS
PIG FEET ADOBO

Serves: 4
Preparation Time: 10 minutes
Cooking Time: 1 hour 20 minutes

This dish is rarely seen on menus but is delicious, especially if the pig feet (trotters) are tender and their gelatinous texture is allowed to permeate the stew.

8 × 7-oz (200-g) pig feet (trotters)
1 bay leaf
2 cloves garlic, 1 whole and 1 chopped
3 tablespoons vegetable oil
2 red onions, chopped
4 tablespoons Panca Chili Paste (see p. 406)
1 teaspoon fresh oregano
½ cup (4 fl oz/120 ml) chicha de jora
2 tablespoons white vinegar
1 rocoto chile, sliced
1 cup (250 ml) Creole Sauce (see p. 416), to serve
salt and pepper

Place the pig feet (trotters) in a pot or large pan with the bay leaf, 4 teaspoons salt, and the whole garlic clove. Add enough water to cover the ingredients and place over the heat. Bring to a boil, then immediately remove the pig feet, draining and setting them aside.

Heat the oil in a separate pan over low heat, add the chopped onion and garlic, and sauté for a few minutes, until the onion has softened. Add the chili paste and oregano, season with salt and pepper, and continue to cook, stirring, for 8 minutes until the paste has thickened and become fragrant.

Add the pig feet to the pan, pour in the chicha de jora and vinegar, and add the sliced rocoto chile. Add enough water to cover the ingredients and cook, partially covered, for 1 hour, until the feet are tender.

Transfer the pig feet to large shallow bowls, ladle over the sauce, and serve with Creole sauce.

Pork Adobo

ADOBO DE PESCADO
FISH ADOBO

Serves: 4
Preparation Time: 10 minutes
Cooking Time: 30 minutes

This adobo is cooked briefly over very low heat so that the fish is juicy and really flavorsome.

2¼ lb (1 kg) bonito fish fillets, ¾ inch (2 cm) thick
¼ cup (2 fl oz/50 ml) white vinegar
4 oz (120 g) cornstarch (cornflour)
4 cups (2 fl oz/50 ml) vegetable oil, for deep-frying plus ¼ cup (2 fl oz/50 ml) for sautéing
2 red onions, sliced
2 cloves garlic, chopped
1 teaspoon ground cumin
4 tablespoons Panca Chili Paste (see p. 406)
2 yellow chiles, seeded, membrane removed, and thinly sliced
1 teaspoon fresh oregano
¼ cup (2 fl oz/50 ml) chicha de jora
4 slices rocoto chile, to garnish
salt and pepper

To serve
1 sweet potato, boiled and sliced (optional)
2 cups (14 oz/400 g) Peruvian-Style Cooked White Rice (see p. 178), optional

Thoroughly clean the fish fillets, cut them in half, and season with salt and pepper. Mix together with the vinegar and coat in cornstarch (cornflour).

Heat the oil for deep-frying in a large pan or deep-fryer to 350°F/180°C, or until a cube of bread browns in 30 seconds. Drop the fish fillets carefully into the hot oil and fry until golden. Drain well on paper towels.

In a separate pan, heat the remaining oil over low heat, add the onions and garlic, and sauté for 2 minutes, until the onions have softened. Add the cumin and chili paste, season with salt and pepper, and cook for another 4 minutes until the paste has thickened and become fragrant.

Carefully transfer the fish to the pan and add the sliced yellow chiles, oregano, and chicha de jora. Cook for a few minutes, being careful not to overcook the fish.

Ladle the fish stew into large shallow bowls. Garnish with rocoto chile slices and serve with boiled sweet potato slices or rice.

ADOBO DE LANGOSTA
LOBSTER ADOBO

Serves: 4
Preparation Time: 10 minutes, plus 10 minutes chilling
Cooking Time: 10 minutes

This is a dish that takes the adobo to a whole new level. It can also be prepared with shrimp (prawns) or crab.

8 × 5-oz (150-g) lobster tails
3 tablespoons Panca Chili Paste (see p. 406)
1 tablespoon garlic, finely chopped
1 teaspoon fresh oregano
2 tablespoons chicha de jora or white wine
2 white potatoes, peeled
8 sprigs oregano
1 rocoto chile, seeded, membrane removed, and sliced
½ cup (2 fl oz/120 ml) Creole Sauce (see p. 416), to serve (optional)
salt and pepper

Place the lobster tails in a bowl, add the chili paste, chopped garlic, oregano, and chicha de jora or white wine, and mix together well. Season with salt and pepper and marinate for 10 minutes in the refrigerator.

Bring a pan of water to a boil, add the potatoes, and cook until tender. Drain and cut into slices. Set aside.

Preheat the oven to 400°F/200°C/Gas Mark 6. Place the lobster tails and their juices in the center of a double layer of kitchen foil. Top each tail with some boiled potato slices, an oregano sprig, and a rocoto chile slice, and carefully wrap up the sides of the foil to form an envelope.

Place the foil envelope in the preheated oven and bake for 10 minutes. Remove from the oven, unwrap, and serve the lobster tails in large shallow bowls with the potato slices, cooking juices, and Creole sauce, if desired.

CAUCHE DE QUESO
CHEESE CAUCHE

Serves: 4
Preparation Time: 15 minutes
Cooking Time: 15 minutes

This cauche is a type of stew or chili with cheese as the main ingredient. It is really delicious, simple to prepare, and you can use any cheese to bring out its wonderful flavors.

- 4 white potatoes, peeled
- 4 tablespoons vegetable oil
- 4 red onions, sliced
- 4 cloves garlic, chopped
- 1 tomato, skinned, seeded, and chopped
- 1 teaspoon ground cumin
- 3 tablespoons Panca Chili Paste (see p. 406)
- 1½ cups (13 fl oz/375 ml) whole (full-fat) milk
- 1 sprig huacatay
- 9 oz (250 g) queso fresco, sliced
- salt and pepper

To garnish
- 1 rocoto chile, seeded, membrane removed, and chopped
- 2 teaspoons chopped huacatay leaves

Bring a pan of water to a boil, add the potatoes, and cook until tender. Drain and cut into ½-inch/1-cm slices. Set aside.

Heat the oil in a pan over low heat, add the onion, garlic, and tomato to the pan, and sauté for a few minutes, until the onion has softened. Add the cumin and chili paste, season with salt and pepper, and continue to cook, stirring, for a few minutes, until the onion is translucent.

Add the milk, huacatay sprig, and queso fresco to the pan and continue to cook, stirring, until the cheese melts. Taste and adjust the seasoning if necessary.

Divide the boiled potato slices between large shallow bowls. Ladle over the stew and garnish with the chopped rocoto chile and huacatay leaves.

CAUCHE DE CAMARONES
SHRIMP CAUCHE

Serves: 4
Preparation Time: 20 minutes
Cooking Time: 15 minutes

This shrimp cauche is the festive version of the cheese cauche. It is absolutely delicious and a pleasure to enjoy in the traditional picanterías (inexpensive restaurants specializing in spicy food) of Arequipa.

- 4 white potatoes, peeled
- 4 tablespoons vegetable oil
- 2 red onions, sliced
- 3 cloves garlic, finely chopped
- 2 tomatoes, skinned, seeded, and chopped
- 2 tablespoons Panca Chili Paste (see p. 406)
- ½ cup (2 oz/50 g) Shrimp Head Paste (see p. 29)
- 1½ cups (13 fl oz/375 ml) whole (full-fat) milk
- ¼ cup (2 fl oz/50 ml) shrimp (prawn) broth (stock)
- 1 sprig huacatay
- 9 oz (250 g) queso fresco, grated
- 48 medium shrimp (prawns), peeled and deveined, with tails still intact
- salt and pepper

To garnish
- 1 rocoto chile, seeded, membrane removed, and chopped
- 4 sprigs huacatay, leaves picked

Bring a pan of water to a boil, add the potatoes, and cook until tender. Drain and cut into ½-inch/1-cm slices. Set aside.

Heat the oil in a pan over low heat, add the onion, garlic and tomato, and sauté for a few minutes, until the onion has softened. Season with salt and pepper, add the chili paste, and cook for another 2 minutes, then add the shrimp paste, milk, broth (stock), huacatay sprig, and queso fresco. Cook for a few minutes, stirring, until the cheese has melted. Add the shrimp (prawns) and cook for a few minutes more, until the shrimp are cooked. Taste and adjust the seasoning if necessary.

Divide the potato slices among large shallow bowls. Ladle over the stew and garnish with the chopped rocoto chile and huacatay leaves.

CAUCHE VEGETARIANO
VEGETARIAN CAUCHE

Serves: 4
Preparation Time: 20 minutes
Cooking Time: 40 minutes

You can try this cauche out with different types of cheese. They will enhance the vegetables in different ways and provide you with unique taste sensations.

4½ white potatoes, peeled
4 tablespoons vegetable oil
4 red onions, sliced
4 cloves garlic, chopped
3 tomatoes, skinned, seeded, and diced
1 teaspoon ground cumin
3 tablespoons Yellow Chili Paste (see p. 405)
1½ cups (13 fl oz/375 ml) whole (full-fat) milk
1 sprig huacatay
9 oz (250 g) queso fresco, sliced
1½ oz (40 g) squash, cut into ½-inch (1-cm) cubes
1½ oz (40 g) fava (broad) beans, skins removed
salt and pepper

To garnish
1 rocoto chile, seeded, membrane removed, and chopped
3 teaspoons chopped huacatay leaves

Bring a pan of water to a boil, add 4 of the potatoes and cook until tender. Drain and cut into ½ inch/1-cm thick slices. Set aside. Cut the remaining potato half into ½-inch/1-cm cubes and set aside.

Heat the oil in a pan over low heat, add the onion, garlic, and tomato and sauté for a few minutes, until the onion has softened. Season with salt and pepper, add the cumin and chili paste and cook for another 2 minutes. Add the milk, huacatay sprig, and queso fresco and continue to cook over low heat, stirring, until the cheese melts, about 2 minutes.

Add the cubed potato and squash and cook for 10 minutes, until the vegetables are tender and cooked through. Add the fava (broad) beans and cook for a few more minutes, until the beans are cooked. Taste and adjust the seasoning if necessary.

Divide the potato slices among large shallow bowls. Ladle over the stew and garnish with the chopped rocoto chile and huacatay leaves.

ATAMALADO DE QUINUA
QUINOA AND PORK ATAMALADO

Serves: 4
Preparation Time: 20 minutes
Cooking Time: 1 hour 30 minutes

The quinoa from the elevated plateaus of Peru and Bolivia is increasingly prevalent on the menus of the finest restaurants in the world. It is a treasure that works beautifully in recipes such as this atamalado.

4 tablespoons vegetable oil
1 red onion, chopped
4 cloves garlic, finely chopped
2 tomatoes, skinned, seeded, and chopped
1 teaspoon dried oregano
4 tablespoons Panca Chili Paste (see p. 406)
2¼ lb (1 kg) pork belly, cut into 1½-inch (3-cm) pieces
4 cups (34 fl oz/1 liter) vegetable broth (stock)
6 oz (175 g) quinoa grains, washed
salt and pepper

To garnish
1 rocoto chile, seeded, membrane removed, and chopped
huacatay leaves

Season the pork pieces with salt and pepper. Heat 2 tablespoons of the oil in a skillet or frying pan over high heat, add the pork, and brown on all sides. Remove from the pan and place on paper towels to drain.

In the same pan, add the remaining oil and the onion, garlic, and tomato, and sauté for 2 minutes, until the onion has softened. Add the oregano and chili paste, season with salt and pepper, and cook for another 2 minutes. Set aside.

Add the browned pork pieces to the pan with the onion and chile mixture and pour in the vegetable broth (stock). Bring to a simmer and cook gently over low heat for 1 hour, or until the pork is tender.

Add the quinoa to the pan and cook for 15 minutes, or until the quinoa grains split. Taste and adjust the seasoning, if necessary. Spoon into large shallow bowls and garnish with the chopped rocoto chile and huacatay leaves.

ATAMALADO DE QUINUA CON MARISCOS
QUINOA AND SEAFOOD ATAMALADO

Serves 4
Preparation Time: 15 minutes
Cooking Time: 25 minutes

An atamalado is not a tamale or a risotto. It is an atamalado. It develops when the stew thickens and little treasures are hidden among its juices—in this case, seafood delicacies—which combine wonderfully with the quinoa.

- 9 oz (250 g) quinoa, washed
- ¼ cup (2 fl oz/50 ml) vegetable oil
- 1 red onion, chopped
- 4 cloves garlic, finely chopped
- 1 tomato, skinned, seeded, and chopped
- 1 teaspoon dried oregano
- 4 tablespoons Yellow Chili Paste (see p. 405)
- 4 cups (34 fl oz /1 liter) vegetable broth (stock)
- 4¼ oz (120 g) clean shrimp (prawns), peeled and deveined
- 12 scallops
- 2¼ oz (60 g) squid, cut into rings
- 4¼ oz (80 g) Cooked Octopus, sliced (see p. 406)
- 2 tablespoons huacatay leaves, to garnish
- salt and pepper

Heat the vegetable oil in a pan over low heat, add the onion, garlic, and tomato, and sauté for 2 minutes, until the onion has softened. Add the oregano and chili paste, season with salt and pepper, and cook for another 2 minutes until thickened and fragrant. Add the washed quinoa and broth (stock) to the pan and cook for about 15 minutes, or until the quinoa grains split.

Add the shrimp (prawns), scallops, squid, and octopus, and cook for a few minutes, stirring, until the scallops and shrimp are cooked through. Taste and adjust the seasoning if necessary. Serve in large shallow bowls and garnish with huacatay leaves.

ATAMALADO VERDE DE QUINUA CON PAVITA
GREEN QUINOA AND TURKEY ATAMALADO

Serves: 4
Preparation Time: 15 minutes
Cooking Time: 1 hour 30 minutes

- 6 oz (175 g) quinoa, washed
- 2¼ lb (1 kg) turkey meat, both white and brown meat
- 4 tablespoons vegetable oil
- 1 red onion, chopped
- 4 cloves garlic, finely chopped
- 2 tomatoes, skinned, seeded, and chopped
- 1 teaspoon dried oregano
- 4 tablespoons Yellow Chili Paste (see p. 405)
- 4 cups (34 fl oz/1 liter) vegetable broth (stock)
- 3 tablespoons Blended Culantro (see p. 407)
- salt and pepper

To garnish

- 4 tablespoons chopped rocoto chile, seeded and deveined
- 2 tablespoons chopped parsley

Cut the turkey meat into 3½-oz/100-g pieces. Season with salt and pepper. Set aside. Heat 2 tablespoons vegetable oil in a skillet or frying pan over low heat, add the turkey, and brown on all sides. Remove from the pan and place on paper towels to drain.

Heat the remaining oil in the pan, add the onion, garlic, and tomato, and sauté for 2 minutes, until the onion has softened. Add the oregano and chili paste, season with salt and pepper, and cook for another 2 minutes until the paste has thickened and become fragrant. Set aside.

Add the browned turkey pieces to the pan with the onion and chile mixture and pour in the broth (stock) and blended culantro. Bring to a simmer and cook gently over low heat for 1 hour, or until the turkey is tender.

Add the washed quinoa to the pan and cook for 15 minutes, or until the quinoa grains split. Taste and adjust the seasoning, if necessary. Ladle into large shallow bowls and garnish with chopped rocoto chile and parsley. Serve.

CAPCHI DE GRANOS
MULTIGRAIN CAPCHI

Serves: 4
Preparation Time: 10 minutes
Cooking Time: 20 minutes

Capchi is a flavorsome Andean dish in which the cheese and milk subtly combine with the vegetables and Andean grains. You can also try preparing it with different local vegetables.

1 white potato, peeled
4 tablespoons vegetable oil
1 red onion, chopped
2 cloves garlic, chopped
2 tablespoons Mirasol Chili Paste (see p. 405)
2 cups (18 fl oz/500 ml) vegetable broth (stock)
1½ oz (40 g) canihua
1½ oz (40 g) amaranth
1½ oz (40 g) multicolored quinoa
1 sprig huacatay
1 sprig wormseed
1 sprig mint
½ cup (4 fl oz/120 ml) heavy (double) cream
1½ oz (40 g) queso fresco, cut into ½-inch (1-cm) cubes
salt and pepper

To garnish
1 tablespoon chopped huacatay leaves
1 tablespoon chopped wormseed
1 tablespoon chopped mint

Bring a pan of water to a boil, add the potatoes, and cook until tender. Drain and cut into ½-inch /1-cm cubes. Set aside.

Heat the vegetable oil in a pan over low heat, add the onion and garlic, and sauté for 2 minutes, until the onion has softened. Add the chili paste and cook for another 2 minutes until the paste has thickened and become fragrant.

Pour in the broth (stock) and bring to a boil, then add the canihua, amaranth, quinoa, and herb sprigs. Reduce the heat to a simmer and cook for 10 minutes, until the grains are cooked. Add the boiled potato cubes, cream, and cubed queso fresco and remove the herb sprigs. Taste and adjust the seasoning, if necessary.

Ladle into large, shallow bowls and garnish with the chopped huacatay, wormseed, and mint. Serve.

CAPCHI DE HABAS
FAVA BEAN CAPCHI

Serves: 4
Preparation Time: 15 minutes
Cooking Time: 35 minutes

This is one of my favorite vegetarian dishes. If you allow the fava (broad) beans to slowly combine with the other ingredients, they will soak up their flavors and take on a wonderful texture.

2 white potatoes, peeled
11 oz (300 g) fava (broad) beans
4 tablespoons vegetable oil
1 red onion, chopped
2 cloves garlic, chopped
2 tablespoons Yellow Chili Paste (see p. 405)
½ tablespoon Panca Chili Paste (see p. 406)
½ cup (4 fl oz/120 ml) vegetable broth (stock)
1 cup (8 fl oz/250 ml) whole (full-fat) milk
½ cup (4 fl oz/120 ml) heavy (double) cream
4 oz (120 g) queso fresco, grated
4 eggs, beaten
1 teaspoon chopped huacatay leaves
1 teaspoon chopped mint
1 teaspoon chopped wormseed
salt and pepper

To garnish
2½ oz (65 g) queso fresco, cut into ½-inch (1-cm) cubes
4 sprigs huacatay, leaves picked

Bring a pan of water to a boil, add the potatoes, and cook until tender. Drain and cut into ½-inch /1-cm cubes. Set aside. Boil the fava (broad) beans until tender, drain, and remove the skins.

Heat the vegetable oil in a pan over low heat, add the onion and garlic, and sauté for 2 minutes, until the onion has softened. Season with salt and pepper, add the chili pastes, and cook for another 8 minutes until the paste has thickened and become fragrant.

Pour in the broth (stock) and bring to a boil, then add the fava (broad) beans, cubed potatoes, milk, and cream. Reduce the heat to a simmer and cook for another 5 minutes, until the mixture begins to thicken. Add the grated queso fresco, beaten eggs, huacatay, mint, and wormseed, and cook for another 2 minutes. Taste and adjust the seasoning as desired.

Ladle into large shallow bowls and garnish with the cubed queso fresco and huacatay leaves. Serve.

CAPCHI DE SETAS
MUSHROOM CAPCHI

Serves: 4
Preparation Time: 10 minutes
Cooking Time: 30–35 minutes

- 2 white potatoes, peeled
- 8 oz (225 g) fava (broad) beans
- 4 tablespoons vegetable oil
- 1 red onion, chopped
- 2 cloves garlic, chopped
- 1 teaspoon ground cumin
- 1 teaspoon oregano
- 2 tablespoons Yellow Chili Paste (see p. 405)
- ½ tablespoon Panca Chili Paste (see p. 406)
- 11 oz (300 g) white (button) mushrooms
- 1½ cups (13 fl oz/375 ml) whole (full-fat) milk
- ½ cup (120 ml) heavy (double) cream
- 4 oz (120 g) queso fresco, grated
- 4 eggs, beaten
- 2 teaspoons chopped huacatay leaves, plus extra to garnish
- 2 teaspoons chopped mint
- salt and pepper

Bring a pan of water to a boil, add the potatoes, and cook until tender. Drain and cut into cubes. Set aside. Boil the fava (broad) beans until tender, drain and remove the skins.

Heat the vegetable oil in a pan over low heat, add the onion and garlic, and sauté for 2 minutes, until the onion has softened. Add the cumin, oregano, and chili pastes, season with salt and pepper, and cook for another 4 minutes.

Add the button (white) mushrooms, potatoes, and fava beans, followed by the milk and cream, and cook over low heat until the mixture thickens. Add the queso fresco, beaten eggs, huacatay, and mint and cook for another 2 minutes.

Ladle into large shallow bowls and garnish with huacatay leaves. Serve.

CARAPULCRA CHINCHANA
CHINCHA-STYLE PORK AND POTATO STEW

Serves: 4
Preparation Time: 20 minutes
Cooking Time: 1 hour 20 minutes

Potatoes are Peru's most prolific and varied agricultural export, so it is no surprise that they have been cooked and prepared in every way possible: sun-dried, dehydrated on ice, fermented, and so on. This dish, which in Lima is prepared with dried (dehydrated) potatoes, is made with fresh potatoes in Chincha.

- 3 oz (80 g) peanuts
- 2¼ lb (1 kg) pork ribs
- 1 oz (25 g) lard
- 1 small red onion, chopped
- 4 cloves garlic, chopped
- 3 cloves
- 1 cinnamon stick
- pinch of ground cumin
- 3 tablespoons Panca Chili Paste (see p. 406)
- 2 tablespoons Mirasol Chili Paste (see p. 405)
- 2 quarts (67½ fl oz/2 liters) pork broth (stock)
- 1 lb 5 oz (600 g) white potatoes, cut into ½-inch (1-cm) cubes
- salt and pepper

Place the peanuts in a mortar or *batán* (Peruvian grinder) and grind until fine. Set aside.

Cut the pork ribs into 2 × 2-inch/5 × 5-cm pieces and season with salt and pepper.

Melt half the lard in a pan over medium heat, add the pork rib pieces, and brown on all sides. Once browned, remove from the pan and set aside.

Add the remaining lard to the pan with the onion and garlic and sauté for a few minutes, until the onion has softened. Add the cloves, cinnamon stick, cumin, and chili pastes and season with salt and pepper. Cook over low heat, stirring, for 5 minutes until the onion is cooked and soft and the ingredients are well mixed.

Return the browned pork pieces to the pan and pour in the pork broth (stock), ensuring that the liquid covers the meat (you can add a little water if necessary). Bring to a simmer and cook over low heat, covered, for 40 minutes, until the meat is tender.

Add the white potato cubes and simmer for another 10 minutes, until the potato is cooked. Add the ground peanuts, taste, and adjust the seasoning if necessary. Spoon into large shallow bowls and serve.

CARAPULCRA
PORK AND DRIED POTATO STEW

Serves: 4
Preparation Time: 15 minutes, plus overnight soaking
Cooking Time: 2 hours 55 minutes – 3 hours 55 minutes

When cooked, dried potatoes give off a starchy substance similar to that produced when cooking risotto, which helps to thicken the stew. Each piece of potato gradually develops a lovely al dente texture as it is rehydrated.

4 cups dehydrated, flaked potatoes
2¼ lb (1 kg) pork ribs
3 oz (80 g) peanuts
1 oz (25 g) lard
1 small red onion, chopped
4 cloves garlic, chopped
3 cloves
1 cinnamon stick
pinch of ground cumin
4 tablespoons Panca Chili Paste (see p. 406)
2 tablespoons Yellow Chili Paste (see p. 405)
2 quarts (67½ fl oz/2 liters) pork broth (stock)
salt and pepper

Preheat the oven to 300°F/150°C/Gas Mark 2.

Toast the dried potatoes in the oven for 6 minutes until they start to brown. Place the toasted potatoes in a bowl, cover with water, and let soak overnight.

The next day, cut the pork ribs into 2 × 2-inch /5 × 5-cm pieces and season with salt and pepper. Place the peanuts in a mortar or *batán* (Peruvian grinder) and grind until fine. Set aside.

Melt half the lard in a pan over medium heat, add the pork rib pieces, and brown on all sides. Once browned, remove from the pan and set aside.

Add the remaining lard to the pan with the onion and garlic, and sauté for a few minutes, until the onion has softened. Add the cloves, cinnamon stick, cumin, and chili pastes and season with salt and pepper. Cook over low heat, stirring, for 10 minutes until the paste thickens and the onions are well cooked.

Drain the soaked potatoes and add to the pan with the browned pork pieces. Pour in the pork broth (stock), ensuring that the liquid covers the ingredients (you can add a little water if necessary). Bring to a simmer and cook over low heat, uncovered, for 2–3 hours, until the meat is tender.

Add the ground peanuts and cook for another 30 minutes. Taste and adjust the seasoning if necessary. Spoon into large shallow bowls and serve.

Pork and Dried Potato Stew

Corn-thickened Turkey Stew

CHANFAINITA
BEEF LUNG STEW

Serves: 4
Preparation Time: 15 minutes
Cooking Time: 35 minutes

This is a dish born of the people, which takes beef or lamb lungs and turns them into a delicious stew. Serve it with plenty of blended chiles, toasted corn kernels, and lemon juice to enjoy it as Peruvians enjoy it.

- 1 lb 2 oz (500 g) cows' lungs
- 2 tablespoons vegetable oil
- 1 red onion, chopped
- 4 cloves garlic, finely chopped
- pinch of ground cumin
- 2 tablespoons Panca Chili Paste (see p. 406)
- 1 tablespoon Yellow Chili Paste (see p. 405)
- 1 lb 2 oz (500 g) white potatoes, cut into ½-inch (1-cm) cubes
- 2 cups (18 fl oz/500 ml) vegetable broth (stock)
- 1 tablespoon chopped mint
- 4 scallions (spring onions), green part only, chopped
- salt and pepper

To serve
- 1 cup (7 oz/200 g) cancha (toasted corn)
- ½ cup (4 fl oz/120 ml) Rocoto Chili Paste (see p. 407)

Thoroughly wash the lungs. Once clean, cut each lung into three pieces. Bring a pan of water to a simmer, add the lungs, and cook for 10 minutes. Remove from the pan and cut into ½-inch/1.5-cm cubes. Set aside.

Heat the oil in a pan over low heat, add the onion and garlic, and sauté for 2 minutes, until the onion has softened. Add the cumin and chili pastes, season with salt and pepper, and cook over low heat, stirring, for 10 minutes until the paste thickens and the onions are well cooked.

Add the cooked lungs and cubed white potatoes to the pan. Pour in the broth (stock), bring to a simmer, and cook for 10 minutes, until the potatoes are cooked. Taste and adjust the seasoning, if necessary.

Add the mint and chopped scallions (spring onions) and spoon into large shallow bowls. Serve with cancha and rocoto chili paste on the side.

ESPESADO DE PAVITA
CORN-THICKENED TURKEY STEW

Serves: 4
Preparation Time: 15 minutes
Cooking Time: 1 hour 35 minutes

The corn in this recipe acts as a thickening agent, which gives this dish its name. It also adds flavor and color and is, in fact, the star ingredient of this dish.

- 9 oz (250 g) corn kernels
- bunch of culantro or cilantro (coriander) leaves
- 2 tablespoons vegetable oil
- 1 onion, chopped
- 4 cloves garlic, finely chopped
- 2 oz (50 g) loche squash, grated
- 1 caigua, chopped
- 2 tablespoons Yellow Chili Paste (see p. 405)
- 1 × 2¼-lb (1-kg) turkey, cut into 2¾-oz (80-g) pieces
- 2 cups (14 oz/400 g) Peruvian-Style Cooked White Rice (see p. 178), to serve
- salt and pepper

Put the corn kernels and culantro or cilantro (coriander) leaves in a blender or *batán* (Peruvian grinder) and blend or grind to form a thick paste. Set aside.

Heat the oil in a large pan over low heat, add the onion and garlic, and sauté for 2 minutes, until the onion has softened. Season with salt and pepper. Add the grated squash, caigua, and chili paste, and cook, stirring, for 10 minutes until the ingredients are cooked. Pour in 8½ cups (68 fl oz/2 liters) water and simmer over low heat for 30 minutes until the stew has thickened and reduced.

Season the turkey pieces with salt and pepper. Add the turkey to the stew and cook for 40–45 minutes over low heat until tender. Add the corn paste to the pan and cook for 10 minutes, stirring continuously, until the stew thickens. Taste and adjust the seasoning if necessary. Serve with rice.

Stewed Duck with Kumquats

ESTOFADO DE PATO CON NARANJITAS CHINAS
STEWED DUCK WITH KUMQUATS

Serves: 4
Preparation Time: 20 minutes, plus 10 minutes marinating
Cooking Time: 2 hours 30 minutes

This is a delicious stew, mainly due to the depth of flavor added by the kumquats. They bring a bittersweet flavor to the stew that is really unique.

1 × 4½-lb (2-kg) duck, cut into 6 pieces
1 tablespoon ground cumin
3 cloves garlic, finely chopped
1 cup (8 fl oz/250 ml) orange juice
½ cup (4 fl oz/120 ml) vegetable oil
1 cup (8 fl oz/250 ml) beef or duck broth (stock)
1 cup (8 fl oz/250 ml) white wine
4 tablespoons Yellow Chili Paste (see p. 405)
Fried Yucca-Root Batons (see p. 80), to serve
salt and pepper

Kumquats in syrup
2 cups (10½ oz/300 g) kumquats
7 oz (200 g) granulated sugar

For the kumquats in syrup, thoroughly wash and dry the kumquats and cut them in half. Place in a pan with 1½ cups (13 fl oz/375 ml) water, bring to a boil, and cook until softened. Add the sugar and continue to cook, without stirring, until a syrup forms. Set aside.

For the stew, place the duck pieces in a bowl, add the cumin and half the chopped garlic, and season with salt and pepper. Pour in the orange juice and marinate for 10 minutes, covered in plastic wrap (clingfilm) and placed in the refrigerator.

Heat the oil in a skillet or frying pan over medium heat, add the duck pieces, reserving the marinade, and brown on all sides. Once browned, remove the duck from the pan and drain on paper towels.

Place the browned duck pieces in a pan and pour in the broth (stock), white wine, and marinade. Bring to a simmer, cover, and cook for 2 hours, until the duck is tender. Set aside.

In a separate pan, heat the remaining oil over low heat, add the chili paste and remaining chopped garlic, and season with salt and pepper. Cook gently, stirring, for 6 minutes until the paste has thickened and become fragrant. Add the cooked duck pieces to the pan and pour in 1 cup (8 fl oz/250 ml) of the duck cooking liquid. Bring to a simmer and cook for a few minutes. Taste and adjust the seasoning, if necessary.

Ladle the duck stew into large shallow bowls and serve with the kumquats in syrup and fried yucca-root batons.

ESPESADO DE PECHO
CORN-THICKENED BRISKET STEW

Serves: 4
Preparation Time: 20 minutes
Cooking Time: 1 hour 20 minutes

The key to success when it comes to this dish is to cook the meat very slowly to ensure that it is nice and tender.

9 oz (250 g) corn kernels
bunch of culantro or cilantro (coriander) leaves
2¼ lb (1 kg) beef brisket, cut into 1½-inch (3-cm) cubes
4 cloves garlic, chopped
2 onions, 1 cut in half and 1 chopped
1 leek, chopped
2 celery stalks
2 tablespoons vegetable oil
2 oz (50 g) loche squash, grated
1 caigua, chopped
2 tablespoons Yellow Chili Paste (see p. 405)
7 oz (200 g) yucca root (cassava), peeled and cut into 2 × 1-inch/5 × 2-cm pieces
salt and pepper

To serve
2 cups (14 oz/400 g) Peruvian-Style Cooked White Rice (see p. 178)
1 cup (250 ml) Creole Sauce (see p. 416)

Put the corn kernels and culantro or cilantro (coriander) leaves in a blender or *batán* (Peruvian grinder) and blend or grind to form a thick paste. Set aside.

Put the brisket, half the garlic, the onion halves, leek, celery stalks, and enough water in a pan to come 2 inches/5 cm above the ingredients. Simmer for 1 hour over moderate heat until the meat is tender. Strain, setting the broth (stock) and the meat aside. Discard the vegetables.

Heat the oil in a pan over low heat, add the chopped onion and remaining garlic, and sauté for 2 minutes, until the onion has softened. Season with salt and pepper. Add the squash, caigua, and chili paste and cook, stirring, for 5 minutes until the paste has thickened and is fragrant. Add the meat and yucca root (cassava) pieces to the pan, pour in the broth and continue to cook until the yucca root is tender. Add the corn paste and cook for another 10 minutes, stirring continuously, until the stew thickens. Taste and adjust the seasoning, if necessary.

Serve with rice and Creole sauce.

CHARQUICÁN
PORK JERKY AND BEEF STEW

Serves: 4
Preparation Time: 20, plus overnight soaking
Cooking Time: 1 hour 10 minutes

Charquicán is a southern Peruvian dish that also features on menus in northern Chile. The secret is to stew the delicious dried and fresh meats very slowly with potatoes and Peruvian spices.

7 oz (200 g) shredded pork jerky
2 tablespoons vegetable oil
1 red onion, chopped
4 cloves garlic, finely chopped
pinch of ground cumin
2 tablespoons Panca Chili Paste (see p. 406)
1 tablespoon Yellow Chili Paste (see p. 405)
14 oz (400 g) brisket beef, cut into 1-inch (2.5-cm) cubes
2 cups (18 fl oz/500 ml) beef broth (stock)
¼ cup (2 fl oz/50 ml) chicha de jora
11 oz (350 g) white potatoes, cut into ½-inch/1-cm cubes
salt and pepper

Put the pork jerky in a bowl, cover with water, and let soak overnight. Drain and set aside.

Heat the oil in a pan over low heat, add the onion and garlic, and sauté for 2 minutes, until the onion has softened. Add the cumin and chili pastes, season with salt and pepper, and cook over low heat, stirring, for 10 minutes until the paste thickens and the onions are well cooked.

Add the cubed beef, pork jerky, broth (stock), and chicha de jora. Bring to a simmer and cook for 45 minutes, until the meat is tender. Add the potatoes and simmer for 10 minutes, until the potatoes are cooked. Taste and adjust the seasoning, if necessary. Serve.

ESTOFADO DE PATITAS
PIG FEET STEW

Serves: 4
Preparation Time: 15 minutes
Cooking Time: 1 hours 30 minutes

Peruvians love any type of stew and slow cooking is celebrated most. A stew prepared with pig feet (trotters) throws a wrench in the works because not everyone loves gelatinous textures—this is something I have never understood as a chef.

4 × 7-oz (200-g) pig feet (trotters)
1 bay leaf
4 cloves garlic, 1 whole and 3 chopped
3 tablespoons vegetable oil
1 small red onion, chopped
3 tablespoons Panca Chili Paste(see p. 406)
3 tablespoons Yellow Chili Paste (see p. 405)
2 tablespoons chicha de jora
11 oz (300 g) yellow potatoes, cut into ½-inch (1-cm) cubes
1 carrot, sliced
2 cups (14 oz/400 g) Peruvian-Style Cooked White Rice (see p. 178), to serve
salt and pepper

Place the pig feet (trotters) in a large pan with the bay leaf, whole garlic clove, and a pinch of salt. Cover with water and place over the heat. Bring to a boil, then immediately remove the pig feet, draining and setting them aside.

Heat the oil in a separate pan over low heat, add the chopped garlic, onion, and chili pastes, and season with salt and pepper. Cook gently, stirring, for 10 minutes until the paste has thickened and become fragrant. Add the pig feet, chicha de jora, and enough water to cover the ingredients, and simmer for 1 hour, until the feet are tender. Add the yellow potatoes and sliced carrot and continue to simmer for around 20 minutes until the vegetables are cooked and the stew has thickened. Remove the pig feet and cut the meat into 2-inch/4-cm chunks. Serve with rice.

ESTOFADO DE POLLO CASERO
HOMEMADE CHICKEN STEW

Serves: 4
Preparation Time: 20 minutes, plus 15 minutes soaking
Cooking Time: 50 minutes

Every household in Peru—even the most humble—knows how to prepare a delicious chicken stew. The aroma that fills a house while this stew bubbles away brings back happy memories of a mother's love.

10 g (¼ oz) dried mushrooms, any type, not too aromatic
½ cup (4 fl oz/120 ml) vegetable oil
1 × 3¼-lb (1.5-kg) chicken, cut into 8 pieces
1 onion, chopped
6 cloves garlic, finely chopped
2 tablespoons Panca Chili Paste (see p. 406)
2 tablespoons tomato paste
3 tomatoes, skinned, seeded, and grated
1 bay leaf
½ cup (4 fl oz/120 ml) red wine
4 cups (34 fl oz/1 liter) chicken broth (stock)
1½ oz (40 g) raisins
scant ¾ cup (2¾ oz/70 g) peas
4 oz (120 g) carrots, sliced
4 white potatoes, halved
2 cups (14 oz/400 g) Peruvian-Style Cooked White Rice (see p. 178), to serve
salt and pepper

Soak the dried mushrooms in a bowl of hot water for 15 minutes, then squeeze to drain, and slice into bite-size pieces.

Heat half the oil in a skillet or frying pan over medium heat. Season the chicken pieces with salt and pepper, add to the pan, and brown on all sides. Remove from the pan and set aside.

Heat the remaining oil in a separate pan over low heat, add the onion and garlic, and sauté for a few minutes, until the onion has softened. Add the chili and tomato pastes and cook gently, stirring, for 10 minutes until the paste has thickened and become fragrant. Add the grated tomato, bay leaf, mushrooms, and chicken pieces, pour in the wine and chicken broth (stock), and season with salt and pepper. Bring to a simmer and cook for 10 minutes, then add the raisins, peas, carrots, and potatoes. Cover and continue to simmer for 15 minutes, until the potatoes are tender. Taste and adjust the seasoning, if necessary. Serve with rice.

FREJOLADA
BEAN STEW

Serves: 4
Preparation Time: 20 minutes, plus overnight soaking
Cooking Time: 2 hours 15 minutes

Peruvians love beans. We often serve them with rice and creole sauce, but we also love drenching them in stew juices to combine different flavors and textures.

14 oz (400 g) canary beans
7 oz (200 g) pork jowl (cheek), diced
2 onions, 1 cut in half and 1 chopped
4 cloves garlic, 2 left whole and 2 chopped
1 carrot
2 tablespoons olive oil, plus extra for drizzling
1 cooking chorizo sausage, sliced
1 smoked pork sausage, sliced
1 × 7-oz (200-g) bacon joint, cut into 1-inch (2.5-cm) cubes
1 teaspoon ground cumin
1 teaspoon dried oregano
3 tablespoons Panca Chili Paste (see p. 406)

To serve
2 cups (14 oz/400 g) Peruvian-Style Cooked White Rice (see p. 178)
1 cup (250 ml) Creole Sauce (see p. 416)
salt and pepper

Place the beans in a large bowl, cover with water, and let soak overnight.

The next day, drain the water and place the beans in a pot or large pan. Add the diced pork jowls (cheeks), onion halves, whole garlic cloves, carrot, and enough water to cover the ingredients. Bring to a boil, then reduce the heat and simmer for at least 45 minutes, until the beans are cooked. Remove the pan from the heat and drain, setting aside the beans and the cooking liquid.

In a separate pan, heat the oil over medium heat, add the sausages and bacon, and brown on all sides. Remove the browned meat from the pan and set aside. Lower the heat, add the chopped onion and garlic, and sauté for 2 minutes, until the onion has softened. Season with salt and pepper, add the cumin, oregano, and chili paste, and cook, stirring, for 10 minutes until the sauce has thickened and become fragrant.

Add the beans, bean cooking liquid, sausages, and bacon to the pan and simmer over moderate heat for 1 hour until the stew has thickened and reduced and the sausages are cooked through. Taste and adjust the seasoning if necessary.

Ladle the bean stew into an earthenware pot, drizzle over a little olive oil, and serve with rice and Creole sauce.

FREJOLES BATIDOS
SMOKY BLENDED BEANS

Serves: 4
Preparation Time: 20 minutes, plus overnight soaking
Cooking Time: 1 hour 10 minutes

The great Peruvian chef Teresa Izquierdo set an example with her humility, perseverance, gratitude, and respect and blessed us with many delicious bean recipes such as this one.

- 14 oz (400 g) black beans
- 3½ oz (100 g) pork jowl (cheek)
- 7 oz (200 g) smoked bacon, cut into 1-inch (2.5-cm) cubes
- 2 tablespoons olive oil, plus extra for drizzling
- 1½ oz (40 g) bacon, diced
- 1 red onion, chopped
- 2 yellow chiles, seeded, membrane removed, and thinly sliced
- 4 cloves garlic, finely chopped
- pinch of ground cumin
- 2 tablespoons Yellow Chili Paste (see p. 405)
- salt and pepper

To serve

- 2 cups (14 oz/400 g) Peruvian-Style Cooked White Rice (see p. 178)
- 1 cup (250 ml) Creole Sauce (see p. 416)

Place the beans in a large bowl, cover with water, and let soak overnight.

The next day, drain the water and place the beans in a pan. Cover with cold water and place over the heat. Bring to a boil and simmer for a few minutes, then drain.

Return the beans to the pan, cover with hot water, and return to a boil. Drain again and return to the pan with the pork jowl, smoked bacon pieces, and more hot water to cover. Bring to a simmer and cook for at least 45 minutes, until the beans are cooked.

Put the bean and pork mixture in a blender, reserving the bean cooking liquid separately. Blend until smooth and set aside in a pan.

Heat the olive oil in a skillet or frying pan over medium heat, add the diced bacon, and brown on all sides. Lower the heat, add the onion, chiles, and garlic, and sauté for 2 minutes, until the onion has softened. Season with salt and pepper, add the cumin and chili paste, and cook, stirring, for 5 minutes until the paste has thickened and become fragrant.

Put the bacon mixture in the pan with the blended beans and ¼ cup (2 fl oz/50 ml) of the reserved bean cooking liquid. Simmer for 4 minutes, until the mixture thickens. Taste and adjust the seasoning, if necessary.

Ladle the bean stew into an earthenware pot, drizzle over a little olive oil, and serve with rice and creole sauce.

Serves: 4
Preparation Time: 15 minutes, plus overnight soaking
Cooking Time: 1 hour 55 minutes

My mother used to make this dish at least once a week. The smell of the escabeche sauce and vinegar would fill the whole house. The sauce and the beans in this dish complement each other beautifully.

2 cups (1 lb 1 oz/480 g) canary beans
1 lb 2 oz (500 g) smoked pork ribs
11 oz (300 g) pork jowl (cheek) cut into 3 even-size pieces
2 tablespoons vegetable oil
1 onion, chopped
2 cloves garlic, chopped
1 teaspoon dried oregano
1 tablespoon Panca Chili Paste (see p. 406)
2 cups (14 oz/400 g) Peruvian-Style Cooked White Rice (see p. 178), to serve
salt and pepper

Sauce
2 red onions, sliced
2 yellow chiles, seeded, membrane removed, and thinly sliced
2 tablespoons vegetable oil
3 cloves garlic, finely chopped
2 tablespoons Panca Chili Paste (see p. 406)
1 teaspoon honey
2 bay leaves
3 tablespoons red wine vinegar
½ cup (4 fl oz/120 ml) vegetable broth (stock)

FREJOLES ESCABECHADOS
BEAN ESCABECHE

Place the beans in a large bowl, cover with water, and let soak overnight.

The next day, drain and place the beans in a large pot or pan. Cover with cold water and add the smoked pork ribs and pork jowls (cheek). Bring to a boil, then reduce the heat and simmer for at least 45 minutes, until the beans are cooked. Set aside the bean mixture and bean cooking liquid.

Heat the oil in a pan over low heat, add the chopped onion and garlic, and sauté for 2 minutes, until the onion has softened. Add the oregano and chili paste, season with salt and pepper, and cook gently, stirring, for 5 minutes until the paste has thickened and become fragrant.

Add the beans and bean cooking liquid to the pan, bring to a simmer, and cook, covered, for 45 minutes. Uncover, add more liquid, and cook for another 15 minutes until the sauce has thickened and reduced.

For the sauce, sauté the red onion and chiles in the oil over high heat for a few seconds. Reduce the heat, add the chopped garlic and chili paste, and cook for 1 minute, then add the honey, bay leaves, red wine vinegar, and vegetable broth (stock). Cook for 2 minutes, until thickened and reduced. Taste and adjust the seasoning, if necessary.

Ladle the beans into an earthenware pot and pour over the sauce. Serve with rice.

Bean Escabeche

GUISO DE TRIGO
WHEAT BERRY STEW

Serves: 4
Preparation Time: 10 minutes
Cooking Time: 45 minutes

This is a homey dish that most Peruvians have grown up with. It is delicious served with a fried egg on top.

14 oz (400 g) wheat berries, washed
2 tablespoons vegetable oil
1 small red onion, chopped
1 clove garlic, chopped
2 tablespoons Yellow Chili Paste (see p. 405)
2 tomatoes, seeded and chopped
2 cups (18 fl oz/500 ml) chicken broth (stock)
1 white potato, cut into ½-inch (1-cm) cubes
1 tablespoon chopped huacatay leaves
2½ oz (65 g) queso fresco, cut into ½-inch (1-cm) cubes
2 cups (14 oz/400 g) Peruvian-Style Cooked White Rice (see p. 178), to serve (optional)
salt and pepper

Place the wheat berries in a pan, cover with water, and bring to a boil. Reduce the heat and simmer for 25 minutes, or until the wheat berries soften. Set the wheat berries and cooking liquid aside.

Heat the oil in a pan over low heat, add the onion, garlic, and chili paste, and sauté for a few minutes, or until the onion has softened. Season with salt and pepper, add the tomatoes, and cook for a few minutes more, then add the cooked wheat berries along with the broth (stock) and 1 cup (8 fl oz/250 ml) of the reserved cooking liquid. Add the white potato cubes and simmer for 10 minutes, until the potato is tender.

Stir in the chopped huacatay and queso fresco, ladle into large shallow bowls, and serve with rice, if desired.

LOCRO DE LANGOSTINOS
SHRIMP STEW

Serves: 4
Preparation Time: 15 minutes
Cooking Time: 20 minutes

This stew contains potatoes instead of squash and the trick is to allow them to disintegrate so that they blend into the stew and absorb the rich shrimp (prawn) flavor.

3 tablespoons vegetable oil
1 red onion, chopped
4 cloves garlic, finely chopped
1 teaspoon ground cumin
4 tablespoons Panca Chili Paste (see p. 406)
2 cups (18 fl oz/500 ml) vegetable broth (stock)
2 cups (18 fl oz/500 ml) shrimp (prawn) broth (stock)
11 oz (300 g) white potatoes, cut into ½-inch (1-cm) cubes
1 sprig oregano
40 medium shrimp (prawns), peeled and deveined
1 teaspoon chopped parsley leaves
2 cups (14 oz/400 g) Peruvian-Style Cooked White Rice (see p. 178), to serve
salt and pepper

Heat two thirds of the oil in a pan over low heat, add the onion and garlic, and sauté for 2 minutes, or until the onion has softened. Add the cumin and chili paste, season with salt and pepper, and cook gently, stirring, for 5 minutes until the paste has thickened and become fragrant.

Pour in the vegetable and shrimp (prawn) broths (stocks) and add the potatoes and oregano. Bring to a simmer and cook for 10 minutes, or until the potatoes become tender.

Heat the remaining oil in a separate pan. Season the shrimp (prawns) with salt and pepper, add to the pan, and sauté for 2 minutes until cooked. Add the shrimp to the potato stew with the chopped parsley and stir together. Serve in large shallow bowls with rice.

Shrimp Stew

LOCRO DE HABAS
FAVA BEAN STEW

Serves: 4
Preparation Time: 15 minutes
Cooking Time: 25 minutes

The combination of fava (broad) beans and squash in this dish is a winning one, which gives this humble stew an interesting and flavorsome touch.

2 tablespoons vegetable oil
1 red onion, chopped
4 cloves garlic, finely chopped
4 tablespoons Yellow Chili Paste (see p. 405)
2 cups (8 oz/250 g) macre or calabaza squash, cut into ½-inch (1-cm) cubes
½ cup (3 oz/80 g) corn kernels
3 cups (26½ fl oz/750 ml) vegetable broth (stock)
1 sprig oregano
1 lb (450 g) fava (broad) beans, shelled and peeled
½ cup (4 fl oz/120 ml) whole (full-fat) milk
2½ oz (65 g) queso fresco, cubed
salt and pepper

To serve
4 poached eggs
2 cups (14 oz/400 g) Peruvian-Style Cooked White Rice (see p. 178)

Heat the oil in a pan over low heat, add the onion and garlic, and sauté for 2 minutes, until the onion has softened. Add the chili paste, season with salt and pepper, and cook gently, stirring, for 5 minutes until the paste has thickened and become fragrant.

Add the squash pieces, corn kernels, broth (stock) and oregano, bring to a simmer, and cook for 15 minutes, until the squash disintegrates. Add the fava (broad) beans, milk, and queso fresco, and cook for 2 minutes. Taste and adjust the seasoning, if necessary. Ladle the stew into large shallow bowls and serve with poached eggs and rice.

LOCRO DE QUINUA
QUINOA STEW

Serves: 4
Preparation Time: 15 minutes
Cooking Time: 45 minutes

The quinoa in this dish should be cooked for longer than usual until the stew starts to thicken slightly. As well as adding texture, it will absorb all the flavors.

14 oz (400 g) multicolored quinoa grains
scant ½ cup (1½ oz/40 g) peas
1½ oz (40 g) fava (broad) beans
3 tablespoons vegetable oil
1 red onion, chopped
4 cloves garlic, chopped
2 tablespoons Yellow Chili Paste (see p. 405)
5 oz (150 g) squash, cut into ½-inch (1-cm) cubes
1 white potato, cut into ½-inch (1-cm) cubes
1 sprig huacatay
1 sprig oregano
¼ cup (2 fl oz/50 ml) whole (full-fat) milk
2½ oz (65 g) queso fresco, cubed
2 cups (14 oz/400 g) Peruvian-Style Cooked White Rice (see p. 178), to serve (optional)
salt and pepper

Bring a pan of salted water to a boil. Add the quinoa, reduce the heat to a simmer, and cook for 10 minutes until it is cooked but not too tender. Drain and spread the quinoa out on a plate to cool. Set aside. Boil the peas and fava (broad) beans until tender, drain, and set aside.

Heat the oil in a pan over low heat. Add the onion and garlic, season with salt and pepper, and sauté for a few minutes, until the onion has softened. Add the chili paste and continue to cook, stirring, for 4 minutes until the paste has thickened and become fragrant.

Add the squash, potato, huacatay, and oregano. Cover with water and simmer for 15 minutes, until the squash is soft and the potatoes disintegrate. Mash any remaining vegetable pieces together with a fork.

Add the quinoa and cook for another 5 minutes. Season with salt and pepper and stir in the milk, peas, fava beans, and queso fresco. Serve on plates with rice, if desired.

LOCRO DE PECHO
VEAL BRISKET STEW

Serves: 4
Preparation Time: 15 minutes
Cooking Time: 1 hour 45 minutes

This is a laborious dish that nevertheless is undoubtedly worth the effort. When the brisket becomes lovely and tender and blends with the potato stew, the result is delicious.

1 × 3¼-lb (1.5-kg) veal brisket
1 lb 2 oz (500 g) beef marrow bones
2 large celery stalks, chopped
1 leek, chopped
1 turnip, sliced
3 red onions, 1 whole and 2 chopped
7 cloves garlic, 3 crushed and 4 chopped
1 sprig oregano
1 teaspoon black peppercorns
3 tablespoons vegetable oil
1 teaspoon ground cumin
4 tablespoons Panca Chili Paste (see p. 406)
2 cups (18 fl oz/500 ml) vegetable broth (stock)
2¼ lb (1 kg) white potatoes, cut in half
1 sprig mint
salt and pepper

To serve
2 cups (14 oz/400 g) Peruvian-Style Cooked White Rice (see p. 178)
1 cup (250 ml) Creole Sauce (see p. 416)

Place the veal brisket, marrow bones, celery, leek, turnip, whole onion, crushed garlic, oregano, and peppercorns in a pan with 3 quarts (101 fl oz/3 liters) water. Bring to a simmer and cook for 1½ hours, until the meat is tender. Use a slotted spoon to remove any froth and sediment that floats to the surface while the meat cooks.

Once cooked, remove from the heat. Strain and reserve the cooking liquid, discarding the bones and vegetables. Cut the brisket into 1-inch/2.5-cm cubes and set aside.

Heat the oil over low heat, add the chopped onion and garlic, and sauté for 2 minutes, until the onion has softened. Add the cumin and chili paste, season with salt and pepper, and cook gently, stirring, for 5 minutes until the paste has thickened and become fragrant.

Pour the reserved cooking liquid and broth (stock) into the pan and add the chopped brisket, potatoes, and mint. Season with salt, bring to a simmer, and cook for 8 minutes, until the potatoes are tender. Mash any remaining potato pieces together with a fork. Taste and adjust the seasoning if necessary. Ladle into large shallow bowls and serve with rice and Creole sauce.

LOCRO DE ZAPALLOS
SQUASH STEW

Serves: 4
Preparation Time: 20 minutes
Cooking Time: 20 minutes

Loche squash is a variety of squash found in northern Peru and, although Peru exports many different types of squash and gourd, any local varieties you can find will be just as delicious. Don't hesitate to use them in this stew.

scant ½ cup (1½ oz/40 g) peas
3 tablespoons vegetable oil
1 red onion, chopped
4 cloves garlic, chopped
5 oz (150 g) macre squash, cut into ½-inch (1-cm) cubes
5 oz (150 g) loche squash, cut into ½-inch (1-cm) cubes
1 white potato, cut into ½-inch (1-cm) cubes
1 corncob, cut into 1-inch (2.5-cm) slices
1 sprig huacatay
1 sprig oregano
¼ cup (2 fl oz/50 ml) whole (full-fat) milk
2½ oz (65 g) queso fresco, cubed
2 cups (14 oz/400 g) Peruvian-Style Cooked White Rice (see p. 178), to serve
salt and pepper

To garnish
4 eggs, hard-boiled
2 tablespoons purple olives, finely chopped
¼ cup (2 fl oz/50 ml) Creole Sauce (see p. 416)

Bring a pan of water to a boil, add the peas, and cook until tender. Drain and set aside.

Heat the oil in a pan over low heat, add the onion and garlic, and season with salt and pepper. Sauté for a few minutes, until the onion has softened. Add the squash pieces, potato, corncob, and herb sprigs, cover with water, and simmer over moderate heat for 8 minutes, until the squash is soft and the potato cooked. Mash the vegetable pieces together with a fork to form a rustic mash. Season with salt and pepper.

Stir in the milk, peas, and queso fresco, spoon onto plates, and garnish with the hard-boiled eggs and chopped olives. Top with a little Creole sauce and serve with rice.

MONDONGO CON GARBANZOS
STEWED TRIPE WITH CHICKPEAS

Serves: 4
Preparation Time: 10 minutes, plus overnight soaking
Cooking Time: 2 hours 10 minutes

To prepare this dish you'll need to stew the tripe until it is almost coming apart, which will allow it to blend beautifully with the chickpeas.

7 oz (200 g) dried chickpeas
2¼ lb (1 kg) tripe
2½ oz (65 g) bacon, diced
1 red onion, chopped
4 cloves garlic, chopped
3 tablespoons Panca Chili Paste (see p. 406)
1 teaspoon Yellow Chili Paste (see p. 405)
salt and pepper

Place the chickpeas in a large bowl, cover with plenty of water, and let soak overnight. Drain and set aside.

Thoroughly wash the tripe and place in a pan of water. Bring to a simmer and cook for 1 hour, until tender. Remove from the pan, reserving the cooking liquid, drain, and cut into ½-inch/1-cm cubes. Set aside.

Place the diced bacon in a separate pan and brown over medium heat with no additional oil. Add the onion, garlic, and chili pastes and cook gently, stirring, for 5 minutes until the paste has thickened and become fragrant.

Add the soaked and drained chickpeas to the pan with 1 cup (8 fl oz/250ml) of the cooking liquid, bring to a simmer, and cook for 45 minutes, or until the chickpeas soften. Add the cooked tripe and simmer for another 15 minutes. Season with salt and pepper. Ladle into large shallow bowls and serve.

LOCRO DE TUBÉRCULOS
MIXED TUBER STEW

Serves: 4
Preparation Time: 10 minutes
Cooking Time: 20 minutes

You can use any tubers you have to hand to prepare this dish. Jerusalem artichokes and globe artichokes also make a tasty addition.

scant ½ cup (1½ oz/40 g) peas
3 tablespoons vegetable oil
1 red onion, chopped
4 cloves garlic, chopped
3 oz (80 g) squash, cut into medium-size pieces
1 corncob, cut into 1-inch/2.5-cm slices
1 small yellow waxy potato, cut into ½-inch (1-cm) cubes
1 white potato, cut into pieces
3 oz (80 g) oca, cut into ½-inch (1-cm) cubes
3 oz (80 g) arracacha, cut into ½-inch (1-cm) cubes
1 sprig huacatay
1 sprig oregano
¼ cup (2 fl oz/50 ml) whole (full-fat) milk
2½ oz (65 g) queso fresco, cubed
2 cups (14 oz/400 g) Peruvian-Style Cooked White Rice (see p. 178), to serve (optional)
salt and pepper

To garnish
4 eggs, hard-boiled
¼ cup (2 fl oz/50 ml) Creole Sauce (see p. 416)

Bring a pan of water to a boil, add the peas, and cook until tender. Drain and set aside.

Heat the oil in a pan over low heat, add the chopped onion and garlic, and season with salt and pepper. Sauté for a few minutes, until the onion has softened. Add the squash, corncob, yellow and white potatoes, oca, arracacha, and herb sprigs, cover with water and cook over moderate heat for 8 minutes, until the squash is soft and the potatoes cooked. Mash the vegetable pieces together with a fork to form a rustic mash. Season with salt and pepper.

Stir in the milk, peas, and queso fresco, ladle onto plates, and garnish with hard-boiled eggs. Top with a little Creole sauce and serve with rice if desired.

MONDONGUITO A LA ITALIANA
STEWED TRIPE A LA ITALIANA

Serves: 4
Preparation Time: 20 minutes, plus 15 minutes soaking
Cooking Time: 1 hour 25 minutes

This is perhaps my favorite of all the stews typically served in Lima. The a la Italiana part of the name is due to the fact that the recipe includes Parmesan cheese and because it is most likely a version of a dish introduced by the Italian immigrants who are now part of Peruvian society.

2¼ lb (1 kg) tripe
¼ oz (10 g) dried mushrooms, any variety
1 white potato, cut into 2 x ¼-inch (4-cm × 5-mm) strips
3 tablespoons vegetable oil, plus extra for deep-frying
1 red onion, thinly sliced
4 cloves garlic, chopped
2 tomatoes, sliced
4 tablespoons Yellow Chili Paste (see p. 405)
2 bay leaves
¼ cup (2 fl oz/50 ml) beef broth (stock)
½ cup (2 oz/50 g) peas
2 carrots, cut into 3-inch (7-cm) batons
1 tablespoon chopped parsley, plus extra to garnish
¼ oz (10 g) Parmesan cheese, grated
2 cups (14 oz/400 g) Peruvian-Style Cooked White Rice (see p. 178), to serve
salt and pepper

Thoroughly wash the tripe and place it in a pan of water. Bring to a simmer and cook for 1 hour, until tender. Remove from the pan, reserving the cooking liquid, let cool, and cut into ½ x 1-inch (1 × 3-cm) strips. Set aside.

Soak the dried mushrooms in a bowl of hot water for 15 minutes, then squeeze to drain and slice into bite-size pieces.

Heat enough vegetable oil for deep-frying in a large pan or deep-fryer to 350°F/180°C, or until a cube of bread browns in 30 seconds. Drop the potato strips carefully into the hot oil and cook until crispy and golden. Drain on paper towels and set aside.

Heat 3 tablespoons oil in a pan over low heat, add the onion, garlic, and tomatoes, and sauté for 1 minute. Season with salt and pepper, add the chili paste and gently cook, stirring, for a few minutes until the paste has thickened and become fragrant.

Add the soaked and drained mushrooms, bay leaves, beef broth (stock), and ½ cup (4 fl oz/120 ml) of the tripe-cooking liquid to the pan with the tripe pieces, peas, and carrot sticks and cook over moderate heat for 5 minutes until the vegetables are tender. Stir in the fried potatoes, parsley, and Parmesan cheese and serve in large shallow bowls with rice and more chopped parsley to garnish.

OLLUQUITO CON CAMARONES
SHRIMP AND ULLUCO MEDLEY

Serves: 4
Preparation Time: 15 minutes
Cooking Time: 40 minutes

You can also prepare this dish with Jerusalem artichokes and potatoes — it will be just as delicious.

1 lb 5 oz (600 g) ulluco root
2 tablespoons vegetable oil
1 small red onion, chopped
3 cloves garlic, chopped
1 tablespoon Panca Chili Paste (see p. 406)
3 tablespoons Yellow Chili Paste (see p. 405)
1 teaspoon ground cumin
2 cups (18 fl oz/500 ml) shrimp (prawn) broth (stock)
1 tablespoon Shrimp (Prawn) Head Paste (see p. 29)
40 medium shrimp (prawns), peeled and deveined, with tails still intact
1 tablespoon chopped parsley leaves
1 tablespoon chopped huacatay leaves
salt and pepper

Wash the ulluco roots and cut into 1 × 2-inch (2 × 5-cm) strips. Set aside.

Heat the oil in a pan over low heat, add the onion, garlic, and chili pastes and sauté for a few minutes, until the onion has softened. Add the cumin, season with salt and pepper, and cook for a few minutes more, until the paste has thickened and become fragrant.

Add the ulluco strips, pour in the broth (stock), and add the shrimp (prawn) paste. Season with salt and pepper and cook, uncovered, for 25 minutes over low heat until the ulluco is tender and the stew is ready. Add the shrimp (prawns), parsley, and huacatay and cook for 2 minutes, until the shrimp are cooked. Serve in large shallow bowls.

OLLUQUITO
CURED MEAT AND ULLUCO MEDLEY

Serves: 4
Preparation Time: 10 minutes, plus overnight soaking
Cooking Time: 1 hour

The ulluco is a delicious Peruvian tuber that is almost always used in this homey dish. You can substitute the ulluco for very tender white potatoes as an alternative.

2 oz (50 g) beef jerky
2 oz (50 g) dried cured beef or lamb
1 lb 5 oz (600 g) ulluco root
2 tablespoons vegetable oil
1 small red onion, chopped
3 cloves garlic, chopped
1 tablespoon Panca Chili Paste (see p. 406)
3 tablespoons Yellow Chili Paste (see p. 405)
1 teaspoon ground cumin
1 sprig oregano
1 tablespoon chopped parsley leaves
salt and pepper

Put the beef jerky and cured beef or lamb in a bowl, cover with water, and let soak overnight.

The next day, wash the ulluco roots and cut into long 1 × 2-inch/2 × 5-cm strips. Set aside. Drain the jerky and cured beef or lamb strips and set aside.

Heat the oil in a pan, add the onion, garlic, and chili pastes, and sauté for 2 minutes, until the onion has softened. Add the cumin, season with salt and pepper, and cook, stirring, for a few minutes until the paste has thickened and become fragrant.

Add the previously soaked jerky and cured beef or lamb and cover the ingredients with water. Bring to a simmer and cook, uncovered, for 30 minutes until the jerky and cured beef are tender. Add the ulluco strips, season with salt and pepper, and cook for another 25 minutes over low heat until the ulluco is tender and the stew is ready. Stir in the oregano and chopped parsley and serve in large shallow bowls.

MORUSA DE PALLARES
LIMA BEAN MORUSA

Serves: 4
Preparation Time: 15 minutes, plus overnight soaking
Cooking Time: 35 minutes

Stewing lima (butter) beans requires time and patience but transforming them into a delicious morusa requires the perfect seasoning.

14 oz (400 g) lima (butter) beans
2 red onion, 1 cut in half and 1 chopped
1 bay leaf
2 tablespoons olive oil
2 cloves garlic, chopped
½ oz (15 g) butter
salt and pepper

To serve
3½ oz/100 g Fried Pork Rind (see p. 81) or grilled steak
2 cups (14 oz/400 g) Peruvian-Style Cooked White Rice (see p. 178)
1 cup (250 ml) Creole Sauce (see p. 416)

Place the lima (butter) beans in a large bowl, cover with plenty of water, and let soak overnight. Drain and set aside.

The next day, peel the soaked lima beans and place in a pan with the onion halves and bay leaf. Cover with water, bring to a simmer, and cook for 30 minutes, until the beans turn to puree. Remove from the heat and beat vigorously with a wooden spoon until smooth.

Heat the olive oil in a separate pan over low heat, add the chopped onion and garlic, and sauté for a few minutes, until the onion has softened. Season with salt and pepper, add the butter and beaten butter beans, and mix together well. Taste and adjust the seasoning, if necessary.

Serve with fried pork rind or grilled steak, rice, and Creole sauce.

PEPIÁN DE ARROZ
GROUND RICE AND HAM STEW

Serves: 4
Preparation Time: 10 minutes, plus 2 hours soaking
Cooking Time: 1 hour 10 minutes

Pepián is a thick stew that can be prepared with rice, chickpeas, or beans. The idea is to allow the starch from these ingredients to thicken the stew and add texture.

14 oz (400 g) white long-grain rice
½ small white potato, cut into cubes
1 × 1 lb-2-oz (500-g) uncooked ham
2 tablespoons vegetable oil
1 small red onion, chopped
4 cloves garlic
2 oz (50 g) loche squash, grated
3 tablespoons Yellow Chili Paste (see p. 405)
2 quarts (67½ fl oz/2 liters) pork broth (stock)
salt and pepper

Put the rice in a bowl, cover with water, and let soak for 2 hours. Drain, spread on a plate, and dry. Place the rice in a mortar or *batán* (Peruvian grinder) and grind until fine. Set aside.

Bring a pan of water to a boil, add the potato, and cook until tender. Drain and set aside.

Cut the ham into 1-inch/2.5-cm chunks and season with salt and pepper. Heat half the oil over medium heat, add the ham chunks, and brown on all sides. Remove from the pan and set aside.

Add the onion and garlic to the same pan with the remaining oil, lower the heat, and sauté for a few minutes, until the onion has softened. Season with salt and pepper and add the grated squash and chili paste. Cook the mixture over low heat, stirring, for 5 minutes until the paste has thickened and become fragrant.

Add the browned ham to the pan and pour in the pork broth (stock). Cook over low heat for 30 minutes, until the ham is tender. Add the ground rice and cook for another 10 minutes, until the rice is cooked, then add the cooked potato cubes. Taste and adjust the seasoning, if necessary, and serve in large shallow bowls.

PEPIÁN DE GARBANZOS
CHICKPEA STEW

Serves: 4
Preparation Time: 10 minutes
Cooking Time: 1 hour 10 minutes

You can also prepare this dish with beans or lentils and serve it with a steak on top. The combination is delicious.

14 oz (400 g) chickpeas
4 cups (34 fl oz/1 liter) beef broth (stock)
2 tablespoons vegetable oil
1 red onion, chopped
4 cloves garlic, finely chopped
1 teaspoon ground cumin
3 tablespoons Yellow Chili Paste (see p. 405)
1 tomato, skinned, seeded, and diced
½ cup (4 fl oz/120 ml) Creole Sauce (see p. 416), to serve
salt and pepper

Preheat the oven to 300°F/150°C/Gas Mark 2. Spread out the chickpeas on a tray and roast for 15 minutes.

Put the chickpeas in a blender or *batán* (Peruvian grinder) with ¼ cup/60 ml beef broth (stock) and blend or grind to form a thick paste. Set aside.

Heat the oil in a pan over low heat, add the onion and garlic, and sauté for 2 minutes, until the onion has softened. Add the cumin and chili paste, season with salt and pepper, and cook gently, stirring, for 5 minutes until the paste has thickened and become fragrant.

Add the tomato, chickpea paste, and remaining beef broth. Bring to a simmer and cook, covered, for 45 minutes until the stew is creamy. Taste and adjust the seasoning if necessary. Serve with creole sauce.

PEPIÁN DE CHOCLO
CORN-THICKENED PORK STEW

Serves: 4
Preparation Time: 15 minutes
Cooking Time: 35 minutes

This is a delicious stew that can be prepared with any type of corn sold in your local area. If the corn is very sweet, combine it with a little potato to enhance the flavor.

- 1 lb 2 oz (500 g) corn kernels
- 12 oz (350 g) pork shoulder
- 4 cloves garlic, finely chopped
- 4 tablespoons vegetable oil
- 1 red onion, chopped
- 1 teaspoon ground cumin
- 3 tomatoes, skinned, seeded, and grated
- 2 sprigs oregano
- 4 cups (34 fl oz/1 liter) beef broth (stock)
- 1 teaspoon chopped parsley leaves, to garnish
- 2 cups (14 oz/400 g) Peruvian-Style Cooked White Rice, to serve (see p. 178)
- salt and pepper

Put the corn kernels in a blender or *batán* (Peruvian grinder) and blend or grind to form a thick paste. Set aside.

Cut the pork into 1-inch/2.5-cm cubes, rub with half the garlic, and season with salt and pepper. Set aside.

Heat half the oil in a pan over low heat, add the onion and the remaining garlic, and sauté for a few minutes. Add the cumin, season with salt and pepper, and cook gently for 2 minutes, until the onion has softened. Add the tomato and oregano and continue to cook for 10 minutes until the tomato disintegrates.

Heat the remaining oil in a separate pan over medium heat, add the pork cubes, and brown. Drain and add to the onion and tomato mixture. Stir, and pour in the broth (stock), then add the corn paste. Cook over moderate heat, stirring continuously, for about 10 minutes, or until the pork is tender. Taste and adjust the seasoning if necessary. Garnish with chopped parsley and serve with rice.

PEPIÁN DE MARISCOS
CORN STEW WITH MIXED SEAFOOD

Serves: 4
Preparation Time: 20 minutes
Cooking Time: 30 minutes

You can add clams, crustaceans, or any other seafood to this dish for a wonderful seafood medley.

- 1 lb 2 oz (500 g) corn kernels
- 1½ tablespoons vegetable oil
- ½ red onion, chopped
- 2 cloves garlic, finely chopped
- 1 teaspoon ground cumin
- 1 tablespoon Yellow Chili Paste (see p. 405)
- 2 sprigs oregano
- 3 cups (26½ fl oz/750 ml) vegetable broth (stock)
- 1 tablespoon huacatay leaves, to garnish
- salt and pepper

Mixed seafood

- 1½ tablespoons vegetable oil
- ½ red onion, chopped
- 2 cloves garlic, finely chopped
- 1 tablespoon Panca Chili Paste (see p. 406)
- 12 medium shrimp (prawns), peeled and deveined
- 8 medium scallops, washed
- ½ cup (5½ oz/160 g) Cooked Octopus, cut into 1-inch (2.5-cm) pieces (see p. 406)
- 4 tablespoons white wine
- 1 teaspoon chopped parsley leaves
- juice of 1 small lemon

Put the corn kernels in a blender or *batán* (Peruvian grinder) and blend or grind to form a thick paste. Set aside.

Heat the oil in a pan over low heat and add the chopped onion and garlic. Add the cumin, season with salt and pepper, and sauté for a few minutes, until the onion has softened. Add the yellow chili paste and oregano and continue to cook, stirring, for 5 minutes until the paste has thickened and become fragrant. Add the corn paste and broth (stock) and simmer over moderate heat for 10 minutes, stirring continuously, until the mixture has thickened and become creamy.

For the mixed seafood, place the oil, onion, and garlic in a separate pan, add the panca chili paste and cook over low heat for a few minutes. Add the shrimp (prawns), scallops, octopus, and white wine and cook for 1–2 minutes, until the liquid has reduced and the shrimp turn pink and are cooked. Stir in the parsley and lemon juice.

Ladle the corn stew into a large serving bowl, top with the seafood, and garnish with huacatay leaves.

PEPIÁN DE PAVITA
TURKEY AND CHICKPEA STEW

Serves: 4
Preparation Time: 20 minutes
Cooking Time: 1 hour 45 minutes

This is in fact two dishes in one: the first is a chickpea pepián, a type of stew, and the second is a turkey stew. You mix them at the very end for a powerful and extremely flavorsome dish.

Turkey stew
1 × 3¼-lb (1.5-kg) turkey
1 tablespoon vegetable oil
1 small red onion, chopped
4 cloves garlic, chopped
3 tablespoons Mirasol Chili Paste (see p. 405)
1 yellow chile, seeded, membrane removed, and thinly sliced
101 fl oz (3 liters) vegetable broth or water
salt and pepper

Chickpea stew
14 oz (400 g) chickpeas
4 cups (34 fl oz/1 liter) vegetable broth (stock)
2 tablespoons vegetable oil
1 red onion, chopped
4 cloves garlic, finely chopped
3 tablespoons Yellow Chili Paste (see p. 405)
1 tomato, skinned, seeded, and diced

To garnish
1 sprig culantro or cilantro (coriander)

To serve
1 cup (8 fl oz/250 ml) Creole Sauce (see p. 416)
8 pitted black olives, halved

Preheat the oven to 300°F/150°C/Gas Mark 2. Spread the chickpeas on a tray and roast for 15 minutes.

For the turkey stew, cut the turkey into 2 × 1½-inch/4 × 3-cm pieces. Season with salt and pepper and set aside.

Heat the oil in a pan over low heat, add the onion and garlic, and sauté for 2 minutes, until the onion has softened. Add the mirasol chili paste, season with salt and pepper, and cook gently, stirring, for 5 minutes until the paste has thickened and become fragrant. Add the turkey pieces to the pan with the stock or water and cook for 45 minutes, until the turkey is tender. Add the sliced yellow chile, taste, and adjust the seasoning. Set aside.

For the chickpea stew, put the chickpeas in a blender or *batán* (Peruvian grinder) with 2 tablespoons of the vegetable broth (stock) and blend or grind to form a thick paste. Set aside.

Heat the oil in a separate pan over low heat, add the onion and garlic, and sauté for 2 minutes, until the onion has softened. Season with salt and pepper, add the yellow chili paste and cook gently, stirring,for 5 minutes. Add the tomato and cook for 1 minute, then add the chickpea paste and remaining vegetable broth. Bring to a simmer and cook, covered, for 45 minutes until the stew is creamy. Taste and adjust the seasoning.

Ladle the chickpea stew into a large serving bowl, top with the turkey stew and garnish with culantro or cilantro (coriander). Serve with Creole sauce and olives.

Turkey and Chickpea Stew

Serves: 4
Preparation Time: 25–30 minutes, plus 2 hours chilling
Cooking Time: 20 minutes

The wonderful ritual of cooking fish stew over a flame grill is common throughout the Amazon region. We call this dish patarashca.

2 × 2¼-lb (1-kg) freshwater fish (such as Mediterranean rainbow wrasse, dorade, red porgy, or comber), cleaned, heads removed, and halved
2 teaspoons turmeric or chili powder
4 cloves garlic, chopped
2 sweet peppers or rocoto chiles, seeded, membrane removed, and chopped
2 tablespoons white wine
1 sprig culantro or cilantro (coriander) or sacha culantro
1 red onion, sliced
1 tablespoon lemon juice
2 tablespoons vegetable oil
8 bijao leaves
salt and pepper

To serve
1 yucca root (cassava), peeled, boiled, and cut into ½ x 2-inch (1 × 5-cm) batons
¼ cup (2 fl oz/50 ml) Cocona and Chili Salsa (see p. 409)

PATARASHCA
FLAME-GRILLED FISH PARCELS

Place the fish halves in a bowl, cover with the turmeric or chili powder, garlic, peppers or rocoto chiles, white wine, culantro or cilantro (coriander) or sacha culantro, onion, lemon juice, and oil. Season with salt and pepper and mix together well. Cover with plastic wrap (clingfilm), transfer to the refrigerator, and marinate for 2 hours.

Place a bijao leaf briefly over a naked flame to soften and bring out its aroma. Repeat with the remaining leaves.

Take 2 bijao leaves and lay one over the other to form a cross. Place a portion of the fish in the middle and pour some of the marinade over it. Carefully wrap up the leaves around the filling to form a parcel and tie with string. Repeat with the remaining ingredients.

Cook the bijao parcels in a ridged pan over medium heat for 15 minutes. To serve, open the parcels and place on plates with yucca root (cassava) batons and cocona and chili salsa.

PUCHERO
MIXED MEAT PUCHERO STEW

Serves: 4
Preparation Time: 20 minutes, plus overnight soaking
Cooking Time: 2 hours 10 minutes

Puchero stew is a version of the famous sancochado limeño (stewed beef in clear broth with vegetables). The main difference is the variety of ingredients used, which sometimes even include fruit.

7 oz (200 g) chickpeas
1 lb 2 oz (500 g) beef brisket, cut into 3-inch (7.5-cm) pieces
1 lb 2 oz (500 g) pork shoulder, cut into 3-inch (7.5-cm) pieces
1 lb 2 oz (500 g) lamb rib, cut into 4 pieces or shoulder, cut into 3-inch (7.5-cm) pieces
2 white onions, chopped
4 cloves garlic
½ celery stalk
1 tablespoon oregano
2 white potatoes
3½ oz (100 g) turnip, sliced
2 carrots
2 corncobs, cut into 1½-inch (3-cm) slices
2 sweet potatoes, cut into 2-inch (4-cm) chunks
3½ oz (100 g) blood sausage
3½ oz (100 g) chorizo
7 oz (200 g) slice of squash, cut into 2-inch (5-cm) chunks
1 cabbage, cut in half
salt

Soak the chickpeas in cold water overnight. Drain.

Place the beef, pork, and lamb in a large pan with the onions, garlic cloves, celery, and oregano. Cover with 202 fl oz/6 liters water, bring to a simmer, and cook for 2 hours until the meats are tender, skimming off any impurities and froth that float to the surface with a slotted spoon. After 1 hour, add the chickpeas.

Add the potatoes, turnip, carrots, corncob slices, sweet potatoes, blood sausage, and chorizo and simmer over low heat for 10 minutes until the potatoes are just tender. Add the squash and cabbage and simmer for another 10 minutes until all the ingredients are cooked, adding a little more water if necessary to prevent the stew from drying out.

Season with salt and ladle into large shallow bowls. Serve.

Stewed Beef with Clear Broth and Vegetables

SANCOCHADO
STEWED BEEF WITH CLEAR BROTH AND VEGETABLES

Serves: 4
Preparation Time: 10 minutes
Cooking Time: 1 hour 40 minutes

The sancochado reigns supreme in Lima. It is closely related to the Italian bollitomisto, French pot-au-feu or Spanish cocido madrileño. The main difference is that the sancochado is served with delicious Peruvian sauces.

1 × 1¾-lb (800-g) beef brisket, cut into 4 equal-size pieces
1 lb 5 oz (600 g) beef chuck ribs
1 leek, halved
1 celery stalk
2 carrots
½ yucca root (cassava), peeled and cut into ½ x 2-inch (1 × 5-cm) pieces
4 potatoes
2 corncobs
5 oz (150 g) squash, cut into 1½-inch (3-cm) cubes
leaves of ½ green cabbage
salt

To serve
1 cup (8 fl oz/250 ml) Creole Sauce (see p. 416)
¼ cup (2 fl oz/50 ml) Carretilla Sauce (see p. 415)
¼ cup (2 fl oz/50 ml) Yellow Chili Cream (see p. 411)
¼ cup (2 fl oz/50 ml) Chicken Condiment (see p. 410)

Wash the brisket and chuck ribs and trim the fat, leaving just enough to flavor the broth.

Place the meat in a pot or large pan with the leek, celery, and carrots and cover with water. Season with salt and bring to a boil. Reduce the heat and simmer for 1½ hours, or until the meat is tender, removing any foam or impurities that float to the surface every 10 minutes with a slotted spoon.

Once the meat is cooked, add the yucca root (cassava), potatoes, corncobs, and squash and simmer for 10 minutes, until the yucca root and potatoes are tender. Add the cabbage leaves and simmer for a few more minutes.

Ladle the broth into large shallow bowls. Divide the meat and vegetables between plates and serve with Creole sauce, carretilla sauce, yellow chili cream, and chicken condiment on the side. Serve together.

POLLO AL HORNO ESTILO A LA BRASA
ROAST CHICKEN

Serves: 4
Preparation Time: 15 minutes, plus 18 hours soaking and 5 hours chilling
Cooking Time: 1 hour, plus 15 minutes resting

There are tens of thousands of chicken shops in Peru, where you see chickens—marinated in Peruvian spices—roasting or gently rotating on spits for an hour at a time. Peruvians love going out with their families to enjoy some golden and juicy roasted chicken. This is most often served with traditional fries!

5 oz (150 g) salt
1 × 3½-lb (1.8-kg) chicken

Marinade
2 tablespoons black pepper
3 tablespoons oregano
3 tablespoons ground cumin
¼ cup (2 fl oz/50 ml) stout
1 teaspoon mustard
5 tablespoons white wine vinegar
1 teaspoon chopped rosemary

To serve
French fries
1 cup (8 fl oz/250 ml) Chicken Condiment (see p. 410)

Put the salt in a bowl and mix together with 2 cups (18 fl oz/500 ml) water until the salt dissolves completely. Immerse the chicken in the brine and let soak for 18 hours.

Prepare the marinade by mixing the black pepper, oregano, cumin, stout, mustard, white wine vinegar, and rosemary in a bowl.

Remove the chicken from the brine and transfer it to the marinade bowl. Cover with plastic wrap (clingfilm) and marinate for 5 hours in the refrigerator.

Preheat a rotisserie oven to 350°F/180°C/Gas Mark 4.

Once marinated, remove the chicken from the bowl and slide it onto the spit of the oven, tying the legs with kitchen string to secure them. Roast the chicken for 1 hour, or until golden. Remove from the oven, let the chicken rest for 15 minutes, and cut it into quarters.

Serve the roast chicken with fries, chicken condiment, and any sauce of your choice.

POLLO DE POLLADA
BARBECUED CHICKEN

Serves: 4
Preparation Time: 10 minutes, plus 2 hours chilling
Cooking Time: 16 minutes

Peruvians have inherited a sense of community from the Incas. Whenever a family needs financial support to make a dream come true or start a new venture, the whole neighborhood lends a hand by organizing a *pollada*, a party where chickens are barbecued in true Peruvian style.

1×4-lb (1.8-kg) whole chicken, cut into quarters

Marinade
1 teaspoon pepper
1 teaspoon ground cumin
1 teaspoon mustard
12 cloves garlic, finely chopped
2 tablespoons Panca Chili Paste (see p. 406)
2 tablespoons Yellow Chili Paste (see p. 405)
¼ cup (2 fl oz/50 ml) soy sauce
¼ cup (2 fl oz/50 ml) vinegar
¼ cup (2 fl oz/50 ml) water
pinch of salt

To serve
4 boiled white potatoes, halved
½ cup (8 fl oz/120 ml) Chicken Condiment (see p. 410)
½ cup (8 fl oz/120 ml) Carretilla Sauce (see p. 415)

To make the marinade, put all the ingredients in a bowl, and mix together well. Add the chicken to the bowl and marinate for 2 hours with ¼ cup/50 ml water, covered with plastic wrap (cling film), in the refrigerator.

Heat a barbecue until very hot. Put the chicken quarters on the barbecue and cook for 8 minutes on each side until browned and cooked through.

Serve with boiled potatoes, chicken condiment, and carretilla sauce.

Roast Chicken

PATO EN AJÍ
PERUVIAN DUCK CHILI

Serves: 4
Preparation Time: 15 minutes, plus 1 hour 30 minutes chilling
Cooking Time: 1 hour 40 minutes

This is one of the tastiest Peruvian stews ever invented. The key to this dish is to be extra generous with the chili and to cook it very slowly.

1 × 5½-lb (2.5-kg) female duck, cut into 8 pieces
3 tablespoons vegetable oil
1 red onion, chopped
4 cloves garlic, chopped
2 sprigs culantro or cilantro (coriander)
4 cups (34 fl oz/1 liter) duck broth (stock) or water
7 oz (200 g) yucca root (cassava), peeled, boiled, and cut into 4 thick batons, to serve
salt and pepper

Marinade
1 cup (8 fl oz/250 ml) beer
4 tablespoons Yellow Chili Paste (see p. 405)
2 tablespoons Mirasol Chili Paste (see p. 405)
1 tablespoon Panca Chili Paste (see p. 406)

To make the marinade, mix the ingredients together in a bowl.

Season the duck pieces with salt and pepper, add to the marinade, and mix together well. Cover with plastic wrap (clingfilm) and marinate in the refrigerator for 1½ hours.

Heat the oil in a pan over low heat, add the onion and garlic, and sauté for 2–3 minutes until the onion has started to soften. Season with salt and pepper and cook, stirring, for another 5 minutes until the onion is golden.

Add the duck pieces and culantro or cilantro (coriander) sprigs to the pan, pour in the duck broth (stock) or water, and bring to a simmer over low heat. Cook for 1½ hours, or until the duck is tender.

Serve with a side of boiled yucca root (cassava).

TALLARINES CON PICHONES
PASTA WITH STEWED BABY PIGEONS

Serves: 4
Preparation Time: 15 minutes
Cooking Time: 1 hour

Pasta with stewed baby pigeons is truly delicious. This recipe also works very well with quail, guinea fowl, pigeon, or chicken.

2 tablespoons vegetable oil
1 oz (25 g) butter
6 × 10½–14-oz (300–400-g) baby pigeons, cleaned and halved
1 red onion, chopped
2 tomatoes, skinned, seeded, and grated
1 carrot, grated
1 bay leaf
4 cups (34 fl oz/1 liter) vegetable broth (stock)
2 tablespoons red wine
1 oz (25 g) grated Parmesan cheese
2¼ lb (1 kg) linguine or any other long, thin pasta
salt and pepper

Heat the vegetable oil and 1 teaspoon of the butter in a pan over medium heat, add the pigeons, and brown on all sides. Remove the pigeons from the pan and set aside.

Add the onion to the same pan and sauté for 2 minutes until the onion is starting to soften. Add the tomatoes and grated carrot and cook for another 2–3 minutes, then return the baby pigeons to the pan with the bay leaf and pour in the vegetable broth (stock). Bring to a simmer and cook over medium heat for 25 minutes, until the pigeons are tender.

Season to taste with salt and pepper. Add the red wine, remaining butter, and Parmesan cheese to the pan and cook for 2 minutes. Remove from the heat and keep warm.

Boil the pasta in a separate pan in plenty of salted water according to the package instructions until al dente. Drain and divide between bowls. Spoon the baby pigeon stew over the pasta and serve.

TALLARINES ROJOS CON POLLO
PASTA WITH CHICKEN AND TOMATO SAUCE

Serves: 4
Preparation Time: 20 minutes, plus 15 minutes soaking
Cooking Time: 30 minutes

This is a dish that is clearly influenced by Italian cuisine that has gradually taken on a Peruvian flavor. The chicken is cooked slowly in the tomato sauce, which gives it a distinctive taste, and the addition of Huancaína sauce gives it a Creole touch.

¼ cup (½ oz/15 g) dried mushrooms, any variety
¼ cup (4 fl oz/60 ml) vegetable oil
1 × 4-lbs (1.8-kg) whole chicken, cut into 8 pieces
1 onion, chopped
3 cloves garlic, chopped
4 tomatoes, skinned, seeded, and grated
2 carrots, grated
2 tablespoons Panca Chili Paste (see p. 406)
1 bay leaf
4 cups (34 fl oz/1 liter) vegetable broth (stock)
2¼ lb (1 kg) linguine or any other long, thin pasta
½ oz (15 g) butter
salt and pepper

To serve
½ cup (8 fl oz/120 ml) Huancaína Sauce (see p. 413)
2 oz (50 g) Parmesan cheese, grated

Soak the dried mushrooms in a little warm water for 15 minutes. Drain.

Heat the oil in a pan over medium heat. Season the chicken pieces with salt and pepper, add to the pan, and brown on all sides. Remove from the pan and set aside.

Add another 3 tablespoons oil to the pan, add the onion and garlic, and sauté for 2 minutes over low heat until the onions have started to soften. Season with salt and pepper and add the tomatoes, carrots, chili paste, bay leaf, and soaked and drained mushrooms. Cook for another 5 minutes, then add the browned chicken pieces and vegetable broth (stock). Bring to a simmer and cook for 20 minutes until the vegetables are tender and the mixture has reduced to a thick sauce.

Meanwhile, boil the pasta in a separate pan in plenty of salted water according to the package instructions until al dente. Drain and transfer to a shallow pan, add the butter and a little of the pasta sauce, and mix together well.

Divide the pasta between plates and spoon over the remaining sauce. Serve with Huancaína sauce and Parmesan cheese.

TALLARINES VERDES CON APANADO
PASTA WITH BREADED STEAK AND PERUVIAN PESTO

Serves: 4
Preparation Time: 20 minutes
Cooking Time: 20 minutes

Tens of thousands of Genovesi immigrants arrived in Peru chasing their dreams, and with them came their pesto. The original recipe was gradually adapted to include spinach and milk, giving birth to Peruvian green pasta.

8 oz (225 g) linguine
½ oz (15 g) unsalted butter
½ cup (8 fl oz/120 ml) chicken broth (stock)
½ oz (15 g) grated Parmesan cheese, plus extra to serve
salt and pepper

Pesto
3 oz (80 g) spinach leaves
4 oz (120 g) basil leaves
2 cloves garlic
½ cup (8 fl oz/120 ml) vegetable oil
½ cup (8 fl oz/120 ml) extra virgin olive oil
1 oz (25 g) grated Parmesan cheese
1 tablespoon salt

Breaded steak
1 × 1-lb 8½-oz (700-g) beef tenderloin (fillet)
1 clove garlic, finely chopped
1 tablespoon flour
2 eggs, beaten
7 oz (200 g) dry, fine bread crumbs
¼ cup (2 fl oz/60ml) vegetable oil
salt and pepper

For the breaded steak, cut the tenderloin (fillet) into 4 medallions. Place the medallions on a clean work surface, lay some plastic wrap (clingfilm) over the top, and press the meat with a rolling pin or meat mallet to stretch it out until the steaks are approximately 4 inches x ¼ inch/10 cm x 5 mm thick.

Season each steak with salt and pepper and rub with the chopped garlic. Coat the steaks in the flour, then the beaten egg, and finally the bread crumbs. Heat the oil in a nonstick frying pan or skillet, add the steaks to the pan, and cook for 5 minutes on each side until crispy and golden. Set aside and keep warm in the oven at a low setting.

For the pesto sauce, wilt the spinach and basil leaves in a hot pan with a few drops of the oil, then transfer to a food processor along with the remaining ingredients. Blend until the sauce is smooth and set aside.

Boil the pasta in a separate pan in plenty of salted water according to the package instructions until al dente. Drain and transfer to a shallow pan, add the pesto sauce, butter, broth (stock), and Parmesan cheese and mix together well. Taste and adjust the seasoning as necessary.

Divide the pasta between plates, topping each with a breaded steak. Sprinkle over a little extra Parmesan cheese and serve.

SOPA SECA
DRY SOUP

Serves: 4
Preparation Time: 10 minutes
Cooking Time: 25 minutes

This is a traditional Peruvian pasta dish that is closely related to the Catalan fideua. The pasta should be cooked in the sauce or juice to absorb all the flavors.

2 tablespoons vegetable oil
2 tablespoons Panca Chili, Garlic and Onion Condiment (see p. 403)
1 teaspoon ground cumin
1 teaspoon dried oregano
1 tomato, skinned, seeded, and chopped
1 carrot, grated
1¾ lb (800 g) dried spaghetti
4 cups (34 fl oz/1 liter) vegetable broth (stock)
salt and pepper

Basil paste
1 cup (2 oz/50 g) basil leaves
2 tablespoons olive oil
salt

Heat the vegetable oil in a pan over low heat, add the chili, garlic, and onion condiment, and sauté for 2 minutes. Stir in the cumin and oregano and season with salt and pepper. Add the chopped tomato and carrot and cook for another 10 minutes until fragrant and the carrot is soft.

To make the basil paste, put the basil, a pinch of salt, and oil together in a small bowl and blend together.

Snap the spaghetti in half and add to the pan. Pour in the vegetable broth (stock) and basil paste, adjust the seasoning to taste, and simmer over low heat for 12 minutes until the pasta is cooked. Spoon into large shallow bowls and serve.

SOPA SECA DE PEJESAPO CON CANGREJO
DRY ANGLER FISH AND CRAB SOUP

Serves: 4
Preparation Time: 20 minutes
Cooking Time: 40 minutes

The angler fish—rockfish—used in this recipe is the key to its success. You can also use any very good-quality rockfish sold at your local market. It will be just as delicious.

- 2 tablespoons vegetable oil
- 1 red onion, finely chopped
- 4 cloves garlic, finely chopped
- 3 tablespoons Panca Chili Paste (see p. 406)
- 4 × 10½ oz (300 g) medium crabs, halved and crushed with a meat mallet
- 1¾ lb (800 g) spaghetti
- 1 cup (8 fl oz/250 ml) crab broth (stock), plus extra if necessary
- 3 cups (26 fl oz/750 ml) angler fish or regular fish broth (stock)
- 2 × 1¾ lb (800 g) angler fish, cleaned and cut into fillets
- ¼ cup (4 oz/120 g) crabmeat, either white or brown
- 1 bunch basil leaves, chopped
- salt and pepper

Heat the oil in a large pan over low heat, add the onion and garlic, and sauté for 10 minutes until the onion is soft. Add the chili paste and cook for another 4 minutes until the paste is fragrant. Season with salt and pepper to taste.

Add the crabs to the pan and cook for 8 minutes, then remove the crabs from the pan and set aside.

Snap the spaghetti in half and add to the pan. Pour over the crab and fish broths (stocks) and simmer over low heat for 15 minutes until the pasta is al dente and has absorbed all the liquid.

Return the crabs to the pan along with the fish fillets. Mix carefully and add a little more crab broth (stock) if necessary if the pasta looks like it is drying out. Cover the pan and cook for 2 minutes. Stir in the crabmeat and the chopped basil leaves to finish. Spoon into large shallow bowls and serve.

TALLARINES A LA HUANCAÍNA CON APANADO
PASTA WITH BREADED STEAK AND HUANCAÍNA SAUCE

Serves: 4
Preparation Time: 20 minutes
Cooking Time: 20 minutes

Huancaína sauce goes wonderfully with pasta and, if served alongside a delicious breaded steak, as is done in Peru, you will have a veritable feast.

- 8 oz (225 g) thick linguine
- ½ cup (8 fl oz/120 ml) Huancaína Sauce (see p413)
- 1 tablespoon unsalted butter
- ½ cup (8 fl oz/120 ml) chicken broth (stock)
- ½ oz (15 g) grated Parmesan cheese, plus extra to serve
- salt and pepper

Breaded steak

- 1 lb 8½ oz (700 g) beef tenderloin (fillet)
- 1 garlic clove, finely chopped
- 1 tablespoon white all-purpose (plain) flour
- 2 eggs, beaten
- 7 oz (200 g) dry, fine bread crumbs
- ¼ cup (2 fl oz/60 ml) vegetable oil
- salt and pepper

For the breaded steak, cut the tenderloin fillet into 4 medallions. Place the medallions on a clean work surface, lay some plastic wrap (clingfilm) over the top and press the meat with a rolling pin or meat mallet to stretch it out until the steaks are approximately 4 inches x ¼ inch/10 cm x 5 mm thick.

Season each steak with salt and pepper and rub with the chopped garlic. Coat the steaks in the flour, then the beaten egg, and finally the bread crumbs. Heat the oil in a nonstick frying pan or skillet, add the steaks to the pan, and cook for 5 minutes on each side until crispy and golden. Set aside and keep warm in the oven at a low setting.

Boil the pasta in a separate pan in plenty of salted water according to the package instructions until al dente. Drain and transfer to a shallow pan, add the Huancaína sauce, butter, broth (stock), and Parmesan cheese and mix together well. Taste and adjust the seasoning as necessary.

Divide the pasta between plates, topping each with a breaded steak. Sprinkle a little extra Parmesan cheese and serve.

Dry Seafood Soup

SOPA SECA DE MARISCOS
DRY SEAFOOD SOUP

Serves: 4
Preparation Time: 15 minutes
Cooking Time: 35 minutes

You can use other types of pasta to make this dish, including bucatini, macaroni, or any type of tubular pasta so that the seafood flavor can seep into it.

- 2 tablespoons vegetable oil
- 1 red onion, finely chopped
- 4 cloves garlic, finely chopped
- 3 tablespoons Panca Chili Paste (see p. 406)
- 1¾ lb (800 g) dried spaghetti
- 3 cups (26½ fl oz/750 ml) fish broth (stock)
- 1 cup (8 fl oz/250 ml) crab broth (stock)
- 4 × 7-oz (200-g) squid, cleaned and cut into rings
- 12 shrimp (prawns), peeled and deveined
- 12 scallops, cleaned
- 6 rock mussels, cleaned
- ¼ cup crabmeat, either white or brown
- 1 bunch basil leaves, chopped
- salt and pepper

Heat the oil in a large pan over low heat, add the onion and garlic, and sauté for 10 minutes until the onion is soft. Add the chili paste and cook, stirring, for 5 minutes more. Season with salt and pepper.

Snap the spaghetti in half and add to the pan. Pour in the fish and crab broths (stocks) and simmer over medium heat for about 15 minutes until the pasta is al dente and has absorbed all the liquid.

Add the squid, shrimp (prawns), scallops, and mussels to the pan, cover and cook for 2 minutes until the seafood is cooked. Stir in the crabmeat and chopped basil to finish. Serve in large shallow bowls.

CONEJO CON MANÍ
RABBIT AND PEANUT STEW

Serves: 4
Preparation Time: 20 minutes, plus 2 hours chilling
Cooking Time: 1 hour 10 minutes

Rabbit recipes are hard to find these days, and yet rabbit used to be one of the star ingredients when it came to stew. This rabbit and peanut stew is one of those traditional stews.

- 2 × 4½-lb (2-kg) rabbits, cleaned and cut into 8 pieces
- 1 teaspoon ground cumin
- 3 bay leaves
- 2 tablespoons white wine vinegar
- ¼ cup (2 fl oz/50 ml) vegetable oil
- 2 tablespoons butter
- 4 tablespoons Panca Chili, Garlic, and Onion Condiment (see p. 403)
- 4 cups (34 fl oz/1 liter) vegetable broth (stock)
- 1 cup (8 fl oz/250 ml) white wine
- 40 g (1½ oz) peanuts, toasted and ground
- 1 tablespoon chopped parsley
- 2 cups (14 oz/400 g) Peruvian-Style Cooked White Rice (see p. 178), to serve
- salt and pepper

Put the rabbit pieces in a bowl with the cumin, 2 bay leaves, and vinegar. Season with salt and pepper, cover with plastic wrap (clingfilm), and marinate in the refrigerator for 2 hours.

Heat the oil and butter in a pan over medium heat, add the rabbit pieces, and lightly brown on all sides. Remove from the pan and set aside.

In a separate pan, sauté the chili, garlic, and onion condiment for 2 minutes over low heat. Season with salt and pepper.

Add the rabbit pieces and remaining bay leaf to the pan, mix together thoroughly, then pour in the vegetable broth (stock) and white wine. Bring to a simmer and cook, covered, for 45 minutes over medium heat until the rabbit pieces are tender. Stir in the ground peanuts and cook for another 10 minutes until the ingredients are cooked through and the flavors have blended.

Stir in the chopped parsley and adjust the seasoning to taste. Serve with Peruvian-style cooked white rice.

SOPA SECA AMAZÓNICA DE GALLINA
AMAZONIAN DRY CHICKEN SOUP

Serves: 4
Preparation Time: 20 minutes
Cooking Time: 1 hour 10 minutes

The chicken brings a deep and intense richness to this dish, while the Amazonian ingredients add a delicious and exotic flavor.

6 tablespoons vegetable oil
1 × 4-lb (1.8-kg) chicken, cut into 8 pieces
1 red onion, finely chopped
6 cloves garlic, finely chopped
2 tablespoons turmeric
2 charapita chiles, seeded, membrane removed, and chopped
4 tablespoons Yellow Chili Paste (see p. 405)
4 cups (34 fl oz/1 liter) chicken broth (stock)
1¾ lb (800 g) spaghetti
6 sacha culantro or cilantro (coriander) or culantro leaves, chopped
Chopped chile garnish (optional)
salt and pepper

Heat 2 tablespoons oil in a pan over medium heat. Season the chicken pieces with salt and pepper, add to the pan, and brown on all sides. Remove from the pan and set aside.

Add another 4 tablespoons oil to the pan, add the onion and garlic and sauté for 2 minutes over low heat until the onions have started to soften. Stir in the turmeric, chiles, and chili paste, and cook for another 10 minutes until fragrant. Add the browned chicken pieces and chicken broth (stock), bring to a simmer, and cook over medium heat for 25 minutes until the chicken is tender. Strain and set aside both the chicken pieces and the cooking liquid.

Pour the chicken cooking juices into a separate pan and place over the heat. Snap the raw spaghetti in half and add to the pan. Cook over medium heat for around 15 minutes until the pasta is al dente and has absorbed all the flavors, adding more chicken broth if necessary to prevent the pasta from drying out.

Stir the chicken pieces and chopped sacha culantro or cilantro (coriander) leaves into the pasta, scatter over the chiles, if using, and season to taste with salt and pepper. Spoon into large shallow bowls and serve.

GALLINA CON MANÍ
CHICKEN AND PEANUT STEW

Serves: 4
Preparation Time: 10 minutes
Cooking Time: 55 minutes

Chicken can be a difficult ingredient to cook to perfection. You can also prepare this dish with quail or duck.

1 × 4-lb (1.8-kg) chicken, cut into 8 pieces
¼ cup (2 fl oz/60 ml) vegetable oil
3 tablespoons Panca Chili, Garlic, and Onion Condiment (see p. 403)
1 teaspoon ground cumin
1 cup (250 ml) vegetable broth (stock)
1½ oz (40 g) peanuts, toasted and ground
salt and pepper

To serve
2 cups (14 oz/400 g) Peruvian-Style Cooked White Rice, to serve (see p. 178)
2 potatoes, boiled and sliced

Season the chicken pieces with salt and pepper. Heat the oil over medium heat in a pan, add the chicken pieces, and lightly brown them on all sides. Remove from the pan and set aside.

Place the chili, garlic, and onion condiment in a separate pan. Add the cumin and cook over low heat for 2 minutes until fragrant. Add the chicken pieces and pour in the vegetable broth (stock). Bring to a simmer and cook over low heat for 35 minutes, or until the chicken is tender. Stir in the ground peanuts and cook for another 5 minutes until the stew has thickened and reduced.

Ladle into bowl and serve with rice and sliced boiled potatoes.

Amazonian Dry Chicken Soup

PATITA CON MANÍ
COW'S HOOF, PIG FEET, AND PEANUT STEW

Serves: 4
Preparation Time: 20 minutes
Cooking Time: 2 hours 10 minutes

This is a very old Creole dish that is also a favorite among traditional Lima folk. The secret is to cook the stewfor a long time until the meat is very tender.

- 1 × 4½-lb (2-kg) cow's hoof, cleaned
- 2 × 12½-oz (350-g) pig feet (trotters), cleaned
- 10 cloves garlic, 4 whole and 6 very finely chopped
- 2 bay leaves
- 4 tablespoons vegetable oil
- 1 cup (5 oz/150 g) chopped red onion
- 3 tablespoons Panca Chili Paste (see p. 406)
- 1 tablespoon Yellow Chili Paste (see p. 405)
- 1½ oz (40 g) peanuts, toasted and chopped
- 1 cup (9 oz/250 g) boiled potatoes, cut into ½-inch (1-cm) cubes
- 1 sprig mint
- salt and pepper

Place the cow's hoof and pig feet (trotters) in two separate pans. Add a pinch of salt, 2 whole garlic cloves and 1 bay leaf to each pan and add enough water to cover the ingredients by 2 inches/5 cm. Place over medium heat and bring to a boil. Boil the cow's hoof for 3 hours and the pig feet for 1 hour.

Remove the hoof and feet from their respective pans and continue to reduce the cooking liquids for 50 minutes until nicely concentrated. Set aside.

Separate the meat from the bones and cut into 1-inch/2.5-cm chunks. Set aside.

Heat the oil in a separate pan, add the onion, chopped garlic, and chili pastes and season with salt and pepper. Sauté over low heat for 2–3 minutes until the onion is soft. Add the cubed meat, pour in the cooking liquids, and continue to cook, stirring, for 8 minutes. Stir in the chopped peanuts and boiled potato cubes, adjust the seasoning to taste, and cook for a final 5 minutes.

Stir in the mint to finish and spoon into large shallow bowls. Serve.

CANGREJO REVENTADO
BURST CRAB

Serves: 4
Preparation Time: 20 minutes
Cooking Time: 16 minutes

A visit to the beaches of Northern Peru—especially Huanchaco—is a good opportunity to try this delicious dish made with local crabs.

- 8 × 10½-oz (300-g) large crabs, cleaned
- ¼ cup (2 fl oz/50 ml) vegetable oil
- 4 cloves garlic, chopped
- 3 tablespoons Yellow Chili Paste (see p. 405)
- ¼ cup (2 fl oz/50 ml) chicha de jora or white wine
- ¼ cup (2 fl oz/50 ml) fish broth (stock)
- 2 sprigs culantro or cilantro (coriander)
- 4 eggs, beaten
- 1 scallion (spring onion), chopped
- 1 tablespoon chopped parsley, to garnish
- salt and pepper

Pound the crabs with a meat tenderizer until the shells are crushed but not completely destroyed.

Heat the oil in a pan, add the garlic, and sauté over low heat for 30 seconds until cooked. Add the chili paste and cook, stirring, for another 2–3 minutes until fragrant.

Add the chicha de jora or white wine, fish broth (stock), crabs, and culantro or cilantro (coriander) sprigs, and season with salt and pepper. Bring to a simmer and cook over low heat for 12 minutes until the crabs are cooked.

Remove the crabs from the pan and scoop out the meat from the shells using a fork. Set the shells aside.

Stir the beaten eggs into the pan along with the chopped scallion (spring onion). Return the crab meat to the pan and mix together well.

Put the crab shells in large shallow bowls and add the crab and egg mixture and garnish with chopped parsley. Serve immediately.

Burst Crab

LANGOSTINOS CON MANÍ
SHRIMP AND PEANUT STEW

Serves: 4
Preparation Time: 15 minutes
Cooking Time: 10 minutes

You can also prepare this dish with clean whole shrimp (prawns), leaving the heads on. They will enhance the flavor of the stew.

40 shrimp (prawns), peeled and deveined
2 tablespoons vegetable oil
4 tablespoons Panca Chili, Garlic, and Onion Condiment (see p. 403)
1 tablespoon peanut butter
1 cup (8 fl oz/250 ml) vegetable broth (stock)
1 tablespoon coconut milk
2 oz (50 g) peanuts, toasted and ground
1 teaspoon grated lemon zest
1 teaspoon chopped culantro or cilantro (coriander) leaves
2 cups (14 oz/400 g) Peruvian-Style Cooked White Rice (see p. 178), to serve
salt and pepper

Season the shrimp (prawns) with salt and pepper. Heat the oil over medium heat in a pan, add the shrimp, and brown for 1 minute on each sides. Remove from the pan and set aside.

Place the chili, garlic, and onion condiment in a separate pan and cook for 5 minutes until it is fragrant. Add the peanut butter and pour in the vegetable broth (stock). Bring to a simmer and cook over medium heat for 3 minutes until the flavors blend.

Add the shrimp and coconut milk to the pan, adjust the seasoning to taste, and cook for another minute. Stir through the ground peanuts, lemon zest, and chopped culantro or cilantro (coriander) leaves to finish.

Ladle into large shallow bowls and serve with Peruvian-style cooked white rice.

CHITA AL AJO CROCANTE
PERUVIAN GRUNT WITH CRISPY GARLIC

Serves: 4
Preparation Time: 15 minutes
Cooking Time: 25 minutes

The Peruvian grunt is a delicious type of fish with a lovely flavor. It goes well with garlic and is ideal for frying. This recipe can, however, also be easily adapted to any other white-fleshed fish.

2 bulbs garlic
4 cups (34 fl oz/1 liter) vegetable oil
2 × 2¼-lb/1-kg Peruvian grunts, cleaned and gutted
4 oz (120 g) white all-purpose (plain) flour
4 oz (120 g) butter
1 handful parsley leaves, chopped
1 small lemon, quartered
salt and pepper

Thinly slice half the garlic cloves with a mandolin slicer or sharp knife. Chop the remaining garlic.

Heat the vegetable oil in a deep-fryer or large pot to 350°F/180°C, or until a cube of bread browns in 30 seconds. Drop the garlic slices carefully into the hot oil and cook until crispy and golden. Drain well on paper towels. Season with salt and set aside.

Season the fish with salt and pepper, thoroughly coat them in the flour, and carefully add to the hot oil. Cook until golden. Drain well and set aside.

Heat the butter in a separate pan, add the chopped garlic, and sauté for 2–3 minutes, until the butter has melted and absorbed the garlic flavor. Strain.

Arrange the fried fish on a serving platter. Drizzle over the garlic butter and top with the chopped parsley, crispy garlic, and lemon quarters.

CHITA AL AJONJOLÍ
SESAME-SPICED PERUVIAN GRUNT

Serves: 4
Preparation Time: 15 minutes
Cooking Time: 32 minutes

This is a classic Japanese-inspired dish, born of the amazing fusion of Peruvian and Japanese immigrant cuisine.

- 2 × 2¼-lb/1-kg Peruvian grunts, cleaned and gutted
- 2 cups (18 fl oz/500 ml) fish broth (stock)
- 1-inch (2.5-cm) piece fresh ginger, peeled and chopped
- ¼ cup (1 oz/30 g) shiitake mushrooms
- ½ cup (4 fl oz/120 ml) soy sauce
- 4 tablespoons sesame oil
- salt and pepper

To garnish

- 2 scallions (spring onions), thinly sliced
- 2 limo chiles, deveined, seeded, and thinly sliced
- 2-inch (5-cm) piece fresh ginger, peeled and sliced
- 1 tablespoon white sesame seeds, toasted

Preheat the oven to 350°F/180°C/Gas Mark 4. Season the fish with salt and pepper and place in a roasting pan.

Pour the fish broth (stock) into a pan and add the chopped ginger, shiitake mushrooms, and soy sauce. Bring to a simmer and cook over low heat for 20 minutes until the liquid reduces by half.

Pour the broth mixture over the fish and bake in the oven for 12 minutes until the fish has cooked. Remove from the oven, arrange on a large serving platter, pour over the cooking juices and take it straight to the table.

Meanwhile, heat the sesame oil in a frying pan until very hot.

Top the fish with the sliced scallions (spring onions), limo chile, and ginger slices, drizzle over the hot sesame oil, and sprinkle with the toasted sesame seeds to garnish.

MAJARISCO
MASHED PLANTAINS WITH SEAFOOD

Serves: 4
Preparation Time: 20 minutes
Cooking Time: 17 minutes

You will often find mashed plantains and cassava in northern Peruvian cuisine. It seems only natural to combine these ingredients with wonderful Peruvian seafood in a dish such as this one.

- 1 cup (8 fl oz/250 ml) plus 1 tablespoon vegetable oil
- 4 green plantains, peeled and cut into 1-inch (2.5-cm) slices
- 4 tablespoons Yellow Chili Paste (see p. 405)
- 1 tablespoon Yellow Chili, Garlic, and Onion condiment (see p. 402)
- 1 tomato, skinned, seeded, and grated
- ¼ cup (2 fl oz/50 ml) chicha de jora or white wine
- 12 shrimp (prawns), peeled and deveined
- 12 scallops, cleaned
- ½ cup (4¼ oz/120 g) cooked thinly sliced octopus
- 1 tablespoon chopped culantro or cilantro (coriander) leaves
- salt and pepper

To serve

- 1 cup (8 fl oz/250 ml) Creole Sauce (see p. 416)
- 7 oz (200 g) yucca root (cassava), peeled, boiled, and cut into 4 pieces

Heat 1 cup (8 fl oz/250 ml) of the oil in a pan over medium heat, add the plantain slices, and cook for 8 minutes until tender. Remove the plantain chunks from the pan and mash them with a pestle and mortar. Set aside.

Heat 1 tablespoon oil in a separate pan, add the chili paste and condiment and cook, stirring, for 2–3 minutes until fragrant. Add the grated tomato, chicha de jora or white wine, and season with salt and pepper. Bring to a simmer and cook over low heat for 2 minutes until slightly thickened.

Add the shrimp (prawns) to the pan and mix together well, then stir in the scallops and sliced octopus. Cook for 3 minutes.

Stir in the mashed plantain and mix together well, and sprinkle with the chopped culantro leaves to finish. Serve with Creole sauce and boiled yucca root (cassava).

Quick-Braised Peruvian Grunt

CHITA SUDADA
QUICK-BRAISED PERUVIAN GRUNT

Serves: 2
Preparation Time: 12 minutes
Cooking Time: 20 minutes

In Peru, *sudar* (from the Spanish "sweat") means to quickly braise seafood in its own juices with almost no added liquid. The fact that a whole fish can be cooked in this way shows how refined this technique is.

1 × 1-lb 5-oz (600-g) Peruvian grunt, cleaned and gutted
1 tablespoon vegetable oil
2 tablespoons Panca Chili Paste (see p. 406)
2 tomatoes, 1 grated and 1 sliced
½ cup (4 fl oz/120 ml) vegetable broth (stock)
¼ red onion, sliced
1 yellow chile, deveined, seeded, and thinly sliced
3½ oz (100 g) yucca root (cassava), peeled, boiled, and cut into 4 pieces
1 rocoto chile slice
1 sprig culantro or cilantro (coriander), plus extra leaves to garnish
¼ cup (2 fl oz/50 ml) chicha de jora or white wine
½ cup (3½ oz/100 g) Peruvian-Style Cooked White Rice (see p. 178), to serve
salt and pepper

Season the fish with salt and pepper. Make two cuts of 2 x ½-inch/5 × 1-cm on both fillets to facilitate the cooking process.

Heat the oil in a large pan, add the chili paste and grated tomato and sauté over low heat for 8 minutes until thickened and fragrant. Pour in the vegetable broth (stock) and season with salt.

Add the fish to the pan with the onion, sliced tomato, yellow chile, boiled yucca root (cassava), rocoto chile slice, culantro or cilantro (coriander) sprig, and chicha de jora or white wine. Bring to a simmer and cook, covered, for 6 minutes. Turn the fish over and cook for another 6 minutes until cooked through.

Carefully remove the fish from the pan and divide the flesh between large shallow bowls. Pour over the cooking juices and vegetables, garnish with a few shredded culantro leaves, and serve with Peruvian-style cooked white rice.

HÍGADO A LA CHORRILLANA
CHORRILLANA BEEF LIVER

Serves: 4
Preparation Time: 12 minutes
Cooking Time: 15 minutes

Fish, meat, poultry, and, of course, offal all go well with the delicious chorrillana sauce. Be careful not to overcook the beef liver—it should be succulent.

14 oz (400 g) beef liver, cut into ½-inch (1-cm) slices
2 tablespoons white vinegar
¼ cup (2 fl oz/60 ml) vegetable oil
salt and pepper

Chorrillana sauce
2 tablespoons vegetable oil
2 red onions, thinly sliced
4 tomatoes, skinned, seeded, and sliced
1 yellow chile, seeded, membrane removed, and sliced
4 tablespoons vinegar
1 tablespoon Yellow Chili Paste (see p. 405)
2 tablespoons Panca Chili, Garlic, and Onion Condiment (see p. 403)
1 cup (8 fl oz/250 ml) vegetable broth (stock)
1 teaspoon unsalted butter
2 tablespoons chopped culantro or cilantro (coriander) leaves
salt and pepper

To serve
2 cups (14 oz/400 g) Peruvian Corn Rice (see p. 195), to serve
2 white potatoes, boiled and sliced

Put the liver slices in a bowl, season with salt and pepper, and add the vinegar. Heat the oil in a pan, add the liver slices, and cook for 3 minutes on each side, until browned but still juicy on the inside. Set aside.

For the sauce, heat the oil in a separate pan over medium heat. Add the onion, tomatoes, and sliced yellow chiles and cook for 2 minutes.

Add the vinegar, chili paste and chili, garlic, and onion condiment and mix together well for 1 minute. Add the vegetable broth (stock), bring to a simmer, and cook for 4 minutes until reduced by a quarter. Stir the butter and chopped culantro or cilantro (coriander) leaves into the sauce, and adjust the seasoning to taste.

Divide the liver slices between plates, spoon over the sauce, and serve with Peruvian corn rice and sliced boiled potatoes.

CORVINA A LA CHORRILLANA
CHORRILLANA CROAKER

Serves: 4
Preparation Time: 10 minutes
Cooking Time: 17 minutes

4 × 6-oz (175-g) croaker fillets
¼ cup (2 fl oz/60 ml) vegetable oil
salt and pepper

Sauce
2 tablespoons vegetable oil
1 red onion, sliced
4 tomatoes, skinned, seeded, and sliced or cut into wedges
1 yellow chiles, seeded, membrane removed, and sliced
4 tablespoons vinegar
1 tablespoon Yellow Chili Paste (see p. 405)
2 tablespoons Panca Chili, Garlic, and Onion Condiment (see p. 403)
1 cup (8 fl oz/250 ml) fish broth (stock)
1 teaspoon unsalted butter
2 tablespoons chopped culantro or cilantro (coriander) leaves
salt and pepper

Season the fish with salt and pepper. Heat the oil in a pan, add the fish fillets, and fry for 4 minutes on each side until cooked and lightly golden. Cover and set aside, keeping warm.

For the sauce, heat 2 tablespoons oil in a separate pan over medium heat. Add the onion, tomatoes, and sliced yellow chiles and cook for 2 minutes until the onion has started to soften.

Add the vinegar, chili paste, and chili, garlic, and onion condiment and mix together well for 1 minute. Add the fish broth (stock), bring to a simmer, and cook for 4 minutes until reduced by a quarter. Stir the butter and chopped culantro or cilantro (coriander) leaves into the sauce and adjust the seasoning to taste.

Serve the fillets on plates, spooning over the sauce to finish.

COSTILLAR DE CORDERO FRITO
FRIED RACK OF LAMB

Serves: 4
Preparation Time: 10 minutes, plus 2 hours chilling
Cooking Time: 10–15 minutes

This dish is typical of the Andean region and is usually made with natural grass-fed lamb. It is really tasty with llatán or ocopa sauce.

1 × 3¼-lb (1.5-kg) rack of lamb, cleaned
4 cloves garlic, finely chopped
1 bay leaf
pinch of salt
4 cups (1 liter) vegetable oil

To serve
4 white potatoes, boiled and cut into ¾-inch (2-cm) slices
¼ cup (2 fl oz/50 ml) Llatán Sauce (see p. 413)
1 cup (8 fl oz/250 ml) Ocopa Sauce (see p. 415), optional

Cut the rack of lamb into 4 large chunks, add to a bowl with the chopped garlic, bay leaf, and salt, and marinate for 2 hours covered with plastic wrap (cling film) in the refrigerator.

Heat the vegetable oil in a wide pan. Add the lamb pieces and cook until thoroughly browned and crispy on the outside but still juicy on the inside. Remove from the heat.

Serve the lamb with boiled potatoes, llatán sauce and ocopa sauce, if you prefer.

Chorrillana Croaker

LOMO A LA CHORRILLANA
CHORRILLANA BEEF TENDERLOIN

Serves: 4
Preparation Time: 10 minutes
Cooking Time: 20 minutes

This recipe adds a twist to the traditional chorrillana sauce that is usually served with fish. This version also goes well with poultry.

4 × 7-oz/200-g beef tenderloin (fillet) medallions
salt and pepper
¼ cup (2 fl oz/60 ml) vegetable oil
2 cups (14 oz/400 g) Peruvian Corn Rice, to serve (see p. 195)

Sauce
2 tablespoons vegetable oil
2 red onions, thinly sliced
4 tomatoes, skinned, seeded, and sliced
1 yellow chile, seeded, membrane removed, and sliced
4 tablespoons vinegar
1 tablespoon Yellow Chili Paste (see p. 405)
2 tablespoons Panca Chili, Garlic, and Onion Condiment (see p. 403)
1 cup (8 fl oz/250 ml) vegetable broth (stock)
1 teaspoon unsalted butter
2 tablespoons chopped culantro or cilantro (coriander) leaves
salt and pepper

Season the beef with salt and pepper. Heat the oil in a skillet or frying pan, add the steaks, and cook over medium heat for 3 minutes on each side until medium rare. Set aside and keep warm.

For the sauce, heat the oil in a separate pan over medium heat. Add the onion, tomatoes, and yellow chiles and cook for 2 minutes until the onion has started to soften.

Add the vinegar, chili paste, and chili, garlic, and onion condiment and mix together well for 1 minute. Add the vegetable broth (stock), bring to a simmer, and cook for 4 minutes until reduced by a quarter. Stir the butter and chopped culantro or cilantro (coriander) leaves into the sauce and adjust the seasoning to taste.

Divide the beef medallions between plates, spoon over the sauce, and serve with Peruvian corn rice.

MALAYA FRITA
FRIED FLANK STEAK

Serves: 4
Preparation Time: 10 minutes, plus 2 hours chilling
Cooking Time: 1 hour 40 minutes

Flank steak is distinguished by the fact that it separates into shreds when cooked. This allows it to form a delicious crust around the outside when fried.

3¼ lb (1.5 kg) beef flank steak
1 onion
4 cloves garlic
1 leek
1 turnip
1 sprig oregano
1 teaspoon black peppercorns
½ cup (4 fl oz/120 ml) chicha de jora or white wine
5 tablespoons Panca Chili Paste (see p. 406)
4 white potatoes, boiled, peeled, and cut into ¾-inch (2-cm) slices
5 cups (42¼ fl oz/1.25 liters) vegetable oil
salt and pepper

To serve
½ cup (4 fl oz/120 ml) Llatán Sauce (see p. 413)
½ cup (4 fl oz/120 ml) Creole Sauce (see p. 416)

Place the flank steak in a large pan or pot with the onion, garlic cloves, leek, turnip, oregano, peppercorns, and a pinch of salt. Cover with 12¾ cups (102 fl oz/3 liters) of water, bring to a simmer, and cook over low heat for 1½ hours until the meat is tender.

Let the meat cool in its own cooking juice, then remove it from the pan and cut into 7-oz/200-g chunks. Strain and reserve the broth (stock), discarding the vegetables.

Place the meat chunks in a bowl with the chicha de jora and chili paste. Season with salt and pepper, cover with plastic wrap (clingfilm), and marinate in the refrigerator for 2 hours.

Heat the vegetable oil to 350°F/180°C in a wide pan, add the meat pieces, and cook until thoroughly browned. Remove the meat from the pan and set aside. Repeat with the boiled and sliced potatoes.

Serve the steak pieces with the potatoes, llatán, and Creole sauces.

Chorrillana Beef Tenderloin

CAIGUA RELLENA
STUFFED CAIGUA

Serves: 4
Preparation Time: 25 minutes
Cooking Time: 30 minutes

This is one of Peru's most popular homemade dishes. You can adapt the recipe and use bell peppers or zucchini (courgettes) instead of caiguas if you like—it will be just as delicious.

8 caiguas
4 tablespoons Panca Chili, Garlic, and Onion Condiment (see p. 403)
2 cloves garlic, finely chopped
14 oz (400 g) beef tenderloin (fillet), cut into ½-inch (1.5-cm) cubes
1½ oz (40 g) raisins, soaked in water
scant ½ cup (1½ oz/40 g) fresh peas, shelled
¼ cup (2 fl oz/50 ml) red wine
1 cup (8 fl oz/250 ml) beef broth (stock)
1½ oz (40 g) black olives, chopped
1 tablespoon chopped parsley
4 hard-boiled eggs, cut into quarters
2 cups (14 oz/400 g) Peruvian-Style Cooked White Rice (see p. 178), to serve

Make a cut lengthwise down the center of each caigua to make a pocket and remove the seeds and central vein. Place the caiguas in a pan of boiling salted water and cook for 2–3 minutes until they are blanched. Transfer from the pan to a bowl of iced water. Set aside.

Preheat the oven to 350°F/180°C/Gas Mark 4. Boil the peas in lightly salted water for 5 minutes. Drain.

To make the stuffing, heat the chili, garlic, and onion condiment in a pan over low heat for 2 minutes until fragrant. Add the chopped garlic, cubed beef, soaked and drained raisins, peas, red wine, and broth (stock), bring to a simmer, and cook for 10 minutes over medium heat until the meat is cooked. Stir through the olives and chopped parsley and remove from the heat.

Fill the caiguas with the quartered hard-boiled eggs and as much of the meat stuffing as possible, place on a baking sheet, and cover with the remaining stuffing. Bake for 10 minutes until the caiguas are tender.

Divide the caiguas between large shallow bowls and pour over the cooking juices. Serve with Peruvian-style cooked white rice.

HUATIA
STEAMED BEEF STEW

Serves: 4
Preparation Time: 10 minutes
Cooking Time: 3 hours

This dish is special and unusual due to the way the meat is cooked: almost steamed in its own juices. Use every aromatic herb you can lay your hands on in your local market to prepare this dish.

3¼ lb (1.5 kg) beef flank steak, cut into 2-inch (5-cm) chunks
½ cup (4 fl oz/120 ml) Panca Chili, Garlic and Onion Condiment (see p. 403)
2 red onions, sliced
¼ cup (2 fl oz/50 ml) white wine vinegar
2 cups (18 fl oz/500 ml) vegetable broth (stock)
1 tablespoon ground cumin
2 sprigs culantro or cilantro (coriander)
1 sprig rosemary
1 sprig oregano
2 sprigs mint
7 oz (200 g) yucca root (cassava), peeled and boiled, and cut into 4 pieces, to serve
salt and pepper

Season the beef chunks with salt and pepper and set aside.

Put the chili, garlic, and onion condiment in a pan and sauté for a few seconds until fragrant. Add the onion, vinegar, vegetable broth (stock), cumin, herbs, and beef, bring to a simmer over low heat, and cook, covered, for 3 hours over low heat until the meat is tender.

Ladle the stew into large shallow bowls and serve with boiled yucca root (cassava).

Steamed Beef Stew

Plantain Balls with Chorizo and Smoked Beef

TACACHO DE PLATANO
PLANTAIN BALLS WITH CHORIZO AND SMOKED BEEF

Serves: 4
Preparation Time: 25 minutes
Cooking Time: 35 minutes

This is a tasty dish that is typical throughout the Peruvian Amazon. It can be enjoyed at any time of the day.

6 green plantains, peeled
4 tablespoons chopped bacon into ½ x ¼-inch (1.5-cm x 5-mm) pieces
3½ oz (100 g) lard
2¼ lb (1 kg) smoked or sun-dried beef, cut into 3½ x 2-inch (8 × 5-cm) pieces
1 lb 2 oz (500 g) chorizo, cut into 4 pieces
1 cup (8½ fl oz/250 ml) Creole Sauce (see p. 416), optional
salt

Place the peeled plantains on a hot barbecue and cook for 15 minutes until tender. Remove from the barbecue and mash with a pestle and mortar or *batán* (Peruvian grinder) until they form a coarse paste.

Fry the bacon over medium heat for 8 minutes until crispy. Drain.

Season the mashed plantain with salt, add the bacon and most of the lard (reserve 3 tablespoons for frying) and mix together well. Roll the mixture into 8 balls and set aside.

Melt the remaining lard in a pan, add the beef chunks and chorizo, and fry for 8 minutes until the meat and chorizo are cooked and browned.

Divide the plantain balls and chorizo and smoked beef mixture between plates. Serve with Creole sauce, if you like.

TRIPULINA
OFFAL AND BEEF STEW

Serves: 4
Preparation Time: 15 minutes
Cooking Time: 50 minutes

Butchers in slaughterhouses keep everything that doesn't have much market value: lungs, tripe, and spleen, among other animal offal. These are seasoned and slow-cooked in their own juices, giving rise to the famous "slaughterhouse stew."

11 oz (300 g) beef testicles, cleaned
11 oz (300 g) beef kidney, cleaned
11 oz (300 g) beef lung, cleaned
11 oz (300 g) beef small intestine, cleaned
6 cloves garlic, 2 whole and 4 finely chopped
1 bay leaf
11 oz (300 g) ground (minced) beef
1 tablespoon vegetable oil
1 teaspoon ground cumin
¼ cup (2 fl oz/50 ml) white wine vinegar
2 tomatoes, skinned, seeded, and sliced
1 red onion, thinly sliced
2 cups (18 fl oz/500 ml) beef or vegetable broth (stock)
salt and pepper

To serve
4 white potatoes, boiled, peeled, and cut in to 1-inch (2.5-cm) slices
1 cup (8 fl oz/250 ml) Creole Sauce (see p. 416)
sliced onion
sliced red chiles
chopped cilantro (coriander)

Place the testicles, kidney, lung, and intestines in a pan with the whole garlic cloves and bay leaf. Cover with water and place over the heat. Bring to a boil, then immediately remove from the heat, drain, and let cool.

Once cool, chop the offal and intestines into 1½-inch/4-cm pieces and place in a large pan over medium heat with the beef and 1 tablespoon of vegetable oil. Stir in the cumin, vinegar, and chopped garlic and season with salt and pepper. Stir.

Add the sliced tomatoes and onion and pour in the beef or vegetable broth (stock). Bring to a simmer and cook, covered, over medium heat for 40 minutes, until the offal is tender.

Serve on plates with boiled white potatoes and Creole sauce. Garnish with onion, chiles, and cilantro (coriander).

LENGUA ESTOFADA
STEWED TONGUE

Serves: 4
Preparation Time: 15 minutes, plus overnight soaking
Cooking Time: 1 hour 35 minutes

Tongue is used less and less in mainstream recipes these days, which is a shame because it is one of the most flavorful cuts of meat when it comes to stew.

7 oz (200 g) dried chickpeas
1 tablespoon dried mushrooms
2¼ lb (1 kg) veal tongue, cleaned
2 cloves garlic
2 bay leaves
1 teaspoon peppercorns
1 sprig oregano
2 tablespoons vegetable oil
1 tablespoon Panca Chili Paste (see p. 406)
¾ red onion, chopped
2 tomatoes, skinned, seeded, and grated
½ cup (4 fl oz/120 ml) red wine
2 quarts (56 fl oz/2 liters) vegetable broth (stock)
2 cups (14 oz/400 g) Peruvian-Style Cooked White Rice (see p. 178), to serve
salt and pepper

Put the chickpeas in a bowl, cover with water, and leave to soak overnight. Drain and set aside. Soak the dried mushrooms in a little warm water for 15 minutes.

Thoroughly wash the tongue and place in a pan with the garlic cloves, bay leaves, peppercorns, oregano, and enough water to cover the ingredients. Bring to a simmer and cook for about 45 minutes over medium heat, until the tongue is tender. Drain the cooking liquid and let the tongue cool, then peel and cut into 1-inch/2.5-cm slices.

Heat the oil in a pan, add the chili paste and sauté for 1 minute until fragrant. Add the onion and grated tomato and season with salt and pepper. Sauté for a few minutes until the onion has softened and the mixture is thick and glossy.

Add the cooked tongue slices to the pan, pour in the red wine and vegetable broth (stock), and add the soaked and drained mushrooms and drained chickpeas. Bring to a simmer and cook over low heat for 45 minutes until the chickpeas are tender. Adjust the seasoning to taste.

Serve the stewed tongue with Peruvian-style cooked white rice.

CAU CAU CLÁSICO
CLASSIC BEEF TRIPE CAU CAU

Serves: 4
Preparation Time: 15 minutes
Cooking Time: 1 hour 35 minutes

As children, Peruvians aren't usually too keen on beef tripe. Over time, however, we start to discover its amazing richness and complex texture and flavors.

- 1¾ lb (800 g) beef tripe, cleaned
- 3 sprigs mint
- 4 tablespoons vegetable oil
- 1 red onion, chopped
- 4 cloves garlic, finely chopped
- 5 tablespoons Yellow Chili Paste (see p. 405)
- 4 white potatoes, cut into ½-inch (1.5-cm) cubes
- 2¾ oz (70 g) carrot, cut into ½-inch (1-cm) cubes
- ¾ cup (3 oz/80 g) peas
- 2 cups (14 oz/400 g) Peruvian-Style Cooked White Rice (see p. 178), to serve
- salt and pepper

Remove the fat from the tripe and place in a pan with a sprig of mint. Cover with water and cook, uncovered, for 40 minutes until tender.

Remove from the heat and discard the water. Cover the tripe and half the mint with more water and return the pan to the heat. Bring to a boil and simmer for 20 minutes. Remove from the heat and let cool, reserving the cooking liquid. Cut the tripe into 1-inch/2.5-cm squares.

Heat the oil in a separate pan and sauté the onion and garlic until the onion has started to soften. Add the yellow chili paste, followed by the tripe squares, and simmer for 10 minutes until tender.

Pour in a little of the tripe cooking liquid and season with salt. Cook for about 15 minutes, then add the potatoes, carrots, peas, and remaining tripe cooking liquid, and cook for another 10 minutes. Chop the remaining mint leaves, add them to thepan, stir, and remove from heat. Divide between plates and serve with Peruvian-style cooked white rice.

CAU CAU DE CONCHAS
SCALLOP CAU CAU

Serves: 4
Preparation Time: 10 minutes
Cooking Time: 20 minutes

Unlike classic beef tripe cau cau, this version is really quick to make. Be careful not to overcook the scallops, which should be juicy.

2 tablespoons Yellow Chili, Garlic, and Onion Condiment (see p. 402)
3 tablespoons Yellow Chili Paste (see p. 405)
4 white potatoes, cut into ½-inch (1-cm) cubes
2 cups (18 fl oz/500 ml) mussel or fish broth (stock)
40 scallops, cleaned
¾ cup (3 oz/80 g) fresh peas, shelled
1 tablespoon chopped mint leaves
2 cups (14 oz/400 g) Peruvian-Style Cooked White Rice (see p. 178), to serve
salt and pepper

In a pan, sweat the yellow chili, garlic, and onion condiment with the yellow chili paste for 3 minutes over low heat until the onion is cooked.

Boil the peas in lightly salted boiling water for 5 minutes. Drain.

Add the potato cubes and mussel or fish broth (stock). Bring to a simmer and cook over low heat for 10 minutes until the potatoes are tender, then add the scallops and peas.

Once the scallops are cooked, after about 2 minutes, taste and season with salt and pepper if necessary.

Stir in the chopped mint, divide between plates, and serve with Peruvian-style cooked white rice.

CAU CAU DE CHOROS
MUSSEL CAU CAU

Serves: 4
Preparation Time: 10 minutes
Cooking Time: 20–25 minutes

The secret to success when it comes to this dish is the quality and especially the quantity of mint used. Add generous amounts for a memorable mussel cau cau.

48 mussels, cleaned
½ cup (4 fl oz/120 ml) white wine
2 tablespoons Yellow Chili, Garlic and Onion Condiment (see p. 402)
3 tablespoons Yellow Chili Paste (see p. 405)
4 white potatoes, cut into ½-inch (1.5-cm) cubes
1 tablespoon chopped mint leaves
2 cups (14 oz/400 g) Peruvian-Style Cooked White Rice (see p. 178), to serve
salt and pepper

Put the mussels in a pan with the wine and 1 cup (8 fl oz/250 ml) water. Place over the heat, cover, and cook until they open. Remove one of the shells from each mussel and return the shell with the meat to the cooking liquid.

In a separate pan, sweat the yellow chili, garlic and onion condiment with the yellow chili paste for 1 minute over low heat until the flavors mix.

Add the potato cubes and the mussel cooking liquid. Cook over low heat for 10 minutes until the potatoes are tender, then add the mussels, and cook for another minute. Season with salt and pepper to taste.

Stir in the chopped mint, divide between plates, and serve with Peruvian-style cooked white rice.

Scallop Cau Cau

CAU CAU DE MARISCOS
SEAFOOD CAU CAU

Serves 4
Preparation Time: 15 minutes
Cooking Time: 15 minutes

You can use any type of seafood to prepare this dish provided you adjust the cooking times accordingly.

1 red onion, chopped
4 cloves garlic, finely chopped
4 tablespoons vegetable oil
5 tablespoons Yellow Chili Paste (see p. 405)
4 white potatoes, cut into ½-inch (1.5-cm) cubes
½ carrot, diced
2 cups (18 fl oz/500 ml) mussel broth (stock)
¼ cup (2¾ oz/80 g) cooked octopus, chopped
¼ cup (2¾ oz/80 g) snails
8 shrimp (prawns), peeled and cleaned
8 small scallops, cleaned
2 sprigs mint
salt and pepper
2 cups (14 oz/400 g) Peruvian-Style Cooked White Rice (see p. 178), to serve

To prepare the snails, boil them in plenty of water for 1½ hours. Remove from the shells, cool down, and chop. Refrigerate if not used immediately.

Sauté the onion and garlic in a pan with the oil until the onion is tender. Add the chili paste and cook for a few minutes over low heat until the chili paste is fragrant. Add the potatoes, carrots, and half the mussel broth (stock) and cook for 8 minutes until the potatoes are tender.

Add the octopus, snails, shrimp, and scallops along with the remaining broth (stock). Cook for 1 minute over low heat.

Stir through the mint, taste, and adjust the seasoning, if necessary. Divide between plates and serve with Peruvian-style cooked white rice.

CAU CAU DE CABEZA
PIG'S HEAD CAU CAU

Serves 4
Preparation Time: 25 minutes
Cooking Time: 2 hours 25 minutes

Modern-day chefs aim to make the most of cuts of meat that were shunned in the twentieth century. Luckily all cuts of meat are acceptable again nowadays, as shown by this cau cau. It is truly delicious.

1 × 11-lb (5-kg) pig's head
2 red onions, 1 whole and 1 chopped
7 cloves garlic, 3 whole and 4 very finely chopped
2 whole carrots
3 bay leaves
1 sprig oregano
4 cloves
4 tablespoons vegetable oil
5 tablespoons Yellow Chili Paste (see p. 405)
2 sprigs mint, 1 left whole, 1 leaves removed and chopped
4 white potatoes, cut into ¾-inch (1.5-cm) cubes
½ carrot, diced
2 cups (14 oz/400 g) Peruvian-Style Cooked White Rice (see p. 178), to serve
salt and pepper

Chop up the pig's head into 4 pieces and thoroughly wash the pieces in cold water. Place the pig's head pieces in a large pan with the whole onion and whole garlic cloves, carrots, bay leaves, oregano, and cloves. Season with salt and pepper, cover with water, and bring to a boil over medium heat. Reduce the heat and simmer for 2 hours until the meat is soft and cooked through.

Remove the chunks of meat from the pan and transfer to a platter. Cool and separate the parts you will be using—skin, meat, ears, snout, and tongue—ensuring that as little fat is left on the meat as possible. Cut the meat into 1-inch/2.5-cm cubes and set aside with the cooking liquid.

In a separate pan, heat the oil over low heat and sauté the chopped onion and garlic for 5 minutes, or until softened. Add the yellow chili paste and cook for a 5 minutes, until fragrant.

Add the cubes of meat, 1 cup (8 fl oz/250 ml) cooking liquid, and the whole mint sprig. Season with salt and pepper and cook for a 2–3 more minutes, then add the potato, carrot, and remaining 2 cups (18 fl oz/500 ml) cooking liquid and cook for 10 minutes until the vegetables are tender. Stir in the chopped mint leaves, divide between plates and serve with Peruvian-style cooked white rice.

CAU CAU DE PATITAS
COW'S HOOF AND PIG FEET CAU CAU

Serves 4
Preparation Time: 30 minutes
Cooking Time: 3 hours 25 minutes

This cau cau is rarely served in homes or restaurants, but is one of the most delicious versions of this dish, provided the hoof and feet are well cooked and very tender.

- 1 × 4½-lbs (2-kg) cow's hoof, cleaned
- 2 × 12¼-oz (350-g) pig feet (trotters), cleaned
- 8 cloves garlic, 4 whole and 4 finely chopped
- 3 bay leaves
- 4 tablespoons vegetable oil
- 1 red onion, chopped
- 5 tablespoons Yellow Chili Paste (see p. 405)
- 2 sprigs mint, 1 left whole, 1 leaves removed and chopped
- 4 white potatoes, cut into ½-inch (1.5-cm) cubes
- ½ carrot, diced
- 2 cups (14 oz/400 g) Peruvian-Style Cooked White Rice (see p. 178), to serve
- salt and pepper

Put the cow's hoof and the pig feet (trotters) in 2 separate large pans. Cover each with water and add a little salt, 2 whole garlic cloves, and 1 bay leaf to each. Bring the water in both pans to a boil, then reduce to a simmer (uncovered). Cook until tender: the cow's hoof for 3 hours and the pig feet for 1 hour.

Remove the hoof and the feet from their respective pans and continue to boil the liquids until reduced by half.

Wash the hoof and feet and separate the meat from the bones. Finely chop the meat and set aside.

Heat the oil in a separate pan and sauté the onion and chopped garlic until softened. Add the yellow chili paste, cook for a few minutes until fragrant, and add the cubed meat.

Pour in 1 cup (8 fl oz/250 ml) of the hoof and foot cooking liquid and season with salt and pepper. Stir in the whole mint sprig, add the remaining bay leaf and cook for about 15 minutes, then add the potato, carrot, and remaining 1 cup (8 fl oz/250 ml) hoof and foot cooking liquid, and cook for 10 minutes until the vegetables are tender.

Stir in the chopped mint leaves, divide between plates, and serve with Peruvian-style cooked white rice.

CAU CAU DE POLLO
CHICKEN CAU CAU

Serves 4
Preparation Time: 10 minutes
Cooking Time: 15 minutes

- 4 tablespoons vegetable oil
- 1 red onion, chopped
- 4 cloves garlic, finely chopped
- 5 tablespoons Yellow Chili Paste (see p. 405)
- 2 cups (18 fl oz/500 ml) chicken broth (stock)
- 2 sprigs mint, 1 left whole, 1 with leaves removed and chopped
- 4 white potatoes, cut into ½-inch (1-cm) cubes
- ½ carrot, diced
- ¾ cup (3 oz/80 g) peas
- 1 lb 5 oz (600 g) skinless chicken breast, cut into 1½-inch (4-cm) cubes
- 2 cups (14 oz/400 g) Peruvian-Style Cooked White Rice (see p. 178), to serve
- salt and pepper

Place the oil, onion, and garlic in a pan, add the yellow chili paste, and cook for a few minutes.

Pour in 1 cup (8 fl oz/250 ml) of the chicken broth (stock) and season with salt and pepper. Next, add the whole mint sprig, potato, carrot, peas, chicken, and the remaining broth (stock). Cook for 10 minutes until the vegetables are tender and the chicken is cooked through. Stir in the chopped mint leaves, taste, and adjust the seasoning.

Divide between plates and serve with Peruvian-style cooked white rice.

Serves 4
Preparation Time: 10 minutes
Cooking Time: 25 minutes

This is a wonderful stew typically served in the Peruvian Andes. It is a popular and homey dish infused with love and nostalgia.

4 tablespoons vegetable oil
2 red onions, finely chopped
12 cloves garlic, finely chopped
pinch of cumin
3 tablespoons Panca Chili Paste (see p. 406)
1 tablespoon Mirasol Chili Paste (see p. 405)
1 cup (8 fl oz/250 ml) vegetable broth (stock)
1 lb 5 oz (600 g) fava (broad) beans, peeled
2 white potatoes, cut into ½-inch (1-cm) cubes
1 sprig huacatay
¼ cup (2 fl oz/50 ml) whole (full-fat) milk
1 tablespoon chopped parsley
salt and pepper

To serve (optional)
1 cup (8 fl oz/250 ml) Ocopa Sauce (see p. 415)
1 cup (8 fl oz/250 ml) Llatán Sauce (see p. 413)

PICANTE DE HABAS
SPICY FAVA BEAN STEW

Heat the oil over low heat in a pan and sauté the onion and garlic for 10 minutes until soft. Season with salt and pepper, stir in the cumin and chili pastes, and cook for a few minutes, until fragrant.

Pour in the vegetable broth (stock) and add the fava (broad) beans, potato, and huacatay sprigs. Simmer for 10 minutes until the potatoes and fava beans are cooked. Stir in the milk and chopped parsley to finish.

Ladle the stew into large shallow bowls and serve with ocopa sauce or llatán sauce, if desired.

Serves 4
Preparation Time: 10 minutes
Cooking Time: 25 minutes

Peanuts have been used in Peruvian art for centuries and no less in the culinary arts. They add a very special touch to our stews and sauces.

4 tablespoons vegetable oil
2 red onions, finely chopped
12 cloves garlic, finely chopped
pinch of cumin
3 tablespoons Mirasol Chili Paste (see p. 405)
1 tablespoon Yellow Chili Paste (see p. 405)
1 cup (8 fl oz/250 ml) vegetable broth (stock)
1 lb 5 oz (600 g) fava (broad) beans, peeled
2 white potatoes, cut into cubes
1 sprig huacatay
¼ cup (2 fl oz/50 ml) whole (full-fat) milk
¼ cup (1 oz/30 g) ground peanuts, plus 4 tablespoons chopped peanuts to garnish
1 tablespoon chopped parsley
chopped mint, to serve
1 cup (8 fl oz/250 ml) Llatán Sauce (see p. 413), to serve (optional)
salt and pepper

PICANTE DE HABAS CON MANÍ
SPICY FAVA BEAN AND PEANUT STEW

Heat the oil over low heat in a pan and sauté the onion and garlic for 10 minutes until soft. Season with salt and pepper. Add the cumin and chili pastes and cook over low heat for a few minutes until fragrant.

Pour over the vegetable broth (stock), add the fava (broad) beans, potato, and sprig of huacatay, and simmer over medium heat for 10 minutes until the potatoes and fava beans are cooked. Stir in the milk, ground peanuts, and chopped parsley to finish.

Ladle the stew into large shallow bowls and garnish with chopped peanuts. Serve with chopped mint and llatán sauce, if desired.

Spicy Fava Bean Stew

PICANTE DE CONCHAS
SPICY SCALLOP STEW

Serves 4
Preparation Time: 20 minutes
Cooking Time: 13 minutes

Unlike *cau cau*, this spicy stew includes dairy ingredients that give it a more complex texture. Due to the Italian—and mainly Genovesi—influence, scallops and cheese are often used together in Peruvian cuisine.

1 tablespoon Yellow Chili, Garlic, and Onion Condiment (see p. 402)
2 tablespoons Yellow Chili Paste (see p. 405)
1 tomato, skinned, seeded, and grated
1 cup (8 fl oz/250 ml) vegetable broth (stock)
scant ½ cup (1½ oz/40 g) peas
40 scallops, cleaned
4 slices rocoto chile
2 sprigs culantro or cilantro (coriander)
¼ cup (2 fl oz/50 ml) whole (full-fat) milk
2½ oz (65 g) grated Parmesan cheese
2 tablespoons chopped parsley, to garnish
2 cups (14 oz/400 g) Peruvian-Style Cooked White Rice (see p. 178), to serve
salt and pepper

Gently cook the yellow chili, garlic, and onion condiment with the yellow chili paste in a pan over low heat for 2 minutes, until fragrant. Add the grated tomato and cook for 2–3 minutes, stirring, until the tomato has softened and started to break down.

Pour in the vegetable broth (stock) and cook over medium heat for 2 minutes. Add the peas and cook for another 2 minutes. Finally add the scallops, rocoto chile, and culantro or cilantro (coriander) sprigs, and cook for another 3 minutes over medium heat until the scallops are cooked and the flavors have mixed together. Season with salt and pepper to taste. Stir in the milk and Parmesan cheese to finish.

Divide the stew between plates and garnish with chopped parsley. Serve with Peruvian-style cooked white rice.

PICANTE DE MARISCOS
SPICY SEAFOOD STEW

Serves: 4
Preparation Time: 15 minutes
Cooking Time: 25 minutes

The simplicity of this dish wins people over every time. Feel free to replace the seafood included in the recipe with any locally available seafood of your choice.

4 tablespoons vegetable oil
2 red onions, finely chopped
12 cloves garlic, finely chopped
1 tomato, skinned, seeded, and chopped
pinch of cumin
8 tablespoons Yellow Chili Paste (see p. 405)
1 tablespoon Quebranta pisco
½ cup (4 fl oz/120 ml) evaporated milk
4 white sandwich bread slices
1 sprig fresh oregano
1 cup (8 fl oz/250 ml) vegetable broth (stock)
12 shrimp (prawns), cleaned and peeled
¼ cup (3 oz/80 g) cooked octopus
2 × 7-oz/200-g squid, cleaned and cut into rings
2 limpets, chopped
8 scallops, cleaned
1½ oz (40 g) ground pecans or walnuts
4 white potatoes, boiled and sliced
4 hard-boiled eggs
salt and pepper

Clean the limpets and cook in 4 cups (34 fl oz/1 liter) water for 3 hours until they are tender. Remove the shells, chop, and refrigerate until needed.

Heat the oil in a pan over low heat and sauté the onion, garlic, and tomato for 10 minutes, until softened. Season with salt and pepper. Add the cumin and chili paste and cook over low heat for 5 minutes until fragrant. Add the pisco and allow the alcohol to cook off—about 2 minutes.

Meanwhile, blend the evaporated milk and bread slices together, and add the mixture to the pan along with the sprig of oregano. Cook over medium heat, gradually adding the vegetable broth (stock), for 4 minutes, until thickened and creamy.

Add the shrimp (prawns), octopus, and limpets and cook for 1 minute. Add the squid, scallops and ground nuts. Cook for another 2 minutes until the scallops and squid are cooked. Taste and adjust the seasoning.

Divide the potato slices and hard-boiled eggs between large shallow bowls and ladle over the stew. Serve.

Spicy Seafood Stew

Serves: 4
Preparation Time: 15 minutes, plus 5 minutes soaking
Cooking Time: 18 minutes

4 slices white bread
½ cup (4 fl oz/120 ml) evaporated milk
1 tablespoon Yellow Chili, Garlic, and Onion Condiment (see p. 402)
2 tablespoons Yellow Chili Paste (see p. 405)
2 tomatoes, skinned, seeded and grated
1 tablespoon pisco
1 sprig fresh oregano
1 cup (8 fl oz/250 ml) vegetable broth (stock)
40 shrimp (prawns), peeled and deveined with tails still intact
1½ oz (40 g) ground walnuts
4 white potatoes, boiled and sliced
2 hard-boiled eggs, to serve
salt and pepper

PICANTE DE LANGOSTINOS
SPICY SHRIMP STEW

Soak the bread slices in the evaporated milk for 5 minutes. Blend and set aside.

In a pan, gently cook the yellow chili, garlic, and onion condiment with the yellow chili paste for a few minutes over low heat until the onions have softened. Add the grated tomato and continue to cook for 5 minutes. Add the pisco and allow the alcohol to cook off—about 2 minutes.

Add the evaporated milk and bread mixture to the pan along with the sprig of oregano. Cook over medium heat for 4 minutes until creamy and pour in about 1 cup (8 fl oz/250 ml) vegetable broth (stock) as needed.

Add the shrimp (prawn) tails and ground walnuts and cook for another minute or two until they are cooked. Taste and adjust the seasoning.

Divide the potato slices and hard-boiled eggs between large shallow bowls and ladle over the stew. Serve.

PICANTE A LA TACNEÑA
SPICY TACNA-STYLE STEW

Serves: 4
Preparation Time: 20 minutes
Cooking Time: 3 hours 55 minutes

This scrumptious dish is a favorite in Tacna, a city in southern Peru that borders Chile.

1 × 4¼-lb/2-kg cow's hoof, cleaned
3 cloves garlic
2 bay leaves
1 lb 2 oz (500 g) beef tripe, cleaned
2 tablespoons Panca Chili, Garlic, and Onion Condiment (see p. 403)
¼ cup (5 oz/150 g) beef jerky
1 teaspoon ground dried oregano
4 white potatoes, cut into ½-inch (1-cm) cubes
2 cups (14 oz/400 g) Peruvian Corn Rice (see p. 195), to serve
salt and pepper

Place the cow's hoof in a pan with enough water to cover it, add the garlic cloves and bay leaves, and season with a little salt. Place over the heat and bring to a boil. Reduce the heat and simmer for 3 hours, or until the meat is tender.

Remove the cow's hoof from the pan and continue to boil until the liquid is reduced to about 3 cups (26½ fl oz/750 ml). Set aside.

Wash the hoof and separate the meat from the bones. Cut the meat into ¾-inch/2-cm cubes and set aside.

Remove the fat from the tripe and place it in a pan with enough water to cover it. Place over medium heat and boil for 10 minutes.

Remove from the heat and discard the water. Pour in more water, return to the heat and simmer for 20 minutes until the tripe is tender. Remove from the heat and allow to cool. Chop the tripe into 1¼-inch/3-cm squares.

In a pan, sweat the panca chili, garlic, and onion condiment for a minute over low heat, until fragrant. Pour in the cow's hoof cooking liquid and add the beef jerky, oregano, and cooked tripe cubes. Cook over medium-low heat for 10 minutes.

Next, add the potatoes and cook over low heat for 10 minutes until they are tender. Taste and add more salt and pepper if necessary.

Ladle the stew into large shallow bowls and serve with Peruvian corn rice.

PICANTE DE CARNE
SPICY BEEF STEW

Serves: 4
Preparation Time: 15 minutes
Cooking Time: 1 hour 30 minutes

This stew can also be made with other cuts of beef such as skirt steak, brisket, or neck.

14 oz (400 g) beef (such as flank steak or beef shank), cut into medium chunks
6 tablespoons vegetable oil
2 red onions, finely chopped
12 cloves garlic, finely chopped
pinch of cumin
3 tablespoons Panca Chili Paste (see p. 406)
1 cup (8 fl oz/250 ml) vegetable broth (stock)
5 oz (150 g) fava (broad) beans, peeled
2 white potatoes, cut into cubes
2 slices rocoto chile
1 tablespoon chopped parsley
2 cups (14 oz/400 g) Peruvian-Style Cooked White Rice (see p. 178), to serve
salt and pepper

Season the meat with salt and pepper. Heat half the oil in a pan, add the meat, and brown on all sides over medium heat. Remove from the heat and set aside.

Heat the remaining oil in another pan and sauté the onion and garlic until the onion has softened. Season with salt and pepper, add the cumin and chili paste, and cook over low heat for 10 minutes, stirring.

Pour in the vegetable broth (stock) and add the browned beef. Simmer over low heat for 1 hour until the meat is tender, then add the fava (broad) beans, potatoes, and rocoto chile slices.

Cook for another 10 minutes until the potatoes and fava beans are tender. Remove the rocoto chile slices and stir the chopped parsley into the stew to finish.

Ladle the stew into large shallow bowls and serve with Peruvian-style cooked white rice.

PACHAMANCA DE PESCADOS
FISH PACHAMANCA

Serves: 4
Preparation Time: 20 minutes, plus 5 minutes marinating
Cooking Time: 23 minutes

Unlike meat pachamanca, the fish version needs to be cooked very quickly to ensure that the fish is juicy.

7oz (200 g) yucca root (cassava), peeled and halved
1 corncob
pinch of sugar
1 × 4½-lb/2-kg fish (such as comber, Peruvian morwong, or suckermouth catfish), filleted
24 corn husks, for cooking
½ limo chile, seeded, membrane removed, and chopped
1½ oz (40 g) fava (broad) beans
½ cup (30 g) chopped yuyo seaweed
¼ cup (2 fl oz/50 ml) vegetable broth (stock)
2 cups (14 oz/400 g) Peruvian-Style Cooked White Rice (see p. 178)
salt and pepper

Marinade
1 tablespoon Panca Chili Paste (see p. 406)
3 tablespoons Yellow Chili Paste (see p. 405)
handful of huacatay leaves
3 cloves garlic
1 sprig mint
4 tablespoons white wine vinegar

Put the yucca root (cassava) in a pan with enough water to cover and boil for 15 minutes. Drain and cut into cubes.

Cook the corn in boiling water with a pinch each of salt and sugar and cook for 10 minutes. Drain, then cut into 4 slices.

Put all the marinade ingredients in a blender and blend together until smooth. Place in a bowl with the fish fillets and marinate for 5 minutes.

Next, cover the bottom of a 12-inch/30-cm earthenware pot with 12 corn husks, lay the fish fillets on top, and add the limo chile, yucca root (cassava), fava (broad) beans, corncob slices, yuyo seaweed, and vegetable broth (stock). Cover with the remaining 12 corn husks.

Place the lid on the earthenware pot and cook over high heat for about 8 minutes until the fish is cooked through. Spoon into large shallow bowls and serve with Peruvian-style cooked white rice.

PICANTE DE CHANQUE Y COCHAYUYO
SPICY CHANQUE AND COCHAYUYO SEAWEED STEW

Serves: 4
Preparation Time: 15 minutes, plus overnight freezing and 30 minutes soaking
Cooking Time: 3 hour 25 minutes

You could also try this recipe out with abalones and any local varieties of seaweed instead of chanques or abalone and cochayuyo seaweed.

2 cups (9 oz/250 g) chanque or abalone
1 cup (1½ oz/30 g) cochayuyo seaweed
4 tablespoons vegetable oil
2 red onions, finely chopped
12 cloves garlic, finely chopped
pinch of cumin
2 tomatoes, skinned, seeded, and chopped
5 tablespoons Panca Chili Paste (see p. 406)
1 cup (8 fl oz/250 ml) vegetable broth (stock)
5 oz (150 g) fava (broad) beans, peeled
1 sprig oregano
2 tablespoons chopped parsley
4 boiled white potatoes, to serve
salt and pepper

The day before, wash the chanque or abalone in plenty of cold water. Freeze overnight, then defrost for 2 hours. Boil for 3 hours until tender. Divide into 3 pieces.

Wash the cochayuyo in plenty of cold water. Soak in 2 cups (18 fl oz/500 ml) boiled water for 30 minutes. Drain well and cook in a nonstick pan until dry and lightly roasted.

Heat the oil in a pan and sauté the onion and garlic for a few minutes over medium heat until the onion has start to soften. Season with salt and pepper, stir in the cumin and tomatoes, and continue to cook over low heat for 2 minutes.

Add the chili paste and cook for 10 minutes until the beans are tender and the flavors are combined. Pour in the vegetable broth (stock) and add the fava (broad) beans, chanques, cochayuyo seaweed, and oregano sprig. Cook over medium heat for a few more minutes until the beans are tender.

Adjust the seasoning to taste and stir in the chopped parsley to finish.

Ladle the stew into large shallow bowls and serve with boiled potatoes.

Serves: 4
Preparation Time: 20 minutes, plus 3 hours chilling
Cooking Time: 2 hours

If you don't happen to have any holes in the ground out in the countryside where you can cook a proper pachamanca, this pot-cooked version of the dish is a good alternative.

2 chicken legs and thighs, cut into 1½-inch (4-cm) chunks
5 oz (150 g) pork shoulder, cut into 1½-inch (4-cm) chunks
5 oz (150 g) lamb, cut into 1½-inch (4-cm) chunks
24 corn husks
½ cup (2 fl oz/50 ml) vegetable broth (stock)
4 small sweet potatoes
4 small potatoes
11 oz (300 g) fava (broad) beans
4 sprigs each of huacatay, mint, and wormseed
salt and pepper

Marinade
4 tablespoons Panca Chili Paste (see p. 406)
2 tablespoons Yellow Chili Paste (see p. 405)
handful of huacatay leaves
small handful of chincho leaves
1 sprig mint
small handful of wormseed
3 cloves garlic
¼ cup (2 fl oz/50 ml) white wine vinegar

To serve (optional)
1 cup (8 fl oz/250 ml) Ocopa Sauce (see p. 415)
1 cup (8 fl oz/250 ml) Llatán Sauce (see p. 413)

PACHAMANCA A LA OLLA
POT-COOKED PACHAMANCA

Put all the marinade ingredients in a blender and blend together until smooth. Place in a bowl with the chicken, pork, and lamb chunks, season with salt and pepper and cover with plastic wrap (clingfilm). Marinate in the refrigerator for 3 hours.

Next, cover the bottom of a 12-inch/30-cm earthenware pot with 12 corn husks, place the marinated meat chunks over the husks and pour in the vegetable broth (stock).

Place the sweet potatoes, potatoes, and fava (broad) beans on top and cover with sprigs of huacatay, mint, and wormseed. Cover with the 12 remaining husks. Cover the pot with a lid and cook over low heat for 2 hours until the meat is tender.

Divide the meat and vegetables among 4 plates and serve with llatán or ocopa sauce in separate bowls, if you like.

Pot-Cooked Pachamanca

PACHAMANCA AMAZÓNICA
AMAZONIAN PACHAMANCA

Serves: 4
Preparation Time: 25 minutes, plus 3 hours chilling
Cooking Time: 1 hour

The Amazon rainforest, an undiscovered treasure trove, harbors a huge variety of fruits and herbs that offer a whole new range of flavors to dishes from all over the world, like this pachamanca.

2 medium chickens, each cut into 8 pieces
½ cup (80 g) beef jerky or dried beef, cut into bite-size pieces
24 corn husks, for cooking
¼ cup (2 fl oz/50 ml) vegetable broth (stock)
2 half-ripe bellaco plantains, cut into 1¾-inch (4-cm) pieces, peel left on
5 oz (150 g) fava (broad) beans
salt and pepper

Marinade
4 tablespoons Yellow Chili Paste (see p. 405)
1 tablespoon Panca Chili Paste (see p. 406)
½ tablespoon turmeric or mishkina paste
handful of sacha culantro or cilantro (coriander) leaves
1 sprig mint
4 Charapita chiles, seeded, membrane removed, and chopped
3 cloves garlic
4 tablespoons white wine vinegar

Put all the marinade ingredients in a blender and blend together until smooth. Tip into a bowl, add the chicken pieces and beef jerky, and cover with plastic wrap (clingfilm). Marinate in the refrigerator for 3 hours.

Next, cover the bottom of a 12-inch/30-cm earthenware pot with 12 corn husks and place the marinated chicken and beef jerky on top. Pour over the vegetable broth (stock), add the bellaco plantain pieces and fava (broad) beans, and cover with the remaining 12 corn husks.

Place the lid on the pot and cook over low heat for 1 hour until the chicken is cooked through. Spoon into large shallow bowls and serve.

PACHAMANCA DE CERDO
PORK PACHAMANCA

Serves: 4
Preparation Time: 25 minutes, plus 3 hours chilling
Cooking Time: 1 hour 30 minutes

This pachamanca can be made with pork shoulder, bacon, ribs, chops, and any other cut of pork with high fat and jelly content. You can also use whole suckling pigs.

1 lb 2 oz (500 g) cubed bacon
1 lb 2 oz (500 g) pork shoulder, cut into 2-inch (5-cm) chunks
1 lb 2 oz (500 g) pork ribs, bone in ¼ cup (2 fl oz/50 ml) vegetable broth (stock)
1 sweet potato
4 small potatoes
1 corncob, cut into 4 slices
5 oz (150 g) fava (broad) beans
24 corn husks
4 sprigs each of huacatay, mint, and wormseed
salt and pepper

Marinade
4 tablespoons Panca Chili Paste (see p. 406)
2 tablespoons Yellow Chili Paste (see p. 405)
handful of huacatay leaves
1 sprig spearmint
small handful of wormseed
small handful of chincho leaves
3 cloves garlic
4 tablespoons white wine vinegar
1 cup (8 fl oz/250 ml) Uchucuta Sauce (see p. 417), to serve (optional)

To prepare the marinade, place all the ingredients in a blender and blend together until smooth. Tip into a bowl with the bacon, pork shoulder, lamb, and pork rib chunks. Season with salt and pepper and cover with plastic wrap (clingfilm). Marinate in the refrigerator for 3 hours.

Next, cover the bottom of a 12-inch/30-cm earthenware pot with 12 corn husks, place the marinated meats on top, pour over the vegetable broth (stock), and cover with the remaining 12 corn husks.

Place the sweet potatoes, potatoes, corncob slices, and fava (broad) beans on top and cover with sprigs of huacatay, mint, and wormseed. Place the lid on the pot and cook over low heat for 1½ hours until the meat and vegetables are tender.

Serve with uchucuta sauce.

PACHAMANCA VEGETARIANA
VEGETARIAN PACHAMANCA

Serves: 4
Preparation Time: 25 minutes, plus 3 hours marinating
Cooking Time: 1 hour

This is one of my favorite pachamancas. You can add any vegetables or tubers you like to this dish.

4 native Peruvian potatoes or any small potatoes
4 small oca
4 mashuas
4 small sweet potatoes
¼ cup (2 fl oz/50 ml) vegetable broth (stock)
1½ oz (40 g) Paria cheese, cubed
5 oz (150 g) fava (broad) beans
24 corn husks
4 sprigs each of huacatay, mint, and wormseed
salt and pepper

Marinade
4 tablespoons Panca Chili Paste (see p. 406)
2 tablespoons Yellow Chili Paste (see p. 405)
handful of huacatay leaves
small handful of chincho leaves
1 sprig mint
small handful of wormseed
3 cloves garlic
4 tablespoons white wine vinegar

Humita
5 oz (150 g) corn kernels
4 tablespoons unsalted butter
1 white onion, finely chopped
4 tablespoons Yellow Chili Paste (see p. 405)
pinch of salt
pinch of sugar
24 corn husks

To serve (optional)
1 cup (8 fl oz/250 ml) Uchucuta Sauce (see p. 417)
1 cup (8 fl oz/250 ml) Rocoto Chili Cream (see p. 411)

For the humitas, blend the corn kernels, and set aside. Melt the butter in a pan, add the white onion, and cook until translucent. Add the chili paste, salt, and sugar and cook for 4 minutes. Add the blended corn and cook for 10 minutes over medium heat until the flavors have melded together. Remove from the heat and cool.

Dip the corn husks in boiling water for 30 seconds to soften. Place a serving of the corn mixture in the center of a corn husk and wrap to form a humita, pressing both sides so that the filling is in the center of the parcel. Tie with string to secure and repeat the process with the remaining corn mixture and husks. Set aside.

For the marinade, place all the ingredients in a blender and blend until smooth. Pour into a bowl, add the potatoes, ocas, mashuas, and sweet potatoes and marinate for 30 minutes.

Next, cover the bottom of a 12-inch/30-cm earthenware pot with 12 corn husks, place the marinated potatoes, ocas, mashuas, and sweet potatoes on top, pour in the vegetable broth (stock), and cover with the remaining 12 corn husks.

Place the humitas, cheese, and whole fava (broad) beans on top and cover with the huacatay, mint, and wormseed sprigs. Place the lid on the pot and cook over low heat for 40 minutes or until the vegetable are tender.

Serve with uchucuta sauce or rocoto chili cream, if desired.

Lima-Style Beef Seco Stew

308

SECO DE CARNE A LA LIMEÑA
LIMA-STYLE BEEF SECO STEW

Serves: 4
Preparation Time: 10 minutes
Cooking Time: 2 hours 20 minutes

***Seco* (from the Spanish "dried") stew is actually a moist and juicy dish, so no-one really knows how it got this name. In any case, this version of the dish stands out for its strong culantro or cilantro (coriander) undertones, and was created in Lima.**

- 2 white potatoes
- 4½ lb (2 kg) beef (flank steak, beef shank, or beef cheek)
- vegetable oil, for cooking
- 1 red onion, chopped
- 12 cloves garlic, finely chopped
- pinch of cumin
- ½ cup (4 fl oz/120 ml) Yellow Chili Paste (see p. 405)
- ½ cup (4 fl oz/120 ml) chicha de jora or white wine
- 1 cup (8 fl oz/250 ml) beef or vegetable broth (stock)
- ¼ cup (2 fl oz/50 ml) culantro or cilantro (coriander) juice or extract
- 1 teaspoon oregano
- ½ carrot, cut into ½-inch (1-cm) slices
- scant ½ cup (1½ oz/40 g) peas
- 4 tablespoons chopped culantro or cilantro (coriander) leaves
- salt and pepper

To serve

- 2 cups (14 oz/400 g) Peruvian Corn Rice (see p. 195)
- 2 cups (14 oz/400 g) Smoky Blended Beans (see p. 247)

Cook the potatoes in boiling water for 15–20 minutes, until tender. Drain and peel.

Season the beef with salt and pepper. Heat ½ cup (4 fl oz/120 ml) oil over medium heat and cook until browned. Set aside.

Heat ¼ cup (2 fl oz/50 ml) oil in a pan over medium heat, add the onion and garlic and cook for about 5 minutes, stir continuously, until the onion has softened. Season with salt and pepper, add the cumin and chili paste, and cook the mixture for another 3 minutes, until fragrant. Pour in the chicha de jora or white wine and cook for 2 minutes to evaporate the alcohol.

Place the browned meat in the pan and add the beef or vegetable broth (stock). Bring to a simmer, cover with a lid, and cook over low heat for 1 hour, stirring occasionally. Add the culantro or cilantro (coriander) juice or extract and oregano and cook for another 45 minutes, then add the sliced carrot and peas and cook for a final 15 minutes, until both the vegetables and the meat are tender.

Stir in the boiled potatoes and chopped culantro or cilantro (coriander) leaves and serve with Peruvian corn rice and smoky blended beans.

CABRITO EN AJÍ
GOAT WITH CHILE

Serves: 4
Preparation Time: 15 minutes
Cooking Time: 1 hour 50 minutes

The key to this traditional northern Peruvian dish is to use a very young and tender kid goat. Culantro or cilantro (coriander) sprigs are used rather than blended culantro, which allows the dish to retain the yellow chile color.

1 × 9-lb (4-kg) kid goat, cut into 9-oz (250-g) pieces
vegetable oil, for cooking
1 red onion, chopped
12 cloves garlic, finely chopped
2 oz (50 g) grated loche squash
pinch of cumin
½ cup (4 fl oz/120 ml) Yellow Chili Paste (see p. 405)
1 cup (8 fl oz/250 ml) chicha de jora or white wine
1 cup (8 fl oz/250 ml) vegetable broth (stock)
1 sprig culantro or cilantro (coriander)
scant ½ cup (1½ oz/40 g) peas
salt and pepper

To serve
2 cups (14 oz/400 g) Peruvian Corn Rice (see p. 195)
7 oz (200 g) yucca root (cassava), cooked

Season the goat with salt and pepper and brown it in a pan with ½ cup (4 fl oz/120 ml) oil. Set aside.

Heat ¼ cup (2 fl oz/50 ml) of oil in another pan over medium heat and sauté the onion, garlic, and grated loche squash for about 5 minutes, until the onion has softened. Season with salt and pepper, add the cumin and chili paste, and cook for another 3 minutes. Pour over the chicha de jora or white wine and cook for 2 minutes to evaporate the alcohol.

Place the browned goat pieces in the pan, pour in the vegetable broth (stock), and add the culantro or cilantro (coriander) sprig. Bring to a simmer, cover, and cook for 1½ hours, stirring occasionally, until tender. Add the peas 5 minutes before the end of the cooking time.

Meanwhile, peel the yucca root (cassava) and cut in half. Put in a pan with water and boil for 15 minutes. Drain, then cut into 4 pieces.

Serve with Peruvian corn rice and cooked yucca root.

SECO DE CORVINA
WHITE CROAKER SECO STEW

Serves: 4
Preparation Time: 10 minutes
Cooking Time: 40 minutes

***Seco* stews can also be seafood dishes. Unlike meat *secos*, they are quick to prepare because fish requires a shorter cooking time and should not be overdone.**

4 × 8-oz (225-g) white croaker fillets (skin on)
½ cup (4 fl oz/120 ml) olive oil
¼ cup (2 fl oz/50 ml) vegetable oil
1 red onion, chopped
12 cloves garlic, finely chopped
2 oz (50 g) grated loche squash
pinch of cumin
½ cup (4 fl oz/120 ml) Yellow Chili Paste (see p. 405)
¼ cup (4 fl oz/120 ml) chicha de jora or white wine
1 cup (8 fl oz/250 ml) vegetable broth (stock)
¼ cup (2 fl oz/50 ml) chicken broth (stock)
¼ cup (2 fl oz/50 ml) culantro or cilantro (coriander) juice or extract
½ carrot, parboiled and diced
scant ½ cup (1½ oz/40 g) peas
2 cups (14 oz/400 g) Peruvian Corn Rice (see p. 195), to serve
salt and pepper

Season the fish fillets with salt and pepper and brown skin-side down in a pan with olive oil. Set aside.

Heat ¼ cup (2 fl oz/50 ml) of oil in another pan over medium heat and sauté the onion, garlic, and grated loche squash for about 5 minutes, until the onion has softened. Season with salt and pepper, add the cumin and chili paste, and cook for another 5 minutes, until fragrant. Pour in the chicha de jora or white wine and cook for 2 minutes to evaporate the alcohol.

Pour in the vegetable and chicken broths (stocks), bring to a simmer, and cook for 8 minutes, stirring occasionally, until the liquid reduces by a quarter of its volume. Add the culantro or cilantro (coriander) juice or extract, carrot, and peas, and cook for another 5 minutes until the vegetables are tender.

Add the croaker fillets to the pan and cook for another 4 minutes. Serve with Peruvian corn rice.

Goat with Chile

SECO DE CORDERO
LAMB SECO STEW

Serves: 4
Preparation Time: 15 minutes
Cooking Time: 2 hours 45 minutes

This is another seco stew from Lima that has a lovely green color thanks to the culantro or cilantro (coriander).

2 white potatoes
vegetable oil, for cooking
4½ lb (2 kg) lamb shoulder or rib, cut into 9-oz (250-g) pieces
1 red onion, chopped
12 cloves garlic, finely chopped
pinch of cumin
½ cup (4 fl oz/120 ml) Yellow Chili Paste (see p. 405)
½ cup (4 fl oz/120 ml) chicha de jora or white wine
1 cup (8 fl oz/250 ml) beef broth (stock)
¼ cup (2 fl oz/50 ml) culantro or cilantro (coriander) juice or extract
1 teaspoon oregano
½ carrot, cut into ½-inch (1-cm) slices
scant ½ cup (1½ oz/40 g) peas
juice of 3 small lemons
2 tablespoons chopped culantro or cilantro (coriander) leaves
2 cups (14 oz/400 g) Peruvian Corn Rice (see p. 195), to serve
salt and pepper

Cook the potatoes in boiling water for 15–20 minutes, until tender. Drain and peel.

Season the lamb with salt and pepper and brown in a pan with ½ cup (4 fl oz/120 ml) oil. Set aside.

Heat ¼ cup (2 fl oz/50 ml) of oil in a pan over medium heat, add the onion, and garlic, and cook for about 5 minutes, until the onion has softened. Season with salt and pepper, add the cumin and chili paste, and cook the mixture for another 3 minutes, until fragrant. Add the chicha de jora or white wine and Cook for 2 minutes to evaporate the alcohol.

Place the browned lamb pieces in the pan and pour over the beef broth (stock). Bring to a simmer, cover and cook 1 hour, stirring occasionally. Add the culantro or cilantro (coriander) juice or extract and oregano and cook for another 45 minutes, then add the sliced carrot, peas, and lemon juice and cook for a final 15 minutes, until both the vegetables and the meat are tender.

Stir in the boiled potatoes and chopped culantro or cilantro (coriander) leaves and serve with Peruvian corn rice.

SECO DE CONCHAS
SCALLOP SECO STEW

Serves: 4
Preparation Time: 10 minutes
Cooking Time: 30 minutes

The key to this dish is to use very fresh scallops, which will ensure a wonderful flavor and a juicy texture. You'll end up with one of the most delicious secos possible.

¼ cup (2 fl oz/50 ml) vegetable oil
1 red onion, chopped
12 cloves garlic, finely chopped
2 oz (50 g) grated loche squash
salt and pepper
pinch of cumin
½ cup (4 fl oz/120 ml) Yellow Chili Paste (see p. 405)
¼ cup (2 fl oz/50 ml) chicha de jora or white wine
1 cup (8 fl oz/250 ml) vegetable broth (stock)
¼ cup (2 fl oz/50 ml) chicken broth (stock)
¼ cup (2 fl oz/50 ml) culantro or cilantro (coriander) juice or extract
½ carrot, diced
scant ½ cup (1½ oz/40 g) peas
44 medium scallops, cleaned
2 cups (14 oz/400 g) Peruvian Corn Rice, to serve (see p. 195)

Heat the oil in a pan over medium heat, add the onion, garlic, and grated loche squash, and sauté for 5 minutes, until the onion has softened. Season with salt and pepper. Add the cumin and chili paste and cook for another 5 minutes, stirring, until fragrant. Pour over the chicha de jora or white wine and cook for 2 minutes to evaporate the alcohol.

Pour over the vegetable chicken broths (stocks), bring to a simmer, and cook over low heat for 8 minutes, stirring occasionally, until the liquid reduces by a quarter of its volume. Add the culantro or cilantro (coriander) juice or extract, carrot, and peas, and cook for 5 minutes until vegetables are tender. Add the scallops and simmer for a final 4 minutes until the scallops are cooked. Be careful not to overcook.

Serve with Peruvian corn rice.

SECO DE TRAMBOYO
PERUVIAN BLENNY SECO STEW

Serves: 4
Preparation Time: 20 minutes
Cooking Time: 54 minutes

Unlike white croaker seco stew, this stew uses Peruvian blenny, a type of rockfish. Local varieties of rockfish will work just as well and produce wonderful textures and flavors.

- 14 oz (400 g) yucca root (cassava), peeled and halved
- 4 × 1-lb 8½-oz (700-g) Peruvian blennies, cleaned and gutted
- ¼ cup (2 fl oz/50 ml) vegetable oil
- 1 red onion, chopped
- 12 cloves garlic, finely chopped
- 2 oz (50 g) grated loche squash
- pinch of cumin
- ½ cup (4 fl oz/120 ml) Yellow Chili Paste (see p. 405)
- ¼ cup (4 fl oz/120 ml) chicha de jora or white wine
- 3 cups (26½ fl oz/750 ml) vegetable broth (stock)
- 1 cup (8 fl oz/250 ml) fish broth (stock)
- ¼ cup (2 fl oz/50 ml) culantro or cilantro (coriander) juice or extract
- ½ carrot, diced
- scant ½ cup (1½ oz/40 g) peas
- 1 sprig culantro or cilantro (coriander), plus a few extra leaves to garnish
- 2 cups (14 oz/400 g) Peruvian Corn Rice, to serve (see p. 195)
- salt and pepper

Put the yucca root (cassava) in a pan, add enough water to cover, and boil for 15 minutes. Drain, then cut in 4 pieces.

Season the blennies with salt and pepper all over and set aside.

Heat the oil in a large pan over medium heat, add the onion, garlic, and loche squash and sauté for 5 minutes, until the onion has softened. Season with salt and pepper. Add the cumin and chili paste, and cook for another 5 minutes, stirring. Pour over the chicha de jora or white wine and cook for 2 minutes to evaporate the alcohol.

Pour over the vegetable and fish broths (stocks), bring to a simmer, and cook for 8 minutes over low heat until the liquid reduces by a quarter of its volume. Add the culantro or cilantro (coriander) juice or extract, carrot, and peas, and cook for 5 minutes until the vegetables are tender.

Add the blennies to the pan with the culantro sprig, cover with a lid, and simmer over medium heat for 7 minutes. Add the cooked yucca root and simmer for another 7 minutes until the blennies are cooked through.

Garnish with culantro leaves and serve with Peruvian corn rice.

SECO DE CHAVELO
BEEF AND PLANTAIN SECO STEW

Serves: 4
Preparation Time: 15 minutes, plus 8 hours standing
Cooking Time: 20 minutes

Even though this dish is called a seco, it is actually prepared very differently to a traditional seco stew. Plantain is the main ingredient in this recipe.

4½ lb (1 kg) rump steak, cut into 4 × 9-oz (250-g) fillets
¼ cup (2 fl oz/50 ml) olive oil
1 cup (8 fl oz/250 ml) vegetable oil
4 green plantains, peeled and cut into 2-inch (5-cm) pieces
1 red onion, chopped
12 cloves garlic, finely chopped
2 tomatoes, skinned, seeded, and grated
1 tablespoon cumin
¼ cup (2 fl oz/50 ml) Yellow Chili Paste (see p. 405)
1 cup (8 fl oz/250 ml) Creole Sauce (see p. 416), to serve
salt and pepper

The day before you prepare this dish, season the meat with plenty of salt and hang them out to dry for the whole day. Alternatively, cover the seasoned meat with plastic wrap (clingfilm) and refrigerate overnight.

The following day, coat the fillets with a ¼ cup (2 fl oz/60 ml) olive oil and place them on a hot grill or barbecue until browned and well cooked on each side. Remove the fillets from the heat, and pound them with a meat tenderizer to soften the meat fibers. Cut the fillets into ½ x 1½-inch (1 × 4-cm) strips and set aside.

Heat three-quarters of the vegetable oil in a pan over low heat, add the plantain pieces, and cook for 6–7 minutes until tender. Remove from the heat, transfer to a pestle and mortar, and coarsely mash together.

Heat the remaining vegetable oil in a separate pan over medium heat, add the onion, garlic, and grated tomatoes and sauté for 5 minutes, until the onion has softened. Season with salt and pepper. Add the cumin and yellow chili paste and cook the ingredients for another 3 minutes, stirring, until fragrant. Stir in the strips of meat and cooked plantains and mix together well. Serve with Creole sauce.

SECO DE CAMARONES
SHRIMP SECO STEW

Serves: 4
Preparation Time: 20–25 minutes
Cooking Time: 30 minutes

You can use freshwater shrimp, prawns, crab, lobster, or any other crustaceans for this recipe.

48 shrimp (prawns)
4 tablespoons vegetable oil
1 red onion, chopped
12 cloves garlic, finely chopped
2 oz (50 g) grated loche squash
pinch of cumin
½ cup (4 fl oz/120 ml) Yellow Chili Paste (see p. 405)
¼ cup (4 fl oz/60 ml) chicha de jora or white wine
2 cups (18 fl oz/500 ml) vegetable broth (stock)
¼ cup (2 fl oz/50 ml) culantro or cilantro (coriander) juice or extract
½ carrot, diced
scant ½ cup (1½ oz/40 g) peas
2 cups (14 oz/400 g) Peruvian Corn Rice to serve (see p. 195)
salt and pepper

Peel and devein all but 4 of the shrimp (prawns), leaving the tails intact. Leave the remaining 4 shrimp whole.

Heat the oil in a pan over medium heat, add the onion, garlic, and loche squash and sauté for 5 minutes until the onion has softened. Season with salt and pepper. Add the cumin and chili paste and cook for another 5 minutes, stirring. Pour over the chicha de jora or white wine and cook for 2 minutes to evaporate the alcohol.

Add the vegetable broth (stock), bring to a simmer, and cook over low heat for 8 minutes until the liquid reduces by a quarter of its volume. Add the culantro or cilantro (coriander) juice or extract, carrot, and peas, and cook for 5 minutes until the vegetables are tender.

Add the whole shrimp and cook for about 3 minutes, then add the shrimp tails and cook for the final few minutes until the shrimp are cooked through. Serve with Peruvian corn rice.

SECO DE MARISCOS
SEAFOOD SECO STEW

Serves: 4
Preparation Time: 15 minutes
Cooking Time: 30 minutes

You can prepare this stew with any type of seafood, provided it is fresh and cooked for the appropriate amount of time.

¼ cup (2 fl oz/50 ml) vegetable oil
1 red onion, chopped
12 cloves garlic, finely chopped
2 oz (50 g) grated loche squash
pinch of cumin
½ cup (4 fl oz/120 ml) Yellow Chili Paste (see p. 405)
¼ cup (2 fl oz/50 ml) chicha de jora or white wine
1 cup (8 fl oz/250 ml) vegetable broth (stock)
¼ cup (2 fl oz/50 ml) chicken broth (stock)
¼ cup (2 fl oz/50 ml) culantro or cilantro (coriander) juice or extract
½ carrot, diced
scant 1½ oz (40 g) peas
8 scallops, cleaned
2 × 7-oz (200-g) squid, cleaned and cut into rings
8 shrimp (prawns), shelled and deveined
¼ cup (2 oz/50) g crab meat
¼ cup (3 oz/80 g) octopus, chopped
2 cups (14 oz/400 g) Peruvian Corn Rice (see p. 195), to serve
salt and pepper

Heat the oil in a pan over medium heat, add the onion, garlic, and grated loche squash, and sauté for 5 minutes, until the onion has softened. Season with salt and pepper to taste. Add the cumin and chili paste and cook for another 5 minutes, until fragrant, then pour in the chicha de jora or white wine and cook for 2 minutes to evaporate the alcohol.

Add the vegetable and chicken broths (stocks), bring to a simmer, and cook over medium heat for 8 minutes, stirring, until the liquid reduces by a quarter of its volume. Add the culantro or cilantro (coriander) juice or extract, carrot, and peas and cook for 8 minutes, stirring occasionally, until the vegetables are tender.

Add the scallops, squid, shrimp (prawns), crab meat, and octopus, and cook over low heat for about 4 minutes but be careful not to overcook. Serve with Peruvian corn rice.

Serves: 4
Preparation Time: 25 minutes
Cooking Time: 20 minutes

1¾ lb (800 g) beef tenderloin (fillet), cut into ½ x 1½-inch (1 × 4 -cm) strips
3 tablespoons vegetable oil, plus extra for deep-frying
14 oz (400 g) potatoes, cut into batons
1 red onion, sliced
2 yellow chiles, seeded, membrane removed, and sliced
2 cloves garlic, finely chopped
5 tablespoons white wine vinegar
4 tablespoons soy sauce
3 tablespoons oyster sauce
4 tomatoes, skinned, seeded, and sliced into half-moon crescents
1 scallion (spring onion), cut into 1¾-inch (4-cm) pieces
1 tablespoon chopped culantro or cilantro (coriander) leaves
2 cups (14 oz/400 g) Peruvian-Style Cooked White Rice (see p. 178), to serve
salt and pepper

LOMO SALTADO
BEEF TENDERLOIN STIR-FRY

Season the tenderloin (fillet) with salt and pepper and set aside.

Half-fill a large pan or deep-fryer with vegetable oil and heat to 350°F/180°C, or until a cube of bread browns in 30 seconds. Drop the potato batons carefully into the hot oil and cook until crispy and golden. Drain well on paper towels.

Put 2 tablespoons of oil in a very hot wok, add the meat, and stir-fry in 4 batches until browned and medium-well done, about 2 minutes. Remove from the wok and set aside.

Clean the wok with paper towels and return it to the heat, adding 1 tablespoon oil followed by the onion, yellow chiles, and garlic. Stir-fry for 30 seconds, then add the pre-cooked tenderloin strips, vinegar, soy sauce, and oyster sauce.

Stir-fry the ingredients over high heat for another 30 seconds and finish by adding the tomatoes, scallion (spring onion), and chopped culantro or cilantro (coriander) leaves. Remove from the heat and season with salt and pepper to taste.

Serve on plates with the fried potato batons and Peruvian-style cooked white rice.

PESCADO SALTADO
FISH STIR-FRY

Serves: 4
Preparation Time: 25 minutes
Cooking Time: 20 minutes

The fish in this recipe can also be stir-fried without coating it in flour first, but you'll need to use a firm-fleshed fish such as swordfish.

- 1¾ lb (800 g) fish fillet, cut into ¾ x 1¼-inch (2 × 3-cm) pieces
- 3 oz (80 g) all-purpose (plain) flour
- 1 tablespoon vegetable oil, plus extra for deep-frying
- 14 oz (400 g) potatoes, cut into batons
- 1 red onion, sliced
- 2 yellow chiles, seeded, membrane removed, and sliced
- 2 cloves garlic, finely chopped
- 5 tablespoons white wine vinegar
- 4 tablespoons soy sauce
- 3 tablespoons oyster sauce
- 4 tomatoes, skinned, seeded, and sliced into half-moon crescents
- 1 scallion (spring onion), cut into 1¾-inch (4-cm) pieces
- 1 tablespoon chopped culantro or cilantro (coriander) leaves
- 2 cups (14 oz/400 g) Peruvian-Style Cooked White Rice (see p. 178), to serve
- salt and pepper

Season the fish with salt and pepper and coat in flour. Set aside.

Half-fill a large pan or deep-fryer with vegetable oil and heat to 350°F/180°C, or until a cube of bread browns in 30 seconds. Drop the potato batons carefully into the hot oil and cook until crispy and golden. Drain well on paper towels. Repeat the process with the fish pieces.

Heat the oil in a very hot wok, add the onion, yellow chiles, and garlic and stir-fry for 30 seconds. Add the fried fish, vinegar, soy sauce, and oyster sauce and stir-fry for another 30 seconds. Finish by adding the tomatoes, scallion (spring onion), and chopped culantro or cilantro (coriander) leaves, remove from the heat, and season to taste with salt and pepper.

Serve on plates with the fried potato batons and Peruvian-style cooked white rice.

SALTADO DE MOLLEJITAS
SWEETBREAD STIR-FRY

Serves: 4
Preparation Time: 30 minutes
Cooking Time: 1 hour 12 minutes

Chicken sweetbreads are often avoided in other countries but Peruvians love them. We use them in *anticuchos* (skewered meat dish), soups, and stews. And, of course, in stir-fries.

- 1 lb 5 oz (600 g) chicken sweetbreads, cleaned
- ½ white onion, chopped
- 1 carrot, cut into chunks
- 1 celery stalk, halved
- ¼ leek, chopped
- 1 tablespoon black peppercorns
- 1 bay leaf
- 2 tablespoons vegetable oil, plus extra for deep-frying
- 14 oz (400 g) potatoes, cut into batons
- 1 red onion, sliced
- 2 yellow chiles, seeded, membrane removed, and sliced
- 2 cloves garlic, finely chopped
- 3 tablespoons white wine vinegar
- 2 tablespoons soy sauce
- 4 tomatoes, skinned, seeded, and sliced into half-moon crescents
- 1 tablespoon chopped parsley
- 2 cups (14 oz/400 g) Peruvian-Style Cooked White Rice (see p. 178), to serve
- salt and pepper

Place the sweetbreads, onion, carrot, celery, leek, peppercorns, bay leaf, and a little salt in a pan with enough water to cover them. Bring to a simmer and cook for 1 hour over medium heat until all the ingredients are tender. Drain and set aside the sweetbreads. Discard the other ingredients.

Half-fill a large pan or deep-fryer with vegetable oil and heat to 350°F/180°C, or until a cube of bread browns in 30 seconds. Drop the potato batons carefully into the hot oil and cook until crispy and golden. Drain well on paper towels.

Season the sweetbreads with salt and pepper.

Heat 2 tablespoons oil in a very hot wok, add the sweetbreads, and stir-fry until golden brown, about 3–4 minutes. Add the red onion, yellow chiles, and garlic, stir-fry for 30 seconds, then add the vinegar and soy sauce.

Add the tomatoes and continue to stir-fry the ingredients for another 30 seconds, then finish by adding the chopped parsley. Remove from the heat and season to taste with salt and pepper.

Serve on plates with the fried potato batons and Peruvian-style cooked white rice.

Serves: 4
Preparation Time: 25 minutes
Cooking Time: 30 minutes

A stir-fry made with chicken legs and thighs is always delicious and the meat will be very tender. Avoid using chicken breasts—white meat can quickly dry out.

1¾ lb (800 g) boned chicken legs and thighs, cut into ¾ x 1¼-inch (2 × 3-cm) strips
3 tablespoons vegetable oil, plus extra for deep-frying
14 oz (400 g) potatoes, cut into batons
1 red onion, thickly sliced
2 yellow chiles, seeded, membrane removed, and sliced
2 cloves garlic, finely chopped
5 tablespoons white wine vinegar
4 tablespoons soy sauce
3 tablespoons oyster sauce
4 tomatoes, skinned, seeded, and sliced into half-moon crescents
1 scallion (spring onion), cut into 1¾-inch (4-cm) pieces
bunch of chopped culantro or cilantro (coriander) leaves
2 cups (14 oz/400 g) Peruvian-Style Cooked White Rice (see p. 178), to serve
salt and pepper

POLLO SALTADO
CHICKEN STIR-FRY

Season the chicken strips with salt and pepper and set aside.

Half-fill a large pan or deep-fryer with vegetable oil and heat to 350°F/180°C, or until a cube of bread browns in 30 seconds. Drop the potato batons carefully into the hot oil and cook until crispy and golden. Drain well on paper towels.

Put 2 tablespoons oil in a very hot wok, add the chicken strips, and stir-fry in 4 batches, until golden brown about 4 minutes. Remove from he wok and set aside.

Clean the wok with paper towels and return it to the heat, adding 1 tablespoon oil, followed by the onion, yellow chiles, and garlic. Stir-fry for 30 seconds and add the browned chicken, vinegar, soy sauce, and oyster sauce.

Continue to stir-fry the ingredients for 30 seconds and finish by adding the tomatoes, scallion (spring onion), and chopped culantro or cilantro (coriander) leaves. Remove from the heat and season to taste with salt and pepper.

Serve on plates with the fried potato batons and Peruvian-style cooked white rice.

SALTADO DE RIÑONCITO
BEEF KIDNEY STIR-FRY

Serves: 4
Preparation Time: 25 minutes, plus overnight soaking
Cooking Time: 26 minutes

The most important thing to bear in mind when preparing this dish is not to overcook the kidney. Rare kidneys will ensure a delicious stir-fry.

- 1 lb 2 oz (500 g) beef kidney, cleaned and membrane removed
- 5 tablespoons white wine vinegar
- 2 tablespoons vegetable oil, plus extra for deep-frying
- 14 oz (400 g) potatoes, cut into batons
- 1 red onion, sliced
- 2 yellow chiles, seeded, membrane removed, and sliced
- 2 cloves garlic, finely chopped
- 4 tablespoons soy sauce
- 4 tomatoes, skinned, seeded, and sliced into half-moon crescents
- 1 scallion (spring onion), cut into 1¾-inch (4-cm) pieces
- 1 tablespoon chopped parsley
- 2 cups (14 oz/400 g) Peruvian-Style Cooked White Rice (see p. 178), to serve
- salt and pepper

Soak the kidneys in 4 cups (34 fl oz/1 liter) water and 2 tablespoons of white vinegar and refrigerate overnight.

Half-fill a large pan or deep-fryer with vegetable oil and heat to 350°F/180°C, or until a cube of bread browns in 30 seconds. Drop the potato batons carefully into the hot oil and cook until crispy and golden. Drain well on paper towels.

Drain the kidneys and cut into ¾ x 1¼-inch /2 × 3-cm chunks and season with salt and pepper.

Add 2 tablespoons of oil to a very hot wok, add the kidney chunks and stir-fry until golden brown, about 5 minutes. Add the onion, yellow chiles, and garlic and stir-fry for 30 seconds, then add the vinegar and soy sauce.

Continue to stir-fry for 30 seconds, then add the tomatoes, scallion (spring onion), and chopped parsley. Remove from the heat and season to taste with salt and pepper.

Serve on plates with the fried potato batons and Peruvian-style cooked white rice.

Seafood and Pasta Stir-Fry

SALTADO DE COLIFLOR
CAULIFLOWER STIR-FRY

Serves: 4
Preparation Time: 15 minutes
Cooking Time: 15 minutes

This is a delicious homemade dish that is perfect for vegetarians. The procedure is almost identical to that of the beef stir-fry and the results are just as tasty.

1 large cauliflower, cut into pieces
salt and pepper
14 oz (400 g) potatoes, cut into batons
3 tablespoons vegetable oil, plus extra for deep-frying
1 red onion, sliced
2 yellow chiles, seeded, membrane removed, and sliced
2 cloves garlic, finely chopped
4 tomatoes, skinned, seeded, and sliced into half-moon crescents
1 tablespoon chopped parsley
2 cups (14 oz/400 g) Peruvian-Style Cooked White Rice (see p. 178), to serve

Add the cauliflower pieces to a pan of boiling salted water and cook for 2 minutes until just tender. Remove from the pan and plunge into a bowl of iced water to stop the cooking process. Drain and set aside.

Meanwhile, half-fill a large pan or deep-fryer with vegetable oil and heat to 350°F/180°C, or until a cube of bread browns in 30 seconds. Drop the potato batons carefully into the hot oil and cook until crispy and golden. Drain well on paper towels.

Add 2 tablespoons of oil to a very hot wok, add the cauliflower pieces, and stir-fry until golden brown, about 2 minutes.

Add the onion, yellow chiles, and garlic and continue to stir-fry for 30 seconds. Finish by adding the tomatoes and chopped parsley, then remove from the heat and season to taste with salt and pepper.

Serve on plates with the fried potato batons and Peruvian-style cooked white rice.

TALLARINES SALTADOS CON MARISCOS
SEAFOOD AND PASTA STIR-FRY

Serves: 4
Preparation Time: 25 minutes
Cooking Time: 16 minutes

You can also add a dash of lemon juice and chile or chopped rocoto chiles to this dish at the very end. It will be deliciously reminiscent of ceviche.

1 lb 8½ oz (700 g) spaghetti, linguine, or any other long pasta
12 shrimp (prawns), peeled and deveined
4 × 7-oz (200-g) squid, cleaned and cut into rings
12 scallops, cleaned
½ cup (3 oz/80 g) chopped octopus
4 tablespoons vegetable oil
1 red onion, sliced
2 yellow chiles, seeded, membrane removed, and sliced
2 cloves garlic, finely chopped
5 tablespoons white wine vinegar
4 tablespoons soy sauce
3 tablespoons oyster sauce
¼ cup (2 fl oz/50 ml) vegetable or chicken broth (stock)
4 tomatoes, skinned, seeded, and sliced into half-moon crescents
1 scallion (spring onion), cut into 1¾-inch (4-cm) pieces
1 tablespoon chopped culantro or cilantro (coriander) leaves
salt and pepper

Cook the pasta in a pan of boiling salted water according to the package instructions. Drain and set aside.

Season the shrimp (prawns), squid, scallops, and octopus with salt and pepper.

Add 2 tablespoons of oil in a very hot wok and stir-fry the shrimp over high heat for 1 minute until pink. Remove from the wok and set aside. Repeat the process with the squid and set aside.

Clean the wok with some paper towels and return it to the heat, adding 2 tablespoons oil followed by the onion, yellow chiles, and garlic. Stir-fry for 30 seconds and add the cooked and drained pasta.

Stir-fry for another minute and add the shrimp, squid, scallops, octopus, vinegar, soy sauce, oyster sauce, and broth (stock). Continue to stir-fry the ingredients for 1 minute, then finish by adding the tomatoes, scallion (spring onion), and chopped culantro or cilantro (coriander) leaves. Remove from the heat and season to taste.

Serve in large shallow bowls.

SALTADO DE VAINITAS
BEEF AND GREEN BEAN STIR-FRY

Serves: 4
Preparation Time: 25 minutes
Cooking Time: 20 minutes

Green beans maintain their texture and absorb flavors, making them an excellent stir-fry ingredient.

2¼ lb (1 kg) green or runner beans, cut diagonally into 1¾-inch (4-cm) pieces
2 tablespoons vegetable oil, plus extra for deep-frying
14 oz (400 g) potatoes, cut into batons
14 oz (400 g) beef tenderloin (fillet), cut into ½ x 1¾-inch (1 × 4-cm) strips
1 red onion, sliced
2 yellow chiles, seeded, membrane removed, and sliced
2 cloves garlic, finely chopped
4 tomatoes, skinned, seeded, and sliced into half-moon crescents
1 tablespoon chopped parsley
2 cups (14 oz/400 g) Peruvian-Style Cooked White Rice (see p. 178), to serve
salt and pepper

Add the green beans to a pan of boiling salted water and cook for 1 minute until just tender. Remove from the pan and plunge into a bowl of iced water to stop the cooking process. Drain and set aside.

Half-fill a large pan or deep-fryer with vegetable oil and heat to 350°F/180°C, or until a cube of bread browns in 30 seconds. Drop the potato batons carefully into the hot oil and cook until crispy and golden. Drain well on paper towels.

Add 2 tablespoons oil to a very hot wok, add the beef strips and stir-fry until browned and medium-well done, about 2 minutes. Add the onion, yellow chiles, green beans, and garlic and stir-fry for another 2 minutes, then finish by adding the tomatoes and chopped parsley. Remove from the heat and season to taste with salt and pepper.

Serve on plates with the fried potato batons and Peruvian-style cooked white rice.

Beef and Green Bean Stir-Fry

TALLARINES SALTADOS CON CARNE
BEEF AND PASTA STIR-FRY

Serves: 4
Preparation Time: 15 minutes
Cooking Time: 25 minutes

This is one of my favorite dishes. It's not an Italian or Chinese pasta dish, it's typical Peruvian wok-fried pasta. You'll love it.

- 1 lb 8½ oz (700 g) spaghetti, linguine, or any other long pasta
- 1 lb 5 oz (600 g) beef tenderloin (fillet), cut into strips
- 4 tablespoons vegetable oil
- 1 red onion, sliced
- 2 yellow chiles, seeded, membrane removed, and sliced
- 2 cloves garlic, finely chopped
- 5 tablespoons white wine vinegar
- 4 tablespoons soy sauce
- 3 tablespoons oyster sauce
- ¼ cup (2 fl oz/50 ml) vegetable or beef broth (stock)
- 4 tomatoes, skinned, seeded, and sliced into half-moon crescents
- 1 scallion (spring onion), cut into 1¾-inch (4-cm) pieces
- 1 tablespoon chopped culantro or cilantro (coriander) leaves
- salt and pepper

Cook the pasta in a pan of boiling salted water according to the package instructions. Drain and set aside.

Season the beef with salt and pepper. Add 2 tablespoons of oil to a very hot wok, add the meat, and stir-fry until browned and medium-well done, about 2 minutes. Remove from the wok and set aside.

Clean the wok and return it to the heat, adding 2 tablespoons of oil, followed by the onion, yellow chiles, and garlic. Stir-fry for 30 seconds, then add the cooked and drained pasta.

Stir-fry the ingredients for another minute and add the beef, vinegar, soy sauce, oyster sauce, and broth (stock). Continue to sir-fry the ingredients for 30 seconds, add the tomato, and cook for another 30 seconds. Add the scallion (spring onion) and chopped culantro or cilantro (coriander) leaves. Remove from the heat and season with salt and pepper to taste. Serve in large shallow bowls.

TALLARINES SALTADOS CON POLLO
CHICKEN AND PASTA STIR-FRY

Serves: 4
Preparation Time: 20 minutes
Cooking Time: 25 minutes

You can also coat the chicken in flour before frying it when preparing this dish. This will produce crispy chicken that contrasts beautifully with the juicy pasta.

- 1 lb 8½ oz (700 g) spaghetti, linguine, or any other long pasta
- 1 lb 5 oz (600 g) boned chicken legs and thighs, cut into ¾ x 1-inch (1.5 × 2.5-cm) strips
- 4 tablespoons vegetable oil
- 1 red onion, sliced
- 2 yellow chiles, seeded, membrane removed, and sliced
- 2 cloves garlic, finely chopped
- 5 tablespoons white wine vinegar
- 4 tablespoons soy sauce
- 3 tablespoons oyster sauce
- ¼ cup (2 fl oz/50 ml) vegetable or chicken broth (stock)
- 4 tomatoes, skinned, seeded, and sliced into half-moon crescents
- 1 scallion (spring onion), cut into 1¾-inch (4-cm) pieces
- 1 tablespoon chopped culantro or cilantro (coriander) leaves
- salt and pepper

Cook the pasta in a pan of boiling salted water according to the package instructions. Drain and set aside.

Season the chicken strips with salt and pepper and set aside.

Add 2 tablespoons of oil to a very hot wok, add the chicken strips, and stir-fry until golden brown about 4 minutes. Remove from the wok and set aside.

Clean the wok and return it to the heat, adding 2 tablespoons oil followed by the onion, yellow chiles, and garlic. Stir-fry for 30 seconds and add the cooked and drained pasta.

Stir-fry for another minute, then add the browned chicken, vinegar, soy sauce, oyster sauce, and broth (stock). Continue to stir-fry the ingredients for 30 seconds. Add the tomatoes, continue to stir-fry for 1 minute, and finish by adding the scallion (spring onion) and chopped culantro or cilantro (coriander) leaves. Remove from the heat and season to taste with salt and pepper.

Serve in large shallow bowls.

HÍGADO SALTADO
CALF'S LIVER STIR-FRY

Serves: 4
Preparation Time: 30 minutes
Cooking Time: 23 minutes

Be very careful not to overcook the liver because it will not taste good. It needs to be stir-fried very quickly over a very high heat.

- 1 lb 5 oz (600 g) calf's liver, cleaned and cut into ½-inch (1-cm) wide strips
- 2 tablespoons vegetable oil, plus extra for deep-frying
- 14 oz (400 g) potatoes, cut into batons
- 1 red onion, sliced
- 2 yellow chiles, seeded, membrane removed, and sliced
- 2 cloves garlic, finely chopped
- 4 tablespoons white wine
- 4 tomatoes, skinned, seeded, and sliced into half-moon crescents
- 1 tablespoon chopped parsley
- juice of 2 small lemons
- 2 cups (14 oz/400 g) Peruvian Corn Rice, to serve (see p. 195)
- salt and pepper

Season the liver strips with salt and pepper and set aside.

Half-fill a large pan or deep-fryer with vegetable oil and heat to 350°F/180°C, or until a cube of bread browns in 30 seconds. Drop the potato batons carefully into the hot oil and cook until crispy and golden. Drain well on paper towels.

Heat 2 tablespoons oil in a very hot wok, add the liver strips, and stir-fry until golden brown, about 3 minutes. Add the red onion, tomato, yellow chiles, and garlic, stir-fry for 30 seconds, then add the white wine.

Continue to stir-fry the ingredients for another 2 minutes, then finish by adding the chopped parsley and lemon juice. Remove from the heat and season to taste with salt and pepper.

Serve on plates with the fried potato batons and Peruvian corn rice.

DESSERTS & SWEETS

Makes: 16 cookies
Preparation Time: 30 minutes, plus 1 hour chilling
Cooking Time: 10 minutes

2¾ cups (11 oz/300 g) all-purpose (plain) flour, plus extra for dusting
4 tablespoons confectioners' (icing) sugar
1 teaspoon salt
⅓ cup (5¼ oz/160 g) margarine, plus extra for greasing
2 teaspoons vanilla extract
1¼ cups (11 oz/300 g) Dulce de Leche (see p. 414), for filling

ALFAJOR CLÁSICO
TRADITIONAL ALFAJOR COOKIES

Sift the flour, confectioners' (icing) sugar, and salt into a large bowl, then add the margarine and vanilla extract. Using your hands, combine the ingredients to form a smooth dough. Roll the dough into a ball, wrap in plastic wrap (clingfilm), and refrigerate for 1 hour.

Preheat the oven to 325°F/160°C/Gas Mark 3. Prepare a baking sheet by lightly greasing it and set aside.

Remove the dough from the refrigerator and roll out on a floured surface with a rolling pin to a large circle about ⅛-inch/3-mm thick. Using a 2½-inch /6-cm round cookie cutter, cut out 32 disks. Place the discs on the prepared baking sheet.

Bake in the preheated oven for 10 minutes. Take out of the oven and cool on the baking sheet. Assemble the alfajores by spreading a portion of the dulce de leche on 1 baked disk, sandwiching a second on top, and pressing gently together. The assembled cookies will keep for 2–3 days in an airtight container.

Traditional Alfajor Cookies

ALBARICOCADA
APRICOT-COCONUT LAYER CAKE

Serves: 8
Preparation Time: 30 minutes, plus 1 hour soaking
Cooking Time: 30–35 minutes

Apricot compote
scant 1 cup (7 oz/200 g) dried apricots
½ cup (3 oz/80 g) granulated sugar

Coconut mixture
5 eggs, separated
generous 1 cup (8 oz/225 g) granulated sugar
2½ cups (8 oz/225 g) shredded (dessicated) coconut

Filling and outer layer
generous 1½ cup (13 oz/375 g) Dulce de Leche (see p. 414)
¾–1 cup (3 oz/80 g) shredded (dessicated) coconut, for decoration

Extras
butter, for greasing

To make the apricot compote, put the apricots in a bowl, cover with water, and soak for 1 hour. Once soft, drain and chop into small pieces. Put the pieces in a pan over medium heat with the sugar and cook, stirring, for about 30 minutes, until the mixture thickens into a compote. Remove from the heat and set aside.

For the coconut mixture, place the egg whites in a pan with the sugar, shredded (desiccated) coconut, and 1 cup (8 fl oz/250 ml) water. Place the pan over low heat and cook, stirring continuously, until the sugar dissolves. Remove from heat and let cool.

Preheat the oven to 325°F/160°C/Gas Mark 3. Prepare 4 baking sheets by lightly greasing them, and set aside.

Beat the egg yolks in a bowl until pale, creamy, and doubled in volume. Pour into the egg white, coconut, and water mixture and stir together. Divide the mixture into 4 portions. Taking one portion, spoon into the center of a prepared baking sheet and shape into a round disk. Repeat with the remaining portions and baking sheets.

Transfer to the preheated oven and bake for 8–10 minutes, until cooked but still soft and sticky on the inside.

To assemble the cake, place one of the disks on a platter and spread with dulce de leche. Place a second coconut disk on top and cover with apricot compote. Add another coconut disk, more dulce de leche, and place the final coconut disk on top.

Finally, cover the top and sides of the cake with dulce de leche and decorate with a little coconut to finish.

ALFAJOR DE CHOCOLATE
CHOCOLATE ALFAJOR COOKIES

Makes: 16 cookies
Preparation Time: 30 minutes, plus 1 hour chilling
Cooking Time: 10 minutes

- generous 2¼ cups (9¼ oz/260 g) all-purpose (plain) flour, plus extra for dusting
- generous ¼ cup (1¼ oz/30 g) unsweetened cocoa powder
- 4 tablespoons confectioners' (icing) sugar
- 1 teaspoon salt
- ¾ cup (6 oz/175 g) margarine, plus extra for greasing
- 2 teaspoons vanilla extract
- 1¼ cups (11 oz/300 g) Dulce de Leche (see p. 414) or Chocolate Dulce de Leche (see p. 414), for filling

Sift the flour, cocoa powder, confectioners' (icing) sugar, and salt into a large bowl, then add the margarine and vanilla extract. Using your hands, combine the ingredients to form a smooth dough. Roll the dough into a ball, wrap in plastic wrap (clingfilm), and refrigerate for 1 hour.

Preheat the oven to 325°F/160°C/Gas Mark 3. Prepare a baking sheet by lightly greasing it, and set aside.

Remove the dough from the refrigerator and roll out on a floured surface with a rolling pin to a large circle about ⅛-inch/3-mm thick. Using a 2½-inch /6-cm round cookie cutter, cut out 32 disks. Place the disks on the prepared baking sheet.

Bake in the preheated oven for 10 minutes, until the cookies turn lightly golden. Remove from the oven and cool on the baking sheet. Assemble the alfajores by spreading a portion of the dulce de leche or chocolate dulce de leche on one baked disk, sandwiching a second on top, and pressing gently together.

The assembled cookies will keep for 2–3 days in an airtight container.

ALFAJOR DE COCO
COCONUT ALFAJOR COOKIES

Makes: 16 cookies
Preparation Time: 30 minutes, plus 1 hour chilling
Cooking Time: 10 minutes

- 2¾ cups (11 oz/300 g) all-purpose (plain) flour, plus extra for dusting
- 4 tablespoons confectioners' (icing) sugar
- 5⅓ tablespoons unsalted butter, plus extra for greasing
- 1 teaspoon vanilla extract
- 1¼ cups (11 oz/300 g) Dulce de Leche (see p. 414)
- shredded (desiccated) coconut, for decoration

Sift the flour, confectioners' (icing) sugar, and salt into a large bowl, then add the margarine and vanilla extract. Using your hands, combine the ingredients to form a smooth dough. Roll the dough into a ball, wrap in plastic wrap (clingfilm), and refrigerate for 1 hour.

Preheat the oven to 325°F/160°C/Gas Mark 3. Prepare a baking sheet by lightly greasing and setting aside.

Remove the dough from the refrigerator and roll out on a floured surface with a rolling pin to a large circle about ⅛-inch/3-mm thick. Using a 2½-inch/ 6-cm round cookie cutter, cut out 32 disks. Place the disks on the prepared baking sheet.

Bake in the preheated oven for 10 minutes. Remove from the oven and cool on the baking sheet. Assemble the alfajores by spreading a portion of the dulce de leche on one baked disk, sandwiching a second on top, and pressing gently together. Roll the sides of the cookies in coconut to finish.

ALFAJOR DE LÚCUMA
LUCUMA ALFAJOR COOKIES

Makes: 16 cookies
Preparation Time: 30 minutes, plus 1 hour chilling
Cooking Time: 10 minutes

- generous 2¼ cups (9¼ oz/260 g) all-purpose (plain) flour, plus extra for dusting
- 1½ oz (40 g) lucuma flour
- 4 tablespoons confectioners' (icing) sugar
- 1 teaspoon salt
- ¾ cup (6 oz/175 g) margarine, plus extra for greasing
- 2 teaspoons vanilla extract
- 1¼ cups (11 oz/300 g) Dulce de Leche (see p. 414) or Lucuma-flavored Dulce de Leche (see p. 352), for filling

Sift the flour, lucuma flour, confectioners' (icing) sugar, and salt into a large bowl, then add the margarine and vanilla extract. Using your hands, combine the ingredients to form a smooth dough. Roll the dough into a ball, wrap in plastic wrap (clingfilm), and refrigerate for 1 hour.

Preheat the oven to 325°F/160°C/Gas Mark 3. Prepare a baking sheet by lightly greasing it, and set aside.

Remove the dough from the refrigerator and roll out on a floured surface with a rolling pin to a large circle about ⅛-inch/3-mm thick. Using a 2½-inch/6-cm round cookie cutter, cut out 32 disks. Place the disks on the prepared baking sheet.

Bake in the preheated oven for 10 minutes. Remove from the oven and cool on the baking sheet. Assemble the alfajores by spreading a portion of the dulce de leche or lucuma-flavored dulce de leche on one baked disk, sandwiching a second on top, and pressing gently together.

ALFAJOR DE MAICENA
CORNSTARCH ALFAJOR COOKIES

Makes: 12 cookies
Preparation Time: 30 minutes, plus 20 minutes chilling
Cooking Time: 12–15 minutes

- 1 cup (4 oz/120 g) cornstarch (cornflour)
- 2¼ cup (9 oz/250 g) all-purpose (plain) flour, plus extra for dusting
- ½ teaspoon baking powder
- ⅛ teaspoon salt
- 1 cup (8 oz/225 g) unsalted butter, cut into cubes
- ½ cup (4 oz/120 g) confectioners' (icing) sugar, plus extra for decoration
- ½ teaspoon vanilla extract
- 2 cups (1 lb 1 oz/480 g) Dulce de Leche (see p. 414), for filling
- ⅔ cup (2 oz/50 g) shredded (desiccated) coconut, for decoration

Sift the cornstarch (cornflour), flour, baking powder, and salt into a large bowl, then add the butter. Using your hands, gently combine the ingredients. Add the confectioners' (icing) sugar and vanilla extract and knead to a smooth dough. Set aside for 20 minutes in the refrigerator.

Preheat the oven to 350°F/180°C/Gas Mark 4. Prepare a baking sheet by lightly flouring it, and set aside.

Roll the rested dough out on a floured surface with a rolling pin to a large circle about ⅛-inch/3-mm thick. Using a 2½-inch/6-cm round cookie cutter, cut out 24 disks. Place the discs on the prepared baking sheet.

Bake in the preheated oven for 12–15 minutes until the cookies turn golden. Remove from the oven and cool on the baking sheet.

Assemble the alfajores by spreading a portion of the dulce de leche on one baked disk, sandwiching a second on top, and pressing gently together. Roll the sides of each alfajor in the coconut and dust the tops with confectioners' sugar to finish.

ALFAJOR DE PENCO
PERUVIAN ALFAJOR COOKIE CAKE

Serves: 10–12
Preparation Time: 40 minutes
Cooking Time: 40 minutes

Fruit syrup
1⅓ cup (12 oz/350 g) chancaca sugar
generous ¾ cup (6 oz/175 g) light brown sugar
1 cinnamon stick
8 cloves
1 teaspoon allspice
1 juicing orange, cut into 8 wedges
1 small lemon, halved
1⅓ cup (5 oz/150 g) walnuts or pecans
7 oz (200 g) coquito nuts, ground
generous 1/3 cup (2 oz/50 g) peanuts, ground
2 small sponge fingers, crumbled

Dough
18 egg yolks
¼ cup (2 fl oz/50 ml) anise liqueur
⅓ cup (2½ oz/65 g) butter, melted, plus extra for greasing
2¾ cups (11 oz/300 g) all-purpose (plain) flour, plus extra for dusting
2 teaspoons baking powder

To make the syrup, place the chancaca sugar, light brown sugar, cinnamon, cloves, allspice, orange wedges and lemon in a pan with 2 cups (18 fl oz/500 ml) water. Bring to a boil, then reduce the heat and simmer until thick and syrupy. Remove from the heat and strain into a bowl.

Add the walnuts or pecans, coquito nuts, peanuts, and crumbled sponge fingers to the syrup and mix together well. Set aside.

Preheat the oven to 350°F/180°C/Gas Mark 4. Prepare 3 baking sheets by lightly greasing them, and set aside.

For the alfajor dough, beat the egg yolks in a bowl with a whisk until pale and creamy. Add the anise liqueur a drop at a time, beating all the time, then add the melted butter.

Sift the flour and baking powder into a separate bowl. Slowly add the flour mixture to the egg yolk mixture and, using your hands, knead the dough until small air pockets begin to form.

Roll the dough out on a floured surface with a rolling pin to a thickness of ½ inch/1 cm. Cut 3 large disks from the dough. Place the disks on the prepared baking sheets and bake in the preheated oven for 30 minutes, or until they begin to brown. Remove from the oven and cool.

Assemble the alfajor cake by spooning a layer of syrup on a disk, sandwiching a second disk on top, and repeating with the remaining syrup and alfajor disk. Serve.

Makes: 12 cookies
Preparation Time: 30 minutes, plus 20 minutes resting
Cooking Time: 20–25 minutes

- 2 generous cups (8½ oz/240 g) all-purpose (plain) flour, plus extra for dusting
- ¾ cup (6¼ oz/180 g) unsalted butter
- 4 tablespoons confectioners' (icing) sugar
- ½ teaspoon vanilla extract

Syrup

- 1½ cups (10¼ oz/285 g) chancaca sugar
- 1 cup (7 oz/200 g) granulated sugar
- 1 cinnamon stick
- ½ cup (4 fl oz/120 ml) orange juice

ALFAJORES DE MIEL
SUGAR SYRUP ALFAJOR COOKIES

For the syrup, place the chancaca sugar, 2 cups (18 fl oz/500 ml) water, granulated sugar, and cinnamon in a pan. Bring to a boil and add the orange juice, continuing to cook until thick and syrupy. Set aside.

Sift the flour into a large bowl. Add the butter and, using your hands, gently combine the ingredients. Add the confectioners' (icing) sugar and vanilla extract and knead to a smooth dough. Set aside for 20 minutes to rest in the refrigerator.

Preheat the oven to 350°F/180°C/Gas Mark 4. Prepare a baking sheet by lightly flouring it and set aside.

Roll the rested dough out on a floured surface with a rolling pin to a large circle about ⅛-inch/3-mm thick. Using a 2½-inch/6-cm round cookie cutter, cut out 24 disks. Place the disks on the prepared baking sheet.

Bake in the preheated oven for 12–15 minutes, until the cookies turn lightly golden. Remove from the oven and cool on the baking sheet.

Assemble the alfajores by spreading a portion of the syrup on one baked disk, sandwiching a second on top, and pressing gently together.

Sugar Syrup Alfajor Cookies

Rice Pudding

ARROZ CON LECHE
RICE PUDDING

Serves: 4
Preparation Time: 5 minutes
Cooking Time: 30 minutes

½ cup (3½ oz/100 g) white short-grain rice
4 cloves
1 cinnamon stick
1¼ cups (10 fl oz/300 ml) whole (full-fat) milk
zest of 1 orange
1¼ cups (10 fl oz/300 ml) condensed milk
1 egg yolk
4 tablespoons port
ground cinnamon, for decoration

Place the rice, 2½ cups (20 fl oz/620 ml) water, cloves, and cinnamon stick in a pan. Bring to a boil, then reduce the heat and simmer until the water evaporates completely and the rice is cooked.

Stir in the fresh milk and orange zest and continue to cook until the liquid has reduced and the rice pudding is thick and creamy. Remove the cloves, cinnamon and orange zest, add the condensed milk and continue to cook, stirring, until thickened.

Beat the egg yolk together with the port in a bowl. Remove the rice pudding pan from the heat and pour in the egg mixture, mixing thoroughly. Set aside to cool, covering with plastic wrap (clingfilm) to prevent a skin from forming.

To serve, spoon the rice pudding into dessert glasses and dust with ground cinnamon to finish.

BUDÍN DE PAN
BREAD PUDDING

Serves: 12
Preparation Time: 25 minutes
Cooking Time: 1 hour 10 minutes

10 French bread rolls or any crusty rolls
1¾ cups (14 fl oz/400 ml) evaporated milk
zest and juice of 1 orange
1 tablespoon vanilla extract
2 tablespoons melted butter
5 cups (2¼ lb/1 kg) granulated sugar
5 eggs, lightly beaten
generous 1 cup (5¾ oz/165 g) golden or regular raisins
4 tablespoons port or wine

Fill a bowl with water. Add the bread rolls and submerge in the water until fully soaked. Once soaked, drain in a colander, squeezing out any excess water. Push the soaked bread through a colander or large strainer (sieve) and place in a bowl.

Add the evaporated milk, orange juice and zest, vanilla extract, melted butter, 2½ cups (1 lb 5 oz/600 g) of the sugar, and the eggs to the bowl and mix together thoroughly. Stir in the raisins and the port. Set aside.

Put the remaining sugar in a pan with 3 cups (25 fl oz/750 ml) water and place over the heat. Cook, without stirring, until the liquid turns golden brown. Pour the caramelized sugar into a large Bundt pan or individual cake molds, ensuring the sides are evenly coated. Let cool. Preheat the oven to 350°F/180°C/Gas Mark 4.

Pour the bread mixture into the coated Bundt pan or individual cake molds. Cook in a bain-marie in the preheated oven for approximately 1 hour, until it looks golden and it has set.

Remove from the oven, let cool completely, then remove from the Bundt pan or molds. Serve immediately.

ARROZ ZAMBITO
DARK RICE PUDDING

Serves: 4–6
Preparation Time: 5 minutes
Cooking Time: 30 minutes

¾ cup (4¾ oz/140 g) white short-grain rice
2 cinnamon sticks
6 cloves
¾ cup (3½ oz/100 g) raisins, plus extra for decoration
⅓ cup (1¾ oz/50 g) chancaca sugar, grated
5 cups (40 fl oz/1.2 liters) evaporated milk
½ cup (3½ oz/100 g) granulated sugar

To decorate
⅓ cup (2 oz/50 g) shredded (desiccated) coconut
pinch of ground cinnamon

Place the rice, 4 cups (34 fl oz/1 liter) water, cinnamon sticks, and cloves in a pan. Bring to a boil, then reduce the heat and simmer until the water has evaporated and the rice is cooked.

Remove the cinnamon and cloves. Add the raisins, chancaca sugar, and evaporated milk and cook for 15 minutes, stirring. Add the sugar and continue to cook over low heat, stirring continuously, for another 15 minutes or until the rice pudding thickens to a creamy consistency.

To serve, spoon the rice pudding into dessert glasses and sprinkle with the coconut, ground cinnamon, and a few extra raisins.

CAMOTILLOS
SWEET POTATO COOKIES

Makes: 15 cookies
Preparation Time: 20 minutes
Cooking Time: 2 hours 40 minutes

butter, for greasing
2¼ lb (1 kg) sweet potato
2 cups (14 oz/400 g) granulated sugar
1 cinnamon stick
zest and juice of 2 oranges
1 egg white
multicolored sprinkles, for decoration

Preheat the oven to 300°F/150°C/Gas Mark 2. Prepare a baking sheet by lightly greasing it, and set aside.

Bring a pan of water to a boil, add the sweet potatoes and cook until tender. Drain, peel, and mash thoroughly until smooth and free of lumps. Place the mash in a pan with the sugar, cinnamon, and orange zest and juice, and cook over medium heat, stirring continuously, for 20 minutes or until the mixture thickens and sets to the point where you could almost stand a wooden spoon up in it. Remove from the heat and set aside.

Spoon the sweet potato mixture onto the prepared baking sheet in 2½-inch/6-cm long portions. Brush with the egg white and decorate with multicolored sprinkles.

Bake in the oven for 2 hours, or until dry. Remove from the oven and cool. Wrap the cookies in plastic wrap (clingfilm) until needed for up to 1 week, or place in mini cupcake liners to serve.

Dark Rice Pudding

BUÑUELOS DE CAMOTE
FRIED SWEET POTATO CUBES

Makes: 10 potato cubes
Preparation Time: 25 minutes
Cooking Time: 40 minutes

2 cups (1 lb 2 oz/500 g) chancaca sugar
2 cups (1 lb/450 g) light brown sugar
1 cinnamon stick
juice and zest of 1 orange
1 lb 2 oz (500 g) sweet potatoes, peeled and cut into 1¼-inch (3-cm) cubes
5½ tablespoons butter
5 oz (150 g) all-purpose (plain) flour
4 eggs
2 cups (18 fl oz/500 ml) vegetable oil

Place the chancaca sugar, half the light brown sugar, the cinnamon, and half the orange zest in a pan and cover with water. Bring to a boil, then reduce the heat and simmer until a syrup forms. Remove from the heat and set aside.

Place the sweet potato cubes in a pan with the orange juice, remaining orange zest, and 2 cups (18 fl oz/500 ml) water. Add the remaining light brown sugar and simmer until the sweet potato cubes are soft. Remove from the heat and drain.

Place the butter and ½ cup (4 fl oz/120 ml) water in a pan and bring to a boil. Add the flour and stir together, then remove from the heat and cool slightly. Add the eggs one at a time, stirring vigorously, to form a paste, then transfer to a bowl. Add the sweet potato cubes to the mixture and coat evenly.

Heat the vegetable oil in a deep-fryer or pot to 350°F/180°C, or until a cube of bread browns in 30 seconds. Drop the sweet potato cubes carefully into the hot oil and cook until crispy and golden. Drain well and serve immediately with the syrup drizzled over.

CHAMPUZ
FRUITY HOMINY PUDDING

Serves: 4–6
Preparation Time: 20 minutes, plus 24–36 hours soaking
Cooking Time: 20–30 minutes

3½ oz (100 g) hominy (dried corn)
1 cinnamon stick
3 cloves
1 lb 2 oz (500 g) pineapple, peeled and chopped
1 soursop, peeled, seeded, and chopped
2 large quinces, peeled, seeded, and diced
scant 2 cups (4 oz/400 g) granulated sugar
1¾ cup (7 oz/200 g) cornstarch (cornflour), dissolved in ½ cup (4 fl oz/120 ml) cold water
ground cinnamon, for decoration

Put the hominy (dried corn) in a bowl, cover with water, and soak for 24–36 hours, changing the water at least 3 times. Grind the hominy a little without completely pulverizing the grains.

Place the ground hominy in a pan with plenty of water, the cinnamon stick, and cloves. Bring to a boil, then reduce the heat, and simmer, covered, for 15 minutes, until tender. Remove from the heat.

Place the cooked hominy in a separate pan with a small amount of the cooking water and add the pineapple, soursop, quinces, and sugar. Simmer over medium heat, stirring, until the fruit is cooked, then add the dissolved cornstarch (cornflour) solution.

Continue to cook over low heat, stirring continuously, until the pudding is thick and creamy. Serve in dessert glasses, dusting with ground cinnamon to finish.

Fried Sweet Potato Cubes

CHOCOTEJAS DE MANJAR CON PECANAS Y PASAS

DARK CHOCOLATE CANDIES FILLED WITH DULCE DE LECHE, PECANS, AND RAISINS

Makes: 80 candies (sweets)
Preparation Time: 1 hour 40 minutes, plus 7 days infusing and 3–4 minutes chilling
Cooking Time: 10 minutes

pisco-infused raisins
scant 1½ cups (7 oz/200 g) raisins
1¼ cups (8 fl oz/300 ml) pisco

Ganache
½ cup (4 fl oz/120 ml) heavy (double) cream
13½ oz (390 g) bitter dark chocolate, broken into small pieces
½ cup (4 oz/120 g) unsalted butter, cut into cubes
2½ tablespoons vanilla extract

Outer layer and filling
3¼ lb (1.5 kg) dark chocolate couverture
2 cups (1 lb 2 oz/500 g) Dulce de Leche (see p. 414)
40 large pecans, shelled

To prepare the pisco-infused raisins, wash the raisins thoroughly, drain, and place in a glass jar. Pour in the pisco and let infuse for at least 7 days. Once infused, strain, transfer to a suitable container, and keep refrigerated until needed.

To make the ganache, put the cream in a pan and warm over low heat. Melt the bitter dark chocolate separately in a bain-marie, add to the cream, and mix together. Add the butter and vanilla extract and mix thoroughly. Cool and refrigerate until needed.

To make the outer shell of the candies (sweets), melt the dark chocolate couverture in a bain-marie or in the microwave. Once melted, pour into a chocoteja mold (or small candy mold), gently tapping the mold on the table to eliminate any air bubbles that may have formed.

Turn the mold upside down to drain out, and reserve, any excess chocolate, tapping it gently. Refrigerate for 3–4 minutes so that the chocolate shells solidify.

Mix the dulce de leche together with the drained pisco-infused raisins in a bowl.

Remove the chocolate-coated mold from the refrigerator and fill each individual mold with a little of the dulce de leche and raisin mixture. Place half a pecan inside each one and add a little of the ganache. Refrigerate until firm.

Remove the chocolate candies from the refrigerator, still in their mold, and cover each one with some of the reserved melted dark chocolate couverture, smoothing the bases with a spatula. Refrigerate once again so that the outer layer solidifies. Remove the candies from the mold by lightly tapping it. Keep refrigerated until serving.

Dark Chocolate Candies Filled with Dulce de Leche, Pecans, and Raisins

Makes: 70 candies (sweets)
Preparation Time: 30 minutes, plus chilling
Cooking Time: 15 minutes

Caramelized almonds
1¾ cups (9 oz/250 g) roasted almonds, chopped
scant ¾ cup (5 oz/150 g) granulated sugar

Ganache
¾ cup (6 fl oz/175 ml) heavy (double) cream
14 oz (400 g) bitter dark chocolate
generous ½ cup (4½ oz/130 g) unsalted butter, plus extra for greasing
2½ tablespoons vanilla extract

Outer layer and filling
2½ lb (1.2 kg) dark chocolate couverture
2¾ cups (1 lb 7 oz/650 g) Dulce de Leche (see p. 414)

CHOCOTEJAS DE MANJAR Y GANACHE CON ALMENDRAS
DARK CHOCOLATE CANDIES FILLED WITH DULCE DE LECHE, CHOCOLATE GANACHE, AND ALMONDS

For the caramelized almonds, heat the sugar in a pan, without stirring, until a golden caramel forms. Add the almonds and mix together with a wooden spoon or spatula, then spread the mixture out onto a silicone baking mat or lightly greased surface. Cool.

To make the ganache, put the cream in a pan and warm over low heat. Melt the bitter dark chocolate separately in a bain-marie, add to the cream and mix together. Add the butter and vanilla extract and mix thoroughly. Cool and refrigerate.

To make the outer shell of the candies (sweets), melt the dark chocolate couverture in a bain-marie or in the microwave. Once melted, pour into a chocoteja mold (or small candy mold), gently tapping the mold on the table to eliminate any air bubbles that may have formed.

Turn the mold upside down to drain out, and reserve, any excess chocolate, tapping it gently. Refrigerate for 3–4 minutes so that the chocolate shells solidify.

Mix the dulce de leche together with the caramelized almonds and ganache in a bowl.

Remove the chocolate-coated mold from the refrigerator and fill each individual mold with a little of the dulce de leche, almond, and ganache mixture. Refrigerate until firm.

Remove the chocolate candies from the refrigerator, still in their mold, and cover each one with some of the reserved melted dark chocolate couverture, smoothing the candies with a spatula. Refrigerate once again so that the outer layer solidifies. Remove the candies from the mold by lightly tapping. Keep refrigerated until serving.

COCADAS
COCONUT CANDIES

Makes: 30 candies (sweets)
Preparation Time: 15 minutes
Cooking Time: 20 minutes, plus drying

- 5 cups (40 fl oz/1.2 liters) evaporated milk
- 1 cinnamon stick
- 5 cloves
- 3 cups (1 lb 5 oz/600 g) granulated sugar
- 3 cups (12½ oz/340 g) shredded (desiccated) coconut
- 4 tablespoons anise liqueur
- butter, for greasing
- 1 tablespoon ground cinnamon

Pour the evaporated milk into a heavy pan. Add the cinnamon stick and cloves, bring to a boil, then reduce the heat and simmer for 10 minutes, until the spices are infused. Remove from the heat and strain to remove the spices.

Return the evaporated milk to the heat and add the sugar and shredded (desiccated) coconut. Continue to cook, stirring continuously, until the mixture thickens. Add the anise liqueur and remove from the heat, beating the mixture until it cools.

Spoon small dollops of the cooled mixture onto a greased baking sheet and let firm and dry out. Once dry, dust the coconut candy with the ground cinnamon.

CREMA VOLTEADA
BAKED CARAMEL CUSTARD

Serves: 2
Preparation Time: 10 minutes
Cooking Time: 35–45 minutes

- 2 cups (14 oz/400 g) granulated sugar
- 3½ cups (28 fl oz/800 ml) evaporated milk
- 3½ cups (28 fl oz/800 ml) condensed milk
- 2 eggs, plus 5 egg yolks
- 1 teaspoon vanilla extract

Preheat the oven to 325°F/160°C/Gas Mark 3.

Heat the sugar together with 1 cup (8 fl oz/250 ml) water in a pan, without stirring until a golden caramel forms. Pour the caramel into a 9-inch/22-cm baking dish, ensuring that the base and sides of the dish are evenly coated. Set aside.

Mix the evaporated milk and condensed milk together in a bowl. Beat the whole eggs and egg yolks together with a whisk and add to the milk mixture with the vanilla extract. Mix together thoroughly. Pour into the caramel-coated baking dish.

Transfer the baking dish to a bain-marie and bake in the preheated oven for 30–40 minutes. Remove from the oven and cool completely. Remove from the baking dish and serve in slices.

CREMA VOLTEADA DE COCO
BAKED COCONUT CARAMEL CUSTARD

Serves: 8
Preparation Time: 10 minutes
Cooking Time: 40–50 minutes

1 cup (7 oz/200 g) granulated sugar
1¾ cups (14 fl oz/400 ml) evaporated milk
1¾ cups (14 fl oz/400 ml) condensed milk
5 eggs
1 teaspoon vanilla extract
⅔ cup (2 oz/50 g) shredded (desiccated) coconut

Preheat the oven to 350°F/180°C/Gas Mark 4.

Heat the sugar together with 1½ cups (13 fl oz /375 ml) water in a pan, without stirring, until a golden caramel forms. Pour the caramel into a 9-inch/22-cm baking dish, ensuring that the base and sides of the dish are evenly coated. Set aside.

Mix the evaporated milk and condensed milk together in a bowl. Beat the eggs together with a whisk and add to the milk mixture. Mix together thoroughly. Pour the mixture into a pan and cook over low heat, stirring continuously until it thickens, approximately 5 minutes. Add the vanilla extract and coconut.

Pour into the caramel-coated baking dish and bake in a bain-marie in the preheated oven for 30–40 minutes. Remove from the oven and let cool completely. Remove from the baking dish and serve in slices.

CREMA VOLTEADA DE QUINUA
QUINOA CARAMEL CUSTARD PUDDING

Serves: 8
Preparation Time: 20 minutes
Cooking Time: 50 minutes

1 cup (7 oz/200 g) granulated sugar
⅔ cup (5 oz/150 g) quinoa, cooked
1¼ cups (10 fl oz/300 ml) evaporated milk
1 cup (8 fl oz/250 ml) condensed milk
4 eggs, lightly beaten
2 teaspoons vanilla extract
1 teaspoon ground cinnamon

Preheat the oven to 325°F/160°C/Gas Mark 3.

Heat 5 oz/150 g sugar together with 1½ cups (13 fl oz/375 ml) water in a pan without stirring until a golden caramel forms. Pour the caramel into a 9-inch/22-cm baking dish, ensuring that the base and sides of the dish are evenly coated. Set aside.

Put half the cooked quinoa in a blender and process, then add to a bowl with the remaining quinoa, evaporated milk, condensed milk, beaten eggs,and remaining sugar. Mix the ingredients together thoroughly with a whisk, adding the vanilla extract and cinnamon.

Pour into the caramel-coated baking dish and bake in a bain-marie in the preheated oven for 45 minutes. Remove from the oven and refrigerate overnight. Remove from the baking dish and serve.

FREJOL COLADO
PERUVIAN BEAN PUDDING

Makes: 950 g
Preparation Time: 15 minutes, plus 8 hours soaking
Cooking Time: 1 hour 45 minutes

2¼ lb (1 kg) black-eye peas (beans), soaked overnight
2 cinnamon sticks
8 cloves
scant 1½ cups (12 oz/350 g) chancaca sugar
1¾ cups (12 oz/350 g) light brown sugar
2 tablespooons toasted sesame seeds, for decoration

Drain the soaked beans.

Place the soaked beans in a pan and cover with water. Add the cinnamon sticks and cloves. Cook for 1 hour 30 minutes, until the beans are tender. Remove from the heat and drain.

Remove the cinnamon sticks and cloves and place the beans in a blender. Process to form a smooth paste.

Put the blended bean paste in a heavy pan with the chancaca sugar and light brown sugar over medium heat. Cook, stirring, until the mixture has thickened so that you can see the bottom of the pan when a spoon is drawn over it.

Spoon into a large china bowl and decorate with the toasted sesame seeds. Serve immediately.

ENCANELADO
CINNAMON SPONGE CAKE

Makes: 40 pieces
Preparation Time: 20 minutes
Cooking Time: 35 minutes

butter, for greasing
3½ tablespoons self-rising (self-raising) flour, plus extra for flouring
5 eggs
scant 1 cup (6 oz/175 g) granulated sugar
1½ tablespoons cornstarch (cornflour) or potato starch
2 tablespoons pisco
1½ cups (12 oz/350 g) Dulce de Leche (see p. 414)

To decorate
confectioners' (icing) sugar
ground cinnamon

Preheat the oven to 350°F/180°C/Gas Mark 4. Grease and flour a 9 × 13-inch/22 × 33-cm baking dish.

In a bowl, beat the eggs together with 2½ oz/65 g of the sugar until foamy. Sift the flour with the cornstarch (cornflour) or potato starch and add to the egg mixture, mixing gently to form a batter. Pour the cake batter into the prepared baking dish and bake in the preheated oven for 30 minutes. Remove from the oven, let cool a little, then remove from the baking dish and transfer to a wire rack. Cool completely.

Heat ½ cup (4 fl oz/120 ml) water together with the remaining sugar in a pan, without stirring, until a syrup forms. Remove the syrup from the heat and add the pisco.

Cut the sponge cake into 2 layers. Pour the hot syrup over the cold sponge cake so that it is completely absorbed.

Spread some dulce de leche on one of the syrup-soaked sponge cake layers and sandwich the other layer on top. Cut the two-tiered sponge into small squares.

Mix the confectioners' (icing) sugar and cinnamon together in a bowl and use to dust the cake squares.

GUARGÜEROS
SUGARY TUBES WITH DULCE DE LECHE

Makes: 10
Preparation Time: 25 minutes
Cooking Time: 10 minutes, plus 15 minutes chilling

½ cup (4 oz/120 g) all-purpose (plain) flour, plus extra for dusting
9 egg yolks, plus 1 egg white
½ teaspoon salt
2 tablespoons pisco
vegetable oil, for frying
2½ cups (1 lb 5 oz/600 g) Dulce de Leche (see p. 414)
confectioners' (icing) sugar, for decoration

Pile the flour on a work counter and make a well in the center. Pour the egg yolks and salt into the center of the well and, using your hands, work out from the center to combine the ingredients and form a soft dough. Knead thoroughly, adding the pisco to the dough as you go, for 10 minutes until the dough can form a ball. Form into a ball, wrap in plastic wrap (clingfilm) and refrigerate for 15 minutes.

Roll the rested dough out on a floured surface with a rolling pin as thinly as possible. Cut the dough into 5 × 3-inch/12 × 8-cm rectangles, then roll each rectangle into a tube, sealing it with egg white.

Heat plenty of vegetable oil in a large pan over high heat and fry the tubes for around 5 minutes, until they are lightly golden. Remove from the pan and drain on paper towels. Cool.

Put the dulce de leche in a pastry (piping) bag fitted with a tip (nozzle). Fill the tubes and dust with confectioners' (icing) sugar to finish.

HUEVO CHIMBO
EGGY CAKE

Serves: 10
Preparation Time: 15 minutes
Cooking Time: 20 minutes

butter, for greasing
12 egg yolks, plus 4 egg whites
4 tablespoons potato starch
1 teaspoon cream of tartar
2 tablespoons baking powder
1 cup (7 oz/200 g) granulated sugar
¼ cup (2 fl oz/50 ml) pisco
1 cup (5 oz/150 g) raisins
1½ cups (5 oz/150 g) chopped almonds, toasted

Preheat the oven to 350°F/175°C/Gas Mark 4. Prepare a 14 × 8-inch/35 × 20-cm rectangular baking dish by lightly greasing it and set aside.

In a bowl, beat the egg yolks with the whites together until they triple in volume. Add the potato starch, followed by the cream of tartar and baking powder, and mix together well.

Pour the mixture into the prepared baking dish and bake for 15 minutes until risen and lightly golden. Remove and cool.

Place the sugar in a heavy pan, add enough water to cover, and heat until a syrup forms. Bring to a boil, add the pisco, raisins, and almonds and remove from the heat. Let cool a little, then pour over the eggy cake. Serve.

Sugary Tubes with Dulce de Leche

KING KONG
KING KONG

Serves: 6–8
Preparation Time: 40 minutes
Cooking Time: 10 minutes

4 cups (1 lb 2 oz/500 g) all-purpose (plain) flour, plus extra for dusting
6 egg yolks
½ cup (4 oz/120 g) margarine, plus extra for greasing
1½ cups (12 oz/350 g) Dulce de Leche (see p. 414)
1 cup (5 oz/150 g) chopped dried figs
1 cup (3½ oz/100 g) chopped walnuts, toasted (optional)
1 cup (7 oz/200 g) Jellied Quince (see opposite)
salt

Pile the flour on a work counter and make a well in the center. Pour the egg yolks, ½ cup (4 fl oz/120 ml) water, margarine, and a pinch of salt in the center and, using your hands, work out from the center to combine the ingredients and form a soft dough. Knead thoroughly for 10 minutes until the dough is smooth. Form into a ball, wrap in plastic wrap (clingfilm), and set aside.

Preheat the oven to 350°F/180°C/Gas Mark 4. Prepare a rectangular baking sheet by lightly greasing it and set aside.

Roll the dough out on a floured surface with a rolling pin to a thickness of ¼ inch/½ cm. Cut 4 square or circular pieces of dough measuring 12 inches/30 cm across. Place on the baking sheet and bake for 10 minutes in the preheated oven. Once baked, remove from the oven and cool on the baking sheet.

In a bowl, mix together the dulce de leche with the dried figs and walnuts, if desired.

To assemble the King Kong, place a cooked cookie (biscuit) on a serving plate and spread with half the dulce de leche and fig mixture. Layer a second cookie on top and spread with the jellied quince. Place a third cookie on top and spread with the remaining dulce de leche and fig mixture, then place the fourth layer of cookie on top to finish. Serve.

LECHE ASADA
BAKED MILK PUDDING

Serves: 4
Preparation Time: 10 minutes
Cooking Time: 20–25 minutes

3¼ cups (28 fl oz/800 ml) whole (full-fat) milk
scant ¾ cup (5 oz/150 g) granulated sugar
3 eggs, plus 3 yolks
2 teapoons vanilla extract

Preheat the oven to 375°F/190°C/Gas Mark 5.

Pour the milk into a heavy pan with the sugar and bring to a boil. Remove from the heat and set aside.

Lightly beat the eggs and egg yolks together in a bowl. Stir in the warm milk and the vanilla extract and strain into heatproof ramekins.

Transfer the ramekins to a bain-marie and bake in the oven for 15–20 minutes, until set. Remove from the oven and cool. Serve.

MACHACADO DE MEMBRILLO
JELLIED QUINCE

Serves: 10
Preparation Time: 20, plus 1 hour soaking
Cooking Time: 1 hour

- 1 lb 2 oz (500 g) quince, peeled, seeded (seeds reserved), and cut into chunks
- 1 cinnamon stick
- 2 cups (14 oz/400 g) granulated sugar

Soak the reserved quince seeds in just enough warm water to cover for 1 hour. Set aside.

Place the quince chunks and a cinnamon stick in a pan over the heat. Cover with water, bring to a boil, then reduce the heat and simmer for 40–50 minutes until the quince is cooked. Once cooked, drain and pass through a strainer (sieve) to produce a puree.

Use a measuring cup or scale to measure out the quantity of pureed quince obtained, then measure out the same amount of sugar.

Place the sugar in a heavy pan, cover with water, and heat together, without stirring, until a syrup forms. Bring to a boil, then reduce the heat, add the pureed quince, and simmer until the mixture thickens and the bottom of the pan can be seen when the mixture is stirred with a wooden spoon.

Add the soaked quince seeds and remove from the heat. Pour the mixture into a glass dish and cool completely. Remove from the dish and cut into ¾ × 2-inch/2 × 5-cm strips to serve.

MANÁ
MANÁ CANDIES

Serves: 6
Preparation Time: 15 minutes
Cooking Time: 10 minutes

- 4 cups (34 fl oz/1 liter) whole (full-fat) milk
- 2 cups (14 oz/400 g) granulated sugar
- 1 egg, plus 7 egg yolks
- generous 1½ cups (7 oz/200 g) confectioners' (icing) sugar
- 1–2 drops food coloring

Place the milk, sugar, egg yolks, and whole egg in a heavy pan and bring to a boil. Reduce the heat and simmer, stirring occasionally to prevent the mixture from sticking and burning. Once all the liquid has evaporated, remove the pan from the heat and beat with a whisk until completely cool.

Once cool, add the confectioners' (icing) sugar to the pan and stir to form a firm paste.

To dye the paste, use 1–2 drops of food coloring, the color depending on which fruit you wish to replicate.

Scoop out of the pan and, using your hands, shape into little balls or tiny fruit shapes.

LIMONES RELLENOS
STUFFED CANDIED LEMONS

Serves: 4
Preparation Time: 10 minutes
Cooking Time: 15 minutes

1¾ cups (14 fl oz/400 ml) evaporated milk
1¾ cups (14 fl oz/400 ml) condensed milk
4 oz (120 g) shredded (desiccated) coconut
1 cinnamon stick
4 lemons
scant ¾ cup (5 oz/150 g) granulated sugar

Pour the condensed and evaporated milks into a heavy pan or Dutch oven (casserole dish). Add the coconut and cinnamon and simmer over low heat, stirring continuously, until the mixture thickens and sticks to the spoon. Remove from the heat, pour into a bowl, and cool. Set aside.

Cut the lemons in half. Taking care not to pierce the peels, scoop out the pulp and seeds.

Blanch the lemon halves in boiling water 3 times, changing the water each time.

Place the lemon halves in a pan with the sugar and ¾ cup (7 fl oz/200 ml) water. Simmer over low heat for 1½ hours, until the liquid reduces and a thin syrup forms. Remove the lemons and place on a rack to drain

Spoon the milk and coconut filling into the candied lemon halves. Serve.

MANJAR DE COCO
COCONUT PUDDING

Makes: 2 cups (500 ml)
Preparation Time: 5 minutes
Cooking Time: 10 minutes

2 cups (18 fl oz/500 ml) evaporated milk
2¼ cups (18 fl oz/550 ml) whole (full-fat) milk
1¾ cups (15 fl oz/425 ml) condensed milk
1 teaspoon vanilla extract
⅓ cup (1 oz/25 g) shredded (desiccated) coconut

Put the evaporated milk, fresh milk, condensed milk, and vanilla extract in a heavy pan over low heat. Cook, stirring continuously, until the mixture has thickened and you can see the bottom of the pan when the spoon is drawn across it. Add the coconut and mix together well.

Remove from the heat and cool before serving.

MANJAR DE LÚCUMA
LUCUMA-FLAVORED DULCE DE LECHE

Makes: 3 cups (1 lb 8½ oz/750 g)
Preparation Time: 5 minutes
Cooking Time: 10 minutes

1¾ cups (14 fl oz/400 ml) condensed milk
1¾ cups (14 fl oz/400 ml) evaporated milk
5¼ oz (160 g) lucuma fruit flesh
½ teaspoon vanilla extract

Pour the condensed and evaporated milks into a heavy pan. Place over medium heat and simmer, stirring, until the mixture has thickened and the bottom of the pan can be seen when you draw the spoon across it.

Stir in the lucuma fruit flesh and vanilla extract. Remove from the heat, cool, and refrigerate until needed.

Stuffed Candied Lemons

MAZAMORRA DE QUINUA
QUINOA PUDDING

Serves: 12
Preparation Time: 10 minutes
Cooking Time: 15 minutes

scant 1 cup (6 oz/175 g) quinoa
2 cinnamon sticks
5 cloves
1¾ cups (14 fl oz/400 ml) evaporated milk
1¾ cups (14 fl oz/400 ml) condensed milk
2 teaspoons vanilla extract
3 teaspoons ground cinnamon, for decoration

Wash and rinse the quinoa 3 times in plenty of water.

Place the quinoa in a pan with 3 cups (25 fl oz /750 ml) water, the cinnamon sticks and cloves. Bring to a boil and cook for 10 minutes, until the quinoa is al dente.

Add the evaporated milk and condensed milk. Lower the heat and simmer until the mixture thickens slightly, stirring occasionally to prevent sticking. Stir in the vanilla extract and remove from the heat. Serve in china bowls, sprinkling with the ground cinnamon to finish.

PASTEL DE CHOCLO DULCE
SWEET CORN CAKE

Serves: 12
Preparation Time: 30 minutes, plus 30 minutes soaking
Cooking Time: 1 hour

6 cups (2¼ lb/1 kg) corn kernels
½ cup (4 oz/120 g) butter, plus extra for greasing
2½ cups (1 lb 2 oz/500 g) granulated sugar
1¾ cups (14 fl oz/400 ml) evaporated milk
1 teaspoon anise seeds, toasted and ground
1 teaspoon sesame seeds, toasted and ground
4 oz (120 g) raisins, soaked in 2 cups (18 fl oz/500 ml) water for 30 minutes
all-purpose (plain) flour, for dusting
6 egg yolks, plus 1 egg white
1 teaspoon ground cinnamon
2 cups (1 lb 2 oz/500 g) Dulce de Leche (see p. 414), optional

Grind the corn with a hand mill and place in a pan over medium heat with the butter. Cook, stirring continuously and gradually adding the sugar and evaporated milk, until the mixture no longer sticks to the bottom of the pan. Add the toasted anise seeds and sesame seeds and continue to cook, stirring, until the mixture has thickened and the bottom of the pan can be seen when a spoon is drawn across it. Remove from the heat and add the drained raisins. Mix together thoroughly and cool.

Preheat the oven to 350°F/180°C/Gas Mark 4. Grease and flour a 9-inch/24-cm square baking dish.

Once the corn mixture has cooled, add the egg yolks and cinnamon and stir together. Pour the mixture into the prepared baking dish, brush with egg white, and bake in the oven for 30–45 minutes, or until a toothpick inserted in the center of the cake comes out clean. Remove from the oven and cool. To serve, cut into squares and drizzle with the dulce de leche, if desired.

MARCIANO DE LÚCUMA
LUCUMA POPSICLES

Serves: 4
Preparation Time: 5 minutes, plus freezing

6 oz (175 g) lucuma flesh from around 2 lucumas
1½ cups (13 fl oz/375 ml) whole (full-fat) milk
1¼ cups (9 oz/250 g) granulated sugar

Put the lucuma flesh in a blender with the milk and blend to a puree. Add the sugar and mix together thoroughly until fully dissolved.

Pour the mixture into plastic popsicle pouches or molds and freeze until required.

MARCIANO DE GUANÁBANA
SOURSOP POPSICLES

Serves: 4
Preparation Time: 5 minutes, plus freezing

6 oz (175 g) soursop flesh
1 cup (7 oz/200 g) granulated sugar

Put the soursop flesh in a blender with 2 cups (18 fl oz/500 ml) water and blend to a puree. Add the sugar and mix together thoroughly until fully dissolved.

Pour the mixture into plastic popsicle pouches or molds and freeze until required.

MARCIANO DE CHICHA MORADA
CHICHA MORADA POPSICLES

Serves: 4
Preparation Time: 5 minutes, plus freezing

2 cups (18 fl oz/500 ml) Chicha Morada (see p. 378)
granulated sugar, to taste
juice of 1 lemon

Put the chicha morada in a bowl, add the sugar, and mix thoroughly until fully dissolved. Add the lemon juice, pour the mixture into plastic popsicle pouches or molds, and freeze until required.

MARCIANO DE MANGO
MANGO POPSICLES

Serves: 4
Preparation Time: 5 minutes, plus freezing

5½ oz (165 g) mango flesh
¼ cup (2 oz/50 g) granulated sugar

Put the mango flesh in a blender with 1 cup (8 fl oz/250 ml) water and blend to a puree. Add the sugar and mix together thoroughly until fully dissolved.

Pour the mixture into plastic popsicle pouches or molds and freeze until required.

Serves: 8
Preparation Time: 50 minutes
Cooking Time: 3 hours

butter, for greasing
6 egg whites
2 cups (14 oz/400 g) granulated sugar
2¼ lb (1 kg) cherimoyas
juice of 1 lemon
2 cups (18 fl oz/500 ml) Chantilly cream

To decorate
4 tablespoons (2 oz/60 g) grated or melted chocolate
a few mint leaves

MERENGADO DE CHIRIMOYA
CHERIMOYA MERINGUE CAKE

Preheat the oven to 225°F/110°C/Gas Mark ¼.

Prepare a rectangular baking dish by lightly greasing it, and set aside. Line 3 baking sheets with parchment (baking) paper.

In a bowl, beat the egg whites, slowly sprinkling in the sugar, until stiff. When the mixture takes on a firm meringue consistency, place in a pastry (piping) bag with a plain tip (nozzle). Pipe out 3 large meringue disks onto the prepared baking sheets. (If you don't have a pastry bag, you can spoon out the meringues.)

Bake at a very low temperature for 3 hours, until the meringue disks are cooked through but not browned. Remove from the oven and cool.

For the filling, peel the cherimoyas, remove the seeds, and coarsely chop the flesh. Put the cherimoya flesh in a bowl, add the lemon juice and half the Chantilly cream, and mix together thoroughly.

To assemble the meringue cake, place a meringue disk on a serving plate and spread over half the fruit and cream filling. Top with another meringue and repeat with the remaining filling before finishing with the final meringue disk. Spoon over the remaining Chantilly cream and decorate with grated or melted chocolate and a few mint leaves.

PASTELILLOS DE YUCA
SWEET YUCCA-ROOT PARCELS

Serves: 12
Preparation Time: 1 hour
Cooking Time: 50 minutes

2¼ lb (1 kg) yucca root (cassava)
2 teaspoons anise seeds
1 teaspoon baking powder
all-purpose (plain) flour, for dusting
1 egg white
4 cups (34 fl oz/1 liter) vegetable oil
2 tablespoons ground cinnamon, for decoration
2 tablespoons granulated sugar, for decoration
salt

Sweet potato filling
2¼ lb (1 kg) sweet potato
2 cups (14 oz/400 g) granulated sugar
1 cinnamon stick
zest and juice of 2 oranges

For the sweet potato filling, bring a pan of water to a boil, add the sweet potato, and cook until tender. Drain, peel, and mash thoroughly until smooth and free of lumps. Place in a pan over medium heat with the sugar, cinnamon stick, and orange juice and zest. Cook, stirring continuously, for approximately 20 minutes, until the mixture is almost thick enough to stand a spoon in. Remove from the heat and set aside.

Wash and peel the yucca root (cassava) and boil with the anise seeds in a pan of salted water until soft. Drain and mash thoroughly until smooth, add the baking powder, and mix together.

Roll the yucca root mixture out on a floured surface with a rolling pin in a ½-inch/1-cm layer. Using a 4-inch/10-cm round cutter, cut out 12 disks. Using an 3¼-inch/8-cm round cutter, cut out another 12 disks.

Take a 4-inch/10-cm disk, place a generous dollop of sweet potato filling in the center, and cover with a smaller disk. Repeat with the remaining disks. Brush the edges of the larger disks with egg white and pull the edges up to seal the parcels, making five points with your hands to create little star shapes.

Heat the vegetable oil in a large pan or deep-fryer to 350°F/180°C, or until a cube of bread browns in 30 seconds. Drop the parcels carefully into the hot oil and cook until crispy and golden. Drain well and serve hot or warm, dusted with the cinnamon and sugar.

Serves: 10
Preparation Time: 25 minutes, plus 6 hours soaking
Cooking Time: 30 minutes

¼ cup (2 oz/50 g) dried apricots
¼ cup (2 oz/50 g)) pitted prunes
¼ cup (2 oz/50 g) morello cherries
¼ cup (2 oz/50 g) sun-dried peaches
1 lb 2 oz (500 g) purple corncobs
1 lb 2 oz (500 g) pineapple, peeled and chopped, plus 1 pineapple peel
2 cinnamon sticks
5 cloves
1¾ cups (12 oz/350 g) granulated sugar
¾ cup (5 oz/150 g) sweet potato flour
ground cinnamon, for decoration

MAZAMORRA MORADA
FRUITY PURPLE CORN PUDDING

Place the dried apricots, prunes, morello cherries, and sun-dried peaches in a bowl and cover with hot water. Let soak for 6 hours. Drain, reserving the soaking water. Set aside.

Cut the purple corncobs in half and place in a large pan over the heat with 80 fl oz/3 liters water, the pineapple peel, cinnamon sticks, and cloves. Bring to a boil, then reduce the heat and simmer for about 45 minutes, until the water has turned a deep purple color and the corn kernels have lost their color. Strain the liquid, discard the solids, and return to the heat.

Add the soaked fruits to the pan along with the sugar and simmer for a few minutes. Add the chopped pineapple.

In a bowl, dissolve the sweet potato flour in a little of the reserved soaking water. Pour into the pan, stirring, and simmer over low heat until the mixture thickens.

Serve in bowls, dusting with ground cinnamon to finish.

Fruity Purple Corn Pudding

Serves: 5
Preparation Time: 50 minutes, plus 1 hour 30 minutes proving
Cooking Time: 1 hour

Fig syrup
1¼ cup (10 oz/275 g) chancaca sugar
1½ cups (11 oz/300 g) light brown sugar
1 tablespoon anise seeds
2 cinnamon sticks
5 cloves
3 dried fig leaves

Dough
5 oz (150 g) sweet potato
3 oz (80 g) macre squash, cut into large chunks
3 oz (80 g) loche squash, cut into large chunks
2¾ cups (11 oz/300 g) all-purpose (plain) flour
⅛ oz (4 g) fresh yeast
3 tablespoons granulated sugar
½ teaspoon salt
½ teaspoon anise seeds
¼ cup (2 fl oz/50 ml) cola
⅔ cup (5 fl oz/150 ml) anise seed tea
4 cups (34 fl oz/1 liter) vegetable oil, for frying

PICARONES
SQUASH AND SWEET POTATO DOUGHNUTS

To make the fig syrup, place all the ingredients except the fig leaves in a pan with 3 cups (25 fl oz/750 ml) water and bring to a boil. Let cook until half the liquid has evaporated and the mixture is thick and syrupy. Add the fig leaves and let infuse for a few minutes. Remove from the heat. Strain into a suitable container, cool, and refrigerate until needed.

To make the dough, bring a pan of water to a boil, add the sweet potato, and cook until tender. Drain. Repeat with the macre and loche squash.

Place the cooked vegetables in a blender and blend until pureed. Put the pureed vegetables in a large bowl with the flour, fresh yeast, sugar, salt, anise seeds, cola, and anise seed tea. Using your hands, combine the ingredients to form a dough, then knead for around 20 minutes until smooth. Leave the dough in a warm place to proof for 1½ hours.

Heat the vegetable oil in a large pan or deep-fryer to 350°F/180°C, or until a cube of bread browns in 30 seconds. Take pieces of the dough and shape into rings or doughnuts, then drop carefully into the hot oil, and cook until crispy and golden. Drain well and drizzle with the fig syrup to finish.

Squash and Sweet Potato Doughnuts

PIONONO DE LÚCUMA
LUCUMA ROLL CAKE

Serves: 8
Preparation Time: 25 minutes
Cooking Time: 12 minutes

- 1½ oz (40 g) unsalted butter, plus extra for greasing
- 4 eggs
- ⅔ cup (3 oz/80 g) confectioners' (icing) sugar
- ⅔ cup (3 oz/80 g) all-purpose (plain) flour
- generous ½ cup (2½ oz/65 g) cornstarch (cornflour)
- 1 teaspoon vanilla extract
- 2 cups (1 lb 2 oz/500 g) Lucuma-flavored Dulce de Leche (see p. 352), for the filling
- ½ cup (1½ oz/40 g) confectioners' (icing) sugar, for decoration

Preheat the oven to 375°F/190°C/Gas Mark 5.

Grease a 24 × 16-inch/60 x40-cm edged baking sheet with butter and line it with parchment (baking) paper. Set aside in the refrigerator.

Melt the butter in a small pan or microwave and cool to room temperature.

Put the eggs and sugar in a bowl and beat together until the egg mixture falls from the whisk in ribbons. Sift the flour and cornstarch (cornflour) into the beaten eggs and stir together to form a batter. Add the vanilla extract and cooled melted butter and stir together well.

Using a spatula, spread the batter over the prepared baking sheet. Bake in the preheated oven for approximately 12 minutes, until golden and cooked through. Remove from the oven and cool slightly, then turn over and remove from the baking sheet. Peel away the parchment (baking) paper and place on a wire rack.

Spread the cake evenly with lucuma-flavored dulce de leche, leaving a thin rim around the edge. Roll the cake very carefully into a log. Dust with confectioners' (icing) sugar to decorate and refrigerate until needed.

POSTRE DE QUINUA ZAMBITA
CINNAMON-SPICED QUINOA PUDDING

Serves: 6
Preparation Time: 10 minutes, plus 2 hours soaking
Cooking Time: 25 minutes

- scant ½ cup (3 oz/80 g) quinoa
- 2 cinnamon sticks, plus 4 extra for decoration
- 6 cloves
- zest of 1 orange
- ¾ cup (3½ oz/100 g) raisins
- 2 cups (1 lb 2 oz/500 g) chancaca sugar
- 3 cups (20 fl oz/720 ml) evaporated milk
- ½ cup (1½ oz/40 g) shredded (dessicated) coconut
- pinch of ground cinnamon

Soak the quinoa in a bowl with plenty of water for 2 hours. Rinse well and drain.

Wrap the cinnamon sticks and cloves in a cheesecloth (muslin) cloth and tie together.

Place the quinoa, orange zest, and spice-filled muslin bag in a pan with 2 cups (18 fl oz/500 ml) water. Bring to a boil and cook for 12–15 minutes, until the quinoa is cooked. Remove the orange zest and spice-filled bag. Add the raisins, chancaca sugar, and evaporated milk and boil for around 15 minutes, then reduce the heat and simmer, stirring, until creamy. Remove from the heat and let it cool.

Serve in dessert glasses, decorating each with the coconut, a little ground cinnamon, and a cinnamon stick.

PONDERACIONES
PASTRY SWIRLS

Makes: 15 pastry swirls
Preparation Time: 10 minutes
Cooking Time: 20 minutes

3½ cups (27 fl oz/800 ml) condensed milk
3½ cups (27 fl oz/800 ml) evaporated milk
3 eggs, plus 10 egg yolks, lightly beaten
1 cup (8 fl oz/250 ml) whole (full-fat) milk
4 oz (120 g) all-purpose (plain) flour
4 cups (34 fl oz/1 liter) vegetable oil
confectioners' (icing) sugar, for decoration

Put the condensed milk and evaporated milk in a heavy pan over medium heat and simmer, stirring, until the mixture thickens slightly and you can see the bottom of the pan when you draw a spoon across it. Add the egg yolks and stir to form a custard. Set aside.

Place the eggs, milk, and flour in a blender and blend to form a batter.

Heat the vegetable oil in a large pan or deep-fryer to 350°F/180°C, or until a cube of bread browns in 30 seconds. Heat the spiral-tipped iron utensil used to prepare pastry swirl in the oil.

When the iron utensil is hot, dip the spiral into the batter up to 2 inches/5 cm from the tip of the spiral. Remove and dip in the oil to fry the dough. When it turns golden, remove from the oil. Remove the pastry swirl from the iron utensil in one smooth motion. Return the utensil to the oil to heat.

Repeat with the remaining dough, heating the iron utensil each time.

Spoon a little egg custard onto each plate and place a pastry swirl on top. Dust with confectioners' (icing) sugar and serve immediately.

QUINUA CON LECHE
MILKY QUINOA PUDDING

Serves: 8
Preparation Time: 10 minutes
Cooking Time: 35 minutes

⅔ cup (6 oz/175 g) quinoa
1 cinnamon stick
4 cloves
1½ cups (13 fl oz/375 ml) whole (full-fat) milk
zest of 1 orange
1½ cups (13 fl oz/375 ml) condensed milk
1 egg yolk
1 tablespoon port

To decorate
mint leaves
ground cinnamon

Place the quinoa, cinnamon stick, and cloves in a pan with 2½ cups (20 fl oz/620 ml) water. Bring to a boil, then reduce the heat and simmer for 15 minutes, until the water has evaporated and the quinoa is cooked.

Stir in the milk and orange zest and cook for a little longer until the liquid has thickened and reduced. Remove the orange zest and pour the condensed milk into the pan. Cook stirring, for a few more minutes.

In a separate bowl, beat the egg yolk together with the port. Remove the pan from the heat and add the egg yolk mixture to the quinoa. Set aside and cover with plastic wrap (clingfilm) to prevent a skin from forming, until cool.

Spoon into dessert glasses and decorate with a few mint leaves and a little ground cinnamon.

Frozen Cinnamon Milk

QUESO HELADO
FROZEN CINNAMON MILK

Serves: 4
Preparation Time: 10 minutes, plus 2 hours freezing
Cooking Time: 15 minutes

2 cups (18 fl oz/500 ml) whole (full-fat) milk
2 cups (18 fl oz/500 ml) evaporated milk
3 cinnamon sticks
5 cloves
3 tablespoons shredded (desiccated) coconut
scant ¾ cup (5 oz/150 g) granulated sugar
2 egg yolks
ground cinnamon, for decoration

Pour the fresh milk and evaporated milk into a heavy pan. Add the cinnamon and cloves and bring to a boil. Reduce the heat, add the coconut, and simmer for 5 minutes. Add the sugar, stir together, and remove from the heat.

Add the egg yolks one at a time and stir to combine. Return the pan to the heat and simmer for another 5 minutes.

Remove from the heat, strain to remove the spices, and pour into a suitable container. Put in the freezer for at least 2 hours, until frozen.

Serve in bowls, dusted with ground cinnamon.

RANFAÑOTE
BREAD AND CHEESE PUDDING

Serves: 6
Preparation Time: 15 minutes
Cooking Time: 5 minutes

3 French bread rolls or any crusty rolls
scant ½ cup (3½ oz/100 g) butter
⅓ cup (2 oz/50 g) almonds, toasted and coarsely ground
⅔ cup (3½ oz/100 g) golden raisins
scant 1 cup (3½ oz/100 g) coquito nuts, peeled and finely chopped
¾ cup (5 oz/150 g) chancaca sugar
1 cup (7 oz/200 g) brown sugar
juice of 1 orange
juice of 1 lemon
2 cinnamon sticks
10 cloves
⅓ cup (4 fl oz/120 ml) port
11 oz (300 g) queso fresco
shredded (desiccated) coconut, for decoration (optional)

Preheat the oven to 350°F/180°C/Gas Mark 4.

Cut the bread rolls into small cubes. Place on a baking sheet, dab with the butter, and bake for 10 minutes until golden and toasted. Set aside.

Mix the ground almonds, golden raisins, and coquito nuts together in a bowl. Set aside.

Place the chancaca sugar, brown sugar, orange juice, lemon juice, cinnamon sticks, and cloves in a pan with 1 cup (8 fl oz/250 ml) water over medium heat. When the mixture starts to bubble, remove from the heat and strain. Return the strained liquid to the heat, stir in the raisins, almonds, and coquito nuts and cook until the syrup thickens and has formed a soft, sticky ball.

Remove from the heat, add the port and toasted bread, and crumble in the queso fresco. Serve in dessert glasses, decorated with coconut to taste.

SUSPIRO DE LIMEÑA
PORT-INFUSED MERINGUE PUDDING

Serves: 6–8
Preparation Time: 20 minutes
Cooking Time: 15 minutes

1¾ cups (14 fl oz/400 ml) evaporated milk
1¾ cups (14 fl oz/400 ml) condensed milk
8 egg yolks, plus 2 egg whites
1 tablespoon vanilla extract
scant ⅔ cup (4 oz/120 g) granulated sugar
1 cup (8 fl oz/250 ml) port
ground cinnamon, for decoration

Pour the evaporated milk and condensed milk into a heavy pan over low heat. Cook, stirring, until the mixture has thickened and the bottom of the pan can be seen when you draw a spoon across it.

Remove from the heat and add the egg yolks and vanilla extract. Mix together thoroughly. Refrigerate until needed.

Place the sugar and port in a pan over medium heat and cook, without stirring, until a syrup forms.

Meanwhile, beat the egg whites in a bowl until stiff and doubled in volume. Add the port syrup to the egg whites in a thin stream, beating all the while, until the inside base of the bowl is cool.

Spoon the cooled custard into dessert glasses and top with the port-infused egg whites. Dust with ground cinnamon to finish.

ROSQUITAS
MINI DOUGHNUTS

Makes: 50 doughnuts
Preparation Time: 1 hour
Cooking Time: 15 minutes

4 tablespoons granulated sugar
¼ teaspoon anise seeds
4 cups (1 lb 2 oz/500 g) all-purpose (plain) flour, plus extra for dusting
1¾ cups (7 oz/200 g) vegetable shortening
butter, for greasing
1 egg white
1 tablespoon sesame seeds
salt

Place the sugar in a heavy pan with the anise seeds and ¼ cup (2 fl oz/50 ml) water. Bring to a boil, remove from the heat, and cool.

Pile the flour on a work counter and make a well in the center. Place the vegetable shortening in the center and, using your hands, work out from the center to combine the ingredients. Transfer the dough to a large bowl, slowly add the sugar water, and knead until it becomes a soft dough. Add a pinch of salt and knead thoroughly for 30 minutes until the dough is smooth and elastic.

Preheat the oven to 350°F/180°C/Gas Mark 4. Prepare a baking sheet by lightly greasing, and setting aside.

Roll the dough out into ¼-inch/5-mm strips. Twist 2 strips of dough together at a time, then shape into a circle to form a mini doughnut. Repeat with the remaining dough.

Place the doughnuts on the prepared baking sheet. Brush each one with egg white and sprinkle with sesame seeds.

Bake in the preheated oven until golden. Remove from the oven and cool on the baking sheet before serving.

Port-infused Meringue Pudding

Serves: 8–10
Preparation Time: 50 minutes, plus 30 minutes chilling
Cooking Time: 20 minutes

Pastry
1⅓ cups (11 oz/300 g) unsalted butter
generous ¾ cup (3¾ oz/110 g) confectioners' (icing) sugar
4 cups (1 lb 2 oz/500 g) all-purpose (plain) flour, plus extra for dusting
2 teaspoons ground cinnamon
1 tablespoon vanilla extract
zest of 1 lemon

Passion fruit mousse
1 cup (9 oz/250 g) cream cheese, at room temperature
1½ cups (13 fl oz/375 ml) condensed milk
2 tablespoons vanilla extract
1 cup (8 fl oz/250 ml) fresh passion fruit juice
2 tablespoons powdered gelatin
3 cups (25 fl oz/750 ml) light (single) cream

Passion fruit glaze
1 teaspoon powdered gelatin
1 cup (8 fl oz/250 ml) fresh passion fruit juice
2 tablespoons passion fruit seeds
½ cup (3½ oz/100 g) granulated sugar

TARTA DE MARACUYÁ
PASSION FRUIT TART

For the pastry, put the butter in a bowl and cream with a spatula until light and fluffy. Add the confectioners' (icing) sugar and mix thoroughly. Gradually stir in the flour, ground cinnamon, vanilla extract, and lemon zest until a smooth dough forms. Cover the dough and transfer to the refrigerator and chill for 30 minutes.

Preheat the oven to 325°F/170°C/Gas Mark 3.

Remove the dough from the refrigerator. Roll out on a floured surface with a rolling pin and use to line the base of a 13 -inch/32-cm round spring-form (loose-bottomed) flan ring. Bake in the oven for 15 minutes until cooked. Remove from the oven and set aside.

For the mousse, mix the cream cheese with the condensed milk in a bowl. Add the vanilla extract and passion fruit juice and mix together well.

Moisten the powdered gelatin with a little water in a small pan and then heat until it dissolves. Mix into the mousse mixture.

Whisk the cream until it takes on the consistency of yogurt and add to the mousse, stirring in a circular motion. Fill the baked pastry with the mousse and refrigerate.

For the passion fruit glaze, moisten the powdered gelatin with a few tablespoons of fresh passion fruit juice, and set aside.

Place the rest of the juice in a pan over the heat with the sugar and heat until the sugar dissolves. Add the moistened gelatin and heat until it dissolves. Mix thoroughly and pour the glaze over the tart. Decorate with passion fruit seeds and refrigerate until needed.

TEJAS DE LIMÓN
LEMON FONDANT CANDIES

Makes: 7 candies (sweets)
Preparation Time: 20 minutes, plus draining
Cooking Time: 2 hours 10 minutes

Dulce de leche filling
¼ cup (2½ fl oz/60 ml) evaporated milk
1 cup (8 fl oz/250 ml) whole (full-fat) milk
2 tablespoons granulated sugar
½ teaspoon vanilla extract

Candied lemons
7 large lemons
2½ cups (1 lb 2 oz/500 g) granulated sugar
salt

Fondant icing
1 cup (7 oz/200 g) granulated sugar
½ teaspoon liquid glucose
juice of ¼ lemon

For the dulce de leche filling, pour the evaporated and fresh milks into a heavy pan. Add the sugar and vanilla extract, place over medium heat, and simmer, stirring, until the mixture has thickened and the bottom of the pan can be seen when you draw the spoon across it. Remove from the heat and let cool.

For the candied lemons, cut the lemons in half widthwise and juice them. Bring a pan of salted water to a boil, add the lemon halves, and let cook for 2 minutes. Remove from the heat and drain. Let cool slightly, then remove as much of the pulp from the lemon as you can with a teaspoon. Repeat this process 6 times, changing the water each time, until you are left with just the lemon peel.

Place the sugar in a pan with ¾ cup (7 fl oz/200 ml) water and the lemon peels. Simmer over low heat for 1½ hours, until the liquid reduces and a thin syrup forms. Remove the lemons and place on a rack to drain, reserving the syrup.

When the lemons have dried, bring the syrup to a boil again, then pour it over the lemons while still on the rack. Let dry and set aside.

For the fondant icing, put the sugar, liquid glucose, and ½ cup (4 fl oz/120 ml) water in a pan, and cook over medium heat until it forms a fine syrup, about 10–12 minutes. Pour into a bowl, add the lemon juice and beat vigorously with a spoon until the mixture turns white.

Fill the lemon halves with the dulce de leche filling, sandwich together, and cover with the fondant icing.

Wrap the iced lemon candies (sweets) in tissue paper, twisting the ends to seal.

TEJAS DE PECANA
PECAN FONDANT CANDIES

Makes: 8 candies (sweets)
Preparation Time: 15 minutes
Cooking Time: 20 minutes

8 large pecans, shelled and halved

Dulce de leche filling
¼ cup (2½ fl oz/60 ml) evaporated milk
1 cup (8 fl oz/250 ml) whole (full-fat) milk
2 tablespoons granulated sugar
½ teaspoon vanilla extract

Fondant icing
1 cup (7 oz/200 g) granulated sugar
½ teaspoon liquid glucose
juice of ¼ lemon

For the dulce de leche filling, pour the evaporated and fresh milks into a heavy pan. Add the sugar and vanilla extract, place over medium heat, and simmer, stirring, until the mixture has thickened and the bottom of the pan can be seen when you draw the spoon across it. Remove from the heat and cool.

For the fondant icing, put the sugar, liquid glucose, and ½ cup (4 fl oz/120 ml) water in a pan and cook over medium heat until it forms a fine syrup, about 10–12 minutes. Pour into a bowl, add the lemon juice, and beat vigorously with a spoon until the mixture turns white. Set aside.

Spoon out a dollop of dulce de leche filling and shape into an oval. Stick the pecan halves to either side of the dulce de leche oval and repeat with the remaining pecans and dulce de leche mixture. Cover each candy (sweet) with the fondant icing.

Wrap the candies in waxed (greaseproof) paper, twisting the ends to seal.

TORREJITAS DE PLÁTANO CON MIEL
BANANA FRITTERS IN SYRUP

Serves: 4
Preparation Time: 35 minutes
Cooking Time: 20 minutes

3 ripe bananas
scant ¼ cup (1½ oz/40 g) granulated sugar
1 teaspoon ground cinnamon
2 tablespoons all-purpose (plain) flour
3 eggs, separated
½ cup (4 oz/120 g) butter, for frying
confectioners' (icing) sugar, for decoration (optional)

Chancaca syrup
1 cup (9 oz/250 g) chancaca sugar
¼ cup (2 oz/50 g) light brown sugar
2 teaspoons anise seeds
3 cinnamon sticks
zest of 1 orange

For the chancaca syrup, place the chancaca sugar, light brown sugar, anise seeds, and cinnamon sticks together with 3 cups (20 fl oz/750 ml) water in a pan over low heat and cook until a syrup forms. Add the orange zest and let infuse for 5 minutes. Remove from the heat, strain, and cool.

To make the fritters, place the bananas in a bowl and mash with a fork. Gradually add the sugar, ground cinnamon, and flour until a paste forms. Add the egg yolks and mix together well.

In a separate bowl, beat the egg whites until stiff. Stir into the banana mixture using a circular motion.

Heat the butter in a skillet or frying pan over medium heat. Add tablespoon-size dollops of the banana mixture and cook until you have golden fritters, turning in the oil.

Serve with the chancaca syrup and dust with confectioners' (icing) sugar, if desired.

TURRÓN DE DOÑA PEPA
LAYERED ANISE SEED COOKIE CAKE

Serves: 10–12
Preparation Time: 1 hour
Cooking Time: 18 minutes

scant 1¾ cup (12 oz/350 g) vegetable shortening
2 teaspoons annatto powder
8 cups (2¼ lb/1 kg) all-purpose (plain) flour, plus extra for flouring
1 cup (8 oz/225 g) margarine, plus extra for greasing
4 egg yolks
4½ tablespoons salt
3 teaspoons sesame seeds, toasted
3 teaspoons anise seeds, toasted
½ cup (4 fl oz/120 ml) anise seed tea
4 oz (120 g) multicolored sprinkles, for decoration

Fruit syrup
2½ cups (1 lb 2 oz/500 g) granulated sugar
1 cup (9 oz/250 g) chancaca sugar
9 oz (250 g) golden pineapple, peeled and chopped
1 orange, peeled, seeded, and chopped
2 apples, peeled, cored, and chopped
2 dried figs, chopped
1 tablespoon anise seeds
6 cinnamon sticks

Preheat the oven to 350°F/180°C/Gas Mark 4. Prepare 2 baking sheets by lightly greasing them and set aside.

To make the syrup, place the sugar, chancaca sugar, and 2 cups (18 fl oz/500 ml) water in a pan. Add the peeled and chopped fruit, anise seeds, and cinnamon sticks and cook over low heat for 30 minutes, until the mixture is thick and syrupy. Remove from the heat and strain. Set aside.

Melt a tablespoon of the vegetable shortening in a small pan and mix together with the annatto powder. Strain and put in a large bowl with the flour, remaining shortening, margarine, egg yolks, salt, toasted sesame and anise seeds, and anise seed tea. Using your hands, combine the ingredients and knead together to form a smooth dough.

Shape the dough into sticks the width of a finger and 12 inches/30 cm in length. Transfer to the prepared baking sheets and bake in the preheated oven for 18 minutes, until golden. Remove from the oven and cool.

To assemble the dessert, arrange a quarter of the cookie (biscuit) sticks tightly together side by side on a serving platter. Cover with fruit syrup. Lay a second layer of cookie sticks in the opposite direction over the top and cover again with the fruit syrup. Repeat the process twice more until you have 4 layers.

Cover the last layer with fruit syrup and decorate with multicolored sprinkles to finish.

VOLADOR DE MANJAR
TRIPLE-DECKER DULCE DE LECHE BITES

Serves: 18
Preparation Time: 30 minutes, plus 30 minutes chilling
Cooking Time: 8 minutes

- 2½ cups (11 oz/300 g) all-purpose (plain) flour, plus extra for dusting
- ½ teaspoon baking powder
- 15 egg yolks
- 2 tablespoons pisco
- 2 tablespoons unsalted butter, plus extra for greasing
- 3¾ cups (1 lb 14 oz/860 g) Dulce de Leche (see p. 414)
- confectioners' (icing) sugar, for decoration

Mix the flour and the baking powder together and pile on a work counter. Make a well in the center, pour the egg yolks, pisco, and butter into the well and, using your hands, work out from the center to combine the ingredients and form a soft dough.

Roll the dough into a ball, wrap in plastic wrap (clingfilm), and refrigerate for 30 minutes. Preheat the oven to 300°F/150°C/Gas Mark 2. Prepare a baking sheet by lightly greasing it and set aside.

Remove the dough from the refrigerator and roll out on a floured surface with a rolling pin into a large circle about 1/16-inch/1-mm thick. Using a 2½-inch/6-cm round cookie cutter, cut out 54 disks. Place the disks on the prepared baking sheet. Bake in the preheated oven for 6 minutes. Turn the disks over and bake for another 2 minutes. Remove from the oven and cool.

Use 3 disks to assemble each bite, spooning dulce de leche between each cookie layer. Dust with confectioners' (icing) sugar and serve.

SANGUITO
CORNMEAL PUDDING

Serves: 12
Preparation Time: 5 minutes, plus 1 hour draining
Cooking Time: 25 minutes

- 3 cups (1 lb 2 oz/500 g) finely ground yellow cornmeal
- 1 cinnamon stick
- 5 cloves
- 5 dried allspice berries
- 2½ cups (2¼ lb/1 kg) brown sugar
- 1 cup (8 oz/225 g) butter
- 1 teaspoon vanilla extract

To decorate

- scant 1½ cup (7 oz/200 g) raisins
- 2 oz (50 g) multicolored sprinkles

Place the yellow cornmeal in a bowl and cover with 6 cups (50 fl oz/1.5 liters) water. Soak for 1 hour, then drain.

Place the cinnamon stick, cloves, and allspice berries in a pan over medium heat. Add 6 cups (50 fl oz/1.5 liters) water, and the soaked and drained cornmeal and simmer, stirring, until the cornmeal is cooked. Add the brown sugar, butter, and vanilla extract and continue to cook, stirring, until the mixture has thickened and the bottom of the pan can be seen when you draw a spoon across it.

Spoon the pudding mixture into a bowl and decorate with the raisins and multicolored sprinkles.

Triple-Decker Dulce de Leche Bites

YEMECILLAS
EGG YOLK CANDIES

Makes: 20 candies (sweets)
Preparation Time: 20 minutes
Cooking Time: 10 minutes

10 egg yolks
1½ cups (11 oz/300 g) granulated sugar
2 tablespoons whole (full-fat) milk

Place the egg yolks, sugar, and milk in a heavy pan and cook over low heat, stirring continuously, until the mixture thickens slightly and you can see the bottom of the pan when you draw a spoon across it.

Remove from the heat and beat the mixture with a whisk until cool.

Roll the cooled mixture into 20 little balls and serve in mini cupcake liners.

YEMECILLAS ACARAMELADAS
CARAMEL EGG YOLK CANDIES

Makes: 20 candies (sweets)
Preparation Time: 20 minutes
Cooking Time: 20 minutes

10 egg yolks
2 tablespoons whole (full-fat) milk
3 cups (1 lb 5 oz/600 g) granulated sugar

Place the egg yolks, milk and half the sugar in a heavy pan and cook over low heat, stirring continuously, until the mixture thickens slightly and you can see the bottom of the pan when you draw a spoon across it.

Remove from the heat and beat the mixture with a whisk until cool. Roll the cooled mixture into 20 little balls. Set aside.

Place the remaining sugar in a small pan and cover with water. Cook over low heat until it turns a golden caramel color. Remove from the heat.

Dip the egg yolk balls in the caramel and cool. Serve in mini cupcake liners.

VOLADOR DE MANJAR Y PIÑA
TRIPLE-DECKER PINEAPPLE BITES

Serves: 18
Preparation Time: 30 minutes, plus 30 minutes chilling
Cooking Time: 8 minutes

- scant 2½ cups (11 oz/300 g) all-purpose (plain) flour, plus extra for dusting
- ½ teaspoon baking powder
- 15 egg yolks
- 2 tablespoons pisco
- 2 tablespoons unsalted butter
- 2½ cups (1 lb 5 oz/600 g) Dulce de Leche (see p. 414)
- 1¼ cups (11 oz/300 g) pineapple marmalade
- confectioners' (icing) sugar, for decoration

Mix the flour and the baking powder together and pile on a work counter. Make a well in the center, pour the egg yolks, pisco, and butter into the well and, using your hands, work out from the center to combine the ingredients and form a soft dough.

Roll the dough into a ball, wrap in plastic wrap (clingfilm), and refrigerate for 30 minutes.

Preheat the oven to 300°F/150°C/Gas Mark 2. Prepare a baking sheet by lightly greasing it, and set aside.

Remove the dough from the refrigerator and roll out on a floured surface with a rolling pin into a large circle about 1⁄16-inch/2-mm thick. Using a 2½-inch/6-cm round cookie cutter, cut out 54 disks. Place the disks on the prepared baking sheet.

Bake in the preheated oven for 6 minutes. Turn the disks over and bake for another 2 minutes. Remove from the oven and let cool.

Use 3 disks to assemble each pineapple bite, stacking them with a little dulce de leche and pineapple marmalade between each layer. Dust with confectioners' (icing) sugar and serve.

DRINKS

CHICHA MORADA
PERUVIAN PURPLE CORN PUNCH

Serves: 25
Preparation Time: 20 minutes
Cooking Time: 3 hours

- 10 lb (4 kg) purple corn ears, halved and partially shelled
- 1 lb 2 oz (500 g) quinces, quartered
- 7 cloves
- 1 cinnamon stick, broken into pieces
- peel of 2 golden pineapples
- 6 cups (2½ lb/1.2 kg) granulated sugar
- 1 cup (8 fl oz/250 ml) lemon juice
- apple, peeled, cored, and chopped, to serve (optional)

Place the halved corn ears in a pot. Add the quince, cloves, cinnamon stick, pineapple peels, and 425 fl oz/12.5 liters water and simmer over low heat for around 3 hours, until the liquid has thickened and turned a deep purple color and the corn kernels have opened fully and lost their color.

Remove from the heat, let cool, and strain. Add the sugar, lemon juice, and chopped apple, and keep refrigerated until ready to serve.

CHICHA FROZEN
FROZEN CHICHA

Serves: 1
Preparation Time: 5 minutes

- ½ cup (120 ml/4 fl oz) Chicha Morada (see above)
- ¼ cup (50 ml/2 fl oz) sugar syrup
- 1 tablespoon lemon juice
- 20 ice cubes
- 1 lemon slice, to garnish

Place all the ingredients in a blender. Blend until slushy. Pour into a chilled glass and garnish with a lemon slice.

CHICHA DE JORA
CORN BEER

Serves: 40
Preparation Time: 5 minutes, plus 4–6 days fermentation
Cooking Time: 1 hour 35 minutes

- 3¼ lb (1.5 kg) jora corn kernels
- 2¼ lb (1 kg) barley
- 40 cloves
- 7½ cups (3¼ lb/1.5 kg) granulated sugar

Toast the jora corn kernels and barley in a large clean skillet or frying pan, without oil, until lightly golden.

Place 170 fl oz/5 liters water in a large pan with the barley, jora corn kernels, and cloves and bring to a boil. Stir continuously to ensure that the liquid does not thicken.

Once half the liquid has evaporated, add another 170 fl oz/5 liters water. Simmer for another hour and a half. Remove from the heat and cool.

Add the sugar, stir to dissolve, and strain the liquid. Pour into a large (preferably clay) jug, cover, and let ferment for 4–6 days, at room temperature, stirring at least once a day. The corn beer will keep for around 20 days.

Peruvian Purple Corn Punch

Tamarind Cremolada

CREMOLADA DE MARACUYÁ
PASSION FRUIT CREMOLADA

Serves: 10
Preparation Time: 10 minutes, plus 3 hours freezing

- 1 cup (7 oz/200 g) granulated sugar
- 2¼ lb (1 kg) passion fruit, strained and seeds removed

Pour 4¼ cups (34 fl oz/1 liter) water into a steel bowl, add the sugar and strained passion fruit and mix together thoroughly. Place in the freezer for 3 hours, until frozen.

Remove the mixture from the freezer and put in the blender. Blend to a sorbet like texture, then pour into glasses to serve.

CREMOLADA DE FRESA
STRAWBERRY CREMOLADA

Serves: 10
Preparation Time: 10 minutes, plus 3 hours freezing

- 2¼ lb (1 kg) strawberries, hulled
- 1 cup (7 oz/200 g) granulated sugar

Put the strawberries in a blender and blend to a puree.

Pour 4¼ cups (34 fl oz/1 liter) water into a steel bowl with the sugar and strawberry puree. Mix together thoroughly. Place in the freezer for 3 hours, until frozen.

Remove the mixture from the freezer and put in the blender. Blend to a sorbet like texture, then spoon into glasses to serve.

CREMOLADA DE TAMARINDO
TAMARIND CREMOLADA

Serves: 10
Preparation Time: 10 minutes, plus 3 hours freezing

- 2¼ lb (1 kg) tamarind flesh
- 1½ cups (11 oz/300 g) granulated sugar

Put the tamarind flesh in a blender and blend to a puree. Strain.

Pour 4¼ cups (34 fl oz/1 liter) water into a steel bowl with the sugar and the strained tamarind puree. Mix together thoroughly. Place in the freezer for 3 hours, until frozen.

Remove the mixture from the freezer and put in the blender. Blend to a sorbet like texture, then spoon into glasses to serve.

CREMOLADA DE GUANÁBANA
SOURSOP CREMOLADA

Serves: 10
Preparation Time: 10 minutes, plus 3 hours freezing

2¼ lb (1 kg) soursop flesh
1 cup (7 oz/200 g) granulated sugar

Put the soursop in a blender and blend to a puree.

Pour 4¼ cups (34 fl oz/1 liter) water into a steel bowl with the sugar and soursop puree. Mix together thoroughly. Place in the freezer for 3 hours, until frozen.

Remove the mixture from the freezer and put in the blender. Blend to a sorbet like texture, then spoon into glasses to serve.

CREMOLADA DE TUNA
PRICKLY PEAR CREMOLADA

Serves: 10
Preparation Time: 10 minutes, plus 3 hours freezing

2¼ lb (1 kg) prickly pear flesh
1 cup (7 oz/200 g) granulated sugar

Put the prickly pear flesh in a blender and blend to a puree.

Pour 4¼ cups (34 fl oz/1 liter) water into a steel bowl with the sugar and prickly pear puree. Mix together thoroughly. Place in the freezer for 3 hours, until frozen.

Remove the mixture from the freezer and put in the blender. Blend to a sorbet like texture, then spoon into glasses to serve.

CREMOLADA DE MANGO
MANGO CREMOLADA

Serves: 10
Preparation Time: 10 minutes, plus 3 hours freezing

2¼ lb (1 kg) mango flesh
1 cup (7 oz/200 g) granulated sugar

Put the mango in a blender and blend to a puree. Strain.

Pour 4¼ cups (34 fl oz/1 liter) water into a steel bowl with the sugar and strained mango puree. Mix together thoroughly. Place in the freezer for 3 hours, until frozen.

Remove the mixture from the freezer and put in the blender. Blend to a sorbet like texture, then spoon into glasses to serve.

LIMONADA
FROZEN LEMONADE

Serves: 10
Preparation Time: 5 minutes

½ cup (4 fl oz/120 ml) lemon juice
8½ cups (68 fl oz/2 liters) water, boiled then chilled
3½ oz (100 g) granulated sugar
handful of ice cubes

Pour the lemon juice and half the water into a blender with the sugar and ice. Blend thoroughly, then add the remaining water and stir to combine. Serve in glasses.

EMOLIENTE
HOT BARLEY DRINK

Serves: 8
Preparation Time: 5 minutes
Cooking Time: 10 minutes

3½ oz (100 g) barley
2½ oz (65 g) horsetail
2 oz (50 g) linseed
¾ oz (20 g) boldo leaves
½ cup (3½ oz/100 g) granulated sugar
juice of 2 small lemons

Wash the barley, horsetail, and linseed thoroughly. Pour 6¼ cups (50 fl oz/1.5 liters) water into a pan and add the barley, horsetail, linseed, and boldo leaves. Bring to a boil, simmer for 10 minutes, and strain. Stir in the sugar and lemon juice and serve hot.

RASPADILLAS DE FRUTAS
FRUIT SHERBET

Serves: 12
Preparation Time: 25 minutes
Cooking Time: 15 minutes

4½ lb (2 kg) granulated sugar
1 lb 2 oz (500 g) mango flesh, blended and strained
1 lb 2 oz (500 g) strawberries, blended
250 g (9 oz) blackberries, blended and strained
250 g (9 oz) raspberries, blended and strained
2 teaspoons mint extract
2¼ lb (1 kg) ice

To prepare a base syrup, place the sugar in a pan and pour in 102 fl oz/3 liters water. Bring to a boil and simmer over medium heat for 10 minutes without stirring. Remove from heat and cool.

Combine the mango flesh with 1 cup (8 fl oz/250 ml) of base syrup in a bowl. Repeat the process with the remaining fruits in separate bowls to prepare individual fruit syrups. To prepare a mint syrup, add the mint extract to 1 cup (8 fl oz/250 ml) of base syrup in another bowl.

Grind the ice in a blender and spoon into glasses. Serve immediately, topped with the individual varieties of flavored syrup.

AGUAYMANTO SOUR
PHYSALIS SOUR

Serves: 1
Preparation Time: 5 minutes

¼ cup (2 fl oz/50 ml) Quebranta pisco
¼ cup (2 fl oz/50 ml) fresh physalis juice
2 tablespoons sugar syrup
10 ice cubes
1 physalis, to garnish

Shake all the liquid ingredients in a cocktail shaker with the ice for 6 seconds, then strain into a chilled tall glass. Garnish with a physalis.

ALARACO
PISCO, CAMU CAMU, AND GINGER ALE COCKTAIL

Serves: 1
Preparation Time: 5 minutes

8 ice cubes
2 tablespoons pisco
2 tablespoons camu camu juice
1 tablespoon granulated sugar
1 dash lemon juice
ginger ale, to top off

To garnish
1 camu camu berry
2 mint leaves

Place the ice in a large stemless cocktail glass. Pour in the pisco, then the camu camu juice, and finally add the sugar and lemon juice. Top off with ginger ale. Garnish with a camu camu berry and a few mint leaves.

CHILCANO DE GUINDA
MORELLO CHERRY CHILCANO

Serves: 1
Preparation Time: 5 minutes, plus 5 days infusing

15 ice cubes
¼ cup (50 ml/2 fl oz) Morello Cherry-Infused Pisco (see p. 393)
1 tablespoon lemon juice
ginger ale, to top off
3 drops Angostura bitters (optional)

To make the morello cherry-infused pisco, pour the pisco into a suitable jar or bottle with a tight-fitting lid or cap. Add the morello cherries and infuse for 5 days before removing the fruit with a slotted spoon.

To make the chilcano, place the ice in a tall glass. Pour in the infused Pisco and lemon juice and top off with ginger ale, adding 3 drops of Angostura bitters, if desired. Serve.

ALGARROBINA
CAROB SYRUP COCKTAIL

Serves: 1
Preparation Time: 5 minutes

1½ tablespoons Quebranta pisco
5 tablespoons evaporated milk
1½ teaspoons cocoa liqueur
½ tablespoon sugar syrup
2 tablespoons carob syrup
15 ice cubes
pinch of ground cinnamon, to finish

Shake all the liquid ingredients in a cocktail shaker with the ice for 12 seconds, then strain into a chilled tall glass. Sprinkle with a pinch of ground cinnamon to finish.

CAMU CAMU SOUR
CAMU CAMU SOUR

Serves: 1
Preparation Time: 5 minutes

5 tablespoons Quebranta pisco
6 tablespoons camu camu extract
2 tablespoons sugar syrup
15 ice cubes
1 fresh camu camu berry, to garnish
1 mint leaf, to garnish

Shake all the liquid ingredients in a cocktail shaker with the ice for 7 seconds, then strain into a martini glass. Garnish with a camu camu berry and a mint leaf.

CHOLOPOLITAN
PERUVIAN COSMOPOLITAN

Serves: 1
Preparation Time: 5 minutes

4 tablespoons Quebranta pisco
2 tablespoons Cointreau
1½ teaspoons lime juice
1 tablespoon fresh passion fruit juice
4 tablespoons cranberry juice
15 ice cubes
1 lime peel twist, to garnish

Shake together the liquid ingredients in a cocktail shaker with the ice for 8–10 seconds. Strain into a chilled martini glass and garnish with a twist of lime peel.

Chicha Punch

CANITA AL AIRE
PISCO, LEMON VERBENA, GRANADILLA, AND CAMU CAMU COCKTAIL

Serves: 1
Preparation Time: 10 minutes, plus 9 days infusing

- 16 ice cubes
- 3 tablespoons Lemon Verbena-Infused Pisco (see p. 393)
- 2 tablespoons tangerine liqueur
- 3 tablespoons granadilla or passion fruit juice
- 1 tablespoon camu camu juice
- ½ oz (15 g) granulated sugar

To garnish
- 2 lemon verbena leaves
- 1 cherry

To make the lemon verbena-infused pisco, pour the pisco into a suitable jar or bottle with a tight-fitting lid or cap. Add the verbena sprigs and infuse for 9 days before removing the verbena.

To make your cocktail, place 8 ice cubes in a mixing glass and add the lemon verbena-infused pisco, tangerine liqueur, granadilla juice, camu camu juice, and sugar, in that order. Stir together for 5 seconds.

To serve, strain into a tall glass with the remaining ice cubes and garnish with a few lemon verbena leaves and a cherry.

CHICHA PUNCH
CHICHA PUNCH

Serves: 1
Preparation Time: 5 minutes

- 4 tablespoons pisco
- 2 tablespoons cherry brandy
- 3 tablespoons pineapple juice
- 3 tablespoons Chicha Morada (see p. 378)
- 1 teaspoon lemon juice
- 15 ice cubes
- 1 orange slice
- 1 lime slice
- 1 lemon slice
- 1 tablespoon finely chopped golden pineapple, to garnish

Assemble all the liquid ingredients in a mixing glass with the ice and stir for 8 seconds to ensure they are mixed and chilled.

To serve, place the orange, lime, and lemon slices in the bottom of a cocktail glass and strain and pour in the liquid. Garnish with chopped pineapple and serve with a straw.

CAPITÁN
PERUVIAN MANHATTAN

Serves: 1
Preparation Time: 5 minutes

- 4 tablespoons Quebranta pisco
- 4 tablespoons red vermouth
- 6 drops Angostura bitters
- 15 ice cubes
- 1 cherry, to garnish

Assemble all the liquid ingredients in a mixing glass with the ice and stir for 8 seconds to ensure they are mixed and chilled.

Strain into a chilled large martini glass and garnish with a cherry.

PERÚ LIBRE
PISCO AND COLA COCKTAIL

Serves: 1
Preparation Time: 5 minutes

15 ice cubes
4 tablespoons (60 ml/2 fl oz) Quebranta pisco
cola, to top off
1 Tahiti lime slice, to garnish

Place the ice in a tall glass, pour in the pisco, and top off with cola.

Garnish with a Tahiti lime slice and serve with a straw.

CARRETERO
PISCO, FERNET, AND RED VERMOUTH COCKTAIL

Serves: 1
Preparation Time: 5 minutes

2 tablespoons Quebranta pisco
1 tablespoon Fernet Branca or Jägermeister
1 tablespoon Cinzano Rosso
4 tablespoons cranberry juice
1 tablespoon passion fruit juice
2 tablespoons sugar syrup
10 ice cubes

To garnish
½ orange slice
1 spearmint leaf

Shake all the liquid ingredients in a cocktail shaker with the ice for 8 seconds, then strain into a chilled tall glass. Garnish with an orange slice and a spearmint leaf.

MARACUYÁ SOUR
PASSION FRUIT SOUR

Serves: 1
Preparation Time: 5 minutes

6 tablespoons Quebranta pisco
2 tablespoons lemon juice
1 tablespoon sugar syrup
2 tablespoons fresh passion fruit juice
1 tablespoon egg white
6 ice cubes
1 cherry, to garnish

Put the liquid ingredients with the ice into a blender. Blend for 7 seconds, then pour into a tumbler. Garnish with a cherry.

CHICHA COLADA
PERUVIAN PIÑA COLADA

Serves: 1
Preparation Time: 5 minutes

4 tablespoons Quebranta pisco
2 tablespoons coconut cream
4 tablespoons Chicha Morada (see p. 378)
2 tablespoons pineapple juice
¼ cup (50 ml/2 fl oz) condensed milk
20 ice cubes

To garnish
2 cinnamon sticks
1 tablespoon finely chopped pineapple
1 teaspoon purple corn kernels

Pour the liquid ingredients with the ice into a blender. Blend for a few seconds, then strain into a tall glass. Garnish with the cinnamon sticks, chopped pineapple, and purple corn kernels.

METROPOLITANO
PISCO AND LYCHEE METROPOLITAN

Serves: 1
Preparation Time: 10 minutes

1½ oz (40 g) lychees in syrup
1½ teaspoons lemon juice
1 sprig spearmint
1 tablespoon granulated sugar
3 tablespoons Italia pisco
2 tablespoons lychee liqueur
15 ice cubes
ginger ale, to top off

To garnish
1 lychee
1 cherry

Place the lychees, lemon juice, spearmint, and sugar in a mixing glass. Lightly crush the ingredients with a cocktail muddler or pestle to release the spearmint flavor. Add the pisco, lychee liqueur, and 8 ice cubes and stir together for 10 seconds.

Strain twice and serve in a tall glass with the remaining ice cubes. Top off with ginger ale and garnish with a lychee and a cherry.

MOJITO PERUANO
PERUVIAN MOJITO

Serves: 1
Preparation Time: 5 minutes

1 tablespoon elderberry liqueur
4 spearmint leaves, plus 1 extra to garnish
4 strawberries
2 tablespoons sugar syrup
4 tablespoons Quebranta pisco
15 ice cubes
1 strawberry, to garnish

Place the elderberry liqueur, spearmint, strawberries, and sugar syrup in a mixing glass. Crush the ingredients with a cocktail muddler or pestle and add the pisco. Mix together for 10 seconds.

Strain twice and serve in a tall glass with the ice. Garnish with a strawberry and a spearmint leaf.

CHILCANO CLÁSICO DE PISCO
CLASSIC CHILCANO PISCO

Serves: 1
Preparation Time: 5 minutes

1 Tahiti lime slice
15 ice cubes
4 tablespoons Quebranta pisco
1 dash lemon juice
6 drops Angostura bitters
ginger ale, to top off
lime wedges, to serve

Place the Tahiti lime slice and ice in a tall glass. Pour in the pisco, then the lemon juice and finally the Angostura bitters. Top off with ginger ale, a wedge of lime, and a cocktail stirrer or straw to finish.

CHILCANO DE ANÍS ESTRELLA
STAR ANISE CHILCANO

Serves: 1
Preparation Time: 10 minutes, plus 7 days infusing

15 ice cubes
1 star anise
3 tablespoons Quebranta pisco
1 tablespoon Star Anise-Infused pisco (see below)
1 tablespoon sugar syrup
1 tablespoon lemon juice
ginger ale, to top off

Star Anise-Infused Pisco
Makes: 4¼ cups (1 liter)
4¼ cups (28 fl oz/1 liter) Quebranta pisco
9 oz (250 g) star anise

To make the star anise-infused pisco, pour the pisco into a suitable jar or bottle with a tight-fitting lid or cap. Add the star anise and let infuse for 7 days before removing the star anise.

To make the chilcano, place the ice and star anise in a tall glass. Shake the pisco, infused pisco, sugar syrup, and lemon juice together for a few seconds in a cocktail shaker. Pour it over the ice and star anise and top off with ginger ale.

CHILCANO DE KION
GINGER CHILCANO

Serves: 1
Preparation Time: 5 minutes

¼-inch (5-mm) piece fresh ginger, peeled and cut into slivers
1 tablespoon lemon juice
2 tablespoons sugar syrup
4 drops Angostura bitters
4 tablespoons Quebranta pisco
6 ice cubes
ginger ale, to top off
1 mint leaf, to garnish

Add half the ginger, the lemon juice, sugar syrup, and Angostura bitters to a cocktail shaker. Using a cocktail muddler or pestle, crush the ginger to release its flavor. Pour in the pisco, add the ice cubes, and shake gently for 4 seconds.

Pour into a tall glass and top off with ginger ale. Garnish with the remaining ginger slices and a mint leaf.

Classic Chilcano Pisco

CHOLO PUNCH
PISCO, CRANBERRY, AND PINEAPPLE COCKTAIL

Serves: 1
Preparation Time: 5 minutes

4 tablespoons Quebranta pisco
1 tablespoon passion fruit juice
1 tablespoon orange juice
4 tablespoons cranberry juice
4 tablespoons pineapple juice
20 ice cubes
½ lime slice, to garnish

Shake all the liquid ingredients in a cocktail shaker with the ice for 6 seconds, then strain into a chilled cocktail glass. Garnish with half a lime slice.

COCA SOUR
COCA SOUR

Serves: 1
Preparation Time: 10 minutes, plus 3 days infusing

6–8 ice cubes
6 tablespoons Coca Leaf-Infused Pisco (see p. 393)
2 tablespoons lemon juice
2 tablespoons sugar syrup
1 tablespoon egg white
1 coca leaf, to garnish

To make the coca leaf-infused pisco, pour the pisco into a suitable glass jar or bottle with a tight-fitting lid or cap. Add the coca leaves. Let infuse for three days before removing the coca leaves.

To make your cocktail, place the ice in a blender or cocktail shaker and pour in the liquid ingredients. Blend or shake for 8 seconds, then strain into a chilled, short glass, being careful to limit the amount of froth. Garnish with a coca leaf.

GUËNAZO
PISCO, LEMON, BASIL, AND PASSION FRUIT COCKTAIL

Serves: 1
Preparation Time: 5 minutes

2 tablespoons sugar syrup
1 tablespoon lemon juice
4 basil leaves
4 tablespoons Quebranta pisco
2 tablespoons fresh passion fruit juice
4 tablespoons sparkling water
1 Tahiti lime slice, to garnish

Place the sugar syrup, lemon juice, and 2 basil leaves in a cocktail shaker. Using a cocktail muddler or pestle, crush the leaves to release the basil flavor, then pour in the pisco, passion fruit juice, and sparkling water.

Strain twice and serve in a chilled tall glass. Garnish with the remaining basil leaves and the Tahiti lime slice.

MACERADO DE PISCO CON HIERBALUISA
LEMON VERBENA-INFUSED PISCO

Makes: 4¼ cups (34 fl oz/1 liter)
Preparation Time: 5 minutes, plus 9 days infusing

4¼ cups (34 fl oz/1 liter) pisco
1 lb 2 oz (500g) lemon verbena

Wash the lemon verbena thoroughly and use only the green sprigs.

Pour the pisco into a jar or bottle with a tight-fitting lid or cap. Add the lemon verbena.

Infuse for nine days, then remove the lemon verbena leaves so that the infusion retains its green color but doesn't darken.

MACERADO DE PISCO CON GUINDA
MORELLO CHERRY-INFUSED PISCO

Makes: 4¼ cups (34 fl oz/1 liter)
Preparation Time: 5 minutes, plus 5 days infusing

4¼ cups (34 fl oz/1 liter) Quebranta pisco
11 oz (300g) morello cherries

Pour the pisco into a jar or bottle with a tight-fitting lid or cap. Add the morello cherries.

Infuse for five days, then remove the fruit so that the cherry flavor remains without the pulp.

MACERADO DE PISCO CON COCA
COCA LEAF-INFUSED PISCO

Makes: 4¼ cups (34 fl oz/1 liter)
Preparation Time: 5 minutes, plus 3 days infusing

4¼ cups (34 fl oz/1 liter) pure Quebranta pisco (
1 oz (25g) coca leaves

Pour the pisco into a large glass jar. Add the coca leaves.

Infuse for three days, then remove the coca leaves.

KUNG FU CHARAPA
PISCO AND CAMU CAMU COCKTAIL

Serves: 1
Preparation Time: 5 minutes

3 tablespoons Quebranta pisco
1 tablespoon fresh camu camu juice
1 tablespoon sugar syrup
15 ice cubes

To garnish
3 mint leaves
1 camu camu berry

Pour all the liquid ingredients into a blender and add the ice. Blend until the mixture has a sorbet-like texture.

Pour into a tall glass and garnish with some mint leaves and a camu camu berry.

LA NALANJITA
PISCO, PHYSALIS, AND TANGERINE COCKTAIL

Serves: 1
Preparation Time: 5 minutes

1 tablespoon fresh physalis juice
1 tablespoon fresh tangerine juice
1 mint leaf
3 tablespoons Quebranta pisco
15 ice cubes

To garnish
1 kumquat
2 lemon leaves

Pour the physalis and tangerine juices into a cocktail shaker with the mint leaf. Using a cocktail muddler or pestle, crush the leaf to release the mint flavor, then add the pisco and ice. Shake for 7 seconds, then strain into a chilled tall glass.

Garnish with a kumquat and lemon leaves.

PISCO PUNCH
PISCO PUNCH

Serves: 1
Preparation Time: 5 minutes

6 tablespoons Quebranta pisco
6 tablespoons pineapple juice
1½ teaspoons lemon juice
25 ice cubes

To garnish
1 orange slice
1 lime slice
1 lemon slice
2 oz (50 g) golden pineapple, chopped

Shake all the liquid ingredients in a cocktail shaker with 15 ice cubes for 8 seconds, then strain into a cocktail glass. Add the remaining ice, garnish with the orange, lime and lemon slices,
and chopped pineapple and serve with a straw.

LA PECOSA
PISCO, GRANADILLA, AND TANGERINE COCKTAIL

Assemble all the liquid ingredients with the ice in a mixing glass and stir together for 10 seconds.

Pour into a large martini glass and garnish with a tangerine segment and a mint leaf.

Serves: 1
Preparation Time: 5 minutes

4 tablespoons Quebranta pisco
6 tablespoons fresh granadilla juice
2 tablespoons fresh tangerine juice
2 tablespoons sugar syrup
15 ice cubes

To garnish
1 tangerine segment
1 mint leaf

SANGRÍA PANCHITA
PERUVIAN SANGRIA

Pour the liquid ingredients one by one into a large cocktail glass. Add the ice.

Garnish with the chopped green apple and pineapple.

Serves: 1
Preparation Time: 5 minutes

2 tablespoons Quebranta pisco
6 tablespoons red wine
2 tablespoons orange juice
2 tablespoons pineapple juice
1 tablespoon elderberry liqueur
2 tablespoons Chicha Morada (see p. 378)
2 tablespoons Inca Kola soft drink
20 ice cubes

To garnish
1¼ oz (30 g) green apple, chopped
2 oz (50 g) golden pineapple, chopped

CHIRIPA
PISCO, GRANADILLA, AND PASSION FRUIT COCKTAIL

Shake all the liquid ingredients in a cocktail shaker with the ice for a few seconds until cold, then pour into a chilled large martini glass.

Garnish with the half Tahiti lime slice.

Serves: 1
Preparation Time: 5 minutes

4 tablespoons Quebranta pisco
2 tablespoons sugar syrup
3 tablespoons fresh granadilla juice
3 tablespoons fresh passion fruit juice
8–10 ice cubes
½ Tahiti lime slice, to garnish

CHINITA SEXY
SEXY CHINITA

Shake the pisco, sugar syrup, and lemon juice together for a few seconds in a cocktail shaker. Add the ice and shake together for another 7 seconds.

Place the strawberries in a tall glass. Pour in the cocktail mix and garnish with a sprig of mint.

Serves: 1
Preparation Time: 5 minutes

3 tablespoons Quebranta pisco
2 tablespoons sugar syrup
1½ teaspoons lemon juice
15 ice cubes
2 oz (50 g) strawberries
1 sprig mint, to garnish

LUCURRUBINA
PISCO, RUM, AND CAROB SYRUP COCKTAIL

Serves: 1
Preparation Time: 5 minutes

1 tablespoon pisco, infused with dried fruits
3 tablespoons rum cream
2 tablespoons carob syrup
2 oz (50 g) lucuma fruit, chopped
2 tablespoons condensed milk
10 ice cubes
carob syrup, for decoration
pinch of ground cinnamon, for decoration

Put the fruit-infused pisco, rum cream, carob syrup, lucuma fruit, and condensed milk into a blender with 4 ice cubes. Blend for a few seconds, then pour into a cocktail shaker and add the remaining 6 ice cubes. Shake together for 6 seconds.

Trickle a little carob syrup around the sides of a tall glass for a marbled effect. Strain in the drink and sprinkle with a pinch of ground cinnamon to finish.

PISCO SOUR
PISCO SOUR

Serves: 1
Preparation Time: 5 minutes

15 ice cubes
6 tablespoons Quebranta pisco
2 tablespoons lemon juice
2 tablespoons sugar syrup
1 tablespoon egg white
2 drops Angostura bitters, to finish

Place the ice in a blender or cocktail shaker and pour in the liquid ingredients. Blend for 3 seconds or shake for 8, then strain into a chilled stemless cocktail glass. Drop the Angostura bitters in the center of the drink to finish.

QUÉ BUENOS MANGOS
PISCO AND MANGO COCKTAIL

Serves: 1
Preparation Time: 5 minutes

4 tablespoons Quebranta pisco
6 tablespoons mango juice
4 tablespoons pineapple syrup
15 ice cubes
1 strawberry, sliced, to garnish

Shake all the liquid ingredients in a cocktail shaker with the ice for 10 seconds, then strain into a chilled large cocktail glass. Garnish with the sliced strawberry.

Pisco Sour

MÓJATE CHOLO
PISCO, TAMARILLO, AND PINEAPPLE COCKTAIL

Serves: 1
Preparation Time: 5 minutes

Peel of 1 tamarillo, cut into 7 strips
7 mint leaves
4 huacatay leaves, plus 1 extra to garnish
1 tablespoon lemon juice
4 tablespoons Quebranta pisco
6 tablespoons pineapple juice
4 tablespoons ginger ale
10 ice cubes

Put the tamarillo, mint leaves, huacatay leaves, and lemon juice to a cocktail shaker. Using a cocktail muddler or pestle, lightly crush the ingredients to release their flavors. Pour in the pisco, pineapple juice, and ginger ale, add the ice cubes, and shake for 6 seconds.

Strain into a chilled large cocktail glass. Garnish with a huacatay leaf.

PISCOLITAN
PISCO, CRANBERRY, ORANGE, AND PASSION FRUIT COCKTAIL

Serves: 1
Preparation Time: 5 minutes

4 tablespoons Quebranta pisco
5 tablespoons cranberry juice
1 tablespoon passion fruit juice
1 tablespoon orange juice
1 tablespoon sugar syrup
8 ice cubes
1 lime peel twist, to garnish

Shake all the liquid ingredients in a cocktail shaker with the ice for 6 seconds, then strain into a chilled martini glass. Garnish with a twist of lime peel.

TACNA SOUR
APRICOT LIQUEUR AND LEMON COCKTAIL

Serves: 1
Preparation Time: 5 minutes

6 tablespoons apricot liqueur
2 tablespoons sugar syrup
2 tablespoons lemon juice
1 tablespoon egg white
15 ice cubes
1 drop Angostura bitters, to finish (optional)

Assemble all the ingredients in a cocktail shaker with the ice and shake for 7 seconds to ensure they are mixed and chilled.

Strain into a cocktail glass, finishing with a drop of Angostura bitters, if desired.

OLD CHUSCO
PISCO, ORANGE, AND GINGER ALE COCKTAIL

Serves: 1
Preparation Time: 5 minutes

1¼ oz (30 g) granulated sugar
¼ orange, sliced
6 drops Angostura bitters
4 tablespoons Quebranta pisco
15 ice cubes
ginger ale, to top off
1 cherry, to garnish

Place the sugar, orange, and Angostura bitters in a cocktail shaker. Gently crush the ingredients with a cocktail muddler or pestle, then add the pisco and ice. Shake for 5 seconds. Pour into a tall glass and top off with ginger ale. Garnish with a cherry.

SOL Y SOMBRA
PISCO, GINGER ALE, LEMON, AND MORELLO CHERRY COCKTAIL

Serves: 1
Preparation Time: 5 minutes

4 tablespoons pisco
½ cup (4 fl oz/120 ml) ginger ale
½ orange slice
15 ice cubes
1½ teaspoons lemon juice
1½ teaspoons morello cherry liqueur

Pour the pisco and ginger ale into a tall glass and add the half orange slice and ice cubes. Pour in the lemon juice and cherry liqueur to finish.

Serve with a straw.

TRAMPOSITO
PISCO, ORANGE, AND PASSION FRUIT COCKTAIL

Serves: 1
Preparation Time: 5 minutes

1½ teaspoons fresh orange juice
1 sprig huacatay, plus 1 extra to garnish
4 tablespoons Quebranta pisco
1 tablespoon sugar syrup
4 tablespoons fresh passion fruit juice
15 ice cubes
1 orange slice, to garnish

Place the orange juice and huacatay sprig in a cocktail shaker. Using a cocktail muddler or pestle, crush the huacatay to release its flavor. Add the remaining liquid ingredients and ice and shake for 7 seconds. Strain twice and pour into a tall glass.

Garnish with a huacatay sprig and an orange slice.

BASIC RECIPES

ADEREZO DE AJÍ AMARILLO, AJO Y CEBOLLA

YELLOW CHILI, GARLIC, AND ONION CONDIMENT

Makes: 1½ cups (12 oz/350 g)
Preparation Time: 5 minutes
Cooking Time: 20 minutes

⅓ cup (2½ fl oz/75 ml) vegetable oil
½ red onion, finely chopped
12 cloves garlic, finely chopped
1 cup (8 fl oz/250 ml) Blended Yellow Chiles (see p. 404)
salt

Heat the oil in a pan over low heat, add the chopped onion, and sauté until golden. Add the garlic and cook for another 3 minutes, then add the blended chiles and cook gently, stirring, until the mixture browns. Season with salt. After about 15 minutes, the oil will start to separate from the mixture, indicating that you have achieved the desired consistency. Remove from the heat and cool.

This condiment can be frozen and makes the ideal accompaniment to casseroles, rice dishes, soups, and stews.

ADEREZO DE AJÍ MIRASOL, AJO Y CEBOLLA

MIRASOL CHILI, GARLIC, AND ONION CONDIMENT

Makes: 1½ cups (12 oz/350 g)
Preparation Time: 5 minutes
Cooking Time: 20 minutes

⅓ cup (2½ fl oz/75 ml) vegetable oil
½ red onion, finely chopped
12 cloves garlic, very finely chopped
1 cup (8 fl oz/250 ml) Mirasol Chili Paste (see p. 405)
salt

Heat the oil in a pan over low heat, add the chopped onion, and sauté until golden. Add the garlic and cook for another 3 minutes, then add the blended chiles and cook gently, stirring, until the mixture browns. Season with salt. After about 15 minutes the oil will start to separate from the mixture, indicating that you have achieved the desired consistency. Remove from the heat and cool.

This condiment can be frozen and makes the ideal accompaniment to casseroles, rice dishes, soups, and stews.

ADEREZO DE AJÍ PANCA, AJO Y CEBOLLA
PANCA CHILI, GARLIC, AND ONION CONDIMENT

Makes: 1½ cups (12 oz/350 g)
Preparation Time: 5 minutes
Cooking Time: 20 minutes

⅓ cup (2½ fl oz/75 ml) vegetable oil
½ red onion, finely chopped
12 cloves garlic, finely chopped
1 cup (8 fl oz/250 ml) Panca Chili Paste (see p. 406)
salt

Heat the oil in a pan over low heat, add the chopped onion, and sauté until golden. Add the garlic and cook for another 3 minutes, then add the panca chili paste and cook gently, stirring, until the mixture browns. Season with salt. After about 15 minutes the oil will start to separate from the mixture, indicating that you have achieved the desired consistency. Remove from the heat and cool.

This condiment can be frozen and makes the ideal accompaniment to casseroles, rice dishes, soups, and stews.

ADEREZO DE ANTICUCHO
ANTICUCHERA SAUCE

Makes: 4½ lb (2 kg)
Preparation Time: 5 minutes

2 cups (18 fl oz/500 ml) Panca Chili Paste (see p. 406)
¾ cup (6 fl oz/175 ml) Garlic Paste (see p. 406)
½ tablespoon black peppercorns, ground
1 tablespoon whole cumin seeds, ground
1 tablespoon oregano leaves, ground
3¼ oz (90 g) salt
2 cups (18 fl oz/500 ml) red wine vinegar
2½ cups (20 fl oz/600 ml) vegetable oil

Place all the ingredients in a bowl and mix together thoroughly. Set aside for 2 hours before using to allow the flavors to blend.

This sauce will keep for some time if refrigerated—just spoon out the amount you need for each new recipe. Use it to prepare *anticuchos* (grilled meat skewers), marinate chicken, or as an accompaniment to fried chicken and barbecued meat dishes.

ADEREZO DE CEBOLLA
ONION CONDIMENT

Makes: 5½ lb (2.5 kg)
Preparation Time: 5 minutes
Cooking Time: 3–4 hours

2 cups (18 fl oz/ 500 ml) vegetable oil
11 lb (5 kg) red onions, diced

Heat the oil in a pan over very low heat, add the onion and cook, stirring occasionally, for 3–4 hours, until caramelized. Remove from the heat and cool.

Once cooled, drain off any excess oil, put in a blender, and blend together thoroughly. Spoon into a suitable container and refrigerate until needed. This onion condiment acts as a base for other condiments and soups.

AJÍ AMARILLO LICUADO
BLENDED YELLOW CHILE

Makes: 14 oz (400 g)
Preparation Time: 15 minutes

1 lb 2 oz (500 g) yellow chiles, seeded, membrane removed, and cut into pieces
½ cup (4 fl oz/120 ml) vegetable oil

Put the chile pieces in a blender with the oil and blend together for about 5 minutes, until thoroughly blended. Strain the mixture to remove any remaining chile pieces, then transfer to a suitable container.

This condiment is best used immediately, though it will keep refrigerated in an airtight container for 2 days. Use it to prepare *tiraditos* (Peruvian raw fish dishes), tiger milk (lemon, chile, and fish sauce), and Creole sauce.

PASTA DE AJÍ AMARILLO
YELLOW CHILI PASTE

Makes: approx. 14 oz (400 g)
Preparation Time: 25 minutes
Cooking Time: 8–10 minutes

2¼ lb (1 kg) yellow chiles, seeded, membrane removed, and cut into pieces
1 tablespoon vegetable oil

Place the chiles in a pan with enough cold water to cover and bring to a boil, then remove from the heat and drain. Repeat the process 3 times, changing the water each time.

Put the blanched chiles in a blender with the vegetable oil and a tablespoon of water and blend for about 5 minutes, to form a thick paste. Once the mixture is well blended, push it through a strainer (sieve).

This chili paste is best used immediately, though it will keep refrigerated in an airtight container for 2 days. It can be used to prepare dressings and stews.

AJÍ MIRASOL LICUADO
MIRASOL CHILI PASTE

Makes: approx. 1¾ lb (800 g)
Preparation Time: 25 minutes, plus 12 hours soaking

2¼ lb (1 kg) dried Mirasol chiles

Thoroughly wash the mirasol chiles to remove any dust or dirt. Cut in half lengthwise and remove the seeds and veins.

Put the chiles in a bowl, cover with water, and let soak for 12 hours or overnight, changing the water 3–4 times during the soaking.

Once soaked, drain the chiles and put in a blender with ½ cup (4 fl oz/120 ml) boiling water. Blend together thoroughly for about 5 minutes, then strain the mixture to remove any remaining chile pieces.

Transfer to a suitable container and keep refrigerated until needed. This chili condiment acts as a base for other condiments, stews, and soups.

AJÍ PANCA LICUADO
PANCA CHILI PASTE

Makes: 1½ cups (12 oz/350 g)
Preparation Time: 20 minutes, plus 12 hours soaking

1 lb 2 oz (500 g) dried panca chiles

Thoroughly wash the panca chiles to remove any dust or dirt. Cut in half lengthwise and remove the seeds and veins.

Put the chiles in a bowl, cover with water, and let soak for 12 hours or overnight, changing the water 3 or 4 times during the soaking.

Once soaked, drain the chiles and put in a blender with ½ cup (4 fl oz/120 ml) boiling water. Blend together thoroughly for about 5 minutes, then strain the mixture. Transfer to a suitable container and keep refrigerated until needed.

AJO MOLIDO
GARLIC PASTE

Makes: approx. 2¼ lb (1 kg)
Preparation Time: 20 minutes

2¼ lb (1 kg) cloves garlic, peeled

Place the garlic cloves in a blender. Pour in 1 cup (8 fl oz/250 ml) water and blend for about 5 minutes. Once thoroughly blended, transfer to a suitable container and keep refrigerated or frozen until needed.

This paste can be used to prepare other condiments, stews, and soups.

PULPO COCIDO
COOKED OCTOPUS

Makes: 4½ lb (2 kg)
Preparation Time: 15 minutes, plus overnight freezing and thawing
Cooking Time: 1 hour

Quickly blanching the octopus 3 times will mean that it does not shrink when boiled.

4½ lb (2 kg) octopus
1 cup (8 oz/225 g) of fine salt

Wash the octopus well to remove mucus. Freeze for 24 hours then defrost in the refrigerator.

Heat a saucepan with 170 fl oz/5 liters of water. When the water is hot but not boiling, put the octopus into the pot and remove it quickly. Repeat this three times.

Return the octopus into the pot and cook for 45 minutes until tender.

CULANTRO O SACHA CULANTRO LICUADO
BLENDED CULANTRO OR SACHA

CULANTRO

Makes: 3 cups (25 fl oz/750 ml)
Preparation Time: 15 minutes

1 lb 5 oz (600 g) culantro or cilantro (coriander) or sacha culantro

Thoroughly wash the culantro or cilantro (coriander) or sacha culantro to remove any soil or dirt.

Drain and place in a blender. Pour in 1 cup (8 fl oz/250 ml) water and process for about 4 minutes, until thoroughly blended.

Strain into a suitable container and refrigerate until needed. Culantro browns quickly, so it is best to use it on the same day.

Blended culantro can be used to prepare aguaditos (Peruvian chicken soup) and rice dishes.

ROCOTO MOLIDO
ROCOTO CHILI PASTE

Makes: approx. 1 lb 10½ oz (750 g)
Preparation Time: 20 minutes

2¼ lb (1 kg) rocoto chiles, seeded, membrane removed, and cut into pieces
1 cup (8 fl oz/250 ml) vegetable oil

Put the chile pieces in a blender with the oil and blend together for about 5 minutes, until thoroughly blended. Strain the mixture to remove any remaining chile pieces, then transfer to a suitable container.

This condiment is best used immediately, though it will keep refrigerated for 2 days. Use it to prepare *tiraditos* (Peruvian raw fish dishes), tiger milk (lemon, chile, and fish sauce), and ceviches.

CAMARONES COCIDOS
COOKED SHRIMP

Makes: 8 shrimp (prawns)
Preparation Time: 5 minutes
Cook Time: 1 minute

1 tablespoon of fine salt
8 shrimp (prawns), shelled and deveined
iced water

Heat a saucepan with 4¼ cups (34 fl oz/1 liter) of water and the salt.

When the water is boiling, cook the shrimp (prawns) for 1 minute.

Drain and cool immediately in bowl of iced water to stop the shrimp cooking.

Keep in the refrigerator if you are not using the shrimp immediately.

ACEITE DE ACHIOTE
ANNATTO OIL

Makes: 1 cup (8 fl oz/250 ml)
Preparation Time: 2 minutes
Cooking Time: 25 minutes

5 tablespoons annatto seeds
1 cup (8 fl oz/250 ml) vegetable oil

Put the annatto seeds and vegetable oil in a pan and cook over medium heat for 25 minutes, until the oil turns a reddish color similar to that of the seeds. Remove from the heat and cool to room temperature.

Once cool, strain and store the oil in a bottle or jar with a tight-fitting cap or lid. Refrigerate until needed.

PASTA DE ACEITUNAS NEGRAS O ACEITUNAS VERDES
BLACK OR GREEN OLIVE PASTE

Makes: 2 cups (8 fl oz/250 ml)
Preparation Time: 10 minutes
Cooking Time: 10 minutes

12 oz (350 g) pitted black or green olives
2 tablespoons vegetable oil

Bring a pan of water to a boil, add the olives, and blanch for 5 minutes to remove the taste of brine. Drain.

Heat the vegetable oil in a pan over medium heat, add the olives, and sauté for 3 minutes. Remove from the heat, put in a blender, and blend to a thick paste. Once the mixture is well blended, push it through a strainer (sieve) to remove any remaining pieces. Transfer to a suitable container and keep refrigerated until needed.

This olive paste can be used to prepare any type of olive-based dressing or sauce, as well as *causa* potato dishes and many other recipes.

LECHE DE TIGRE BÁSICA
TIGER MILK

Makes: 2½–3 cups (20–25 fl oz/600–750 ml)
Preparation Time: 5 minutes

1 cup (8 fl oz/250 ml) lemon juice
⅓ cup (2 oz/50 g) fish trimmings
½ cup (4 fl oz/120 ml) fish stock
1 small celery
1 red onion
1 teaspoon salt
10 ice cubes
½ limo chile
1 teaspoon chopped culantro or cilantro (coriander) leaves

Place all the ingredients in a blender and blend.

Taste and add more salt if necessary. Strain and refrigerate the mixture for later use.

This basic tiger milk is suitable not only for preparing ceviches, but can also be used to enhance the flavor of *parihuela* (spicy seafood stew), *sudado* (classic Peruvian fish stew), rice and shellfish dishes, and all types of Peruvian seafood dishes.

AJÍ DE COCONA
COCONA AND CHILI SALSA

Makes: 1 lb 4 oz (550 g)
Preparation Time: 20 minutes

3 cocona fruits, diced and juice reserved
3 tomatoes, skinned, seeded, and chopped
1½ tablespoons chopped sweet chile or limo chile
1 teaspoon chopped Charapita chile or yellow chile
1½ teaspoons chopped sacha culantro leaves
1 teaspoon chopped culantro or cilantro (coriander) leaves
juice of 10 small lemons
salt and pepper

Place the chopped cocona fruits, tomatoes, sweet chile, charapita chile, sacha culantro, and culantro or cilantro (coriander) in a bowl. Season with salt and mix together thoroughly.

Add the lemon juice and any cocona juice that was set aside during chopping. Mix together well and season to taste with salt and pepper.

Transfer to a suitable container and keep refrigerated until needed.

This salsa is excellent served with *juanes* (seasoned rice in bijao leaves), *tacacho con cecina* (plantain fritters with smoked pork meat), fresh heart of palm salad, grilled fish, and *patarashca* (stuffed fish wrapped in bijao leaves).

AJÍ DE HUACATAY
GREEN ROCOTO CHILI AND HUACATAY SAUCE

Makes: 4¼ cups (34 fl oz/1 liter)
Preparation Time: 20 minutes
Cooking Time: 10 minutes

1 cup (8 fl oz/250 ml) vegetable oil
1 lb 8½ oz (700 g) green rocoto chiles, seeded, membrane removed, and cut into pieces
1 small red onion, chopped
3 cloves garlic, chopped
8 oz (225 g) roasted peanuts
½ tablespoon chopped huacatay leaves
3¼ oz (90 g) queso fresco
4 saltine crackers or savory crackers
1 tablespoon white wine vinegar
½ tablespoon chopped parsley

Heat the oil in a pan over medium heat, add the chiles, onion, and garlic, and sauté for about 9 minutes until the onion is golden. Remove from the heat and drain the oil without discarding it.

Put the chile mixture in a blender with the roasted peanuts, chopped huacatay, queso fresco, saltine crackers, vinegar, and parsley. Blend together, gradually drizzling in the oil from the sautéed chiles, until you have a smooth emulsion. Transfer to a suitable container and keep refrigerated until needed.

This sauce is best served with potatoes, corn on the cob, fritters, and sandwiches.

AJÍ DE POLLERÍA
CHICKEN CONDIMENT

Makes: 4¼ cups (34 fl oz/1 liter)
Preparation Time: 20 minutes

6 yellow chiles, seeded, membrane removed, and cut into pieces
½ tablespoon mustard
3½ tablespoons Blended Yellow Chiles (see p. 404)
1 egg
1 clove garlic, chopped
pinch of ground cumin
½ teaspoon chopped huacatay leaves
pinch of oregano leaves
salt and pepper
1 tablespoon white wine vinegar
2½ cups (20 fl oz/600 ml) vegetable oil

Place the chile pieces in a blender with the mustard, blended chiles, egg, and garlic. Add the cumin, chopped huacatay leaves, and fresh oregano and season with salt and pepper. Pour in the white wine vinegar and blend for a couple of minutes to combine all the ingredients.

Continue to blend, drizzling in the vegetable oil, until the sauce emulsifies to a mayonnaise-like consistency.

Transfer to a suitable container and keep refrigerated until needed.

This condiment is best served with sandwiches, barbecued chicken, and other recipes such as *tequeños* (cheese-filled wonton fingers), croquettes, and *empanadas* (South American pastries).

CREMA DE AJÍ AMARILLO
YELLOW CHILI CREAM

Makes: 1 cup (8 fl oz/250 ml)
Preparation Time: 10 minutes
Cooking Time: 12 minutes

3 tablespoons vegetable oil
9 oz (250 g) yellow chiles, seeded, membrane removed, and cut into pieces
9 oz (250 g) queso fresco
salt and pepper

Heat the oil in a pan over medium heat, add the chiles, and cook, stirring occasionally, for about 10 minutes, until softened. Remove from the heat and drain the oil without discarding it.

Place the sautéed chiles in a blender. Add the queso fresco and season with salt and pepper. Blend together, gradually drizzling in the oil from the sautéed chiles, until you have a thick cream.

Pour into a suitable container and keep refrigerated until needed. This chili cream is best served with fried yucca root (cassava) and *chicharrones* (fried pork rind).

CREMA DE ROCOTO
ROCOTO CHILI CREAM

Makes: approx. 2¼ lb (1 kg)
Preparation Time: 20 minutes
Cooking Time: 10 minutes

¾ cup (6 fl oz/175 ml) vegetable oil
2¼ lb (1 kg) rocoto chiles, seeded, membrane removed, and cut into pieces
½ small red onion, chopped
2 cloves garlic, chopped
½ tablespoon ground cumin
4 saltine crackers or savory crackers
4 oz (120 g) queso fresco
salt and pepper

Heat the oil in a pan over medium heat, add the chiles, onion, and garlic and cook, stirring occasionally, for 3 minutes. Add the cumin and sauté for another 6 minutes or so, until the onion has softened. Remove from the heat and drain the oil without discarding it. Cool.

Place the sautéed chili mixture in a blender. Add the saltine crackers and queso fresco and season with salt and pepper. Blend together, gradually drizzling in the oil from the sautéed chiles, until you have a thick cream.

Pour into a suitable container and keep refrigerated until needed. This chili cream is best served with fritters and grilled dishes.

HUANCAÍNA A LA ANTIGUA
OLD-FASHIONED HUANCAÍNA SAUCE

Makes: approx. 2¼ lb (1 kg)
Preparation Time: 15 minutes

13 oz (375 g) yellow chiles, seeded, membrane removed, and cut into pieces
⅓ cup (2½ fl oz/75 ml) vegetable oil
7 oz (200 g) queso fresco
1 saltine cracker or savory cracker
1 × 14-fl oz (410-ml) can evaporated milk
1½ teaspoons salt

Place the chiles and vegetable oil in a mortar or *batán* (Peruvian grinder). Slowly start grinding together, gradually adding the queso fresco, saltine cracker, and evaporated milk as you go, to form a chunky, thick paste. Stir in the salt, transfer to a suitable container, and refrigerate until needed.

This sauce is an ideal accompaniment to potatoes and pasta.

MAYONESA
MAYONNAISE

Makes: 4 cups (2 lb/900 g)
Preparation Time: 8 minutes

1 egg
1 teaspoon mustard
juice of 1 small lemon
4¼ cups (34 fl oz/1 liter) vegetable oil
salt and pepper

Place the egg, mustard, and lemon juice in a blender. Season with salt and pepper. Blend together, gradually drizzling in the oil, until thick and creamy. If too thick, thin with a little water.

Transfer to a suitable container and keep refrigerated until needed.

Mayonnaise can be used to prepare the filling for *causas* (Peruvian potato dishes), as a condiment for a number of dishes, and as a base for other sauces.

SALSA TÁRTARA
TARTAR SAUCE

Makes: 1½ cups (13 fl oz/375 ml)
Preparation Time: 5 minutes

8 oz (225 g) Mayonnaise (see above)
1 egg, hard-boiled and chopped
1 tablespoon capers, chopped
1½ oz (40 g) small dill pickles (gherkins), chopped
1 white onion, finely chopped
1 teaspoon mustard
1 teaspoon chopped parsley leaves
salt and pepper

Put the mayonnaise, chopped egg, capers, dill pickles (gherkins), onion, mustard, and parsley in a bowl. Season with salt and mix together well. Season to taste with salt and pepper.

Transfer to a suitable container and keep refrigerated until needed. This sauce is generally served as an accompaniment to fish chicharrones (fried fish dishes) and fritters, as well as sandwiches and snacks.

HUANCAÍNA ACTUAL
HUANCAÍNA SAUCE

Makes: approx. 2¼ lb (1 kg)
Preparation Time: 10 minutes
Cooking Time: 10 minutes

¼ cup(2½ fl oz/75 ml) vegetable oil
9 oz (250 g) yellow chiles, seeded, membrane removed and cut into halves
¼ red onion, chopped
2 cloves garlic, chopped
1¾ cups (14 fl oz/400 ml) evaporated milk
4½ oz (130 g) queso fresco
4 saltine crackers or savory crackers
salt

Heat the oil in a skillet or frying pan over high heat, add the chile halves, onion, and garlic and cook, stirring, for 7 minutes, until softened. Place in a blender, and add the evaporated milk, queso fresco, and saltine crackers. Season with salt and blend to a smooth, creamy puree.

Transfer to a suitable container and refrigerate until needed. This sauce is an ideal accompaniment to pasta, hot appetizers, and nibbles.

LLATÁN
LLATÁN SAUCE

Makes: approx. 1 lb 8½ oz (700 g)
Preparation Time: 10 minutes
Cooking Time: 10 minutes

½ cup (4 fl oz/120 ml) vegetable oil
2 green rocoto chiles, seeded, membrane removed, and halved
1 red onion, chopped
4 cloves garlic
2 tablespoons chopped huacatay leaves
1 tablespoon chopped wormseed
salt

Heat the oil in a skillet or frying pan over medium heat, add the rocoto chiles, onion, garlic, huacatay, and wormseed, and sauté for 7 minutes, until the onion has softened. Remove from the heat and drain the oil without discarding it. Cool.

Place the sautéed mixture in a blender and season with salt. Blend together, gradually drizzling in the reserved oil, until you have a thick cream.

Pour into a suitable container and refrigerate until needed. This sauce is an ideal accompaniment to stews, *chicharrones* (fried pork rind), and fried guinea pig.

MANJAR BLANCO CLÁSICO
CLASSIC DULCE DE LECHE

Makes: 1 lb 7 oz (650 g)
Preparation Time: 2 minutes
Cooking Time: 1 hour 30 minutes

2 cups (18 fl oz/500 ml) evaporated milk
2 cups (18 fl oz/500 ml) full-fat (whole) milk
1¾ cups (15 fl oz/ 425 ml) condensed milk
1 teaspoon vanilla extract

Pour the evaporated milk, fresh milk, condensed milk, and vanilla extract into a heavy pan. Place over medium heat and simmer, stirring, until the mixture has thickened and the bottom of the pan can be seen when you draw the spoon across it.

Remove the heat, cool, and refrigerate until needed. This dulce de leche can be eaten on its own or used as a filling for various desserts and sweets.

MANJAR DE CHOCOLATE
CHOCOLATE DULCE DE LECHE

Makes: 1 lb (450 g)
Preparation Time: 2 minutes
Cooking Time: 1 hour

1¾ cups (14 fl oz/400 ml) condensed milk
1¾ cups (14 fl oz/400 ml) evaporated milk
3 oz (80 g) bitter dark chocolate, broken into pieces
1½ tablespoons cocoa paste (cocoa mass)
1 teaspoon vanilla extract

Pour the condensed and evaporated milks into a heavy pan. Place over medium heat and simmer, stirring, until the mixture has thickened and the bottom of the pan can be seen when you draw the spoon across it.

Add the dark chocolate and the cocoa paste and stir together until the chocolate has melted. Add the vanilla. Remove from the heat, cool, and refrigerate until needed.

OCOPA
OCOPA SAUCE

Makes: approx. 3¼ lb (1.5 kg)
Preparation Time: 15 minutes
Cooking Time: 8 minutes

¾ cup (6 fl oz/175 ml) vegetable oil
1 lb 10½ oz (750 g) Mirasol chiles, seeded, membrane removed, and finely chopped
½ red onion, finely chopped
4 cloves garlic
7 oz (200 g) queso fresco
2¾ oz (70 g) animalito cookies
1 tablespoon chopped huacatay leaves
¾ oz (20 g) roasted peanuts
1 cup (8 fl oz/250 ml) evaporated milk
salt

Heat the oil in a skillet or frying pan over medium heat, add the chiles, onion, and garlic, and sauté for a few minutes, stirring, until the chiles have softened and the onion have cooked. Remove from the heat and cool.

Place the cooled chile and onion mixture in a blender, add the queso fresco, animalito cookies, huacatay leaves, and peanuts. Season with salt and blend, gradually adding the evaporated milk and 1 cup (8 fl oz/250 ml) water, until creamy. Transfer to a suitable container and keep refrigerated until needed. Ocopa sauce is the ideal accompaniment to *causas* (Peruvian potato dishes), cooked potatoes, and pasta.

SALSA CARRETILLA
CARRETILLA SAUCE

Makes: approx. 2¼ lb (1 kg)
Preparation Time: 20 minutes

3 rocoto chiles, seeded, membrane removed, and cut into pieces
¼ red onion, chopped
1 clove garlic, chopped
a pinch of ground cumin
a pinch of oregano
½ tablespoon chopped huacatay leaves
1 tablespoon red wine vinegar
2½ cups (20 fl oz/600 ml) vegetable oil
½ tablespoon chopped scallion (spring onion), green part only
salt and pepper

Put the rocoto chiles in a blender with the red onion, garlic, cumin, oregano, huacatay, and vinegar. Season with salt and pepper and blend together, gradually drizzling in the oil, until creamy. To prevent the sauce from becoming too hot and splitting, pause the blending every 3 minutes.

Once creamy, transfer to a suitable container, add the chopped scallion (spring onion), and keep refrigerated until needed. Carretilla sauce is the ideal accompaniment to *anticuchos* (grilled meat skewers), fritters, and *empanadas* (South American pasties).

SALSA CRIOLLA
CREOLE SAUCE

Makes: 5 oz (150 g)
Preparation Time: 5 minutes, plus 5 minutes soaking

½ red onion, thinly sliced
ice cubes
1 limo chile, seeded, membrane removed, and thinly sliced
1 tablespoon chopped culantro or cilantro (coriander) leaves
juice of 3 small lemons
salt

Soak the onion slices in iced water for 5 minutes to crisp. Remove from the water, drain, and place in a bowl.

Add the sliced chile, culantro or cilantro (coriander), and lemon juice to the onion. Season with salt and mix together thoroughly. This sauce is best served immediately and is the ideal accompaniment to *chicharrones* (fried pork rind), rice dishes, stews, fish and other dishes. A different variety of Creole sauce is made in northern Peru, which is pickled for longer and includes chopped radish and blended yellow chiles as additional ingredients.

SALSA DE AJÍ AMARILLO
YELLOW CHILI SAUCE

Makes: approx. 1½ cups (13 fl oz/375 ml)
Preparation Time: 5 minutes

1 cup (8 fl oz/250 ml) Blended Yellow Chiles (see p. 404)
juice of 3 small lemons
2 tablespoons chopped scallion (spring onion), green part only
salt and pepper

Put the blended chiles in a bowl with the lemon juice and season with salt. Mix together thoroughly. Add the chopped scallion (spring onion) and adjust the seasoning to taste.

Transfer to a suitable container and keep refrigerated until needed. This sauce is the ideal accompaniment to baked potatoes, corn on the cob, and grilled meats.

SALSA DE ROCOTO POPULAR
POPULAR ROCOTO CHILI SAUCE

Makes: approx. 2¼ lb (1 kg)
Preparation Time: 20 minutes

2¼ lb (1 kg) red rocoto chiles, seeded, deveined, and cut into pieces
3 cloves garlic
¼ cup (2 fl oz/50 ml) white wine vinegar
2 tablespoons chopped scallion (spring onion), green part only
1 red onion, finely chopped
salt and pepper

Put the chile pieces in a blender with the garlic, vinegar, and 1 tablespoon of salt and blend together until smooth.

Add the chopped scallion (spring onion) and red onion, taste, and adjust the seasoning if necessary. Transfer to a suitable container and keep refrigerated until needed. This sauce is the ideal accompaniment to stews, rice dishes, and grilled dishes.

UCHUCUTA
UCHUCUTA SAUCE

Makes: approx. 1¾ lb (800 g)
Preparation Time: 15 minutes

4 green rocoto chiles, seeded, membrane removed, and chopped
1 cucumber, peeled, seeded, and grated
¾ oz (20 g) peanuts
3 tablespoons chopped huacatay leaves
2 tablespoons evaporated milk
¼ red onion, chopped
1 tablespoon chopped culantro or cilantro (coriander) leaves
2 oz (50 g) queso fresco
salt

Put all the ingredients in a blender, season with salt, and blend until the mixture becomes a creamy sauce. If it thickens too much, thin with a little more milk or water. The texture will depend on the blending time: less time will give it a coarser texture and more time will make it smoother.

Transfer to a suitable container and keep refrigerated until needed.

Uchucuta sauce is the ideal accompaniment to cooked potatoes, *pachamanca* (marinated meat baked on hot stones), *huatia* (Peruvian slow-cooked beef), and *chicharrons* (fried pork rind).

GLOSSARY

AMARANTH
Tiny seed of an Andean plant packed with amino acids and nutrients. Used in soups, stews, and sauces, it can also be toasted and used in desserts, cookies (biscuits), and breads. It has been consumed since pre-Hispanic times.

ANIMALITO COOKIES
Sweet, crumbly, animal-shaped cookies (biscuits) with a mild vanilla flavor. Used to prepare certain Peruvian dishes, such as *carapulcra* (pork and potato stew) and various sauces.

ANNATTO
Seed of an Amazonian tree used as a condiment. The seeds produce a reddish paste, which is used as a food dye in Peruvian cuisine. It is this ingredient that gives *jamón del país* (Peruvian ham) its characteristic color.

ARRACACHA
An Andean root vegetable whose flesh can be white, yellow, or purple. Arracachas are very starchy, have a slightly sweet taste and can be boiled, fried, or added to soups, stews, and desserts. Its cultivation pre-dates the Incas.

BANANA LEAVES
Leaves of the banana tree used to wrap and steam traditional Peruvian tamales.

BANANA PASSIONFRUIT
A medium-size, oval-shaped fruit with very pleasant-tasting, bitter-sweet, and slightly sour pulp. In Peru, banana passionfruits produced in the north and in the jungle are the largest and sweetest; those grown in the mountains are small and sour. They are used in juices, desserts, ice creams, and cocktails.

BEANS
Dried or fresh legumes (pulses) used to prepare soups, salads, and desserts. A wide variety of beans are used in Peruvian dishes such as the tacu tacu (fried rice and bean cakes). Canario (canary) beans and black beans are among the most popular.

BEAN SPROUTS
Ingredient used in Chinese-Peruvian or chifa cuisine also known as soy sprouts.

BIJAO LEAVES
Leaves of an Amazonian plant used in Peruvian cuisine to wrap and cook dishes such as tamales (corn-based dough and meat wrapped in bijao leaves) and *juanes* (rice and meat /fish wrapped in bijao leaves), which infuse the food with a certain flavor and aroma.

BITTER ORANGE
A fragrant orange with a very distinctive taste cultivated along the Peruvian coast and in the Peruvian highlands and Amazon. Decades ago, it was regularly used to make ceviche until it was replaced by lemons. It is still used for this purpose in northern Lima, however.

CACAO
Cacao was originally cultivated by pre-Hispanic peoples and is currently cultivated in Cusco, Ayacucho, Junín, Huánuco, San Martín, the Amazon, and Piura. Organic Peruvian cacao is used more and more by chocolatiers around the world due to its richness and flavor.

CAMU CAMU
An Amazonian fruit native to Peru that is round, smooth-skinned, and plum-colored. It is sour and rich in vitamin C, containing more than thirty times the amount of vitamin C as an orange. It is used in jams, ice creams, drinks, and in cocktails due to its very distinctive taste and sharpness.

CAÑIHUA
An Andean plant whose seeds are packed with protein. Cañihua seeds are toasted and ground to produce flour that is used in soups, breads, cakes, and cookies (biscuits).

CAROB SYRUP
An extremely flavorsome extract obtained from carob fruit which is dark brown in color, thick, and sweet. It is typically found in northern Peru and has energizing and fortifying properties. Carob syrup is used in desserts, sauces, drinks, and in the famous carob syrup cocktail.

CHANCACA
Dark brown unrefined sugar or sugar cane molasses, which is shaped into a half-ball or block when solid. This half-ball or slab of chancaca is traditionally sold in pairs, making a full ball. It is used in desserts, drinks and to prepare syrups for *picarones* (doughnut-like dessert) or *alfajores* (double-decker cookies).

CHARAPITA HOT CHILE
A small, round, orange Amazonian chile that is aromatic and very spicy. It is used to prepare sauces and can be preserved or pickled. It is widely used in Peruvian jungle regions, where it is believed to be an aphrodisiac.

CHERIMOYA
Fruit with a thin green peel and white flesh that is sweet, juicy, and slightly tart. The cherimoyas of Cumbe, east of Lima, are renowned for being large, fleshy, and delicious, with very few seeds. Can be eaten fresh and used in desserts, drinks, and ice creams.

CHICHA DE JORA (PERUVIAN CORN BEER)
An alcoholic beverage made from jora or germinated corn kernels that are sun-dried and ground. It has been brewed throughout the Andes since pre-Hispanic times. Today, it is made using traditional methods and consumed across Peru, and also used in recipes such as goat stew.

CHIFLES
A snack consisting of finely sliced green plantains that are fried in vegetable oil and seasoned with salt. Chifles can be savory, sweet, or spicy.

CHILE PEPPER
Fruit with a spicy flavor that varies in intensity, depending on the type of chilli. Peruvian chiles come in various colors, shapes, and sizes and are originally from the Andes and Amazon region. They can be eaten whole or ground (minced), fresh or dried, pickled or in their natural state. The seeds and veins are removed to reduce the intensity of the heat. Chile peppers are the foundation of Peruvian cooking and distinguish it from other cuisines.

CHINCHO
An extremely aromatic herb used to flavor dishes such as *pachamanca* (meat dish cooked on hot stones) and typical mountain region soups.

CHUÑO (FREEZE-DRIED POTATOES)
Potatoes that are dried through exposure to ice and sun. Different varieties of Andean potatoes are frozen outdoors, then exposed to sunlight and pressed until dry. There are two types of *chuño*: *chuño negro* (black chuño) and *chuño blanco* (white chuño), also known as *moraya*, which is run under water after drying.

COCONA
A tart, bittersweet Amazonian fruit that is oval-shaped and yellow-orange in color. Used in juices, jams, compotes, cocktails, ice creams, and sauces. It has been cultivated in Peru since ancient times.

CORN HUSKS
Soft green leaves that surround corn cobs and are used to wrap traditional Peruvian *humitas* (fresh corn cakes).

CORN NUTS
Corn kernels that are toasted in a pan with oil and salt until golden brown. Corn nuts are eaten in the Andean region as a snack or nibbles and are used to garnish seafood dishes such as ceviche. They are also served with cocktails and aperitifs. The most well-known type of corn nut is known as *chulpi*.

CORNCOB
Young corncobs with milky and slightly sweet kernels. These are cultivated in different regions of Peru, but those produced in Cusco are famous for their extraordinary flavor and size. The best Andean corncobs are produced between December and April, while corncobs produced on the coast are harvested all year round.

CULANTRO
An aromatic herb used in many Peruvian dishes due to its distinctive flavor and aroma. A key ingredient in sauces and recipes such as goat stew, rice with duck, and various chowders. Some people also like to add small amounts of culantro to ceviches. Cilantro (coriander) may be used as a substitute.

DRIED MEAT (CECINA)
Pork or beef that has been preserved with salt and air-dried or smoked. This process prevents it from hardening and gives it a pleasant taste when fried or grilled. In the Amazon, dried meat can also be made from peccary meat and other types of game.

DRIED MUTTON/ALPACA/ LLAMA (CHALONA)
Dried mutton/alpaca/llama, which is processed in a similar way to cecina, in other words, salted and sun-dried. It is consumed mainly in the southern highlands of Peru.

DRIED POTATOES
These are dehydrated potatoes that are cubed and appear to be crystallized. One of the main ingredients in traditional *carapulcra limeña* (Lima-style pork and dried potato stew), these potatoes need to be soaked and rehydrated before cooking.

DRIED POTATOES
These are dehydrated potatoes that are cubed and appear to be crystallised. One of the main ingredients in traditional *carapulcra limeña* (Lima-style pork and dried potato stew), these potatoes need to be soaked and rehydrated before cooking.

DULCE DE LECHE
A creamy confection prepared with milk and sugar that traditionally requires hours of cooking. Other ingredients such as almonds and fruit pulp, among others, can also be added. It is served as a dessert or can be used as a filling or topping for cakes, alfajor cookies (biscuits), *guargüeros* (fried sugary tubes filled with dulce de leche), and other sweets.

FIG-LEAF GOURD
A fruit similar to pumpkin with a green and white speckled skin. The flesh of the fig-leaf gourd is white and is used to prepare stews, *ajiacos* (potato and chili stew) and traditional soups, such as spicy fig-leaf gourd.

FRENCH BREAD ROLLS
Very popular bread rolls that are widely consumed in Peru. They are small and round with a slash or dent in the middle. The bread inside the rolls is white and dense and the crust can be either crispy or soft. It is sold in all Peruvian bakeries.

FRESH TURMERIC LEAVES
Used in Peruvian cooking and also known as "Amazonian saffron."

GRANADILLA
Fruit of a tropical plant cultivated in Peru since pre-Hispanic times. Oval-shaped with a brittle outer rind, the inside of the fruit contains a cluster of seeds surrounded by sweet, gelatinous pulp. It is used to prepare juices, desserts, and cocktails.

GINGER
Ginger is used in numerous Peruvian-Chinese or chifa dishes and is also added to soups, stews, and ceviches.

HEART OF PALM
A vegetable harvested from the inner core and growing bud of certain palm trees. Due to its fresh and mild taste, it is used to produce *chicha* (corn drink), creamed dishes, *juanes* (rice and meat/fish wrapped in bijao leaves) with *paiche* (type of fish) and salads.

HOMINY OR HOMINY CORN
Corn kernels that have been dried and treated with an alkali solution, originally consumed by pre-Hispanic peoples. Hominy grains are large and meaty.

HUACATAY
Aromatic herb that grows along the coast, in the highlands and jungles of Peru. Its intense aroma and flavor make it the ideal herb for soups, stews, sauces, and dishes such as *ocopa* (boiled potatoes in a creamy huacatay and chili sauce) or *huatia* (slow-cooked beef with herbs). It is a staple of Peruvian cuisine.

HUACHO SAUSAGE
A finely minced, cured pork sausage seasoned with salt, herbs, and spices. It has a distinctive orange color and is produced in Huacho, north of Lima. It can be fried, eaten uncooked, or mixed with scrambled eggs.

JERKED MEAT
Meat that is salted and sun-dried, originally produced in the Andes. It is prepared using a technique passed down from ancient Peruvians, who used llama and deer meat, beef, pork, and poultry to produce jerked meat. It is used in a number of typical dishes such as *ulluku* with jerked meat, jerked meat with rice, and *charquicán* (pork jerky and beef stew).

KUMQUAT
A tiny fruit measuring only 2 inches/ 5 cm in diameter that is both sweet and sour. It is used in Peru to prepare juices, sweets (cooked in syrup), jams, and traditional dishes such as stewed duck a la Chepén.

LEMON/LIME
A small, round acidic fruit with a yellow or green peel. Peruvian cuisine generally calls for a variety known as "key lime," which is widely used to prepare ceviches, sauces, desserts, and other dishes due to its tartness and refreshing taste.

LIMA (BUTTER) BEAN
A flat, kidney-shaped, cream-colored bean that is very popular in Peru. It has been consumed since pre-Hispanic times and is cultivated mainly on the coast, but also in the mountains. The lima beans of the Ica region are particularly well known. Peruvian markets sell dried lima beans, which need to be soaked prior to cooking, and also green or fresh lima beans.

LIMO HOT CHILI
A very spicy and aromatic chile. It comes in red, yellow, green, orange, white, and purple varieties and is commonly used to prepare ceviches due to its aroma and flavor.

LOCHE SQUASH
An elongated fruit with a dark green skin and golden orange flesh; it has a powerful aroma and delicious taste and is native to northern Peru. It is used in stews, purees, sweets and dishes such as *cabrito a la chiclayana* (goat à la chiclayana). Its cultivation can be traced back to 4,200 B.C.

LUCUMA
A small, round fruit measuring approximately 4 inches/10 cm in diameter, with a green peel and yellow, dry flesh that is sweet and very pleasant-tasting. Fresh lucuma can be used in drinks and cocktails or added to desserts, sweets, and also ground into flour for certain dishes.

MACRE SQUASH
A large, dark green pumpkin with bright yellow/orange flesh. It is used in soups, stews, puddings, purees, and desserts. It is the main ingredient of *locro* (type of stew) and *picarones* (doughnut-like dessert).

MANGROVE COCKLE
A dark bivalve mollusk found in Tumbes, on the northern coast of Peru, that lives beneath muddy soil or among mangrove roots. Due to its ability to exist outside water, it can live for up to seven days in humid environments. Mangrove cockles are used to prepare dishes such as ceviche and rice with mangrove cockles.

MANTECOSO CHEESE
Cheese with a distinctive texture and fat content that allow it to melt and add a very special texture to dishes.

MASHUA
Andean tuber of which over a hundred varieties are known, the most popular being the yellow mashua and the red speckled mashua. Eaten raw it has rather a sharp taste, but when exposed to sun and parboiled it has a sweet flavor.

MIRASOL HOT CHILE
These are yellow hot chiles that have undergone a sun drying process. They are used whole or minced to prepare condiments and add flavor to foods and sauces. The seeds and membrane are usually removed and then the chiles are soaked and used to prepare a paste.

MOCHERO HOT CHILE
A chile from the Moche river valley, in the La Libertad region. It is a medium-size chile that is either yellow or green. It is often used to prepare ceviches on the northern coast of Peru as it is widely produced in the region.

OCA
An Andean tuber cultivated at 9840–13,125 ft/3,000–4,000 m above sea level. Consumed raw it has a somewhat sharp taste, but exposure to sunlight gives it a sweet and pleasant flavor. There are around 50 different types of oca, with the most well-known grown in the regions of Áncash, Cusco, Puno, and Junín. The best way to cook oca is to boil or roast it.

PANCA HOT CHILE
A red chile that is dried in the sun while still on the plant. It is dark red in color and is not as spicy as yellow hot chiles. It can be used whole or as a paste and is the basis for various condiments and stews, such as adobo stew.

PARIA CHEESE
A cheese typical of southern Peru produced with a mixture of cow and sheep's milk. It is a firm, flavorsome, and salty cheese.

PASSION FRUIT
A round fruit with a tough green/yellow skin containing a cluster of seeds and plenty of golden-colored juice. It has a pleasant tartness and intense flavor and aroma, so is frequently used to prepare juices, soft drinks, sweets, jams, ice creams, sweet-and-sour sauces, and cocktails.

PHYSALIS
A small, round, yellow Andean fruit that is encased in a calyx of thin leaves, similar to a cocoon. It has a mild bittersweet taste and is used in jams, desserts, sauces, juices, and cocktails.

PISCO
A spirit made from pure fermented grape juice, which is distilled in copper stills. pisco has been produced in Peru since the seventeenth century and contains only grapes, with no added alcohol, water, or other ingredients. It is produced in the regions of Ica, Lima, Tacna, Moquegua, and Arequipa using Quebranta, Italia, Mollar, Torontel, Moscatel, Negra Criolla or Negra Corriente, Albilla, and Uvina grapes. There are three types of pisco: pure pisco, prepared from a single strain; "blended" pisco, produced by combining two or more strains; and mosto verde pisco, produced by distilling the grape juice prior to fermentation, which makes it particularly smooth. It is drunk in cocktails and used in desserts.

PLANTAIN/BANANA
Different types of banana/plantain are consumed in Peru. The silk banana, whose flesh is yellow and soft, is eaten raw and used in juices and desserts. The bellaco plantain is long and thick with orangey flesh and is boiled, roasted or fried. The bizcocho banana is 2–2¾ inches/5–7 cm in length and has a pleasant taste and, finally, the de la isla banana has pinkish flesh and is extremely tasty.

POTATO
A typical Peruvian tuber, of which there are thousands of varieties. Of the 3,000 plus varieties of potato that exist in the world, the majority are found growing in the wild in Peru. Two of the most popular types of potato are the yellow potato, the color of egg yolks, which take on a very soft and crumbly texture when cooked; and white potatoes, which are very pale, firm and do not disintegrate as easily when cooked. Native potatoes were also domesticated thousands of years ago by ancient Andean peoples and come in many different shapes and colors.

POTATO STARCH (FLOUR)
Used in small quantities to thicken sauces and broths (stocks). It is also widely used in Chinese-Peruvian or chifa cuisine as a thickening agent.

PRICKLY PEAR
A fruit with a fairly thick peel, fine prickles, and juicy pulp filled with tiny seeds. It can be eaten fresh if the peel and prickles are removed, or in salads, juices, sorbets, and jams.

PURPLE CORN
Corn that acts as a powerful colorant and grows on the Peruvian coast/in the Andes. The cobs are a dark purple, almost-black color, and are used in desserts and drinks such as *mazamorra* (corn pudding) or *chicha morada* (Peruvian purple corn punch), to which it adds a beautiful purple color. It was discovered by pre-Columbian peoples.

QUESO FRESCO
A white cheese that is used in various dishes and sauces, such as *huancaína* and *ocopa* sauce. Industrially produced queso fresco is moist and has a mild taste, but you can also get rustic, traditionally made varieties of queso fresco. These are extremely flavorsome and vary in salt content and texture.

QUINCE
A somewhat dry-fleshed fruit that has a slightly sharp, but pleasantly bittersweet taste. It grows along the coast and in the Peruvian highlands, and has been used to make compotes, jellied quince, jams, and soft drinks since colonial times.

QUINOA
A small, round, pale Andean grain. Colored varieties of quinoa can also be found in Peru, including: pink, red, orange, brown, and black. It is a highly nutritious grain that is used in various dishes, stews, soups, soft drinks, desserts, and breads. It has been cultivated since 5,800 BCE.

RED ONION
Red onions are favored above all others in Peruvian cuisine due to their intense flavor. Among the most well-known are the red onions from Arequipa, from Lurín, red Creole onions, and Italian red onions. They are used in the base condiments of various dishes and are also the main ingredients in certain dishes such as ceviche, *escabeche* (marinated dishes), stir-fried beef tenderloin, and Creole sauce.

ROCOTO HOT CHILE
A large, red, extremely spicy chile similar in appearance to the bell pepper, only slightly smaller. This chile is native to the Andes and can have a red, green, or yellow skin. Rocoto hot chiles grow in different regions of Peru including Arequipa, where they are considered iconic, and in Huarochirí, in Lima province. It is used as a condiment, in sauces, stuffings, and salsas and in dishes such as stuffed Rocoto hot chile or *escribano* (potato, tomato, and Rocoto hot chile dish).

SACHA CULANTRO
A strongly aromatic Amazonian herb similar to culantro. It is used mainly as a condiment and to prepare sauces.

SARANDAJA BEAN
A small, cream-colored bean that is cultivated on the northern coast of Peru. It is often served as an accompaniment to various dishes typical of the region, such as ceviche.

SAUCO
A Peruvian elderberry with a very dark purple berry that grows in clusters. These berries are extremely juicy and have a somewhat bitter-sweet taste. Native to the Andes, they are used in jams, desserts, cocktails, and sauces.

SCALLION (SPRING ONION)
A type of onion with thin white stems and long green leaves. They have a delicate taste, although the white parts have a sharper flavor. Spring onions are used in soups, sauces, Creole and Andean stews or sauces, in Chinese-Peruvian (*chifa*) cuisine and in dishes such as *sangrecita* (cooked chicken blood) and Peruvian fried rice.

SHRIMP (PRAWN)
A crustacean measuring up to 12 inches/30 cm in length which lives among rocks on riverbeds, particularly of fast-moving rivers, along the Peruvian coast. The shrimp (prawns) of the Arequipa region, in particular Majes, Camaná, Ocoña, and Tambo, are famous and their exquisite meat can be added to soups, stews, and ceviches. They are also wonderful in dishes such as shrimp (prawn) chowder. To protect the species, shrimp fishing is forbidden in Peru between January and April.

SOURSOP
A white-fleshed, bittersweet fruit encased in a thin green rind. Used in drinks, desserts, and ice creams due to its strong aroma and pleasant taste. Also used as a base for traditional *champuz* (fruity hominy dessert).

SOY SAUCE
Used in Peruvian–Chinese, or *chifa*, cuisine.

STUFFING CUCUMBER
A Peruvian fruit that is about 6 inches /15 cm long, with a thick green peel and soft spines. It is often cooked and stuffed with meat and other ingredients, but can also be enjoyed in salads and dishes such as *ajiaco* (potato and chili stew).

SWEET POTATO
An edible root vegetable that is soft and sweet when cooked. Two of the main varieties found in Peru are the yellow and purple sweet potatoes, both used in soups and stews. Sweet potatoes are also traditionally used to garnish ceviches. You can also fry them and serve with *chicharrones* (fried pork rind) or as nibbles or snacks. Sweet potato flour is also used in sweets and breads.

TAMARILLO
An Andean fruit with a distinctive taste and subtle aroma, similar to the tomato, but with a slightly elongated shape. It is normally dark red and fleshy and can be eaten raw or cooked; it is often used in compotes, candies (sweets), drinks, condiments, and sauces.

TAMARIND
Dark-colored pod measuring 4 to 6 inches/10–15 cm in length that contains a blackish pulp. The pulp has a pleasant, bittersweet taste, contains seeds and is mainly used in juices, drinks, sauces, sweets, and ice creams.

TRIPE
Beef tripe, which is thoroughly washed and cut into chunks. Used to prepare soups, chili stews, spicy dishes, and grilled dishes. Has been used as an ingredient since the early days of Afro-Peruvian cuisine.

ULLUKU
An oval-shaped tuber cultivated in cold Andean regions at altitudes above 9,840 ft/3,000 m. It comes in different varieties with peels that vary in color, ranging from yellow to red, pink, purple, and blue. It can be added to stews, soups, purees, and typical dishes such as the famous *ulluku* with jerked meat.

WORMSEED
An aromatic herb with a very distinctive taste that is used as a condiment in soups, broths, chowders, and particularly *pachamanca* (meat dish cooked on hot stones).

YELLOW HOT CHILE
Although referred to as "yellow," this chile is actually orange in color. It is cultivated throughout Peru and is the most frequently used chile in Peruvian cuisine. Many dishes use yellow hot chile condiment as a base as it adds flavor and color. It can either be minced or cut into strips.

YUCCA ROOT (CASSAVA)
A long tuberous root measuring up to 39½ inches/1 m in length. It has a brown skin and the flesh is white or pale yellow, depending on the variety. Yucca root (cassava) can be boiled or fried and is typically served in Peru as an accompaniment to many Creole and seafood dishes.

YUYO SEAWEED
Seaweed that is used in ceviches and spicy dishes, or to garnish Peruvian seafood dishes.

INDEX

Q

Phaidon Press Limited
Regent's Wharf
All Saint Street
London N1 9PA

Phaidon Press Inc.
65 Bleecker Street
New York, NY 10012

www.phaidon.com

First published 2015

ISBN: 978 07148 6920 9

A CIP catalogue record for this book is available from the British Library.

Commissioning Editor: Emilia Terragni
Project Editor: Ellie Smith
Production Controller: Mandy Mackie

Translation by Lingoleaf

Designed by Julia Hasting
Artworked by Studio Chehade

All photographs by Andy Sewell except those on pages: 162, 179, 184, 191, 207, 210, 219, 229, 251, 277, 320, and 323 taken by Pocho Caceres.
Illustrations by Julia Hasting

Printed in China

The publisher would like to thank Diego Alcántara, Theresa Bebbington, Liz Clinton, Fabricio Cano Davila, Simon Davis, Albitres Antonio Farfán, Jodie Gaudet, Laura Gladwin, Roberto Grau, Sophie Hodgkin, Michelle Lo, Begoña Velasco Oliart, Pene Parker, Juan Périco, Rosa Reyes, Emma Robertson, Raúl Rosas, Kathy Steer, and Anthony Vasquez for their contributions to the book.

RECIPE NOTES

Unless otherwise stated, eggs and individual vegetables and fruits, such as onions and apples, are assumed to be medium.

Unless otherwise stated, pepper is freshly ground black pepper.

Cooking times are for guidance only, as individual ovens vary. If using a fan oven, follow the manufacturer's instructions concerning oven temperatures.

Exercise a high level of caution when following recipes involving any potentially hazardous activity, including the use of high temperatures, open flames, wiping hot pans, and when deep-frying. In particular, when deep-frying, add food carefully to avoid splashing, wear long sleeves, and never leave the pan unattended.

Some recipes include raw or very lightly cooked eggs, meat, or fish, and fermented products. These should be avoided by the elderly, convalescents, infants, pregnant women, and anyone with an impaired immune system.

When no quantity is specified, for example of oils, salts, and herbs used for finishing dishes, quantities are discretionary and flexible.

Both metric and imperial measures are used in this book. Follow one set of measurements throughout, not a mixture, as they are not interchangeable.

All spoon and cup measurements are level, unless otherwise stated. 1 teaspoon = 5 ml; 1 tablespoon = 15 ml. Australian standard tablespoons are 20 ml, so Australian readers are advised to use 3 teaspoons in place of 1 tablespoon when measuring small quantities.

ACKNOWLEDGEMENTS

To all Peruvian peasants and fishermen, who through their daily labor make it possible for us to obtain the best products, produce, and fish. To everyone who works in their kitchen with outstanding passion and love, so that Peruvian gastronomy is alive and expanding throughout the world. This book is for them all, with my gratitude.

Many thanks as well to my kitchen staff: Roberto Grau, Diego Alcántara, Anthony Vásquez, Rosa Reyes, and Raúl Rosas, as well as my Peruvian editorial team: Begoña Velasco, Antonio Albitres, and Juan Périco. Thank you to those who accompanied me researching and creating this book which has allowed me to share with the world the enormous variety and richness of our Peruvian cuisine.

Gastón Acurio